Across the Great Divide

To Lynne and Stephen

Beatrice C. Pappa

Across the Great Divide
The Selected Essays of Abraham Coralnik

Translated by
Beatrice Coralnik Papo

Volume I
Reflections on Jewish Civilization

Volume II
Culture and Philosophy from Europe to America

Across the Great Divide

✦

The Selected Essays of Abraham Coralnik

Volume I
Reflections on Jewish Civilization

Translated by
Beatrice Coralnik Papo

With a foreword by
Daniel Schifrin

iUniverse, Inc.
New York Lincoln Shanghai

Across the Great Divide
The Selected Essays of Abraham Coralnik

iUniverse books may be ordered through booksellers or by contacting:

iUniverse
2021 Pine Lake Road, Suite 100
Lincoln, NE 68512
www.iuniverse.com
1-800-Authors (1-800-288-4677)

Cover design by David Avidor

ISBN-13: 978-0-595-34573-1 (pbk)
ISBN-13: 978-0-595-79320-4 (ebk)
ISBN-10: 0-595-34573-5 (pbk)
ISBN-10: 0-595-79320-7 (ebk)

Printed in the United States of America

To my children Ruth and Ari Schifrin and Michael and Dorothy Papo
To my grandchildren Dara, Joel and Sharon Papo,
Debra Schifrin, Daniel Schifrin and Abby Friedman
To my sister Zoe Coralnik Kaplan
To my niece Caroline Kaplan
To my great-grandsons Aviv and Lior Schifrin
and to all the great-grandchildren yet to come.

B.C.P.

Contents

Jewish Culture and Politics

Zionism and the Land of Israel

The Religious Experience

Texts and Histories

Travels in Europe

Travels in the Americas

A Detour to Egypt

Foreword

It is an irony worthy of the Yiddish language that the miserable years between World Wars I and II, a time of extreme terror and dislocation for Eastern European Jews that eclipsed almost everything in Jewish history (except for what was about to happen), was also a period of enormous cultural productivity. In Europe, as well as in America, Yiddish literature, letters and journalism were in full flowering; Jewish political expression existed in stunning varieties, from Zionism to communism to the Bund; and theaters, art centers and cultural societies blossomed. It was a time of fierce — perhaps desperate — creativity, which the Jewish community needed to confront the myriad choices and dilemmas that confronted it.

Onto the scene stepped Abraham Coralnik — Dr. Coralnik to his readers — beloved and respected columnist for the New York Yiddish daily *Der Tog* (The Day), former editor of Theodore Herzl's newspaper *Die Welt*, a philosopher, inveterate traveler, and master of European languages and literatures. In his German articles in *Die Welt*, in his correspondence for the Russian press, in his English essays in the pro-Zionist *The New Palestine*, and especially in his Yiddish writings for *Der Tog*, Coralnik attempted to bring clarity to a people at a historic crossroads.

Born in the Ukrainian town of Ouman in 1883 — the same year Sholem Aleichem published his first short story "Two Stones" — Coralnik grew up in a traditional Jewish household. His mother ran the family jewelry store, while his father stayed home and studied both Jewish texts and European philosophy. Coralnik attended a Jewish school, becoming well versed in the canon of Jewish religious texts, but he also absorbed from his father a love of, and familiarity with, the German philosophical tradition. He eventually left the Ukraine to study at the University of Vienna, where he took his Ph.D. in philosophy, focusing on the skeptics.

Coralnik never taught in a university. Instead, he was captivated by the extraordinary political and cultural turmoil already shaking the Jewish world. In 1904, at the tender age of 21, he began working at *Die Welt* — the official journal of the Zionist movement — and after Herzl's death became one of its editors. Between that job and the outbreak of World War I, Coralnik traveled throughout Europe as a correspondent for Russian newspapers, seeing firsthand the tremendous changes in cultural and political life taking place for Jews and for Europeans in general.

Coralnik was in Berlin when World War I started. As a Russian national, he felt it would be prudent to leave Germany, and he took his family to neutral Copenhagen. Stuck without work, and deeply curious about the United States, he decided to go to America, and joined the newly formed Yiddish daily *Der Tog*. When the czar was overthrown in February of 1917, however, Coralnik returned to Russia, full of optimism for a new society. His contacts among the Menscheviks, who had initiated the revolution, were excellent, and he soon found himself a senior government official in the Ukraine, a job for which he was probably not well suited. The next year, after Lenin had displaced the feckless Menscheviks, Coralnik wisely decided to return to New York, where for the next 20 years he wrote for *Der Tog*.

In the 1920s and 1930s, the role of the Yiddish periodical functioned in ways hard for today's newspaper readers to fully understand. Subscribers to *Der Tog* or its competitor the *Forvertz* [Forward] were mostly new immigrants trying to make sense of America, and these papers gave them an "education" in the broadest sense of the word. Whereas in the *Forvertz* Abraham Cahan's *bintel briefs* — a kind of "Dear Abby" for immigrants — helped Jews solve practical problems, Coralnik's essays in *Der Tog* focused on more cultural, political, historical and theological advice. His goal was twofold: to put Jewish culture in a more universal context, providing some background for the changes overwhelming a still poor and transitional community; and to put universal culture in a more Jewish context, demonstrating the Jewish influence on cultural and political movements throughout history, and thus encouraging Jewish interest in the broader intellectual world.

Coralnik's essays can be read for their value as journalistic documents, offering a snapshot of Jewish cultural and religious life over two decades. As Chaim Greenberg, the editor of Coralnik's 1928 collection of essays, put it, "there was no important political event or social phenomenon to which he had not responded." Reading his work today, then, we re-experience the key phenomena of the period: the continuing development of Jewish life in the land of Israel, the cancerous growth of anti-Semitism in Europe, and the spectacular transformation of Jewish life in America.

The essays endure, however, the way most journalism does not, because Coralnik's writings are saturated with historical and religious context. In "David Lubin," for instance, we learn how a Polish Jew transformed himself from an immigrant into a Sacramento department store owner, and then into the Prophet-quoting head of the powerful International Institute of Agriculture in Rome. From the success of this one man Coralnik squeezes out a parable for the continuing power and relevance of Jewish texts, as well as the social and political possibilities of a new age.

The essays in this two-volume collection, culled from *Der Tog* during the 1920s and 1930s, fall into several broad categories: culture, politics, religion, travel and philosophy. But these divisions are somewhat arbitrary, since part of Coralnik's intellectual — and even spiritual — mission was to break down boundaries between categories; to show, for instance, the unexpected connections between the mystical and the political, or between the philosophical and the geographic.

Many of Coralnik's essays explore the bewildering variety of political choices facing Jews during this period, and many are striking in their prescience about the fate of European Jewry and the still developing State of Israel, neither of which Coralnik, who died in 1937, lived to see.

Writing in 1923 about a possible Jewish homeland, Coralnik is already concerned that the spiritual and moral lessons of Judaism would be lost if the country-to-be adopted the negative characteristics of what Herzl hoped would be a nation like all other nations. Will Israel merely become another European colony, Coralnik asks in "About the Wide and the Narrow Road," adding one vineyard, bank and factory after another? "Is the entire meaning and purpose of the great Jewish tragedy," he writes, "merely [to become] a small Eastern republic?" Many Jews continue to ask this question today.

In "A Time for Soul Searching," a 1933 essay written just a few months after Hitler was elected to power, Coralnik excoriates those German Jews who couldn't see how bad their situation was. The Jews, "more than anyone else in this time of crisis, need a critical self-assessment, a soul searching that will allow no cover-up or whitewash," he writes. And in his essay "The Middle Way" he expresses his concern with the normal Jewish response to trouble — a "penetration into our own depths" — by pointedly asking: "Is this, perhaps, the last time we will lower the pitcher into the well before it runs dry?"

Coralnik was a sharp critic of Jewish religious and spiritual trends throughout history, usually with an eye toward how they shaped the contemporary Jewish consciousness. In some essays, as in "Henri Bergson" and the two-part "Between Job and Ezekiel/Hermann Cohen's Way to God," Coralnik delves into the mostly positive influence of the spiritual or non-rational in the work of contemporary philosophers. For Coralnik, finding the correct balance between the rational and the supra-rational was of the utmost importance. Sometimes, as he informed his readers, the pendulum had swung too far toward the rational. For instance, as he explains in "Lacking Pepper," the Jewish community had become enraptured with Hasidic ideas, but without bothering to study the rigorous scholarship that lay beneath it. This insight is familiar to those today who observe the proliferation of superficial classes on the Kabbalah and Jewish mysticism, which offer little in the way of philosophical, theological or historical context.

Coralnik was also fascinated by Yiddish as a language, the love-hate relationship that Jews have had with it, and the lives of the writers and cultural figures who brought it to such a high art. On the one hand, Coralnik, like many Jews familiar with both Hebrew and major European languages, observed that Yiddish "considers itself to be a mere accident, an unnecessary ballast, to be overthrown at the first opportunity." On the other hand, it was a language that in its very quirkiness and flexibility recapitulated the modern history of the Jewish people.

We see these ideas developed in the essay "The Lonesome Language," in which Coralnik describes Yiddish symbolically as "The child of an Eastern father and a Western mother…a language saturated with pain…a reflection of the Jews, the most widespread, the most enterprising and the most solitary of peoples." Yiddish insists, then, that its Jewish speakers are by definition wanderers and boundary-breakers, constantly reinventing the world even as they are grounded in the most ancient of living cultures. Less metaphysically, in essays like "Hersh David Nomberg," "About Yehoash," and "Baal Makhshoves," Coralnik helps us see what the daily lives of these Yiddish writers were like as they speak to us (sometimes through the filter of Coralnik's imagination), from the cafés, apartments and newspapers where they lived and worked.

Coralnik was fascinated by the political and philosophical personality — especially, as in the case of Karl Marx, when they came together in the same person — and he wrote passionately about figures like Socrates, Plato, Machiavelli, Abraham Lincoln, Woodrow Wilson, and Herbert Asquith. These essays are fascinating in their own right, but become even more compelling when one considers the audience — a poor, struggling, yet culturally and intellectually vibrant community of immigrants. With so many Yiddish speakers involved with unions and progressive politics, essays like "Marx and the *Manifesto*" and "Pierre-Joseph Proudhon: The Pathos of Justice," for all their intellectual demands, were of more than theoretical interest to Coralnik's readers.

One of Coralnik's heroes was Michel de Montaigne, the seventeenth-century French writer who pioneered the essay form, and whose motto, Jewish enough in its sensibility, was "What do I know?" Coralnik saw in Montaigne a precursor of his own concerns and style. Like Montaigne, Coralnik viewed the essay as an opportunity for wide-ranging reflection, and, ultimately, as part of an ongoing spiritual autobiography. Seen in this literary context, not knowing The Answer, indeed struggling to formulate the right question, was not a failing but the very essence of the essay — and of life itself. For these reasons, Coralnik's work, although learned and authoritative, was also open-minded and flexible, and therefore remains deeply alive for today's readers. Irving Howe and Eliezer Greenberg included two of Coralnik's essays in their 1972 anthology *Voices from the Yiddish*, noting that his lyrical, impressionistic style added to the freshness of his ideas.

Chaim Greenberg, who edited a posthumous anthology of Coralnik's work, explained that Coralnik's inability to assert definitively the answers to intractable issues was one of his greatest strengths. "The main inheritance we have of him is, as it were, his self-portrait, the portrait of a man in whose mind and soul all the great problems and contradictions of our generation played themselves out," he wrote in the book's introduction. "His work remains the gift of a man whose struggle to find answers to eternal questions has stimulated us to do our own questing."

But Coralnik himself wasn't quite so happy carrying the burden of these contradictions, and in many of his essays he visibly yearns for the political, philosophical or spiritual insight that would show him the one true path, that would bridge all of the contradictions.

In his essay "Upon A Repudiated Star: At the Grave of Jacob Wassermann," Coralnik notes that the German author's central flaw was being unable to come to terms with the bifurcation between his two identities, between German and Jew: "He sought a path for the German and Jew within himself. But these are two distinct paths, and he found neither one...Somewhere, at a certain point, an artist must feel secure, must be sure of himself. There must be an inner core where the pilgrim feels at home or is on his way towards it."

Implied in this criticism of Wassermann is Coralnik's own anxiety about contradiction and ambiguity, about not having a "home," and he saw those qualities simultaneously as a blessing and a curse. As Greenberg notes, however, Coralnik's true home was Judaism, even if he felt it to be a constricting and well-worn house he sometimes longed to leave behind.

In his articles on writing itself, Coralnik is even more explicit about his existential struggle. For instance, in "The Essayist," Coralnik's own introduction to his 1928 anthology (and reprinted in this volume), he discusses himself in the third person:

...essayists stumble around in the world of spiritual values, wander through the vast, rich world and do not know what it is they are called on to do. They are like visitors in a museum, moving from picture to picture, from one statue to the next, gathering an impression here, a mood there, experiencing ecstasy and disappointment. When the museum closes and they are back on the street, with all its lack of awareness and its triviality, they feel lonely and miserable. In the museum there is art, an arbor filled with fruit; be it ripe or green, it is still fruit. On the street, on the other hand, there is naive, unquestioning life. Essayists alone are in-between, neither bringing forth fruits nor naively enjoying life, always in search, always questioning and forever lacking self-confidence, forever dissatisfied with themselves.

What we see, then, is a lone man, searching and skeptical, forever locked between the museum and the street. If there is a master theme in Coralnik's work, it is the attempt to cross or at least explore what he saw as a few key unbridgeable chasms in life: Judaism and the European humanist tradition; the rational and the mystical; the past and the future; high and popular culture; the intimate and the remote.

Coralnik adored travel writing, and in a way all of his essays are records of voyages, describing in Yiddish — the language of the perennial exile — humanity's search for safe harbor in a world of storms. It is only, perhaps, in passages describing a future Jewish state that Coralnik believed he could glimpse an actual and metaphysical Promised Land. But, like Moses, Coralnik never made it. A fatal heart attack in New York in 1937 prevented him from seeing what "civilized" Germany did to the Jews or how the world, after 2,000 years, grudgingly allowed them to bloom again in the desert of Israel.

◆   ◆   ◆

Over the last fifteen years, Coralnik's essays have been making their transition *en masse* from Yiddish to English, thanks to the efforts of Coralnik's elder daughter, Beatrice Coralnik Papo. A native speaker of German and Russian, who learned to read and write Yiddish as a teenager, she rediscovered the richness of the language as she followed her father's ideas from one century, culture and book to the next. Begun in large part to better understand her father's life, as well as to pass on his work to her non-Yiddish speaking descendants, Papo became increasingly interested in the essays for their own sake. Initially it was only a small group of friends and family, gathering periodically to listen to her newest translations, who were privy to these essays. Their excitement prompted the publication of *Across the Great Divide*.

At some point during this period I became a part of the conversation as well. As Papo's grandson and Coralnik's great-grandson, I was drawn to these essays not just for their humanity and intellectual force, but as my literary patrimony. Like my great-grandfather, I am a columnist for a New York Jewish newspaper hoping to bridge Jewish and universal culture through essays and cultural criticism. And so the family has come full circle, having passed through the cataclysm of the Holocaust and the triumph of Israeli statehood.

The philosopher David Hartman has described the history of Jewish life as the continuation of a holy conversation one generation holds with another. Abraham Coralnik spoke to his daughter, Beatrice, who spoke to my mother, Ruth, who spoke to me — only one line of conversation in a family where everyone shared and everyone spoke. And I write this foreword for my children, who will hopefully find their own way back to their history.

Daniel Schifrin
Berkeley, California
December, 2004

Acknowledgements

"And if not now, when?"

Rabbi Hillel's injunction really hit home 15 birthdays ago. Realizing that my grandchildren do not speak Yiddish (mea culpa), I wanted to make their heritage available to them by translating the essays of my father, Abraham Coralnik, from Yiddish into English. Then I remembered hearing, after my father's death, from a wide variety of people, how eagerly they used to look forward to his essays, how he had broadened their horizons, and enriched their lives. In fact, *Der Tog* — the Yiddish daily where my father's articles had appeared — used to reprint one of his essays each July 16th (the day of his death) as long as the paper existed. And so I decided to widen the audience for these essays, hoping to give them new life with new readers in a new language. I hope the content of my father's thoughts come through in this translation; nevertheless, I'm sure that his exquisite style has to be enjoyed in the original Yiddish.

I have been blessed with the moral support of my late husband Joseph M. Papo, and with the practical assistance of all of my family, during the years of struggling with the task of doing justice to my father's profound and complex thoughts, written in elegant Yiddish, as I translated them into English. My very special thanks are due to my grandson Daniel Schifrin for editing these essays, and the invaluable help he received from his wife Abby Friedman in organizing them for publication.

Beatrice Coralnik Papo
December, 2004
San Jose, California

Without a Preface[1]

There is a custom, long grown stale, to start a book with a preface. This is especially incongruous when the book is not an organic entity, but one that has been woven together; not a tree, but a collection of leaves — loose leaves, fallen leaves. I would almost say a herbarium.

I have never been able to understand the need for a preface, for an introduction, especially when there are only leaves, only moods and opinions which, dictated by the moment, are often blown away by the next. Let me reiterate: These are only leaves that are collected here. The issues of the day addressed me, and I have responded. The questions were often curt and harried ones, and the answers came in the same staccato tempo. There is no completion, no following up on themes to their conclusion. The motifs are touched upon with but a light stroke of the brush. A portrait remains a mere silhouette; a consideration of an issue turns into a dialogue with myself. This may derive from my basic attitude: I do not believe in exhaustive answers, or in examining issues from all sides. My worldview is not a linear one. The facets of a crystal look differently to me each time a ray of light illuminates them. Had I chosen a motto, it would have been the famous saying by Heraclitus the Dark: "You never step in the same water twice."

Loose leaves, some of them still green and fresh, recently fallen, and others already yellowed, bearing the stamp of their time on their curling edges. They had fallen off the tree in hard times, in years filled with crisis, transitions and destruction. Years of yearning and of unsuccessful attempts to build a better world. Once again, they are the children of their time. Or perhaps not? Perhaps they contain, after all, an imprint of the timeless that is in each one of us. I do not know, and it does not concern me. I do not want to be their advocate or their promoter. I have fulfilled my obligation to them; I have been their companion. I have entrusted my words to them, my sighs and my daydreams. Now they are on their own, free to find their own way as best they can. I will continue along my path, and who knows, perhaps we may yet meet again.

---

1.   From Abraham Coralnik's introduction to his 1928 Warsaw edition of *Selected Essays*

The Essayist

✦

Dedicated to Reuben Brainin

There are so many confident, self-assured men of thought and action in the world, but only a few who lack self-assurance — and each one of them pursues his own, separate way. Each of the self-confident ones know what task he was created to fulfill, knows the meaning of his life and of his labor. Each one of them plants his particular seed, then waits for the fruit to ripen, spiritually and materially. This planting and waiting is called a vocation, becomes their goal in life. The politician has a vocation — to govern his society, to lead his contemporaries, to make history. The explorer, the thinker, they dedicate their lives to rethinking old problems, to finding new explanations, to discovering new paths. As to artists, they are, of course, the ones most deeply sustained by their belief in themselves, in their task, in their message. Their ability to create — the privilege, as Goethe once said, "to tell what they suffer" — is enough to exhilarate them, to raise their self-esteem, to confirm their knowledge that their art is their steady goal, their prescribed way of life.

But essayists stumble around in the world of spiritual values, wander through the vast, rich world and do not know what it is they are called on to do. They are like visitors in a museum, moving from picture to picture, from one statue to the next, gathering an impression here, a mood there, experiencing ecstasy and disappointment. When the museum closes and they are back on the street, with all its lack of awareness and its triviality, they feel lonely and miserable. In the museum there is art, an arbor filled with fruit; be it ripe or green, it is still fruit. On the street, on the other hand, there is naive, unquestioning life. Essayists alone are in-between, neither bringing forth fruits nor naively enjoying life, always in search, always questioning and forever lacking self-confidence, forever dissatisfied with themselves.

But there are some human beings who wander through the vast, rich world of spiritual values and do not know what it is they are called upon to do. They are like visitors in a museum, moving from picture to picture, from one statue to the next, gathering an impression here, a mood there, experiencing ecstasy or disappointment. When the museum closes and they are back on the street, with all its lack of awareness and its triviality, they feel lonely and quite miserable. In the museum there is art, an arbor filled with fruit; be it ripe or green, it is still fruit. On the street, on the other hand, there is naive, strong, unquestioning life. And these people alone are in between, neither bringing forth fruits, nor naively enjoying life, always in search, always questioning and forever lacking self-confidence, forever dissatisfied with oneself.

The seeker tries to come up with a cast into which to pour his own thoughts and impressions, but the cast melts in his hands, for he lacks the vessel which might contain the hot, flowing stream. Not having planted any seeds, he is not entitled to any of the ripening fruit, so all he can gather are leaves, although often very beautifully shaped and colorful ones. He may gather the brightly colored leaves of a southern tree in summer, but, more often than not, they will be the reddish-golden or cinnamon-colored leaves of fall. Trying, starting, but not completing — this is the only thing he can give. Only the leaves of his soul.

The poet creates a work; the musician honors his achievement with the Latin word *opus*; and the thinker follows Aristotle in creating an "organon," an instrument, a structure. The essayist alone writes essays, or "try-outs"; with characteristic modesty he does not even presume to call it a "work." He does not demand of the world: Accept my teaching, learn from me, or else let yourself be charmed by my tone, by my personality, let my life become yours — for this is the plea of the artist. The essayist knows his limitations; he offers no teaching, nor does he become part of anyone's life, only offering a little bit of himself, some leaves from his branches. The leaves fall and are often stepped on without receiving even a glance. And no one knows, no one senses how much suffering, how much personal life experience is to be found in a cinnamon-colored leaf that is lying on the ground.

Then there comes a day when a man of acute sensitivity and an observant eye notices a leaf, picks it up and places it in an album, and then one more and yet another one until he has a kind of herbarium, but a herbarium not of blossoms, albeit dried ones, but of leaves, leaves which have never graced a fruit tree. Yet should someone happen to weave such leaves into a wreath, who would wear it?

Let us take a look at the greatest essayists in the world. In France we have the father of the genre, Montaigne. In England, Walter Pater and Charles Lamb have, of course, attained an indisputable place in world literature, their names found in all encyclopedias and all textbooks, their writings on all library shelves.

But are they being read? And if they are read, out of curiosity, can the reader share their feelings, become involved in their thoughts?

Ovid, Dante and even minor poets can still be read today, because they brought forth human beings and spun out stories that survive throughout the ages, just as we still look at statues and listen to music, no matter how old. What matters is less the enjoyment of these works than their ability to make an impression, elicit a response, stimulate new growth. Montaigne and Lamb, on the other hand, are merely companions who sit at your fireside on a wintry night or walk with you in the woods and converse. The conversation might range from soul-searching to humor to a goodly deal of skepticism, but their most characteristic feature would be intimacy. The essayist's mission is to help us retain intimacy, say, with a piece of music when the tones dim into an aftertone, or with a painting after a painter's line and colors cede their shape and clarity, losing themselves somewhere in the distance. The essay and essayist brings us back to the past where, in the end, all things rest.

The essayists do have a place and a vocation, only they do not know it. They are, perhaps, the only ones whose writing flows out of their love for their fellow men. And this, in the final analysis, is the greatest, most human artistic achievement. How many human beings are capable of loving others? Who can turn to God asking, "Forgive me, for having always loved too much?" Few people possess this talent, least of all the creative artists. The creator is blinded to anything but his own work. He looks at the world not through open but through narrowed eyes, and he perceives, therefore, great wonders. The sunrays have the most beautiful colors when seen through narrowly contracted eyes. But to look at the sunlight with wide-open eyes, unafraid of being blinded, this is love and this is the way of the essayist. He loves the world even when he feels pessimistic; he loves the light, even though on occasion he must pull the shade down. He loves human beings and what they achieve, even when he speaks of it ironically. The irony itself is merely an expression of, or perhaps a cover-up for, his love. It is the embarrassment of a lover who fears that his intense love may be seen as sentimentality, may give rise to ridicule, and so he disguises his feelings, hides behind an elaborate style, denies them.

The only thing that the essayist actually has to offer is his great love of the world's beauty and spirituality. He does not even strive to become a guide to the beauty he perceives, nor to interpret or teach it, because he is not at all sure that his interpretation is the correct one. He only wants to point out to his fellow beings: Look at the sun, see how beautiful that scenery is! He feels the magnificence, and he perceives the limitations of a medium — any medium — to express it. There is no vessel large enough to contain the world's splendor.

Montaigne once described himself as "a man who is merely a face, a face that perceives, that reacts to everything; a face which masks a depth where words can no longer penetrate." He has, thus, created an image for the essayists of all generations. Perhaps the world really needs such a face. Perhaps an album of beautiful, dried leaves does have a cultural value. What do I know?

Jewish Culture and Politics

A Time for Soul Searching

Every catastrophe, each of life's stunning blows, tends to drive those who are given to reflection, those who sincerely and earnestly want to get at the root of matters, toward self-criticism. Prior to summoning life and fate before the heavenly tribunal, such a man calls himself to judgment — he is the plaintiff and he is the judge. Poets are given to such soul-searching. Ibsen claimed that "to write poetry is to judge oneself." Yet, it is more accurate, more true, to say that self-judgment is an act of poetic creation which finds its expression not in rhymed or free-verse poems, not even in dramas or short stories, but in the idiosyncratic art of coining words which hover on the dividing line between science and poetry, between thought and imagination — the art which we call critique, the critique of life.

There are times when ideas become petrified, when the prevalent views and attitudes lose their vitality and their meaning, when their continued existence is owed to mere inertia and to the force exerted by the past. Those venturing into the analysis and critique of ideas need to possess the great artistic skill of finding a crack in the petrified surface of the organism and widening it sufficiently to release its component parts, setting them free to explore other possible modes of thought and to create new designs. As we examine the history of all cultured nations, we find that the most momentous periods of their national existence were also times of self-criticism, with perhaps one exception — the Jews. This despite the fact that Jews, more than anyone else in this time of crisis, need a critical self-assessment, a soul-searching that will allow no cover-up or whitewash.

Can we conceive of Job the accuser and protester, the Job of the first part, without the Job who turns his gaze inward, the Job who conducts a searching dialogue with himself? And it is most unfortunate that just now, in our new Job-period, we stay within the first part; we accuse, but are at peace with ourselves. We are angry at the whole world while remaining self-satisfied. Even when we do feel twinges of dissatisfaction and when we do venture into a self-analysis, this analysis turns out to be terrifyingly shallow.

I have been waiting to hear how German Jews will respond to the catastrophic events now underway. The liberals keep silent, while the radicals look forward to better times and write polemical anti-Nazi articles from Prague or Zurich. The Zionists are the only ones who talk. Every issue of the *Jüdische Rundschau*, the Central Zionist Organ of Germany, features philosophical discussions on Jews and Judaism. Each week the Zionists subject themselves and the Jewish people to a moral stocktaking and, to tell the truth, I do not know if it would not be better if they, too, would remain silent. It might be much better because theirs is not a soul-searching that descends into its own spiritual depth. Instead they look at Judaism through the eyes of outsiders, and their critique remains a superficial one — they subject German Jewry to the critique of their enemies.

The German nationalist says: Germans and Jews are two historically disparate nations that cannot co-exist; they must be separated from each other. Then come the Zionists with their own variation on the theme: Of course, we have always said the Jews must lead their own life, must follow their historically conditioned way of life, and the tragedy of German Jewry is that they have forgotten, have wanted to forget, their Jewishness. A different premise, a different background, but the conclusion is practically the same — we must isolate ourselves and retreat into our biblical four cubits. The conclusion is — nationalism.

As close and as dear as Zionism is to me (close and dear not because of its nationalistic element but because of its historical elements), I must confess that I do not find myself attracted by the reasoning which propelled German Jews toward Zionism — counsels of despair and anger do not lead us to the core of the problem. And the problem is: What is Jewishness in our day and age? This is, surely, not a brand new question, and I do not intend to come forth with an answer, either now or in the future, since I do not feel strong enough to shoulder such a burden. There was a time, eighteen or twenty years ago, when the self-confidence of youth led me to believe that I possessed sufficient strength to uncover the ancient well, to lift the weighty stone. Those were the days when I used to ponder, and wax poetic on, the essence of Judaism, its substance and its core. But I also felt that this critique lacked a firm foundation, and that neither I nor any of my contemporaries would succeed in pursuing an analysis of Judaism to its very end, to a solution. Not only because we may have lacked the perceptual and creative energy needed for the task, but because we wanted to unite extremes, to combine into one organic entity two mutually exclusive substances: a critical study of Judaism and the foundation of Jewish nationalism. The negative and the positive, thought and will, were tripping each other up. I came to understand that a true, courageous, abyss-deep exploration of Judaism could only take place either in *Eretz Yisrael,* where the national will has been, at least potentially, realized, or in a communist society, where the nationalist ideal has been pushed aside by socialism.

In Russia, Jewish thought is dead, as is any other thought, communist dogma and phraseology having choked off all free critical thinking in general, and Jewish thought in particular. Can we expect a critical analysis of Judaism from the few Jewish poets who are rhapsodizing about the greatness of Stalin and the achievement of tractors? In *Eretz Yisrael,* however, Judaism does not depend on any outside forces. There, being Jewish is a matter of course and is, therefore, an internal problem. There begins anew the spiritual work that the Jews of the last few generations have avoided, the work of continuing the Jewish thought process, of following Judaism's dialectical path, a path which has led us, in turn, to the Kabbalah, to Hasidism and to Reform — the three mainstreams of Judaism — until it came up against the wall of nationalism. We were facing a dead end, until national fulfillment in *Eretz Yisrael* opened the way. The fulfillment, limited as it may be, has freed the Jews in *Eretz Yisrael* from the millstone of nationalism, and the ancient source has been let free again.

In the press and literature of *Eretz Yisrael* I have noted, more than once, comments and observations that could not possibly have appeared in the Jewish press of any other country, because they would have been deemed ill-advised and ill-timed. Even a book like Joseph Klausner's *Jesus the Nazarene,* which looks on Jesus as a Jew and interprets him from a Jewish viewpoint, could not possibly originate in any other country. I still remember the time in Vienna, when a Mr. Friedlander brought out a book on Christianity. He was attacked and denounced as an anti-Semite, as a "troubler of Israel," only one step removed from being a missionary. Yet, basically, Friedlander's view of Jews had not been so different from Dr. Klausner's.

Klausner is a historian and philologist rather than a critical analytical thinker, and he fails to penetrate very deeply into the problems of Judaism. He merely because we have not built a new temple, and we are afraid to destroy the old one. But the builders are not afraid.

The Paradox of Judaism

It was shortly before the outbreak of World War I when a group of Jewish writers and thinkers came together in Berlin to discuss the question of "What is Judaism, its essence and manifestations?" and published a symposium in the Hebrew journal *Ha-atid*. At that time we were asked, both seriously and mockingly: Have you run out of real problems? Why are you seeking answers to questions that were answered long ago? Do you intend, as it were, to prove anew all the old axioms? This cannot be done even in geometry or physics, and the task you are proposing to shoulder is equivalent to scooping out an ocean. Other nations also endure spiritual crises and people everywhere are struggling to discern the fundamental forces which govern our universe, yet we do not see Catholics, Protestants or the Eastern Orthodoxy tormenting themselves with such queries. And rightly so, because faith, like love, is not subject to the dictates of our will; we can no more decide to have faith than we can decide to love someone. In both cases, we either have it or we do not, there is no in-between. There were of course some 19th century philosophers who had wanted to persuade the world that it is possible to evolve a religion based on reason, just as Hegel had been teaching that the relationship between men and women must be based on reason and calculation rather than on emotions. Why look for answers to the problems within Judaism when the problems besetting the Jews from the outside remain unsolved?

The outbreak of World War I and the catastrophic post-war years unleashed troubles of such intensity as to cast all previous concerns aside, and thus we are devoting less thought today than ever before to the foundation and essence of Judaism.

Whenever, in the course of the last two years, I have listened to or have read sermons delivered by American rabbis on Shabbat or on holidays, or if I even looked at the titles of these sermons, I felt that the rabbis were the only ones to derive some benefit from the advent of Hitler and the re-emerging of anti-Semitism in the world. They found themselves freed from the responsibility of finding the right theme and of weighing the words they utter, freed from the heavy task of thinking, for they had been presented with a ready-made theme with its endless variations. Sometimes, however, a speaker would stray from the prevailing trite discourse and would strike a dissonant chord. This happened not long ago in a sermon (or it might better be termed a declamation) delivered by one of our best-known American rabbi-politicians titled "Hitler and the Jews" — a familiar subject, to be sure, and opening in quite a familiar way. But as he proceeded, the rabbi became heated, his oratory catching fire, and his language taking on a prophetic cadence. "The Jew will…the Jew wants to…the Jew must save the world…He must establish *Gan Eden* on earth, bring about fairness, justice, equality, righteousness." A remarkable word, this last one, a word which exists only in the lexicon of priests and rabbis. And the rabbi addressed the Jews sitting in his synagogue, and those who were listening over the radio. "Remember, fellow Jews, what the prophet has demanded of you and what I require of you now," namely, being a beacon of fairness, justice and "righteousness."

I listened and tried to visualize "the Jew" on the receiving end of this sermon. We know him, of course, we see him day-in and day-out — the diamond merchant, the glove manufacturer, the bank director, the Wall Street broker, the lawyer and the doctor. But as I tried to discern among those someone who might be engaged in the pursuit of the above-enunciated high ideals, I could not find him. But even if there were some willing and capable of pursuing them, I cannot see any way for them to do so, since they are small cogs in a powerful social machinery. And stationed, as they are, on the side of the well-to-do and the strong, how can one demand from them, how can one even hope that they should harbor such feelings as expressed by the Prophets? When we look toward the other side of the fence, we see the masses who still live in the traditional, non-assimilated way, the so-called Jewish Jews, the small shopkeepers struggling for their livelihood and the workers who have to safeguard their class interests, and I ask again: Are the sons of the Prophets to be found among them, and am I failing to recognize them?

Long ago Rabbi Lev Itzhak of Berdichev raised the question: "There are the Greeks, Persians and the Romans, so why do the commandments, on all occasions, specify: Speak to the children of Israel? Why is the entire burden always put on us?" At this point, the Berdichever Rabbi broke off his query and began to recite "*Yisgadal v'yiskadash...*", the prayer glorifying God, and which was for him perhaps the final answer. It is possible that this may be the final answer for us as well, only how do we find our way to the "*yisgadal?*" Or to put it differently, where is our way to Judaism?

And this is, of course, the paradox of Judaism — its mathematical paradox, if you will — that its parts have grown larger than its whole. The whole, i.e. Judaism as a worldview, as a way of life, as a metaphysical concept, has shrunk considerably, while its component parts, the political, temporal, historical aspects, have taken over the empty space. Why do we modern Jews experience so tragically the re-emergence of anti-Semitism? We are, one would imagine, inured to all kind of trials, seeing that our entire emancipation dates only from yesteryear. Yet, compare the hysteria which has swept through today's Jewish community with the calm and the courage demonstrated by Jews in the past, even though they suffered more than we do. At that time Judaism had been a strong organism, a living force, a spiritual unity and everything surrounding it remained at the outskirts of its existence. In our time the situation is exactly the opposite — Judaism finds itself on the periphery, relegated to a distant, cloudy horizon, while at the core of its being there is constant movement, which means that there is really no core at all.

It is time, therefore, to renew the old discussion at the point it was broken off some 120 years ago. We must probe ever deeper, using thought the way a diamond cutter uses his scalpel. Let us forget for the moment Hitler and anti-Semitism and the destructive, negative forces over which we have no control, and give thought to concerns that are subject to our jurisdiction: the floor is open for discussion. And the first one to take the floor is Professor Mordechai M. Kaplan with his book *Judaism as a Civilization*, which is an attempt to reconstruct American Jewish life.

Dr. Kaplan's views are not unknown, and he has previously expressed them in a number of writings. The kernel of his thought is that Judaism is an inheritance from preceding generations, which must be preserved, but which must also be re-adapted to the demands of present times. To put it graphically, let us think of a man inheriting a treasure chest filled with gold coins and ornaments. He would feel ridiculous wearing any of the ancient ornaments, and he could make little practical use of the coins. The only thing he could do with such an inheritance would be to donate it to a museum. And this has been the position of the old German-Jewish reformer Haldheim and, even more strongly, that of Abraham Geiger. For them Judaism was a museum piece, such as a Tutankhamen mummy, or, in the best case, an old Grecian urn, beautiful and artistic. You cannot, however, take a mummy to a tea party, marry Tutankhamen, or drink beer out of a Grecian urn. Their fate is to stand in glass cases in a tastefully arranged museum, and from time to time on a Sabbath or a major holiday, the heirs will file by the glass cases, led by a guide who will explain to them everything they need to know about the mummy and the urn. And should some of the heirs not want to visit the museum because they know all about the exhibits already, or because they simply are not interested in archeology, they know that the treasures are in the glass boxes and the boxes are reposing safely in the museum.

Let us now picture another kind of heirloom, such as the famous Palazza Maxima Castle in Rome. It has been standing for more than 800 years already, passed on from one generation to the next within the same family. It is a gigantic structure, built of slabs of grey stone, a relic of the past which also houses the living. It is not a very comfortable place to live in; the rooms are either too big or too small, intended for ceremonial use rather than for the comfort and intimacy of daily living. It is not really a home. In several of the novels of Gabriel D'Annuzio we find variations on the following theme: A modern, hot-blooded young man, the last of a long line of princes or noblemen, rebels against the grey walls of the palace and the deep shadows which hover over it. But then necessity forces the heir to fit himself into the ancient house; there is no other choice left to him. At that point he begins to reach out to his past and, as he comes to learn about his ancestors he begins to experience a feeling of kinship with them and sets out to incorporate them into his own life, not by offering them romantic veneration but by making them a part of his daily life.

Dr. Kaplan views the problem of the Jewish heritage and Jewish civilization in just such terms. There is no need for me to subject Dr. Kaplan's newly published work to a detailed analysis. I agree completely with his criticism of the various religious currents in modern Judaism: Reform, New-Orthodoxy, etc...They are, unfortunately, not even currents, but rather dammed-up pools, having lost their initial spark of religious ecstasy or, one might say, their interest in the metaphysical problems posed by religion. They have preserved only the cadences of prayer recitation, and chant over and over again, but always in the wrong key. What I am mostly interested in are the positive, pragmatic aspects of Dr. Kaplan's book. He wants to arrive at a synthesis, and he wants to show the Jews of today and those of tomorrow what constitutes Judaism, encompassing in his synthesis the national, cultural and social elements, as well as the religious ones. I say "as well" because the religious element is not at the center of his concept of Judaism, but only one of its component parts. Judaism is not a civilization built upon and around its religion. Rather it contains religion as a part of the totality of Jewish life. Dr. Kaplan divests Jewish religiosity of its metaphysical element. The role played by religion is more important to him than its essence, or, as he puts it in a characteristic phrase, "The *tehillah* is more important than the *tefillah*," meaning that the act of praying is more important then the content of the prayer. Religion thus becomes again the indissoluble part of folk-consciousness and folklore; it ceases to be an end in itself; it ceases to be the meaning and purpose of Judaism.

It seems to me, however, that the old skeptic Renan had reached deeper into the essence of the problem when he said that prayer represents a unique and ultimate experience of human consciousness, a submerging of oneself in a communion with God, and the intoxication of eternity. No religion or civilization can be tailored to the temporal requirements of any given people, just as there can be no art created for the masses. Any great creation grows out of the life and aspirations of its creator and contains its own intrinsic value, is an end in itself. Friends and neighbors of the artist come to view the work of art and begin to respond to the essence of his creation, and as the circle grows, it gradually evolves into a civilization. This is how all civilizations come into being, including Judaism. The problem of Judaism, says Dr. Kaplan, is the problem of "otherness," of being different. But this is viewing Judaism from the outside. Only to others do "I" appear different; to myself I constitute the norm, and it is the others who are "different." The Jewish problem cannot be solved from without. We have to tackle it from within, searching for answers not outside our perimeters but within the very depth of Judaism. This entails a long and far-reaching exploration, demanding much effort and much time. The Jewish paradox is more acute today than when it first emerged more than a century ago, and it is imperative for us to continue the debate, and search for a resolution.

Civilization and "Kugelization"

There was a time when the excommunication of a "heretic" was a highly ceremonial rite. Dressed in white robes and prayer shawls, rabbis and officials gathered around a black lamp holding shofars. The shofars were blown, the black light extinguished, and the poor heretic was cast out from both worlds, expelled from his holy congregation and, of course, from the world to come. Today we go about it in a less dramatic way. We don't blow the shofar, we only harangue from a platform; we don't light black lamps, we merely fill our fountain pens with black or blue ink and "pound out" an editorial.

It is rather a pity, this loss of the dramatic impact, because it deprives Judaism of its *grande geste*. It is possible that we may regain it some day. The Orthodox rabbis and the various "keepers of the faith" are already preparing for the battle. They are sharpening their swords and pointing their darts as they gird their loins to enter the battle in defense of God. The Jewish atmosphere is crackling with electricity. In Europe and in America the conditions for a struggle are not too favorable, but, sooner or later, a battle will erupt in Palestine, and it will be a major one, as old Judaism confronts the new. Old Judaism has forgotten nothing of the past and has learned nothing new, while modern Judaism has passed through all the seven regions of Hell, has wrangled with man and with God, has learned a great deal, but has also forgotten a great deal as well.

In olden days, when two armies faced each other, it was customary for both sides to dispatch an emissary to challenge the opponent to a fight. Sometimes the

13

armies engaged in a bit of gallows humor, sending out their puniest soldiers to confront each other. There are similar tactics at play today. The bulk of the army is preceded by minor forces, by "boy scouts" charged with the task of reconnoitering the enemy's strategic positions. I do not believe that Orthodox Judaism has worked out elaborate battle plans or any new strategies, nor do I believe that the Orthodox camp has begun to send out "boy scouts," but there are already volunteers eager for adventure, especially since they very safe. It is, actually, Judaism's misfortune that it has so few heretics. Other religions have struggled with doubters, but, in the end, have made their peace with them. Other belief systems have matured theologically and have broadened their metaphysical horizons. But Judaism has put an end to its development. Anyone having the courage to put forth any new idea was excommunicated, and the community returned to its traditional, comfortable ways. This fate befell Spinoza and the mystics and could have been the fate of the Hasidim had they not lacked the courage for a final showdown and, fortunately, were able to retreat in time.

I would truly understand it if an Orthodox thinker came forward with his own precepts, because Judaism does find itself in a most precarious condition. It has lost the ground beneath its feet. It once had a spiritual and cultural unity. But the spiritual element has vanished, and what remains is a feeling that eludes a rational formulation, a feeling of peoplehood, a will for survival. But is this enough? It may suffice for the collective, but the individual needs to find in Judaism more than nationalism. Other people's moving to Palestine, speaking Hebrew, and hoping to find a way of getting the Arabs to compromise cannot invest the lives of individual Jews with Jewish content, cannot bring them a greater fulfillment. As long as Zionism was a utopia, it could be an ideal, and as such it had the power of breathing new life into other, seemingly dead ideals, because men do yearn to believe. The dogma is less important than the process, and the goal is of less moment than the way of reaching it. But once one's yearning is fulfilled, what remains?

In Palestine Jews can contend with each other without the element of fear. Here, in the *galut*, one hears the panicky: "Don't touch...Judaism may fall apart!" If one offers a critical view of Judaism, one is called to task: "Stop, you enemy of Israel, the Jewish people is in danger!" Such an accusation was leveled at Moses Mendelssohn, at all reformers, at all dissenting Jewish thinkers. A magic circle surrounds Jews and Judaism, Jewish nationalism and Jewish culture. Now is the time to step out of the circle, to break down the wall, to find our way. We cannot always live in fear, suppressing our thoughts and moods, swallowing all doubts and avoiding all discussions. In the realm of the spirit, a good war is better than a bad peace.

It is not worthwhile to discuss and critique in detail Mr. Bublik's *Cry of Distress*. It is bad theology, expressed in journalese, with every page filled with "universalism," "conditioning," "assimilation," and "civilization." One can be versed in all of modern Jewish literature and still use the present-day Yiddish vocabulary, just as one may write a book proving the unimportance of grammar, but the book itself must be grammatically correct. I will, however, forgive him his language, since he suffers from a general failing of modern Yiddish writers when they tackle "sacred issues." They lack linguistic discrimination; their dogma kills their style. What I cannot overlook, however, is the content, is Mr. Bublik's cavalier way of debunking Western cultural history. In the first chapter, he denigrates the Greeks, then in Chapter Two the Romans, and after that the Russians, Socialism, Naturalism, the *Haskalah,* Mendelssohn, Achad Ha'Am, Hebrew literature…. He literally does not leave a stone unturned: "Greeks have no morals," says Mr. Bublik, and "The load which weighted Greek civilization down to the ground, and kept it from attaining higher human ideals, was the Greek affinity with nature." Should you ask him what this means, he would answer that the Greeks practiced revenge, failed to honor their elders, etc., etc. And what about the Stoics, Plato, the whole Socratic thought process? And what about the way the Greeks provided for the welfare of their elders? This is of no interest to the historian Mr. Bublik; he doesn't want to recall this; he doesn't want to know about it. The Greeks are enchained; the Jews are free. He accepts as proof the writings of a second-rate German philosopher, Professor Radner, who wanted to elevate Protestant Christianity. The Jews are free, because it says in the Torah that God said to man: You may choose to walk the way of life or you may choose to walk the way of death. Some choice!

If this is a manifestation of Orthodoxy, then I truly pity Orthodox Jewry. And I am also afraid that no one will come forth to struggle with it. It is too weak, and the rule of fairness says: Do not attack a man who has hit the ground. But what is it that this boy scout of Orthodoxy wants? What are his positive values? He has excommunicated all of us; we are no good, and our nationalism, our Jewish thinking, is ruled by the concern: "What will the non-Jews say?" And this, in turn, leads to assimilation and conversion. What, then, are we to do? How are we to save ourselves and the Jewish people? Out of the entire Exodus-long book I was able to derive only one directive: You must pray, you must go to the *mikvah,* observe all the holidays and rituals; in short, the world-demolishing critic enjoins us to replace civilization with what David Frishman has dubbed "kugelization."

Why did he need to fill so many pages to say something that we know well already? Akiba Rabinowitz from Poltawa told that to us twenty years ago. Jews have learned *Gemarah* and swayed in prayer to atone for their sins without the admonition of Professor Radner, while Socialism has been denounced by venerable God-fearing rabbis. What then is the message that Gedaliah Bublik delivers at such length and in a Germanic Yiddish? One cannot help but pity Orthodox Jewry for being ignored by its opponents and compromised by its friends. Its proponents must do a lot of thinking and learning before they will be ready for the battle. And who knows? Thinking and learning may make it an easier battle for us. We are no longer afraid of excommunication performed by black-inked editorials. They harm no one. Let us wait until the Orthodox camp is ready. We can afford to wait.

Over the Abyss

This is a fragment of a yet unformed vessel, a chapter of a book which, undoubtedly, will never be written, a segment of a thought-process which never stops, which, perhaps, never can stop: thoughts about Judaism.

Beset by the needs of the times, by the overwhelming pressure of countless problems facing us each day, each one clamoring for exclusive attention, we often tend to forget about the heart of the matter. Only a few, select spirits have the inner strength to shoulder the whole of the heavy burden and, refusing to put down the heavy yoke, cling to it joyfully. But for the rest of us ordinary human beings this is too difficult a task. For who can bear the constant sight of an abyss, who can bear standing close to its edge? Yet this is at the base of all our problems — the abyss.

About 300 years ago, a young Parisian scientist, a mathematician and physicist, a scholar of genius, was crossing the Pont Neuf in Paris when suddenly he saw before him an abyss. A gulf had opened up before his eyes, just for a second, in a lightning-like vision, but its effect persisted throughout his entire life, transforming the mathematician and physicist Pascal into, perhaps, the greatest religious thinker of Western European culture. It was the beginning of his inner struggle for faith, and he was filled with a yearning to be close to God, "…not the God of the philosophers, but the God of Abraham, Isaac and Jacob."

When questions about Judaism's role in the world, about the supra-historical phenomenon called "Israel," begin to nag at me anew, I always arrive at a juxtaposition of two concepts: the abyss and the God of Abraham. Then Judaism begins to rise above the problems of the passing day, begins to transcend accidental historical events, and focuses, once again, on a metaphysical question, the question of the abyss. Abyss means chaos, formlessness, infinity, an ever further downward descent, a dimension of bottomless depth. A lack of foundation means also a lack of meaning, means being outside the reign of causality; the world becomes a conglomeration of disconnected, unrelated phenomena.

The beginning. The formless, shapeless, unstructured matter existing in timelessness, is, in a creative moment, subjugated by the will into cohesion. Link by link, a chain of causality is forged, a form takes shape, the abyss is covered up, the infinite becomes finite, the world comes into being, meaning and purpose begin to merge, and life becomes filled with content. The abyss is being filled up, but the abyss struggles; the incomplete and unfinished is in a state of constant warfare against the formed and attracts the weakening elements. The rallying cry of the abyss is death: death that breaks the mold, destroys the completed form, dissolves wholeness; death which is also a part of life.

These thoughts and comments arose as I was leafing through the latest book by the Jewish scholar Dr. Moses Wartman, *The Jewish Teaching of Creation*, a book on Jewish cosmogony. I am sure that I am not doing justice to either the author or his book, but my interest was captured by a single statement (even though unsubstantiated by any factual documentation or philosophical discourse): "This is the fundamental difference between the Jewish monotheistic concept of God and the concept of other nations. In Babylon the abyss had become a symbol of chaos and of evil. In Judaism God fought the abyss and conquered it. There is, therefore, no more evil in the world." This interpretation has the hallmark of an apology, of justification, and an aggrandizement of Jewish theology, of a kind of philosophical nationalism. The author is entitled to his opinion, he may even have some historic justification for it, but he fails to provide sufficient data, nor does he consider the fundamental problem contained within Judaism, one that it has still not carried to term. Yet even in his discourse defending philosophy we find a resonance of the Jewish voice, of the leitmotif that has dominated all of Jewish thought: the struggle with the abyss, the triumph over chaos, and the concern with good and evil.

I have come across very few references to the fact that, fundamentally, the Hebrew words for good and bad, *tov* and *ra*, do not express moral values but are rather a description of an organic, structural state of being, as it were. *Ra*, in the last analysis, means nothing more than broken, unfinished, that is, unformed. Now, as we follow the creation of the world in Genesis, we find, at the end of each day, that "God saw that this was good." I have no exact knowledge of the origin, roots or linguistic nuances of the word *tov*, but its meaning in this context is not "good" in our sense of being just and charitable, but rather whole, completed, formed into shape. Both concepts eventually underwent changes, acquiring different colorations and shadings, becoming infused with moral, social components; "good" came to mean being weak and fractured, while "bad" came to mean being strong and intact. Jewish history politicized the Jewish religious vision; it required this change, and thus it came into being.

Yet a deeply rooted contradiction maintained a constant spiritual struggle within the Jewish psyche, between two basic currents of thought, which accounts for the peculiar sterility of Jewish religious philosophical thought. The teaching of the closed-off abyss gradually sank into oblivion, and the concept of basic evil triumphed even within Jewish thought. And in the very moment that Judaism accepted the *ra*, opened the abyss, it lost its normative impetus, fettering its creative force. Wherever basic problems are being misunderstood or misinterpreted, free and productive thinkers are stymied, and instead of a vision of the world we get the interpretation of symbols.

I may be wrong, but it seems to me that at this very moment we are about to witness a new phenomenon of world-historic import: a third uprising of the Jewish spirit. All indications point that way, the signs are clear; too much hatred against Jews has been ignited throughout the world, the enmity burns too strongly. I say the third uprising because Judaism has waged a constant struggle against the world, a struggle over the abyss. In the ancient Greek world, Greek thought pivoted around the concept of negation; the Platonic concept of non-being was, so to speak, the root of being, a world which arises out of non-existence and which contains, even in its affirmation, elements of negation. But Judaism opposed all negation; its credo was: The world is complete and totally affirmative. Its theory was that evil is merely error, error meaning a state of being torn asunder, which has no legitimacy, and no longer exists in the world. The second struggle was waged against Christianity and, again, around the abyss. A horror of suffering and of evil had fallen on the world, placing an almost unbearable burden on human shoulders. And now comes the third struggle: Chaos, once again, has taken hold of the human spirit, and the abyss is once more devouring life, life that has been formed, completed. We now see mere beginnings, change, incompleteness, and dissolution holding sway, in theory as well as in reality.

And the Jew wanders around the world as in a maze. He senses his truth; it is in his blood, contained in his heritage, but he does not have the courage to accept his own view of the world. The ancient Jewish concepts and formulations are too old, too historically conditioned, and there are, as yet, no new ones. But here and there a Jewish voice is heard, a summons to battle against the abyss, demanding a formed, whole world. This is, in the final analysis, the deepest meaning of socialism, as Marx formulated it, and this is the path that the new Jewish religious thought is beginning to clear for itself, albeit without the courage to pursue it. The thinkers are oblivious to the fact that there exist, after all, only two religious systems in the world today, Hindu and Jewish: the teaching of the halted wheel and the teaching of the covered abyss. All that is in between is mere ritual, is no more religiously creative. And Pascal created no paradox in aligning the concept of bottomless depth with the "spirit of the abyss." He perceived and drew his conclusions. We are seeing the abyss anew, and we must draw our own conclusions, because the abyss has magnetic powers, and the forces of negation are prevailing in the world.

About the Jewish Spirit

The other day I was in the office of a Jewish philanthropic institution when my friend the director engaged me in a conversation about "Jewish charity." "Why do Jews," he asked, "have such peculiar notions of charity? Especially Eastern European Jews? Why are they so dissatisfied with our Western or American methods? I can see no other explanation for it than their utter lack of a sense of organization, of systematic, orderly work methods. They are too individualistic, they proceed without order, without any system."

I was his guest and, wanting to be polite, as is the way among "civilized Anglo-Saxons," I proceeded to agree with him. "You are right, of course, our Eastern European Jews do lack a sense of order and of organization, they act on impulse, from their heart, they do not think systematically. They are...but why should I go on enumerating what you know yourself. The only time a Jew is at his best is when he serves you chicken soup." My words, however, did not fool my friend. Human eyes have a language of their own, and my eyes tend to be rather expressive. To mask them with glasses came to naught because I cannot see a thing through them and get dizzy.

"All right, all right," he said, "you did your gentlemanly duty and agreed with me. Now tell me the truth."

"The truth — if only I knew it. Had I been vouchsafed just a glimpse of it, I would not be sitting here with you, I would not be here at all, doing what I am doing, writing what I write, and doing it so often with a heavy heart because I know that 'this is not it,' that this is not what our age is waiting for, and that I am falling short of fulfilling my allotted task.

"You know, medieval scholastic philosophers said something which has been reverberating within me from the moment I began to concern myself with such problems a long, long time ago. What they said was: The differences between things are countless and nameless. Each individual is unfathomable, (although a better translation of the Latin term might be "ineffable," which really means that it cannot be expressed in words.) The words we do use must match in depth the unique entities they represent, and such words are not to be found in any dictionary. Perhaps the most difficult to fathom among the many species is the Jewish one. All those who claim to have found the key to the "secret of the Jewish soul," to understanding Jewish philosophy, or as a philosophizing hack has once written, to knowing the "philosophy of the Jewish spirit," are either climbing up a slippery slope, or simply engaging in a chatter about all and everything, as is the German wont.

"You ask me why is it that Eastern European Jews have this peculiar view of charity, and why don't they want to accept the general practice? Your question touches on many issues that need to be considered. Charity is a relationship between man and man. It is an ethical and not a social concept. But ethics must have its roots somewhere; it must receive its nurture from deep within the soil in which its roots are imbedded, from the relationship between man and the universe. This, really, is where the true problem lies, and had our generation been able to deal with the tremendous events that we have been slated to experience, we would be concentrating on only one consideration: What is our Jewish way? What is the purpose and meaning of Jewish life, of the Jewish spirit?

"We really should take pride in the fact that a culture has unleashed a fight to the death against us. Let us not fool ourselves or seek comfort in the belief that this is merely a "flicker of anti-Semitism," brought on by economic or political events. They do play a role, of course, but they do not fully account for it. The causes lie deeper. The great dispute between the "Rabbi" and the "Priest" which Heine held up to ridicule was neither funny nor witty, and whatever "odor" he may have attributed to the disputants was the odor of reality, an odor best not to be inhaled since life rarely exudes intoxicating perfumes. It was a serious, bloody dispute that was interrupted for a while by historical upheavals and by an ensuing general normalization. When new difficulties arose and events reached critical proportions, the dispute recommenced, with this difference: Today's "Priest," today's fanatic, poses iron-clad and often dynamite-laden questions, yet today's

"Rabbi" does not know the answers, does not even understand what it is he is being asked.

"The question with which history confronts us now is: What does Judaism want, which is its road to life? In Germany this question is raised with hatred and scorn by Rosenberg and, in a civilized way, by Spengler. This question is being raised indirectly by the Communists, by the Christian theologians, and lastly by the Liberals, seeking an integrated view of the world and an end to the domination by old, inherited books. Their quiet, at times barely articulated questions contain their share of irony and derision. We are asked historical questions, and our reply is couched in political formulae and public relations phraseology. We close our ears even to our own inner voice. Every now and then someone will choose to walk away from the multitude, to weave his own pattern of Jewish thought. Such a one was Franz Rosenzweig, the Jewish philosopher from Frankfurt. It was with an aching heart and after much soul searching that he tackled the Jewish problems, yearning to infuse Judaism with renewed vitality and vigor. He wanted to transform it from being of concern to merely "one nation" to becoming a "Star of Redemption" for the entire modern world. He wanted it to be a spiritual power rather than a mere cipher in the antiquated annals of the history of nations. But Rosenzweig was also merely interpreting Judaism, interpreting it in the light of Hegelianism; he had not sought to go back to the ancient source of Judaism.

"You ask me, my friend (and if you do not, you certainly should), what is the spirit of Judaism? If you had the time and the needed learning, even just a basic linguistic proficiency and historical knowledge, I would have set you down with a book that I have been reading for the last five months. I read and read and am unable to fathom it. It is no more and no less than the *tanach* of the "Rav," the founder of Chabad. Do not think that I have either the required scholarship or the patience to read the *Likuti Momim* (*Collected Writings*), which is the historical book's rightful name. This is a task for only those among us who work in this field and can devote their entire time to it, or for those who harbor such an intense interest in the matter as to overcome all obstacles. The rest of us who lead busy lives earning a living lack the time and the patience to tackle the old text, which, like all original Jewish texts, is written in an ornate, inelegant style.

"Fortunately, a Hasidic scholar and writer, Hayim Itzhak Bunin, has girded his loins, as he states in his preface, to rescue the spirit of the *Tanya* from oblivion by recreating the philosophy of the Chabad and its system of values. It is in this, to a certain extent, stylized form that the *Mishnat Chabad* has become accessible to those of us who lack the patience to explore it in its original form. At first reading you gain the impression of being not in the presence of anything very old, such as medieval philosophy, or the teachings of the saintly Ari and his pupils, but rather of being in an adjacent time and space. And while modern Jewish scholars have shed some light on the pupils, the Ari himself has remained an enigma, a locked treasure chest. Some of the grandchildren of Rabbi Shneur Zalman, the old Rav of Liadi, still live among us, and the aura of tradition still permeates the air. And even in present day New York there are Jews who proclaim themselves "Tamimim," the spiritual heirs of Chabad. Yet we are divided from them by a deep chasm. We may, by dint of the greatest effort, get to the edge and peer over it, but is it possible for us to plumb its depth?

"First of all, we must change our entire terminology. Each of us is accustomed to using certain words and established clichés in our thought process. Philosophy has built up a kind of lexicon of clichés, ready-made words and expressions, and the greatest misunderstandings are apt to arise from the fact that we take traditionally defined words and interpret them in new, yet untried ways. The philosophy of Chabad, however, does not use the terminology of modern philosophy, or even that of Jewish Scholasticism, i.e. that of the Rambam, or of Cresca, or even that of Rabbi Levi Ben Gerson, the 14th century author of *The Wars of God*. Instead, the Hasidic thinkers have taken over the obscure terminology of the Kabbalah, have "popularized" it, have infused the old Chaldaic words with a live Jewish spirit, with "Jewishness." And because Hasidism turns only to its own sources, and because its thought process is immune from all alien influences, it truly mirrors the "spirit" that struggles within the Jew, that struggles with the universal problem.

"What is the struggle about? About the bridge between the 'One' and the 'Multitude,' a problem that is as old as human thought, but which has reached its highest peak, attained its most tragic theme, in Judaism — a struggle raging, I would say, around 'One-ness.' When one speaks of Judaism as 'Monotheism' one uses a Rabbinic formula that is only a shallow rendition of Jewish thought. Mathematically speaking, One is a number, a beginning, the beginning of a numerical chain or the completion of another one, and both numerical chains are infinite, composed of smaller numbers (halves, quarters, etc.). The positive number One on the one side faces the negative, Minus One, on the other, and in the infinite space between them reposes the Zero. But this is not the Jewish metaphysical concept of 'One-ness.' Nothing precedes the One, nothing follows it, the One stands alone, and nothing can exist outside of it. If we peel away the terminology of the Kabbalah, we find its essence — the world is God because God is the world. But how does the world come into being? How does the multitude issue from the One? The Ari provided the concept, and the Chabad theory spun it out. It is the concept of *tzimtzum*, in which the One, the Infinity, which is time and space and yet not contained in either time or space, has 'shrunk' like a dress that has been taken in. The dress is still the same, but there is a new seam where the taking-in took place, and this seam, this 'shrinking into oneself,' is the act of creation, is the world.

"Pursued logically, this idea should lead us rather close to Spinoza's thinking, which is that there is no will, or ethics, and that man is an integral part of existence, like the glimmer produced by a ray of light. How can there be a link between the infinite and the finite? And there is the tragic leap of Jewish thought — it leaps over the abyss, fastens itself like a spangle on the eternal garment, as the *Tanya* puts it, and therefore is a part of it, yearning for it. The world is merely an opening-up of the seam, a yearning to open up. And since human beings alone are granted this yearning, it is the duty of every man to see in each passing minute a new unfolding and to yearn for its realization. From the above theory flow the ethics and the moral code of Judaism, based on humility, the equality of all human beings, and a partnership that unites all men. Since we all stand merely on the threshold, 'all lives are of equal worth, and no one may consider his own life more important than that of any fellow man. Equality, absolute equality, this is the absolute decree.' This is the ethical philosophy of Chabad; this is the deepest conception of the ethical philosophy of Judaism.

"I do not want to burden you too much, my friend. I believe that metaphysics is a difficult matter, which does not lend itself to casual conversation. Nor do I want to unroll before you the entire philosophy of Hasidism and the essence of the Chabad. Perhaps there will arise a new, profound Jewish thinker who will pick up the threads and weave a system out of the loose conceptual strands. Or is it better to leave them loose? For perhaps thinking is akin to the circulation of blood, which circulates only when the arteries are kept open.

"You ask me: What is the 'Jewish spirit?' I can only tell you that it is a spring that is so deeply embedded that only rarely can anyone find his way to it. You ask: What is 'Jewish charity?' And I answer: It is a network of human relationships that could have saved the world, if the world truly wanted to be saved."

My friend had finished smoking his cigar and was looking at me through his thick lenses. "Well, well," he sighed, "you surely have mastered the art of obfuscating the simplest matters. I am afraid that your philosophy is too lofty for me. I shall ask some college professor to write an article on charity." My friend wished for greater clarity, but alas, we are able to perceive clearly only the things that stretch out before us, on level ground. Our tragedy, indeed, lies in the fact that we are afraid to scale the mountains or to descend into the chasm.

Prescriptions for Judaism

Once again Judaism! Once again the eternal question about the future, the fate, the path of Judaism. It is a question which has grown more than tiresome already, and yet, one must raise it. It is a moral obligation imposed by one's conscience. One must, from time to time, or perhaps always, think, talk, and concern oneself with that question. They may be idle thoughts, they may, perhaps, be boring, but this is the essence of all spiritual life. To think about truly important matters is never "interesting," nor is it "amusing"; it is a sacrificial labor.

The question is often raised, mostly by single-minded nationalists of various hues: Why and for whose sake must one always concern oneself with such "sterile" problems? Do other nations do it? Do the French, the Germans or the Americans pound their heads against the wall and wrack their brains questioning their own "existence," their "essence," and the "meaning" of their lives? Is it not enough to be alive? Does this fact demand any justification? Is not the "I am, therefore I am" a sufficient declaration?

The questioners do not see, however, that their views are inaccurate, and that they do not understand the fundamental question. When we say that the French, the Americans, and all the other nations do not, day in and day out, question, explore, or analyze the foundations of their being, we are talking about the average Frenchman or American, about the multitude, the masses. What about the Jewish masses? When a Jew recites, once a year: "What am I, what is our life?" he does so automatically. And even if he does think about the meaning of what he is

27

intoning, he thinks of it in terms of personal, general human life. Should he broaden his thinking to include a specifically Jewish content, his thoughts turn to the external aspects of Jewish life, to its political, social and economic manifestations.

Other nations, however, also include a group of people whose life work consists in thinking for and about the collective. The entire cultural work of other nations, furthermore, is nothing more than an endeavor to find a way to define their national individuality, to affirm the meaning of their existence. This has been the life work of Goethe; this has been his gift to Germany. This has been the role of the creative work of Victor Hugo, Balzac and Flaubert in France. This has been, until recently, the aim of all of Russian culture. To seek a path is to live; those who are about to die do not search for one. Only those search for a path who are still in the midst of life. Therefore, the fundamental question facing the Jewish thinker is: Where do we stand? The hallmark of a philosopher being the constant exploration of his inner self, the eternal Jewish self-questioning is, then, not a symptom of decadence or weakness, but rather a sign of its vitality.

The greatest difficulty of the problem is posed, actually, not by Judaism but by the multiplicity of Judaisms. Each country has its own, idiosyncratic Judaism. Because the problem Judaism faces in Germany is different from the one it faces in England, in Italy or in Russia; one is frequently faced with the need to look not for one but for diverse answers, for solutions appropriate to different countries. But it is in America that Judaism is facing its most complicated and severe problem.

It is not anti-Semitism which threatens us most. More important, more difficult, and more consequential than the way in which others see us, is the way in which we view ourselves. We must come to grips with the questions: What is it we want? What do we expect from ourselves? Why should we continue on our historic path? I say "why," not "how," and therein lies the radical difference between us and others, between American Jews and other American national groups, because for them there is only the "how." If a German or an Italian cannot find a way to maintain his German or Italian national culture, he simply becomes an American like all others, he relinquishes his historic identity, because he has no answer to a "why." For us, however, the "why" is of fundamental concern, even though up to now it had not been an acute one.

The attention and energies of American Jewry have been totally absorbed by the ongoing process of renewal, by the arithmetic progression, by the influx of immigrants, by the hard, physical labor of adaptation and adjustment, by securing an economic foothold, by all these purely individual tasks. This process is now almost at an end. The flow of humanity has slowed down to a trickle. The immigrants have "adjusted," they have gained a more secure foothold. It may not be quite the way they would have wished or expected from their vision of the "New World." Their foothold may not be deep enough to protect them from any approaching storms, but yet…but still…

As American Jewry came to feel sufficiently secure to release its spiritual forces, it gave birth to the American Jewish question. It is no accident that so much has been written of late about Judaism, especially in English. Much of the writing is foolish, childishly immature and superficial, but the very fact that people write shows that people think, that people feel a need to immerse themselves more deeply in Judaism. What interests me are not the answers but the questions that are being asked. I look at questionnaires issued by Jewish "dignitaries" such as Adolph Ochs from the *Times,* by rabbis and community leaders, trying to find a solution to the question: What shall we do if we want to remain as we are? If we want to keep the immigrants at bay? I see them furrowing their brows and I hear them talk nebulously about "Jewish education," about "Jewish character," about remaining Jewish in America, etc., etc. And I see the tragic emptiness that has developed in the Jewish consciousness, how it has shed all its values.

I do not see a religious renaissance anywhere in the world, except, perhaps, in India. And there it is due to the influence of a deeply religious, ecstatic man, Mahatma Gandhi. By his example, his life, his personality, he has awakened in India forces which were already on the verge of somnolence. What he did was to reinterpret religious concepts and to infuse a new ethical enthusiasm into the religious thought of India. And this is the only way to inject new life into religious beliefs, wherever they may be. This holds true for Jews as well. And this is, exactly, what we are lacking. We do not have the personality, the impetus, the ecstasy, the new approach. We lack the spiritual teachers and leaders. We have "Doctors of Divinity" who sermonize in temples about everything in the world and who repeat, week in and week out, the same worn-out theological phrases. They are theological functionaries hired by their congregations, subject to their presidents. They are splendid representatives to the outside world, but their role in the community is an insignificant one, and they don't fulfill very well whatever function they still have.

We even have propagandists on behalf of Judaism, but what we do not have are propagandists within and about Judaism. Theology urges us to practice the commandments, but the Jewish individual wants more than pragmatic religion; he also wants a foundation and pathos. The Jew longs for ecstasy. Jews have always longed for it, even when the danger of disintegration did not loom so threateningly. And they have created mysticism, in the form of Hasidism. The Hasidic ecstasy enlivened Judaism, infusing it with new courage, uncovering a deeper source. This source is now covered over, sealed up. We are again being offered clichés about Judaism's irrelevance, about its great fatigue, about our inability to advance and to achieve. Let all the advocates of seminaries and Jewish Sunday schools and Hebrew classes, let them not fool themselves, let them not entertain illusions that words, books and dozens of new rabbis will be able to sustain Judaism in America. The Catholic Church learned its secret from their thinker Thomas Aquinas: "Love is above all knowledge." Their entire system is, therefore, a different one. They did not want to spread theological knowledge among the masses; they infused them with ecstasy, the ecstasy of love.

The Hasidim also knew the secret, and that is why they so quickly prevailed. Now it must become clear to us that in America the Jewish personality is disintegrating into its component parts. This is a fact, you cannot stop it, it is a historic process. Palliative measures, old-fashioned prescriptions, grandmothers' remedies are all useless. One must turn to scientific methods, to the newest ones. One must gather the split elements again and create a new spiritual organism, a new Jewish personality, even at the risk of losing an entire group of adherents. Because Judaism is not defined by numbers, Judaism is still a spiritual process, is creativity, and creativity is an act of constant renewal. Creativity is unafraid, is not teleological; it is not compelled to keep an eye on the "Thou shalt not." For too long we have been focusing on the prohibitions, reluctant to touch upon sensitive matters, lest it cause us pain, lest it harm us. What we are left with, therefore, is only history, only apologia, i.e. politics. If in former times philosophy, and thought in general, was said to be "in the service of theology," religion now can be said to be in "the service of pragmatism."

We are, however, living in a time of emancipation. History has emancipated the Jew, and the Jew must now emancipate Judaism. He must free it from the chains of history and restore its freedom of movement, its right to autonomy. If one is looking for a prescription for Judaism, it requires only one: inner freedom.

"Au bon entendeur — salut"

My article "Prescriptions for Judaism" has elicited a few letters from readers. The Jewish world, the Jewish reader, is still more profound than the average Jewish writer. He has not yet acquired the professional cynicism, the scorn of all thought, the supercilious attitude to everything that is not crystal clear, to everything that is "non-literary." This is, perhaps, the only consolation a writer has. Were it not for a soul here and there, for unknown, troubled, searching souls determined to do their own thinking, all the writing would, truly, be a mere drop of water falling into the ocean. The letters I have received are all different from one another. Some are excited and troubled, others well thought through and admonishing. And all of them want an answer, a personal answer.

This would be, perhaps, the right approach to follow. To address not everyone, not just an abstract multitude, but to speak to the individual, to a concrete human being. And not only to talk to him but to draw closer to him, and to draw closer to one another all those who search, all those who ask something from life, all those who suffer in their Jewishness. But the time for this has not come yet, not for me and not for them. None of us yet sees the way. We are following different paths. Perhaps someday we shall meet at an intersection. Perhaps not. But I do not want to bar anyone's path, nor do I believe in leapfrogging over bars. It does not matter; let it be painful, let it make life more difficult. "Living is not important, what is important is traversing the ocean."

One reader, one questioner, wants to know: What are the remedies that I prescribe for Judaism? And when I speak of prescriptions, do I mean that Judaism is sick? Is it really sick? What are the symptoms? And if it is sick, must one heal it? He reminds me of a new law just passed in Denmark, a law which allows a physician to speed up the death of an incurably ill patient. And he reminds me, further, of the dictum of the ancient Greek physician Galen: "What fire cannot cure, the knife can, and if the knife cannot do it then death is the cure." According to ancient medicine, a wound has to be cauterized, and a tumor has to be cut out, otherwise the organism dies and the "cure" comes about on its own.

I do not know if I can provide answers to all the questions and all the doubts, here and now, in one sitting. But I am obliged to give my diagnosis. Why sick? What are the symptoms? It is true, no sooner does one make a diagnosis, take down a "medical history," than one is besieged from all sides by analyses and warnings and remedies. From solicited and unsolicited sources come offers of patented and over-the-counter medicines. "Nature-doctors," especially, beseech us to return to nature, to the earth, to work, certainly to rest, and to observe physically and spiritually wholesome diets. Another category are the professional God-knowers, if one may call them that, the rabbis, the "shamans," who have discovered that an evil spirit, a *dybbuk*, has invaded us and must be exorcised with amulets, with imprecations, with ancient words and ancient formulae. And they think that these incantations can heal the illness of Judaism.

Then there is a group of Jews standing on the side who do not feel bound by any formulae, who feel no fear of a final ending and its consequences. This is the Jewish intelligentsia, dispersed throughout the world, often without any contact with each other, often alienated from each other by their different cultural environments. And yet, be it in Berlin or in London or even in New York (and surely soon in Tel Aviv), Jewish intellectuals agree on the need of a moral stocktaking. Are the works of Jacob Wassermann, Ber Hoffman, Buber, Claude Montefiore and even Joseph Klausner, not a kind of an on-going self-analysis of the Jewish soul, an attempt to reaffirm Jewish values? I mention these names with respect. Each of them is a string, giving forth its own tone, without, however, arriving at a harmonic unity. Ber Hoffman asks: What is Jacob's mission? Wassermann asks: What is the role of the Jew in the world order? Buber is looking for the source of Jewish ecstasy. And Klausner, perhaps unaware that his inner urge has led him to become an echo of generation-long deliberations, has returned to the old parting of the ways, to the point where, thousands of years ago, the Jewish and the non-Jewish world went their separate ways. Perhaps forever?

From all these analyses flows one answer, though often disguised, though often neither formulated nor even intended: Jews suffer from a spiritual inhibition. They are walled off from life by thousands of years of "Thou shall not," by a constant rule of "It is forbidden." Upon the portal of Judaism is engraved the word *asur* — it is prohibited. And even that which is not prohibited is, really, not quite permissible. This is the reason that Judaism became such a tremendous cultural power and, more than that, became culture itself, because it is founded upon the "it is forbidden." All of culture, after all, is nothing more than restrictions placed upon the "free" man, placing him within a desired framework, surrounding him with a given atmosphere; it is, in a word, what we call religion.

The Greeks, the Romans, all of classical culture, labored to create a "religion," and they did not succeed. They issued laws, but those laws lacked moral authority. They ruled men, not man. The only culture that was able to do it, which had managed to do it, was the Jewish one. Jews laid down the foundation for religion, just as they formulated the concept of God. This is why all of Jewish culture, from its beginning, had been a purely religious one. But then a branching out took place. The religious motif was joined by the national, historic one. That meant imposing limits on what had been limitless and fettering man with two chains. The Jew has been imprisoned by history more than any other people in the world. Everyone else is free to forget, to renounce the past, and to live merely in the present. The Jew was not free to do it, he was not allowed. Never advancing, always held back, he would repeatedly pull at the chain; but he was unable to break it, because a break would have meant descending into an alien, chaotic world. He was forced to carry history on his shoulders in order to protect a world which he himself helped to build.

Rudolf Borchardt, in his wonderful booklet *The Book of Servitude*, expresses a genuinely Jewish thought when he has his yeoman address God: "If you do not do what I want, I will erase your name from my memory." Wittingly or unwittingly, Borchardt expressed, in his way, what the Hasidim and the rabbis said in their words and their rulings: The Jew must maintain mastery over himself in order for the world to exist. He was even afraid to look too deeply into his own depth for fear that he might lose his foothold.

I have recently read in a biography of Freud a remarkable saying about Jews. "We Jews," he said at a meeting of psychoanalysts, "are the seeds of culture, and seeds are trodden into the ground." They know that this is their fate, and they accept that it must be so, that this is the meaning of their life.

But one cannot forever be content being an instrument towards reaching a prescribed goal. There comes a time when one wants to work towards a goal of one's own making. The urge is always there, but it is suppressed and barred from coming to the fore by a process of "inhibition," by a lack of freedom, by a dependence on something that exists outside of us. We therefore cannot react simply, naturally, to whatever happens around us. This is why all of our reactions to world events are so muted, and this is why we react to our own events in such secretive, whispering asides. We do not allow ourselves to think through to the end the concerns of our present and our future. We have, therefore, ceased being the universal factor we once were and that we should be: the religious factor.

What is the role we are playing in spiritual life today? We have scholars, we have explorers and artists, so why, then, are we so noncreative? Because we have withdrawn from the field that is peculiarly our own. The world is anxiously waiting for a word; it yearns and it suffers and it is so grateful when it hears one. Is Spinoza's great cultural impact not due to the fact that he addressed the world as a Jew? Unlike Maimonides, who used Aristotelian concepts in an attempt to understand, interpret and maintain Jewish tradition, Spinoza chose a free, creative approach to the world, to God and to himself. And why did Henri Bergson have such an impact on the world? His theories may be based on wrong premises, his philosophy may be more poetry than reasoning, but it is, once more, a religious doctrine of life, and this is more important than a logically correct theoretical system.

It is true, of course, that Spinoza, Bergson and other more or less important thinkers and seekers have often fought against Judaism, openly or in disguised ways. But what they fought against was a Judaism that had settled into tradition and history and had stopped being a spring. A spring never stops; the water that flows forth today is not the water of yesterday. And the spring is still alive. Somewhere in the depth is its origin, a boundary beyond which we cannot go. But the spring releases water that can feed rivers and fertilize dry land.

We have now reached a point in time when the modern Jew wants to find a way out of his spiritual entanglement; he wants to begin anew; he yearns, once again, for religion, now that he is no longer bound by "religion"; he wants to arrive at a Jewish view of life such as united us once but does no more. A view of life which does not depend on the language one speaks, nor on The Book, nor on the admonition: "This may threaten the survival of Judaism."

We must, therefore, release our strength and throw ourselves into the battle. During the last few centuries Judaism withdrew from the battle, draping itself in the *tallit*, pulling the prayer shawl over its head and secluding itself in a corner. Nothing mattered except the preservation of Jewish tradition. Then the question arose: What it is that we want to preserve, a museum relic? A mummy?

Let the Albanians be apprehensive about their survival; the Jews need not be afraid. A spiritual element of universal import may subject itself to analysis, and even if it should split into its component parts, will this process not result in a new configuration? When my reader, my questioner, wants to know what I mean by "inner freedom" and of what avail it will be, my answer is: The freest man is the one who masters himself, who subjects himself to his own penance, who chooses not to be content, cocooned and happy. The way of freedom leads from the merits achieved by our ancestors to merits we achieve on our own. At the point when one reaches that plateau, one, in turn, becomes a "Father"; one, in turn, becomes a beginning.

We Jews have too long depended upon the merits of our Fathers. Now it is up to us to be a beginning — or an end.

Josephus and Simeon

In the editorial office of the Zionist organ *Die Welt* at 9 Tirkenstrasse in Vienna, there was, in the early years of the movement, no name more frequently evoked and vilified than that of Josephus Flavius. It served as a sobriquet condemning all anti-Zionists, all assimilators, all representatives of the Jewish cultural community, and all German-nationalist journalists.

Josephus' main antagonist was a Bohemian Jew of bear-like stature and clumsiness, an ardent Zionist but a boor and a complete ignoramus. Not only could he not read Hebrew script and had no knowledge at all of Jews and of Judaism, but he had no desire to learn or to know. Furthermore, he disliked all Jewish scholars and was capable of tearing them to pieces, would we but let him. But what a good job he did at knocking down anti-Semitic students at the University of Vienna! Every Saturday he would don long, polished boots, drape a white and blue cummerbund around his chest, put on his hat at a rakish angle and sally forth with other Jewish-nationalist students to engage in ferocious battle with any German-nationalist students they might come across. It was a real pleasure to watch them. After the battle this most dedicated contributor to *Die Welt* would return to the office, at times with a bandaged head or limb, but always beaming with satisfaction and joy, and sit down to write a scalding article against Josephus Flavius.

◆   ◆   ◆

A few years later I met another Jewish writer. This one did not come from Bohemia, was not endowed with bear-like strength and bearing, nor was he an ignoramus. Just the opposite: he was small, thin, feeble and a veritable Pharisee. He was as desiccated as the fig which served as nourishment for the legendary Rabbi Zadok, and he seemed to be altogether a reincarnation of him. He was the son of an old-fashioned, unworldly, small-town rabbi who had little awareness of there being any other places in the world than his native town and Jerusalem. He lived his life not in the small city located between Ouman and Kiev but in Babylon, or, perhaps, in Jerusalem, among the Pharisees.

His son became enthralled by Josephus Flavius. He was so captivated that he chose as his pen name "Ben Gurion," the lion cub, which was the Hebrew name his contemporaries had bestowed upon Josephus Flavius, or Joseph ben Mattatiah ha-Kohen. Small wonder, then, that Micah Joseph Berdyczewski became himself a Josephus among modern Jews, one of the few who were still dreaming of a Judaism free from all earthly fetters, free from all legalistic boundaries imposed by cities and counties, who yearned for a Judaism as a spiritual force and nothing more. From Podolia his path led to Weimar, from the prayer house to Friedrich Nietzsche. And he turned hostile towards the modern-day "zealots," the various Simeon bar Gioras. He branded them as half-Jews, converts themselves or children of converts, Jews who lacked roots in Jewish culture, Jews who lacked tradition and, therefore, lacked all ability to view Judaism critically, or even the will to renew it. He could see a bridge connecting the Pharisees to Nietzsche, but he could see no bridge connecting him to the old Judaism of Simeon bar Giora.

Berdyczewski entertained the dream that Josephus might reenter the stream of Jewish culture, that he might be accepted back into Jewish life, that he might be freed from his Greek imprisonment. For until now we have known Josephus only in his Greek disguise. But this Pharisee, the priest of Jerusalem, had written his books *The Antiquities of the Jews* and *The Wars against Apion* in "the language of his people," as he had said, i.e. in Hebrew or in Aramaic. But the original was lost, just as almost all ancient Jewish books dealing with the life and history of the Jewish people were lost. Jews seem to have disliked history. The people with the most remarkable history, the people who have left the deepest imprint on world-history, have not taken the least care to preserve their historic documents. History is action, but following the destruction of the Second Temple, after the Jewish spirit prevailed against the restrictions imposed on Judaism, the Jewish mind withdrew from all action. The past is acceptable, but only as long as it is "Godly," as long as it can serve as a moral guideline, as long as it can be fitted into a sermon. The future is up to the messiah, that is to God, and once more to legends. But the present, random daily life was of little interest to the Jews. All that has remained from the old, traditionally accepted history are the Midrashim and Lamentations, either poetry or dirges.

There once was a profusion of literature about Jews and Jewish life in the remarkable, eventful, tumultuous period of the Second Temple. Josephus Flavius mentions a number of them — the Book of Nicholas of Damascus and the Book of Julian, among others — books written in "Jewish" as well as in Greek. There were books written in Jerusalem, in Antioch, in Alexandria, but only one book has remained, one monument, and that is the work of Josephus.

The time has truly come for Jews to recapture their history. Each new document that comes to light opens up a new vista on Jewish life and Jewish thought. Jews also need to acquaint themselves with the historical literature that has survived. Dr. Berdyczewski's dream to return Josephus to the Jewish people, to change Josephus Flavius back into Joseph ben Mattatiah Ha-Kohen, has come true. Dr. I.N. Shmichuni has undertaken this task, being the first to publish *The Jewish War*, the history of the tragic end of Jewish independence.

◆   ◆   ◆

It is not my intent to enter into a critique of the translation, into a comparison of texts or, even, into an assessment of Josephus Flavius himself. Was he a traitor, an assimilated Greek, a sycophant, a man in whose veins flowed ink instead of blood? Or was he a far-seeing politician with a broader outlook on Jewish history, a kind of prophet who had foreseen the course of world history? It is futile to try to account for historic acts and for the people who committed them. History is assessment, but not a moral one. To render judgment on the basis of our current perspective is meaningless. We must look at events and at men through the lens of their own time and then fit them into the overall framework.

As I reread the history of the destruction, of the end of Jerusalem in a good, clear Hebrew translation, a question arose in my mind: Do we have to regret this outcome? What if history had taken a somewhat different turn? What if Titus had not been as skillful a strategist as Josephus portrays him, or if a miracle had occurred, such as the sudden uprisings in other Roman provinces which forced Vespasianus to cut short his attacks on the Jews? What if the Jerusalemites had listened to the well-informed speeches of Joseph ben Mattatiah and submitted for a time to Roman domination, in order to save the Temple and the entire old order? Might it have been better, might Judaism have gained more from it? Whom does history vindicate? Joseph Ha-Kohen, the nobleman, the Pharisee, the scholar and the polished orator, or the coarse half-Jew from Geshur in the Trans-Jordania, Simeon bar Giora, who stood up for the Jewish people, for Jewish freedom? Historical tools now at our disposal do not help us understand what it was that Simeon bar Giora, Johanan Gush Halev and their followers — the zealots and destroyers as Josephus called them — actually meant to achieve. Why had they been so enraged, why had they attacked so many people, especially the priests and the nobility? Had they not understood what was commonly known at the time, that tiny Judea could not withstand the Roman colossus, that the struggle was a hopeless one?

Josephus does not offer us any reasons, but from what he does tell us, and even from the abuse he heaps upon the "destroyers," we can deduce that this was a struggle not only for political freedom but also for social equality, a struggle for the integrity of Judaism.

In one of the last, most tragic chapters in Josephus' history, there is a casually sketched yet wonderfully depicted moment. Josephus, with some other Jews who had escaped captivity by going over to Titus, are walking beneath the walls of Jerusalem, pleading with their beleaguered brethren: "Stop, submit! You are sacrificing the Holy City in vain, you are destroying the Temple!" The city is burning, and the towers are about to collapse. The desperate fighters are barricaded in the Temple. They know already that they are lost; they know it and will not submit. And they answer: "Why are you always speaking about the Temple? Whose house is it, if not the House of God? And does God, do we, not have another Temple? The entire world is our Temple. Let our Temple burn down, if this is its fate. If we live and remain free, we will build a new one. And if we die, if we are conquered, of what concern is the Temple to us?"

Josephus pays scant attention to these utterances. His own long orations and those of the High Priests seem much more important to him. But to those of us who see the results of the struggle and who still bear the scars of the catastrophe, to us these words are of a very different import. They offer us the key to Jewish history; they shed light on the meaning of our life. Is Judaism a petrified institution or a living, driving force? Does the Jew live in a prayer house whose foundations are to be eternally preserved, or in a prayer house that can be destroyed, burned down and rebuilt — a prayer house that is bigger and wider than a building, that encompasses the whole world?

This dualism, this split in the Jewish soul, is still with us today. Joseph ben Mattatiah and Simeon bar Giora are two sides of the Jewish coin, two shapers of the Jewish world. Josephus remained a prisoner of Titus and wrote books. Simeon was captured by Titus, brought to Rome and thrown off the parapets of the Roman Capitol to be impaled upon the Tarpeian Rock. Josephus, the defender of Judaism as the established order, has remained a literary figure. Simeon, the ignorant one, the "half-Jew" who wanted to be a whole one, who, with whole-hearted naiveté and pathos, believed in the possibility of a Judaism whose prayer house would encompass the world — Simeon has survived Rome, the Capitol and the Tarpeian Rock. From the burning towers of Jerusalem he leapt into the depth of the Jewish soul — and there he still lives.

All of us today are reliving the life of Simeon bar Giora and his struggle against Joseph ben Mattatiah. We do so willingly or unwillingly, wittingly or unwittingly.

New Heavens and Old Clothes

They had been neighbors, friends. They had grown up together, attending the same school, learning Torah from the same rabbi. One was Isaiah, the son of Amos; the other was Levi, the son of Simeon. The old Amos was a descendent of one of the grandest families of Jerusalem, with links to the royal house. Rumor had it that he was a brother of the King of Judea. But it was only a rumor, no one knew the true story except for Amos himself, and he kept silent.

Simeon had been a simple Jew, quite an ordinary householder, a merchant who owned caravans and who traveled with them to Sidon, Egypt, and even further. Whenever he returned from his travels with camels laden with a multitude of merchandise, with golden fabrics, silver vessels, Arabic perfumes, and fine, white Egyptian linens, he would tell wondrous tales about the lands he had seen. He talked about foreign customs, about strange beasts and birds, about wild desert-dwellers and, especially, about Jews who were roaming the earth, trading, buying and selling.

Among the listeners at the market or at the house of Simeon, the merchant, the most curious and enraptured ones were the two young boys, Isaiah, the son of Amos, and Levi, the son of Simeon. When they went home from the market or were sitting in a corner of the house of study, they would spin out what they had heard, and their young imaginations would endow Simeon's vague descriptions with brilliant, alluring colors. And both made a vow to go out into the wide world, to traverse the earth.

They grew up and went their separate ways. Isaiah withdrew from the rabbinic domain and joined a group which society had, rather jeeringly, dubbed "The sons of the prophets." Old Amos died, and Isaiah became homeless. He walked the streets of Jerusalem, having renounced all pleasures of life. He retreated to the caves of the Judean mountains to find an answer to his yearnings among the wine growers and their simple way of life. One day found him pacing back and forth, in a dreamy mood, in his small room in a poor part of Jerusalem where he once taught school, when he heard a voice: "Whom shall I send? Who shall represent Me?" He understood what this meant; he knew that this was the call, long-awaited. Until now he felt drawn to go out into the world, but he did not know where: to the deserts of Arabia? to the shores of the river Nile? to Babylon or the mysterious lands on the other side of the ocean? He felt drawn to new heavens, to wider, more majestic ones than the ones rendered ordinary by the pettiness, sameness, provincialism, isolation and limitations of life in Jerusalem. Nothing was original, even the clothes that the women wore were copied from somewhere else. Everything was imported from foreign lands, even thoughts.

The very few who understood him and shared his thoughts, the small number of young, deeply rooted Jewish poets, were in despair. And for good reason. The people played deaf, they refused to listen. When the prophet Micah had come to talk to them, people jostled him on the street. The great, profound poet Amos was ridiculed, his speech was mimicked; people called him the tongue-tied stutterer. And life continued on the same, old, well-trodden path. People went on saying: "Jews are a wearisome, complaining people. They cannot distinguish between their enemies and their friends, those who want to lift them up and lead them onto new paths." Anyone who chose to be a prophet to the Jews had to be prepared for scorn, humiliation and a difficult life.

These were the thoughts which occupied Isaiah, and his heart was filled with sorrow as he paced in his room, struggling with himself. He saw, clearly, the clouds which were gathering above the Judean mountains. There were enemies on all sides. Assyria, Babylon, Egypt, Edom, Moab were merely waiting for the hour when they would attack Jerusalem and conquer it. And the Jews of Jerusalem were paying no heed to the danger, were quite unconcerned. They were content to live for the day, enjoying their possessions, yet ever greedy for more. The few wise Jews who understood the portents of the time, who knew what Jerusalem stood for, what its meaning and its essence were, they were already old and lacked the power to influence people and effect a change in their way of life. This is what the best among the Jewish youth were telling each other, and they grieved for the future of Judea and Jerusalem.

The time demanded young people with courage and the will to sacrifice, people with broad vision and a will to work toward it. But there were none to meet this need. Instead, there were go-betweens rushing like scorched mice from Jerusalem to Egypt, from Jerusalem to Babylon, from one king to the next, bribing one and flattering another and promising each a mountain of gold. Having exhausted all the intrigues and tricks at hand, they proudly returned home, bringing back tiny promises from a king or a court, who, surely, did not mean to keep them. They were eager to save Jerusalem. But should Jerusalem be saved? Jerusalem as it now stands, a city and nothing more than a city? Is this alone its purpose and its end? The walls of Zion, the borders of Judea, a piece of land and the bit of sky above it — is this all?

And Isaiah responded to the voice: "Send me, I will go, I will speak, and may they do to me what they want. I shall offer my body to those who will want to strike me, to those whose hands are outstretched to slap me. Someone must take on the mission, someone must free himself from all fear, must be willing to sacrifice all he cherishes, life itself if necessary. Jerusalem is worthy of it." And he stepped out onto the street, and with his clear, ringing, melodic voice he began his song: "Hear O Heavens, and give ear O Earth, for the Lord has spoken." And fear and wonderment fell on Jerusalem. A new word had been heard, the word of a new heaven, and of a wide, wide world.

As Isaiah ventured out into the streets of Jerusalem, his childhood friend Levi, the son of Simeon, was also making his first appearance on the market place. Old Simeon was dead, and he died a pauper. His last several journeys had reduced him to poverty. Desert Bedouins had attacked his caravan, ransacked his merchandise and taken all the money, everything he had amassed in the course of his long, difficult travels. Borrowing money from friends and from usurers, pledging his house, selling everything he possessed and everything his relatives could give him, he had started anew. But success eluded him once more. His laden ships sank, the slaves carrying the merchandise rebelled and ran off with the wares; old Simeon himself barely escaped with his life. Suffering both in body and mind, he made his way back to Jerusalem where he soon died of a broken heart.

Levi remained an orphan, homeless, poor, without a future. But he did not spend much time lamenting his fate. His father had left him one inheritance: the lust to wander. He still recalled the wondrous tales Simeon had told about the Jewish merchants who wandered through foreign lands, through alien states, beneath other skies, trading and getting rich. They bought and sold everything that came to hand, stopping at nothing, taking on the difficult task of amassing more and more. And Levi decided to go out into the wide world. Jerusalem was too small for him, he was drawn to new horizons and to wide oceans. He followed his father's counsel, that in foreign lands Jews should start trading among the poor who cannot afford to buy from the proud, expensive local merchants. Wealthy people have no need to come to the Jew, but the poor, the people who buy used merchandise at low prices, who like things but cannot afford to pay for it all at once, and need to buy on credit, those are the people the Jew can do business with. A Jew must start slowly, little by little, step by step, he must climb the ladder rung by rung. A Jew must not be conspicuous, must not elbow his way into the ranks of the rich and the great. He must wait until they come to him. And they will come, they must come.

This was the testament Simeon left to his son Levi, and Levi followed it in pious obedience. He used the few remnants of his father's great fortune to purchase old clothes from the ladies and the housewives of Jerusalem, from beautiful women who would not wear a dress more than once. And through the streets of Jerusalem could be heard Levi's voice: "Old clothes, who has old clothes to sell"?

A wind arose, a stormy, hot wind. Its waves spread from one corner of the world to another, over oceans and deserts, from east to west and from south to north. And it scooped up the two voices: "Hear O Heavens," rang out the sweet, melodious voice of Isaiah, the son of Amos. "Old clothes," repeated the dry, low-keyed voice of Levi, the son of Simeon.

Lacking Pepper

Reading the brief wire from Poland gave me a joy and a respect for the Jewish people such as I have not experienced for a long time. In the city of Ostrog in the province of Volhynia, the part of Volhynia that now belongs to Poland, 10,000 Jews paraded in honor of the 300th jubilee of the Maharsha, Rabbi Shmuel Edels. A parade of 10,000 Jews in a small provincial town such as Ostrog is more than a commemoration by scholars and literati; it is a holiday observed by the entire community. This means that in the city of Ostrog, in the province of Volhynia, there survives among the Ukrainian and Polish Jews a veneration of Jewish cultural achievements. There are pogroms in Poland, boycotts, persecution, poverty, suffering, strife between the parties, Jewish disunity. Jews are living beneath a dark cloud, yet, at the same time, they are commemorating the jubilee of the complicated, sharp, mind-taxing exegete Maharsha, who has caused a great deal of trouble for so many generations of Jewish youngsters.

It was 300 years ago, in 1631, that the Yeshivah principal Rabbi Shmuel Edels, son of Rabbi Yehuda Edels, died in the city of Ostrog. On his mother's side he was the great-grandson of the famed Rabbi Yehuda Low of Prague, to whom legend ascribes the creation of the golem. Born in Poznan, he became the town's Yeshivah principal, then moved to Chelm and Tiktin before settling in Ostrog, where he achieved the height of scholarship, becoming the remarkable, idiosyncratic figure in Jewish cultural history, the Maharsha.

I have often wondered why modern Jewish literature, be it Yiddish or Hebrew, has shown so little interest in and understanding of such a genuinely Jewish characteristic as the rabbinate and rabbinical literature. The Jewish press is spilling over with Hasidic stories and biographies of Hasidic rabbis, and there has grown up a voluminous literature on Hasidism in both Hebrew and Yiddish. Every newspaper and magazine contains both serious assessments of and lyrical accolades to Hasidism, but there is almost no mention of the stern, serious explorers of Jewish thought, who have truly carried on the train of thought, who have spun the golden, or, if you will, spider-thin threads with which to bind together the links of thought. There is nary a mention of the highbrow, original thinkers, the scholars, the *geonim*. They are surrounded by silence; their names and their work are forgotten.

It is natural. People are attracted by that which can be grasped easily, and the Agadah, the Midrash, legends and ethics are so easy to grasp. They bring forth the romance, the poetry of life. Whereas the prose is gray and difficult, especially the prose of the rabbis of old, the prose of the Gaon of Vilna, or of the Rami, Rabbi Moshe Issevich, or of the Maharsha, who was, perhaps, the most difficult and most complicated commentator that Jewish literature has brought forth in the last several centuries.

It would have been a gratifying task for a genuine, serious student, highly schooled in modern philosophy, to immerse himself in the works of the old scholars. His approach would not be one of "scholastic" scorn and contempt, but one of a clear, acutely perceptive, scientific analysis, pitting word against word, method against method. And out of the welter of allusions, aphorisms and hints he would fashion a realm of Jewish thought. Jews, however, have grown afraid of themselves. They have for so long been branded "Talmudists" and "Pilpulists," that they themselves have come to believe in the inferiority of their own thought, to deny their uniqueness.

Pilpul. To this day this is a word that highly disturbs German Jews and all those under their influence. Jews are trying to be "realistic," "logical," to be like everyone else. They are, therefore, anxious to extinguish within themselves the one wonderful gift with which they were endowed with at their birth, the gift of the *pilpul*, of acuity. They have thrown away the pepper, and with it went the salt. And Jewish thought has become just as bland as the general thought of our time.

We have no exact knowledge of the origin of the word *pilpul*. Does it, actually, come from the word pepper, or is its root, as Levinson assumes, "*peh, lamed, lamed,*" i.e. speech? What is clear is that from earliest times, the word *pilpul* stood wants to reconcile the two cultures without a critical examination of either one. The thought processes of *Eretz Yisrael*, however, go deeper, and recently I came upon an article in one of the last issues of *Kituvim*, an article by Eliezer Steinman entitled *World Jewry: An Article about the Foundations of Judaism*. Throughout all of their historical existence, Jews have asked: Why are the nations in an uproar? Yet it never occurs to us to ask: Why are the Jews in an uproar? What are we truly saying? What is our voice in the universal choir? And when we do ask: What does the Jewish people want?" we get the answer: The Jewish people want to live, to have food, a roof over their head and a peaceful daily life. But is this all? Is this the entire impetus for the heroic struggle that Jews are waging for the preservation of their essence? Or, are they actually waging a struggle? Is the whole problem a historical fiction, a mere fabrication which we accept as the truth? And what is "the truth about Jews"? Our enemies have often uncovered it, piling confusion upon confusion. Why should we not try to uncover the truth ourselves?

One cannot deny that it is not easy to tell Jews the truth in such difficult, bitter times. Steinman approaches the truth with considerable courage, but also with naiveté — without fear but also without a philosophical perspective. His critique of Jewish faults focuses on what he considers its cardinal sin — its certainty that "it feels free of sin." Jews have come to believe in their greatness, purity and uniqueness and do not feel at all that sin also is cowering on their doorstep, the sin of cruelty, of narrow-mindedness, the eternal motive of blood and sacrifice. Steinman is not frightened by the consequences of his thought. He lays bare the weakest, most atavistic, pre-historic elements of Judaism — the system of sacrifices, of blood, of "expiation"; it is this searchlight that he turns on contemporary Jewish life as well. As we read about sacrifices and about King David, about a time which, according to Steinman, was one of cruel carnage, we are assailed by the question: And what are Jews today? Are we truly better than all of the others? Do we have the right to be proud of ourselves?

The last question is, of course, naive, and the attempt to answer it is even more so. It is very easy to say "no" to history. It is not very difficult to tear down the ancient, gossamer veils that cover the past. But I have no desire to engage in polemics. I have no desire to listen to anyone's lectures on a chapter of religious psychology, not even that of Steinman. What matters is not the accomplishment but the urge toward it, not what is being said, but the courage to say it. Steinman's attempt is, after all, only a symptom. *Eretz Yisrael* has set the Jew free and has returned to him his sense of perspective, enabling him to be introspective. We, here, have been unable to engage in a clear and sincere soul-searching for a thought process that was sharp and challenging, a thought process that was seasoned by pepper as well as by salt. It was an allusion to ideas that were not homegrown, but rather alien and exotic. Yet pepper on its own is not worth a great deal. Thus *pilpul*, in itself, does not constitute thinking, because each thought is, in essence, simple, earthbound, one-dimensional. To think is to remember, to recall. Thus Plato defined the "idea," the thought process. We remember what we have seen, what we have heard. Actual thought is an image or a sound. And the majority of men stop at this level of thought. Even the scholars, the explorers, only rarely rise to a higher level.

There is, one might say, nothing shallower than the so-called "folk wisdom," whatever form it may assume. Be it the form of Proverbs or Lamentations, be it the moral philosophy of Epictetus, or be it folk tales, it is always trite because it stops at the threshold of thought. Real thinking begins with conflict, with contradiction, and with negation, with that which is not, i.e., with that which cannot be seen or heard. Thought deals with matter that is not directly accessible to the senses. Our thought is a laboratory where all "reality" has first to be torn apart, destroyed, negated in order to be reassembled and reshaped in a different form. The ability to perceive that which "is not," to turn away from superficial evidence, has in actuality been the driving force of Jewish thought.

To create "systems" means to assort, to compile, to organize, which is, in the final analysis, a mere mechanical arrangement of objects in a given order. But how can you assort and compile all the deep contradictions, oppositions and differences of reality, of life and of thought? One can build houses out of wood, but not out of spider webs, not out of delicate threads which fall apart at the merest touch. This is why most "systems" of thought are so simple, so awkward. One often wonders at the naiveté of systematic thinkers. Did they themselves not see the weaknesses, contradictions and emptiness of their structures? Many try to respond and to interpret their thinking, and the commentaries are often more profound, more original and more substantive than the system itself. The system builder simply followed a thought, but the commentator pursued it with acuity, with *pilpul*.

Already in olden times, in the times when Jewish thought, that complex spiritual phenomenon known as "Torah," was still a living, ongoing creation, there was an awareness of the great, profound difference between those thinkers who just learn from others, follow tradition, re-think the thoughts of those who went before them, and those who go the way of *pilpul*, who select and renew. As the *Gemarah* says: "Should the Torah, the received, traditional, inherited one be forgotten, *pilpul* would be able to reconstruct it, to recreate it anew." Living thought is creative, but the spoken, rounded-out word becomes petrified, infertile.

It is no accident that *pilpul* gained its greatest authority among Jews in the years of the edicts, at the times of their greatest disappointments. It was at a time when the Torah had begun to be a burden to the people, when old-time certitudes had lost their life-directing authority, when reality had become unbearable, when autonomous, idiosyncratic thought had come into its own. And it was because all of life had become one stark incongruity, that all of spiritual life came to focus on questions and doubts, came to look searchingly at the world and at itself.

This was happening in the medieval Christian world as well, when the contrast between life and faith grew too great. At that time "scholasticism" had come to replace the former Greek thought process, which was characterized by clear affirmation and absolute negation. Scholastics, such as the famed Abelard, were weaving between the "yea" and the "nay," building bridges between the two worlds. Yet building bridges is a very complicated matter; one has to take into account the amount of water that flows beneath them. A small river can be bridged by a few wooden planks, but a large river requires iron and steel and engineering skill.

The deepest and the stormiest of all the rivers was the Jewish one. No other mental realm harbored such contradictions. Everything is ephemeral: society, justice, existence. The present is doubtful and the future an enigma; one is enclosed by mountains, surrounded by opposing barriers. In order to survive, the Jewish spirit had to "uproot mountains and grind them into dust." *Pilpul* became a social tool and not an intellectual requirement.

It was, thus, rather natural that the Maharsha, the last and perhaps the greatest exponent of *pilpul*, of a sharp and challenging approach to knowledge, i.e. thinking, became one of the "central pillars" of the entire Jewish spiritual edifice. Rashi, the Tosafists and the Maharsha are three levels of intellectual development: simplicity, clarity, and a highly developed complexity which often ends in dichotomy. The highest achievement of *pilpul* thus lead to its demise. The sharp knife got duller, *pilpul* gradually lost its prestige, Jewish life became more "normal," and the Jews came to harbor the illusion that they could live a normal life. Jewish thought, in the process, lost its salt and its pepper.

Is the gathering of 10,000 of Jews in Ostrog at the grave of the Maharsha symptomatic of our time? Is the Jewish spirit turning inward because Jewish life, once again, is becoming harder, because reality is growing less intelligible? The old house of the Maharsha in Ostrog bore the inscription: "My house is open to the wanderer." I believe that the present-day Jewish wanderer may do well to enter the old house of the Maharsha, the house of the sharp, contentious thought. Without *pilpul* the world remains unintelligible, and without *pilpul* life loses much of its appeal. It lacks pepper.

The Jewish Intellect

Every country, every people, ought to adopt the following custom: Every fifty years, or at the most, every hundred years, the best, the most beautiful, the most mature writing produced during that time should be assembled and published in a large volume, a kind of a monument to the spiritual Zeitgeist.

It is happening anyway, in one form or another, but those who do it are, usually, private individuals, limited both by a lack of means and also by their subjective viewpoints. This is not an enterprise to be carried out by one man alone. One man cannot be an expert in all areas; he cannot have access to all the nooks and crannies of his culture. This requires an academy, a body of scholars, writers, and thinkers, subsidized by the nation.

I have often thought that it is time for Jews to issue such an opus. Of course, books are issued, from time to time, bearing grandiose titles: *Treasure, Thesaurus, Encyclopedia* or *Monumentum Judaica.* But these books almost never live up to what they promise. They follow a one-sided philological, historical or literary approach. They never mirror the "Jewish intellect." And yet, this is of the greatest importance not only for those of us who strive for greater self-knowledge and self-understanding, but also for everyone else who has to interact with us.

Sixty or seventy years ago, Disraeli wrote the following in his novel *Coningsby:* "At the present moment, in spite of a century, a millennium, of suppression, the Jewish spirit is exerting a great influence upon European affairs. I am not talking merely of laws, of literature; I am talking of the living Jewish intellect." Disraeli

49

knew what he was speaking of, for he was speaking of himself. He felt the great power that the Jewish spirit, the Jewish "intellect" was exerting over the world, how it influenced history, how it shaped the fate of nations.

In Disraeli's time only a few felt this. Today everyone feels it. Never was the "Jewish intellect" so historically creative as today, never has the Jew such a direct impact on the course of history, on cultural development, as he does today. And it is, therefore, more important than ever before, to know and to understand the "Jewish intellect," its essence and its hidden motifs. This should, surely, be the task of the entire Jewish people. It would require the selection of a committee of representative Jewish scholars and writers to undertake an assembly of the best, the most characteristic works created by the Jewish intellect in the course of the last fifty years, when it has become an important cultural factor in the modern world. Such a book should be issued in the two national languages of the Jewish people, in Hebrew and in Yiddish, but it should also be available in English and in German, the two universal languages which have, of all languages, the closest tie to the present and the future of Judaism. But until the Jews get ready for such a monumental work, we must content ourselves with surrogates, with ersatz monuments.

Among these, there is one, I must say, which is both in good taste and thoughtful. It is *The Jewish Anthology*, assembled by the French Jewish poet Edmund Fleg, in French, and translated into English by Maurice Samuels. Good taste, understanding and a poetic instinct have saved Edmund Fleg and Maurice Samuels from tripping over the stumbling block that always lies in the path of all Jewish writers when they address other nations: apologia. Being on the defensive is part of Jewish nature. Jews are always singing their own praises, boasting of their own merits and presenting the world with a statement: Look at us, what we are and what we have accomplished! Look, admire us and treat us well! This is pretty much the tone and the aim of all the Jewish "interpreters" and literary impresarios.

Fleg and Samuels are modern Jews. They do not address "the nations," they do not set out to demonstrate to the world the "beauty" and the "greatness" of Israel. They address the Jews themselves. In the final analysis it is the Jewish people who are the interested party. Jews must, first of all, put forth their own concepts of what Judaism means, what it has achieved, what is its way and what is its goal. Little is accomplished by simply quoting verses from Lamentations and the Bible. Present-day Jewish youth who have no access to the old sources, who can no longer unlock the gates to the past, they must receive a key to the gate which leads to themselves. They must learn what forms the Jewish intellect can assume and has assumed in the course of the remarkable, vibrant, colorful Jewish history.

Modern Jewish youth must learn about Josephus Flavius and about Philo the Alexandrian, the philosopher who wanted to build a bridge between Judaism and Plato; about Ariesto, the Hellenized Jew, and the Hebraic Jews of *Eretz Yisrael* and Babylon; about the Tannaim and Amoraim. They must learn about Yehuda Halevi, and Ibn Gabirol, about the Rambam and Saadia, and all the way up to Heinrich Heine, Emma Lazarus, Herman Cohen, Morris Rosenfeld and Abraham Reisen. They must learn about Abravanel, Disraeli, Herzl and Rathenau. These were poets, thinkers, statesmen, nationalists and assimilationists, believers and skeptics, conscientious Jews and conscientious apostates (such as, for example, Karl Marx) each one having his say in the annals of history.

"Tell me what you think," says Jewish history to every offspring of the Jewish people, whoever he may have been, whatever stance toward Jewish history he may have taken. And each one spoke his piece. Out of all the pronouncements, each one contradicting the other, each one with its own nuances, associations and allusions, there emerges a wholeness, a sort of epos of the Jewish intellect. I would even go further. I would include in such an anthology not only those involved in Judaism but also all those who bear a Jewish imprint. I would include Paul's *Letter to the Hebrews*, the arguments of the heretics of the Shabbatai Tzvi movement and those of the Frankists. And I would also include Moses Mendelssohn's *Phaedon* and Georg Simmel's *Money*, Marcel Schwab's *Essays* and even a chapter or two by Spinoza, Bergson, the physicist Heinrich Hertz, by Einstein and Minkovsky. I would place them all between the covers of a book, and the book would no longer be a Jewish anthology but, rather, a mirror of the Jewish intellect, a monument to the Jewish spirit.

There is no doubt that Jewish history has yet to be written. What we have until now is merely a fragment and a beginning. The history of the Jewish people in ancient, even *ur*-ancient times, must be written anew. Those who have undertaken this task earlier — Graetz, Jost, Wellhausen, Maier, etc. — knew little of ancient Judaism. Each year brings new discoveries, new treasures are found. With the passage of time it will become clearer what we once were and how we became what we are now. The former historians, however, lacked not only knowledge of their material, but also a general overview, an unbiased historic outlook on the Jewish people. The German historians always focused either on defense or accusation, but very rarely did they aim at a simple understanding.

Jewish history must be rewritten. This requires preparation, a critical, knowledgeable review of the material, which will result in a sourcebook of Judaism, a kind of inventory. This is a task for the Jewish people itself. Why should the Hebrew University in Jerusalem not take on this task? This would be its first, most important achievement. And I am sure that if such work were to be started, both means and people would be forthcoming. One only needs to launch the idea and to support it; one only needs to understand that the most important knowledge is self-knowledge. This holds true not only for individuals but for a people as well.

Just to Stay Alive?

This is not a polemic. I am stating this at the outset because I do not want to enter into a debate about the "Ghetto," a debate which my colleague S. Niger began in response to my recent article "Center or Ghetto." There are questions which cannot, and should not, be debated, and one of them is the reality of our national existence. Thus, the current wars of Yiddish versus Hebrew, and Zionism versus *galut*, strike me as idle chatter. They remind me of the contention of the old *maskilim* that Hebrew is the holy language of the Chosen People, transmitting to us the knowledge vouchsafed from heaven, while Yiddish is mere speech, the "jargon." The exaggerated claims of the Yiddishists, for their part, appear to me to be a modern version of the old debate among pious Jews as to who had more money, Rothschild or Baron de Hirsch.

The Hebraists, it is true, are more fanatical in their assertions than are the Yiddishists. Yet this struggle between the two extreme trends exerts very little influence on Jewish life. Except, of course, when Hebraists get up in the Lithuanian or the Polish parliament to denounce Yiddish, thereby impeding, for the sake of their principle, the few national gains that can be achieved in those countries. And when I hear that in Palestine the language that is spoken by millions of Jews is not only looked down upon but is also subjected to a boycott, then I understand why Engels included the Jews among "the peoples who have no history." We are so history-oriented that, ironically, we have lost the sense of living history. We live so much in the past, as well as in the future, that we let the present run through our fingers. It is already an old complaint: We are a people of the past, and of the future.

The extreme Yiddishists also go too far in promoting their position. Exaggeration may, of course, play a positive role if it serves to widen and deepen our perspective, but it becomes useless, if not harmful, when it loses all sense of proportion, all contact with reality. And it seems to me that S. Niger has fallen prey to a loss of proportion in the demands he makes on Jewish culture in its present, historically conditioned form. The main question that I touched upon in my earlier article was, actually, quite limited in scope, namely: Do we need a Jewish university in Europe? And beyond the question of needing one, I wondered about the practicality of implementing such an idea. I was not thinking about language. When Professor Einstein made the proposal of establishing a Jewish university he surely had not given thought to the debate about Hebrew versus Yiddish. He simply had in mind a university established by Jews for Jews. While considering the possibility of such a plan, a question unavoidably arose: What shall be the language of instruction? Yiddish? But is Yiddish, in fact, an "inter-Jewish" language? German Jews would be the first to deny it. The considerations, then, culminated in a principal question: Do we need to "ghettoize," thus giving up, of our own volition, the struggle for our rights?

To state it more clearly: There is no Jewish national problem, i.e., there is no question as to whether Jewish culture can and should exist. Such a question cannot be posed, because what exists, exists. There exists a Jewish nation, there exists a Jewish national — or, rather, a national Jewish — culture. The question, however, is: Where are its boundaries? Niger, surely, has logic on his side when he says that if we can have a Jewish elementary and Jewish high school, why not a Jewish university as well? This is logical, but it is the logic of a straight line. A straight line can, of course, extend to eternity, but only in theory, in abstract thought. In concrete reality the line comes up against boundaries, even on paper. Opening up Jewish elementary and high schools in America sounds like a good idea, but when it comes to its practical implementation, even Niger would have to concede that it is an impossibility, just as we cannot have Jewish national autonomy in America as it exists, on paper, in Lithuania or in Poland.

It may be that we will have to revise the school question in Poland as well. The chaotic struggle between the Hebraists and Yiddishists, between those who identify more closely with Poles and those whose identity lies in Jewish nationalism, forces us to ask the question: Can we possibly continue this kind of national politics? And even if everything were to work smoothly, and a way could be found for the warring elements to arrive at a *modus vivendi*, this still would not solve the problem which faces a national culture when two factions of equal importance oppose each other. Russian Jewry, at least for me, is not the world's *aleph* and *tet*. German and American Jewry are not to be waved aside with the flip of the wrist. They have played a not insignificant role in the history of the Jewish people, and will play an even greater role in the future. But one has to approach German and American Jews differently from the Russian and Polish ones. The question I raised in "Center or Ghetto" concerned chiefly the two important communities where, I think, the Ghetto concept would be unacceptable.

Niger replies: "Do not scare us with the ghetto. If there is a Ghetto, so what? Let there be a Ghetto — just so we stay alive." I did not want to retort with the answer a Jew gave a Russian judge who had accused him of living in Moscow without a permit: "Your Excellency, you call this living?" What does "just to stay alive" actually mean? I can understand the ancient messianic view of Jews as bearers of a universal idea. They, our elders, could allow themselves the luxury of saying "there is life as long as blood is flowing in our veins." Let there be spilling of blood, suffering, sacrifices, as long as one stays alive, because there is a purpose that is higher than life itself. But when we are told that we are not obligated to struggle for a better world, not obligated to carry on our shoulders the yoke of a universal culture, what, then, does it mean "just to stay alive"? Does it mean that we may conduct ourselves any way we want as long as we remain Jews, as long as we speak Yiddish? Is this, truly, the final aim, the purpose of all of Judaism? I know that this is a question which may elicit a derisive smile from our national realists; "final aim," "purpose," these are outlived, outdated, mildewed concepts! That may be so. But in the realm of belief one creed is as valid as the other, and national idealism is not less valid than national realism. At this point I must say that for me Judaism is not a fact but a task. Not everyone who is born a Jew is a Jew. And it is not language alone that is at the core of Judaism. Judaism is a moral category. Judaism, in the final analysis, is "the survival of the fittest." Only the strongest, the most able, the most ethical person can and may be a Jew.

This view opposes the Ghetto mentality of "Let there be shady characters, as long as they are ours." Ghetto implies that we are all part of the same dough. Ghetto is a self-imposed confinement. Can we weather this? Jewish history has, from time to time, undergone a process of purification. For the most part, though not always, this was an involuntary process, and a very painful one. Take Spain, for instance. Reading the history of Spanish Jewry, not in the romanticized version of Graetz but in the objective account of the Spanish historian Amador de la Rios, one can see that already at the time of Ferdinand and Isabella Jews in Spain had begun to undergo the same process of disorganization and disassociation that we are undergoing today. The great intellectual flowering of the Arab-Spanish period had already become a legend. Actual Jewish life had become very sober and often unpleasant. Jews were assimilating, and had it not been for Torquemada's fanatic persecution, the Jews might have fitted themselves into the Spanish-Christian environment. The catastrophe cleared the atmosphere. Those who had the will and the strength remained Jews and suffered for their Judaism; the others submitted to Torquemada's verdict.

Such a process has been taking place, in one form or another, throughout all of Jewish life, and it is doing so now, before our very eyes, everywhere in the world. The tired, the inept, Jewishly inept ones, are falling by the wayside, and the strong ones remain. Tragically, it is the most tired and weak who are staying in the ghetto, too weak even to leave it. They remain Jews out of inertia, a burden to themselves and to Judaism. We need to oppose this inertia with strength and with a confidence in our ability. But such strength and confidence cannot be sustained, cannot blossom in the ghetto.

Let me reiterate: It is not a question of language. One can speak and write Yiddish without living in the ghetto, and one can be a Ghetto-personality while speaking the latest American slang. It is not the form but the content that is at the heart of the matter. It is not life but the meaning of life that is of prime importance. "Life" is altogether an individual endowment, not a collective one. And even an individual may say, as an old Roman did: "It is our duty to spread; we are not obligated to stay alive." But while an individual may succumb to a life without meaning, without beauty and without purpose, letting his empty days be mere stepping-stones toward death, a people may not.

Casanova tells us in his memoirs about coming across an old man in the underground prison of Venice, who had spent 50 years there under the most terrible conditions. But the old man had become accustomed to this way of life and did not want to die. His sufferings were great, yet he still wanted to live. A people, however, may not succumb to such a hunger for life. To spread, to sail the seven seas, to be part of universal history, to contribute to the shaping of the world, to live up to our promises — this is our goal and our task. "To live for the sake of living?"…"Your Excellency, do you call this living?"…Is this worthwhile?

Without a Melody

It is late at night, and I am sitting up with a volume of the Talmud. I am reading the way one reads other books, with my eyes; my lips do not move, my mouth is closed. As I leaf through the Hebrew text of the first volume of Bava Metzia my eye alights on quite an intricate debate. Still, one can disentangle the issues once one grasps the remarkable Talmudic concept of *migo* — this must follow from that. And here, too, help is available, offered not only by Rashi, not only by the old, classic books, but also by a new commentary, in a lively, clear, modern language — clear and legalistically precise. I have before me the first volume of Bava Metzia with English explanations, with literal translations of difficult passages, from the text and from Rashi — a very good work by Abraham, Reuben and Alex Steinbach.

This work is an important beginning, and it needs to be continued. It is necessary not only for the authors' stated purpose of serving as an auxiliary text for rabbinic seminaries and yeshivahs. It is also needed by lay readers who are interested in the Talmud, who want to recall something they learned in their childhood, but who already need glasses to see the fine print, who still want to try swimming in the ocean of Talmuds but who must now resort to a life preserver.

I am looking through the book and am grateful to the Steinbachs. I appreciate when, here and there, I come upon a concept, an interpretation, that has become unfamiliar, that has been mislaid, so that now I must dig into the bottom of the drawer where this piece of teaching has been hiding, together with some enigmas and some crumbs of wisdom. I am grateful. And yet, I soon stop looking at the English commentaries and am even becoming a bit irritated at their presence. And as the course of the debate becomes more difficult to follow, my lips part of their own volition and almost without my awareness, and then there arises, in the still of the night, a singular tune: *Amar Rava* — Rava said — and then nai-nai-naina-nai-ai-ai. Who is singing? Am I the one who is quietly swaying over the page of the Talmud, intoning the Talmudic *migo*, immersing myself in the ancient logic and jurisprudence of ages past, of a world that is gone forever? Is this my voice or the voice of generations upon generations, from Babylon and Persia, from Toledo and Cairo, which is singing in the night? For a while the melody is reawakened, the melody of Judaism.

I know that I am being sentimental, I am giving way to flights of imagination; I know I am responding to an ingrained habit, and still, memories well up from years back in Florence. I am reading Talmud to the students of the Florentine rabbinical seminary. In front of me are my students, or rather fellow-learners, young Italian men who are preparing for the rabbinate or for "Jewish studies." I read the text, read it in the ordinary prosaic, dry tone of our daily speech; the language, and the translation itself, is so un-Talmudic. Something does not fit. Imagine: *Cosi dicce Raba*, meaning *Amar Rava*. And not because the Italian language is less expressive than any other; on the contrary, in its image and style it comes closer to Hebrew than does, say, English. But the difference does not lie in the words, nor in their interpretation, nor on the arrangements of the concepts, nor even in the method of instruction. The difference lies in the tune, in the melody, in the atmosphere that exists around the words, the melody which is, perhaps, the essence and the meaning. It has accompanied "The Book" on all its wanderings. Do you remember the way we, as children, learned the Bible in *cheder*? The melody of the *v'ani*? You read it in your usual voice, and it sounds so different. But when the Rabbi began to intone: *v'ani*, and I your father Jacob have not acted this way with your mother Rachel...it had been just an acre of land...had died, etc., etc., the simple words grew in front of our eyes into a magnificent picture: Jacob sitting on a wagon pulled by oxen or, perhaps, a camel, with a wide road stretching ahead of him, bordered by almond and date trees, and with Rachel, dressed in white, sitting next to him. You felt the stillness of a summer afternoon; the fieldwork was done, and you could hear a prayer-like crooning. And the Bible became so moving, so close to home. And then, do you remember the trumpet-like tones of "Comfort ye, comfort ye, my people," the rousing appeals of Jeremiah? Do you remember the measured, masterful sound of the words of the Mishnah, the convoluted, ornate, hearty melodic tune of the

Gemarah, and the melancholy, pensive, depth of the Zohar? It was an entire symphony with its allegros and vivace, with its scherzo and adagio. It was the music of the soul of Israel; can it be otherwise?

Each culture has its own melody. A physicist, of course, will not be intoning a treatise on atomic theories, nor can one hum Einstein's mathematical formulae. But one step away from pure science, and culture acquires its own coloration, its own special form, its melody. An Italian reads his poetry differently from an Englishman. A Frenchman plays a dramatic role one way, and a Russian another. To Anglo-Saxons it seems that Frenchmen are declaiming, posing, singing, and they do not understand that this is the tone, the rhythm of French culture. And no, it cannot be changed. There is the same rhythm pulsating in each manifestation of a national culture, alive and dynamic in its verbal expression, frozen and static in its architecture and its sculpture, and reaching even further into its political and societal life. If you want to understand a people, its life and its history, you must listen to the rhythm of its speech, to the rise and fall of its intonation, to its logical and musical accents. Put Pushkin next to André Chenier and Gogol next to Voltaire and you will be able to distinguish the Russian Revolution from the French Revolution, you can see Lenin and Robespierre.

The most tragic factor in contemporary Jewish life is that it has lost the rhythm of its melody. True, it is said: "Listen to whatever language you know." But what is it we can hear besides the *Shema,* besides the totally abstract, heaven-reaching formulation of the drama of Jewish faith? Can it nurture Judaism all by itself, can it revitalize it on its own? Of course, the *Shema* remains the same whether it is said in Hebrew or in Greek, in English or in Chinese. But what of the world that surrounds the *Shema,* the mysterious, shadowy, emotional life-experiences which permeate it? And does this not, really, begin there, on the other side of the threshold? From the Rambam to Ahad Ha'am, from the reformers in Germany to American Jews who are letting Judaism wither on the vine: everyone is stressing "logos," reason, the rational substance of Judaism. They are searching for the "meaning," i.e. for the logical interpretation and interconnection.

But culture is not logical, at any rate not exclusively so. One cannot, one may not, seek its sense and its meaning. It is, it exists for its own sake, and it has at all times its own melody, its own inner rhythm. If the melody falls silent, then reason is bereaved, turns into a dry leaf, a withered flower, a word which fades because it finds no echo. And I am hearing how it is fading, the Jewish tune, the melody of the Jewish soul, filled with sweetness, with sorrow, with the yearning for consecration. I hear it already from far, far away, like the music of the "spheres," and the voice becomes more and more faint, losing itself in the abyss into which the entire Jewish life is sinking, step by step, day by day, deeper and deeper.

Pouring Salt on Open Wounds

A New York satirical magazine once paid me a great, albeit undeserved, compliment. At a time when rudeness prevails and when civility in our press stops way below the Eiffel Tower, a compliment is such a rarity that I feel obliged to acknowledge it gratefully. The compliment consisted of a drawing depicting Jewish national culture in the shape of a young woman with whip-inflicted wounds on her bared back. An outstretched hand is holding a saltshaker and pouring salt on the open wounds. The hand, according to the caption, is mine.

Quite unintentionally, they offered me the greatest praise I could have hoped for. And I am, truly, grateful. I am said to be holding in my hand a saltshaker and pouring salt upon the wounds of Jewish culture. My only concern is that I may not have enough salt, or that my salt may lack the acidic, stinging, pain-inflicting capacity that it should have, because this is what we truly need. I do not understand why all Jewish writers, all supporters of Jewish culture, have not armed themselves with saltshakers, why they do not all pour salt on the wounds.

I know, one fears to inflict pain. One is also afraid of the salt. It is, perhaps, the terrifying example of Lot's wife. She looked back and was turned to salt, into a statue of salt. And there is salt in every backward look. Critical analysis is a process of reducing a highly developed organism into its component parts. And were we to ask the organism under analysis whether it enjoys the process, the answer would be a resounding "no." It is, therefore, fortunate that we do not ask. We go on with the work, with the analysis, in order to arrive at a new synthesis.

61

There is no doubt about it. If we want to go on developing, widening, creating Jewish culture, we must subject it to a constant, forthright, pitiless analysis. The majority of our culture builders, unfortunately, do not make the effort to arrive at a clear conception of what needs to be done, to what end and for whose sake.

I am so far talking only about the circle of people involved in the strengthening and development of a Jewish national culture in America or in Europe, in New York or in Warsaw. There is also another group which is pulling in a diametrically opposite direction, concentrating exclusively on Palestine. But this is a chapter in itself, a question that needs separate consideration.

What do the builders of a Jewish national culture actually want? What is their contribution to Jewish life? As far as I can see, it is only literature, only language. There is so far no culture, merely linguistics. The Jewish word, the Jewish sound, is, for them, an end in itself. Had the Jewish people lived under different conditions, had the basic elements of Jewish life not undergone so many shattering rearrangements, then such a linguistic culture would surely have been very productive, very natural. Such was the cultural war led by Greek Yiddishists for their native language against the "Hebrew" language of the Hellenistic state.

But our problem is different. It is not a question of Yiddish versus Hebrew, not even of Yiddish versus English; the problem is much more extensive, more difficult, more tragic. It is the question of the spiritual countenance of the Jewish people. As I look around, and then look backward at the path Judaism has followed, at the events of Jewish history, at the illusions which have been shattered, at the structures which have collapsed, how can I not be assailed by salt, by acrid, burning, stinging salt?

It may be that I am a maximalist in my Jewish demands. It may be that this is a proof of the spiritual assimilation of which people have accused me. I am being asked: Why don't you demand the same of other peoples, why just of Jews? It is true, I demand a great deal less of others just because they are "others" and because I am applying a different measuring rod to the Jewish people than to any other people. Is this a pride, an idée fixe, absorbed in infancy through my mother's milk? Maybe so, but it is an essential part of being Jewish. When you penetrate deeply into the Jewish soul you find the Messiah concept, you find the "You have chosen us." And I am not ashamed to say that I believe that we are the "chosen" people, a called-upon, destined people. It is so because we have willed it, because we have experienced it. We were chosen at the time of our suffering, called upon at the moment of purification, elected to assume leadership, destined to continue to lead.

We know what lies behind us, the entire world knows where we have led it. The question is: Where do we go from here? The past contains obligations; history imposes responsibility upon us. And I cannot accept the thought that we Jews have lived through excruciatingly destructive experiences just for the sake of being "like all other people."

Are we, like cows, simply to follow the herd? Have we not dreamed of being the shepherd who will lead the entire human herd!? (Jewish culture: The meaning depends on where you place the accent, on Jewish or on culture.) My Yiddishist friends think that Yiddish offers us sufficient culture. They are pleased to have Yiddish language and Yiddish letters, reproducing stories, essays, plays and songs composed in other languages, written in Latin or Cyrillic characters. They are content; for them this suffices. But for me this is not enough. Jewish culture must not be a mere incorporation of other cultures; it must emerge out of Jewish life; it must be a universal culture created by Jews in the spirit of Jewish history.

We are, after all, not the only ones seeking a path worthy of pursuit. Take a look at the spiritual life of the Germans, Russians or English and you will see how tired they have grown of things as they are. They are no longer content with "literature," nor even with science. They are searching for meaning; they are searching for their own spiritual content; they are searching for continuity. And if nations who are not facing language problems or the threat of assimilation and disappearance, if they are struggling, then what shall we who are standing at the edge of an abyss be doing? At a time when the whole world is straining toward depth, shall we retreat to the flatlands? When a spirit of disquiet is spreading throughout the world, shall we drape ourselves in contentment and self-approval? I have never believed in the injunction: Leave the Jews in peace. I rather believe that just as a picador tantalizes, enrages and even hurts the bull, so should we inflict spiritual pain and heartache on Israel. A Jew should not be calm; a Jew should not grow old; a Jew should not be content! No one should be content, but the Jew least of all — this is the historic pact between Jews and the world.

How is this reflected in the new Jewish culture? How does the Jewish storm, the Jewish pathos, express itself in the new Jewish national culture? Are the poems of Peretz Markish, stories by Johann Rosenfeld, or the abstract quasi-German literary criticism which appears in our Jewish anthologies and journals a manifestation of the Jewish spirit? Is this the well that nourishes the Jewish soul? It may be that the broad masses look upon it as high literature, but culture is not merely mass culture. And as for those of us who are no longer part of the masses, what do we derive from that culture? Can we live with it, and does it answer our quests? What does it offer our inner self? And, furthermore, Jewish culture cannot and must not depend on the masses. I have said it many times already, and I will say it again: What matters in Judaism is not quantity but quality. The question is not "how many are following it?" but "in what way do they follow?" This is the problem all cultures face, but Jewish culture more than any other because it is the only one that is not a naturally evolved organism; it is an abstraction; it is pure spirit.

England can tolerate "Paterism," i.e. a culture by and for the masses, superficial, banal, popular. It can tolerate it because alongside the journalistic, cheap, condescending, "literature" there is Oxford and Cambridge, there is Bertrand Russell, Aldous Huxley and George Bernard Shaw. Germany can tolerate a mass culture because it is gifted with spiritual and intellectual wealth, because it does not have to struggle to maintain its national culture. But we cannot tolerate a shoddy culture; with us it has to be either a high culture or nothing. Either we manage to create an idiosyncratic, great, heavenward aspiring culture, a continuation of the old Jewish world and a path toward its renewal, or we must bow our head and let the wheel of history roll over our body and crush it.

If this is pouring salt on wounds, so be it. I will pour all the salt that comes to hand. Let it hurt, let it burn, and may the wounds not heal too quickly. Let us not be content too soon. A self-satisfied smile does not belong on a Jewish face.

Achad Ha'am: The Thinker

A few months ago, while in *Eretz Yisrael*, I was asked by a Hebrew newspaper to write an evaluation of the seventy-year-old Achad Ha'am. I agreed and then found myself delaying doing so from day to day. On the boat home, I sat down a couple of times with pen in hand, but the pen did not move, and in the end I gave up. I could not write it. Something in me did not allow it, respect for the old, sick man, respect for *Eretz Yisrael*. I did not want to come to a celebration in workaday clothes, but neither could I don a festive garment. Now Achad Ha'am is dead, all polemics are stilled, all discussion is finished, sunk into the past, already a part of history. And it is from a historical perspective that I want to view Achad Ha'am's work and his personality, since we know but little of his strictly personal life, and since those who did know something about it could not find anything to tell us that would attract our attention or engage our emotions.

Achad Ha'am, "one of the people," one of the thousands, ten thousand Jewish *Maskilim* of the past generations, was born in a small city and reared in the old Jewish tradition. Later on he emancipated himself, studied, read, went out into the world, carried himself as a European, but spiritually he remained bound to his origins. Had chance led him to assume a professorship in Berlin or a law practice in St. Petersburg rather than to conduct business in Odessa and London, his spiritual persona would have remained essentially unaltered, because he was Achad Ha'am, one of the people. He was, to be sure, one of the few, an exceptional figure, yet still one of his people. And even though his generation produced only one Achad Ha'am, it was his generation, and he had been part of it.

We have almost forgotten the atmosphere which prevailed in the past generation, very different from the demands for clarity, simplicity and breadth of vision which inform our present times, with all questions focused on practical feasibility. We want to implement our aims and are partially able to achieve this. A door has been opened, a path has been cleared for anyone who wants to follow it towards a practical, sober, simplified world. Now let us turn the clock back to the period that has just come to an end. It was a period of a kind of twilight, filled with secrets and mystical allusions; the narrow streets of Jewish cities and townlets, with the walls of their synagogues bearing the imprints of memories of suppressed grief, of short-lived ecstasies, of old memories and of eternal questioning. Questions going back to Abaye and Rava in the Babylonian Talmud, questions of a mystical nature raised in the dance-rhythm of the Hasidim. And, from time to time, reverberations of stirring thoughts from the outside world would find their way into those narrow streets.

Out of this background emerged the picture of a *Maskil*, an enlightened intellectual, who is outwardly free but inwardly bound. The *Maskil* believed that his immersion into world literature, his reading books of all cultures and in all languages enabled him to "rationalize" Judaism; but, in fact, he read it all "in Jewish." Be it Kant or Nietzsche or Darwin, he approached them all with an "Abaye has said" and in the spirit of the *Gemarah*. Ancient Judaism commanded, "interpret the world — it is a body of law which must be examined, requires constant commentaries on Heaven and Earth; so, study, my son, study." And he interpreted and examined, he asked questions of life, and he attempted to answer them. He followed the ancient method: building bridges between the old and the new, using all possible means to integrate new concepts into old texts. This was the mood of "the people" and Achad Ha'am was "one of the people." It may be that the *nom de plume* which Asher Ginzberg chose was not truly appropriate. It should have been not "one of the people," but "one of the enlightened," since at that time the people, that great mass that of late has played such a large role in Jewish history, afflicting Jewish life with vulgarity and lack of grace, this mass had not yet begun to make itself felt.

I have been rereading the writings of Achad Ha'am (as well as the "commentaries"), and as I search through them I ask myself: Wherein lies the originality of his thinking? There have been Jewish thinkers, not only in old, distant times but also in times closer to our own, closer to our sphere of interest, and their thoughts have been Jewish in form and in process, but not in aim. Spinoza, the greatest of them all, ventured so far that he was unable to find his way back to Judaism. Shlomo Maimon, Bergson, Simmel, each one of them viewed the world "Jewishly," and they brought new nuances into the stream of thought. Can Achad Ha'am be bracketed with these thinkers? No one could, of course, ascribe to him the same depth and breadth of thought, but did he share their realm of inquiry? Had he grappled with fundamental questions and striven to answer them? To do this, one need not be an academician and write learned books for other academics, but essays and editorials must express a view of the world if these publications are to have a historic value.

What, then, was Achad Ha'am's *Weltanschauung*? I have looked for it in his first essays which express, as it were, his philosophical strivings, his first steps toward forging his own path and formulating his own view of the world. There Achad Ha'am touches on ethics, on faith, on the Torah of the heart, on the petrifaction of the written word, on the philosophy of history, on the further development of faith. But then I began to probe more deeply, demanding, pedantically: What does "further development of the faith" actually mean, or "Torah of the heart?" How does one define the "ethics of Judaism" and the "Jewish spirit?" And, most of all, what path of thought did he follow to reach his conclusions? I could find no answers to my questions.

Achad Ha'am formulated concepts that were part of popular philosophy. So, of course, had Rambam adopted concepts formulated by Aristotle and by Arab Aristotelians. But what divides them from each other is that the Rambam used these concepts as stepping stones to a philosophy of Judaism, while Achad Ha'am set out to fashion a policy for Judaism, or, rather, on its behalf. A rabbi faces Achad Ha'am with justifiable concerns: What does it mean to follow a Torah of the heart? What path shall Judaism adopt if it is to make any progress? And Achad Ha'am's answer is not religious or philosophical but political — a new current will find its way into the heart of the people; the Jewish heart will now beat with renewed vigor and promote the people's growth and development. And the current that will achieve this miracle is — *hovev Tsion*, the love of Zion. Is this an answer? And if so, is it a satisfactory one?

Let us assume that the goal has been reached, that we have attained a focal point, a spiritual center, and that the Jewish people are now "free to develop." What then? No one can, of course, foretell in what way a people will develop, but tell us which way you would have us go! How would Achad Ha'am have responded to such a request? He would have talked, and he did talk — about "Jewish ethics," although he did not penetrate into the depths of Jewish ethics, nor did he look at it with fresh, modern eyes. He talked of "absolute justice," but failed to ask the question: What is justice? And what is absolute? Somewhere he says that the Prophets demanded absolute justice. This is not a new assertion, it is one made by many Jewish theologians. More importantly, though, it is a historically incorrect one. The Prophets preached not absolute justice, but absolute law.

Achad Ha'am, however, is not yearning to achieve an ideal; his aim is to have an impact on reality. He is looking for guidance, not to the Prophets, but to the Priests, since the Prophets stood above all national delineations, while the Priests remained nation-based, creating a harmonious relationship between the people and their spiritual ideal. This was the paradigm Achad Ha'am strove to follow. Only, living in a time of transition between two ages and two realities, he was unable to choose and, instead, bestowed upon the current reality of nationalism the spiritual terminology of the past. And he was unaware of this contradiction and of the hopelessness of such a harmony, or such a compromise. One can achieve political compromises but not spiritual ones. One cannot preach Love of Zion, demand the colonization of Palestine and, at the same time, believe in a mystical destiny of the Jewish people. Heavenly and earthly Jerusalem combined in one program; this really is asking too much, and it therefore failed. This was the underlying reason for the collapse of Achad Ha'am's political system, as well as the collapse of his theoretical worldview.

They had been adversaries, Achad Ha'am and Berdyczewski. Of nearly the same age, born in neighboring towns, of similar Jewish cultural background, Achad Ha'am was the quiet, moderate one, the aristocrat, the "one" among his people. His words were well chosen, well considered, well polished (though not profound) and had a special, parchment-like beauty. Micah Joseph Berdyczewski was a stormy, restless, rugged writer. Lacking linguistic finesse he wrote badly in all languages, ungrammatically but yet in an expansive, dramatic, stirring style. If Achad Ha'am's path led from the Haskalah, via John Stuart Mill and Herbert Spenser, to the Rambam, then Berdyczewski's path went from the Haskalah, to Friedrich Nietzsche, to the Baal Shem Tov. These two neighbors were, at the same time, adversaries and comrades in spirit, because, in the final analysis, both were mystics. Only, Berdyczewski loudly proclaimed his mysticism, whereas Achad Ha'am never wanted to acknowledge being a mystic, not even to himself. He saw himself as a rationalist, a positivist thinker who was directing Jewish life towards an obvious solution, because what can be more natural than nationalism and homeland politics? He failed to notice that what he was truly aiming at was the Messiah.

Only one thing divides him from those whom he castigates in his "Slavery and Freedom": they wanted to free Judaism from national yearnings by denying its existence, whereas he wanted to achieve this freedom by fulfilling the yearning — two ways to the same goal. And, perhaps, he would have dared to follow his path, had it not been for his ties with the older generation, had it not been for his own intellectual captivity. This had always been the fate of Jewish thinkers, namely, when they reach the ultimate thought they hear the injunction: Do not probe any further! One of Achad Ha'am's most endearing traits of character, as well as the outstanding aspect of his leadership, was his awareness of where his boundaries lay, and his never striving to overstep them.

"How do you say lack of tact in Hebrew?" is a question often to be found in Achad Ha'am's letters, having held "tactlessness," this Jewish shortcoming, in strong dislike throughout his whole life. And what is lack of tact if not a lack of moderation, of reverence, of differentiation; if not an expression of scornful familiarity towards everyone? Lack of tact is not limited to speech and behavior, for one can be a tactless thinker as well. And tact is the hallmark of all culture. Achad Ha'am recaptured it and returned to Jewish thought its crowning glory: the sense of tact, of moderation, of limits. And who knows whether his love of Zion had its roots in a sense of tact, of moderation, of boundaries, in a great modesty in the face of the highest demand of Jewish history? He perceived this only from a distance. He and his entire generation were able to glimpse it only from afar, separated by boundaries, and he had the tact, the sensitivity, to maintain the distance, to stay within the boundaries. The charm of his style flows from this reserve, but also the incompleteness of his thinking. There are thinkers who proceed on the basis of logically arrived at positions, and others who reach their conclusions intuitively; but then there are those thinkers whose aim it is to comfort, and their comfort emerges as "half a comfort," and their thoughts are merely half-thoughts. Was it the fault of Achad Ha'am that he was praised to the skies, claimed as a prophet, a priest, a spiritual leader in Judaism? He did not want it, he did not believe it. He was aware of his limitations, and he thus serves as a model in our present-day, chaotic Jewish life. And this is why, for a time, he will be Achad Ha'am, the one among the people, until such time when Judaism will find its new promise, or will be lost with the old one.

Anski: Russia's Negotiator

The first time I met S. Anski was in 1917. Though we belonged to the same political party, we were separated by temperament, education, and age. An idea — the perception of "the people" — stood between us. We both belonged to the Russian Social Revolutionaries, the SR's for short. But just as the Russian Social Democrats were split into Bolsheviks and Mensheviks, and further into strict Marxists and Revisionists, so too was the SR party split into a multitude of groups and sub-groups. All these groups hardly knew each other; there was very little they could agree on. The disagreements were not political ones (the SR's were not great politicians, only pragmatists); theirs was rather a divergence of outlooks and motivations.

Nothing is easier than being a Social Democrat. It is quickly learned; you need not study all the three volumes of Marx's *Das Kapital*, nor even have an inkling of political economy or sociology. All you need is to have read the *Communist Manifesto* and to know that there are two classes engaged in a war, which, according to the decree of history, must result in the victory of the working class.

And yet, as a Social Democrat one has to be able to defend the past as well as the concerns of the present, and one has to be able to present reasonable explanations and justifications for the ills of the world. Not everybody is able to do this. But the most difficult of all is to be a radical thinker with a socialist heart, without becoming a one-sided, dried-out, petrified human being. And what is the Social Revolutionary theory if not an attempt to construct a system of social radicalism that will weld together two concepts that break apart beneath the first of life's onslaughts: the concepts of individual freedom and of mass domination, the concepts of individualism and of socialism?

The Social Democrats had one teacher: Marx. The SR's had a whole academy: Lavrov and Michelovski, Proudhon up to a point, and many others. Marx had the power to erect a categorical system upon a very simple principle, and those who carried on after him were mere commentators. Lavrov and Michelovski were neither powerful nor original thinkers; they were commentators and disseminators, not philosophers. The SR's therefore never had a "dogma" as their core of reference. Everyone struck out in his own direction. One was set on having the SR's adopt the principles of Kant, and another would advocate following some other thinker. One SR writer assured me that we could derive the validity of the SR theory from the work of the great French mathematician Poincaré.

This left the young SR's in disarray and sent them in search of a firm foundation. And the reason for their disarray was that their quest did not come from their heart, from their feelings. The young generation no longer harbored the old sentimental love for "the people," an idealization of "the people." The old concept of *narodnichestvo* — peoplehood — did not appeal to the young ones; only the old SR's remained loyal to the ideal, to the faith in the great, magic, mountain-moving power and the profound truth of the people. Among such narodniks were G. Schreiber, Minor, the old Nathanson-Bobrov, and S. Anski. Most of them were Jews. Who else can believe so wholeheartedly in a "people" (whichever it may be), and so fully idealize it, but a Jew? Because we usually idealize that which is far removed from us, the true Russians — Gleb Ouspenski, Reshetnikov, or, among the young ones, Buni and Sergeiev-Zens — those who lived with the Russian people not as onlookers, but as part of it, who did not study them but were flesh of its flesh, they did not idealize the peasants. Rarely have writers spoken the truth about their people as bitterly and as mercilessly as have the Russian writers. But for the Jews, the Russian people were an abstraction. They got to know them through literature; they learned the language, the folk-language, from Afanasiev's collection of folk-expressions or from Schein's (also a Jew) collection of folksongs. The only time they saw a real peasant was upon their deportation to Siberia, but this again was rather a stage-peasant, not an everyday, simple one.

I am not saying that we of the younger generation were better acquainted with the "people," but at least our illusions were not as great. We did not explain in detail each word and each witty folk saying, nor did we go along with our friend Victor Michaelovich Tchernov in the assumption that the best way to write in Russian was to pepper it with folkisms. It may be that we young SR's were more deeply influenced by Marxist Socialism, which had driven out our sentimentality. And this is why, for a long time, I felt little interest in Anski's political and literary work. I found him too old, too soft, too lyrical.

When I met Anski for the first time in St. Petersburg he made a very strange impression on me. I saw standing before me an old Jew, or rather, an old-fashioned one, straight out of the past. It was not his face, which could have been that of any Russian intellectual, or of a Frenchman à la Anatole France. Nor was it the way he was dressed, his paramilitary jacket and boots giving him the air of a retired military officer. But his posture, his walk, the way he looked at you, were so singularly Jewish, and in such sharp contrast to his military outfit, that he gave the impression of a Jew masquerading as a soldier. And the inner, spiritual man was just as old-fashioned as the outer one. There are, you know, people who attain old age already in their youth. To be old means to draw to a halt at a certain point on one's way, being unable to proceed any further, to pursue neither an ascending nor a descending path. And yet it is the scaling of heights and the danger of losing one's footing and falling that allows one to live life to its fullest. Russians such as Anski were characterized as "men of the sixties," those who were steeped in the atmosphere of the 1860's, a time of good, well-meaning, compassionate, narrowly-focused, folk-loving idealists. Whether a liberal, a socialist, or of any other party, a man of the sixties will remain a man of the sixties, marked by an indelible stamp.

When I first met Anski I tried to discuss the events of the day with him, mostly non-political issues, but I soon gave up. We failed to understand each other. He was too scholarly for me, too good, and too optimistic. The ice was broken, though, when we abandoned the affairs of the day and turned to the past. Anski's knowledge of Hasidic stories seemed limitless, and he told them with great sweetness. Even Hasidic stories have their variety. Some, like those from Bratislav or from Kotzk, challenge the mind, while others are moral legends that affect you like old ballads, like a Sabbath afternoon tea in an old-fashioned Jewish home. The Hasidic stories Anski told were idyllic, dreamy, good-hearted, God of Abraham tales. From then on I often sought out Anski. The more heart-breaking the events and the more wintry the atmosphere prevailing in Russia, the more I was drawn to the past, to seek comfort from the warmth of bygone days.

Only once did I see Anski in a great, tragic role, and this moment has etched itself in my memory as a symbol of Russia. It was the second day after the Bolshevik Revolution. The government had been overthrown. Kerensky had fled. The other ministers, Kishkin, Poltchinski, Tereschtenka, our friend Rutenberg, and Maslov, who had been a minister just for a few days, remained in the Petroslavska

Fortress. In the city shots were being traded as some of the Junkers were still defending themselves and holding off the Bolsheviks. It was a moment of anarchy. A government had fallen, and no successor had yet appeared to take over power.

The natural successor during this time of transition was the Petersburg City Duma, an acknowledged legal authority. And it may well be that the Duma might, indeed, have assumed such power, might have become a bridge to a new Russia, had its leaders not been of the mold of the 1860's, but of the "twenties." It needed a man of the twentieth century to utter the deciding words. But the Duma was headed by G. Schreiber, a fine person, a good SR, a dedicated *narodnik*, but lacking any political skill. Thus, this is what took place at the moment when the fate of Petersburg had to be decided: The Duma sent a delegation to the Bolsheviks to conduct negotiations regarding the takeover of power, and the leader of this delegation, the negotiator between the two Russias, was S. Anski.

The entrance to the Duma was guarded by soldiers. Everywhere on the gray stone steps, in the long hallways, were young men with rifles (the "Red Guard" as they were then called). In the assembly hall reigned noise and chaos. There were three groups. On the right were well known aristocratic faces — Schingarov, the Countess Panina, and others; in the center there were more Jewish countenances; and on the left were the Bolsheviks with their lips twisted in grim fanaticism, cynically smiling eyes, and faces radiating flaming hatred. Slutzkaya, a Jewish woman with piercing black eyes, a former dentist who had studied in Berlin, was unable to sit still. Mamilski, a Jewish looking non-Jew, was sporting an artificial, almost theatrical smile. Insults and invective flew from all sides. On the platform the various parties were talking, except for the Bolsheviks. They did not need to talk; they had acted. It was hysterical, meaningless and purposeless talk. No one knew how the session would end; everyone was waiting for the delegation.

At last it arrived. S. Anski came up to the platform and began to read his report about the negotiation. He was tired and looked old, older than I have ever seen him, a broken man. He read about the failure of his mission in a sing-song voice, almost as if he were praying, enveloping the assembly in a feeling of doom. We realized that everything was lost and that one could not expect anything from the negotiations or from the negotiator. Suddenly Anski raised his voice; he had arrived at a critical point. The entire night, he said, the negotiators had debated and argued with the Bolsheviks. And then toward the end of the night workers from the Abuchov factory came in and pounded the table: "Make an end of it, or we will do it for you!" Greatly agitated, Anski straightened up and in turn pounded on the podium. After that his voice sank, he hunkered down again and he finished his report in a tired monotone. A stillness fell on the assembly. Even the socialists remained quiet. It was as if a black shadow had traversed the hall, the shadow of a mighty black eagle with tumultuous wings — the eagle of death, of destruction, of despair.

And always when I think about Russia, how it all came about, I remember the old, tired, bowed-down figure of Anski on the podium of the Duma. I remember his tragic negotiating mission and his pounding the table: "Make an end of it, or we will do it for you!"

In Whose Name?

From the tree-covered mountains of Transylvania, from the plains of Hungary, from Germany — from everywhere comes again the old Jewish lamentation. And out of all the crevices of the earth, like an outpouring of burning lava, erupts hatred, hatred toward Jews. No country is safe from it; one place today, someplace else tomorrow. In Hungary and in Russia, Jews are being killed today. In Germany, elected politicians are, in all seriousness, proposing that all Jews be herded into a ghetto, made to wear degrading clothes and deprived of all their possessions. Protestantism has taken over the role of former Catholic fanaticism. It has completed the developmental cycle: from the hatred of Rome to the hatred of Jerusalem. So it is in Germany, and so it will be soon everywhere where Christianity is about to perish.

The same motive prevails both at the beginning and the end. It may be that this is a kind of spiritual illness, which psychiatrists call an "endemic psychosis." This is what took place on the eve of the Crusades; thus it was in Spain before the Inquisition; and thus it was in Russia during the pogroms. And no one stopped the psychic epidemic; no one wants to stop it. All right, a psychosis does stop more slowly and with greater difficulty than other epidemics. Still, there comes a time of fatigue, a spell of calm, and the storm is followed by silence. But in the meanwhile? Maybe our children and grandchildren will be more fortunate than we are, just as our parents, some of them at least, the parents of today's West

European and American Jews, enjoyed more fortunate and quieter lives than their parents.

But what about us? This is, after all, our world and no one else's. Everything lies in our hands. Whatever may come after us, an idyllic flowering or a barren graveyard, the present we live in is ours. We are the only ones who can determine what the aim and the meaning of our life is, and what path we must follow to reach it. We have been trying, for years on end, to find the meaning of our existence and our suffering, and we have failed to do so. Every one of us, each in his own way, is knocking at all the gates, and not one of them has opened up for us. The gates are locked, we do not have a key to open them, and we lack the strength to ram them open.

I know it is useless to talk about it. But why should it be? Why should not every Jew, whoever he may be, feel a deep sorrow and pain? Why should a Jew forget? And why not use the time of the terrible crisis through which we are now passing for a profound analysis of all of our values, a kind of inventory of our spiritual and moral possessions? I do not want to enter into such an analysis here. It requires a different atmosphere, an atmosphere of heightened spirituality, of a quiet, serious, passionate religious relationship to life. Religious? This word must be a rather unintentional slip of the pen, because I am still not at peace with it, because my mind has not, as yet, won through to a mature, crystallized relationship with religiosity. And the only things I can offer are sketches, fragments and meditations, but no resolutions.

We, the modern Jewish intelligentsia, have been struggling with this problem for years, and we cannot resolve it. The generations preceding us — the *Maskilim*, leaders of the Haskalah — had it easier. They believed in their ideas; they felt sure of themselves and of the world they were living in. They were, actually, very religious Jews, those old assimilationists, those old "heretics." They thought that they themselves were "naysayers," but what they were opposing was merely the formal manifestations of historical tradition, and even that not wholeheartedly and with regret. They did not deny the "dogma." They completely believed that the Jews were given the mission to spread the light of truth throughout the world, that their lives, that the life of the people and its suffering, has a meaning and a purpose.

"If you want to find an honest Jew, look for him among the heretics," our Jews once used to say. They may, perhaps, have meant it ironically, but the irony was permeated with a tacit respect. Both factions knew that the way was the same, that the same duty applied within the ghetto and outside of it, the duty of fulfilling a mission. And those outside of the ghetto have pursued this task more loyally than those within it.

The old heretics! What a shame that they have vanished and that there is no one to take their place, that they have lived and died without leaving any heirs. It seems to me that there are no more heretics in Jewish life, because — because there are no more believers. This, of course, sounds like an oxymoron. As soon as you set foot on East Broadway, or on any other "Jewish" street, wherever it may be, in Europe or in America, you will see beards and side-locks, a sexton in a top hat on the Sabbath, and a rabbi wearing a fur hat — because for a rabbi everything is still as it used to be, but only as preserved in a museum, in a glass box.

What has remained is a Jewish beard, a Jewish face, often the sound of the Yiddish language, but nothing more. The beard no longer suits the face, nor does the language does reflect thought. It is no longer tradition, merely inertia. The inertia is so great that no one exerts himself anymore, either for or against it. There is a tacit agreement not to disturb the status quo and not to confront each other with the bitter truth. This is the usual way of the world. When a patient is seriously, hopelessly ill, all those around him smile, console him and assure him that life will be beautiful as soon as he gets well. The patient does not believe it, he only stifles his doubt up to his final moment.

We hear a great deal lately about Jewish religion and the need for "religious education." "The Jewish faith is in danger," lament various proponents of the religious faction, presenting us with horrifying views of the future: without God, without Jews, without decent human beings...chaos, destruction, the end of the world. And we hear proposals to combat this trend, and money is collected to implement these proposals. They collect money to rescue God. And whenever I hear these God-defenders, I ask myself: In whose name are they speaking? What do they want? Have the bitter years passed them by without leaving any scars? Have they been untouched by any eroding doubt? Have they not felt the great sorrow of the Jews who have suddenly seen the destruction of all their illusions, hopes and expectations?

I feel intellectually and emotionally very close to the Jews throughout Eastern Europe who have lived through the terrible experiences of the last years, and I am very understanding of their total despair and their questioning: In whose name and for the sake of what are we suffering? The day will come when Jews will have to pose this question and find an answer. The question itself is already a preparation for a renewal, for a revitalization of petrified Jewish thought.

This is a problem that has faced the Jews in all of their exiles, as it was a problem for the Jews of 15th century Spain. They, too, could not reconcile the Jewish concept of universal justice and universal meaning with their brutal, meaningless reality. The thing that mitigated their spiritual suffering, but also helped them to avoid searching for a clear answer, was the religious fanaticism of their enemies. But it truly was a fiction to say that Torquemada was the main culprit in the drama of the Spanish exile, since economic, social and political motives played a much stronger role. Social motives also brought on the Chmelnitzki pogroms. But in both instances there were added religious motives: one faith confronting another in a kind of Armageddon, a fight for God. And Jews, as well as Christians, let themselves be persuaded that the fiction was a fact. In the final analysis, everything is fiction and everything is fact, depending on how it plays itself out. But the veil has been torn, the fiction has been exposed to the Jews and to the whole world. And this is also the tragedy afflicting modern anti-Semites: they do not know why they hate the Jew. Something elicits their antagonism but they do not know how to account for it. People crave certainty, they want to be convinced, and the modern anti-Semite, himself lacks conviction. Take, for example, a present-day German racial anti-Semite, who is no longer a Christian. Protestantism had done away with the Christian dogma that he had believed in, and religion is no longer a part of his life. He is not fighting Jews for the sake of a *Weltanschauung*, and it is just because he does not know what he is fighting against and why that the struggle becomes so feral, so bitter and barbaric, culminating in a spiritual psychosis.

The anti-Semite does not know the reason for his hatred, hence the Jew does not know either. Neither the observant nor the intellectual Jew of today believes any longer that he is engaged in a struggle for God. The believer is an enforcer of inherited tradition, the intellectual Jew feels oppressed by it, and both sides are confronted with a question mark.

Granting my desire to be optimistic, let us believe that history does not repeat itself, and that all the feral, black forces will not succeed in driving the Jews back into the ghetto. Let us believe that the storm will soon abate, and that a normal time will return. Does this mean a return to the *status quo ante*? A return to the same concepts, the same formulae, without a single new, fresh idea? Does this mean a continued lack of meaning and lack of purpose? It seems likely. I cannot see any sign of a renewal. Yet, following the exile from Spain there had been a time of mysticism and of a deep, religious uprising; a destruction of old values and a creation of new ones. The old, rational Judaism was taken over by mysticism in its old, primitive form. It had been a beginning, a new approach. What will come now? A watered-down, English Protestant-colored Judaism that is being propagandized in America, or an "aleph-bet," fundamentalist Judaism that Russia is yearning for?

I am merely posing the question, nothing more. Questions scare, and answers soothe us. And I do not want to be soothed. If Jewish bodies are suffering, let Jewish souls suffer too. This is a creative kind of suffering. It is time to pose the question, the most burning question: In whose name? And if the time for an answer is still far away, so be it. To raise the question is the essential function of life.

The Heaven-Goer

There can be few more boring, unproductive, incomprehensible topics of inquiry than those posed by theology. And yet, there are few more dramatic, suspenseful and gripping questions than the ones posed by that same theology. Dramatic because they are so shadowy, so unrealistic. Suspenseful and gripping because — because the most gripping act in a circus is the performance of a tightrope-walking acrobat.

You know very well that what he is doing is absolutely senseless and ridiculous. You know that walking a tightrope is not a natural way of locomotion, and you surely would not want to imitate such an act. All of us are capable of walking, but only a circus performer can walk a tightrope. And every theologian is, in essence, a tightrope walker. He climbs higher and higher, and for a while he is suspended above us. We are enraptured, and for that moment we are lifted up from the earth, are spiritually freed from the inexorable law of gravity, becoming a part of the tightrope acrobatic balancing act.

Following that act, we become most appreciative of being able to land on hard, solid, matter-of-fact ground. And did you notice another thing? An acrobat must wear tights. Thus it has been since men started climbing glass walls and walking on tightropes. It s a sort of uniform, a performance costume. Should a circus acrobat venture on a tightrope in ordinary clothes, such as he wears on the street, he would immediately seem ridiculous, just as it would be ridiculous to see someone walking the street dressed in tights, white silk socks and shoes with silver buckles. You can climb towards heaven only in a tradition-sanctioned uniform.

◆   ◆   ◆

I may be harboring an unacknowledged conservative attitude, even though I tend to reject all religious observances, because whatever religious feelings I may have are too deeply buried within me to allow for any outward manifestation. Yet, it is a fact that I cannot imagine a theologian of any religion any other way than in a long black coat, a turned-around collar, and a certain bearing. He cannot be just like you or me, just a regular person without a distinguishing mark. He is, according to a characteristically English appellation, a "sky-pilot," a heaven-goer. His concern is with immaterial matters, with final meanings and mysteries, concerns that do not fall into the realm of science or philosophy.

It is true, of course, that the scholar, the thinker, also deals with hidden matters, with the unknown; that he, too, is searching for the meaning of life, of the universe. But the scholar is seeking for answers; the theologian knows the answer. The thinker inquires; but to the theologian, of whatever faith, everything is clear, and he has ready answers. His tightrope is already in place, and he only needs to walk it. Sometimes the rope is woven of sunrays. If so, then the theologian becomes a great spiritual personality. But more often it is a more ordinary one, and then the theologian does nothing more than perform tricks. This is a difference in degree, not in substance.

The scholar, the thinker, is a man among men; he does not claim the right to be a guide or mentor, nor does he presume to preach to us, to "bring us the truth," to speak "in the name." And, therefore, he does not need to be different from us. But the theologian does separate himself from us, he positions himself above us. Every Sabbath, every Sunday (as in the Free Synagogue) and every Friday night, the theologian rises and holds forth on everything that is timely, and he scolds. He is a castigator, and as such he must wear a hair shirt, have long hair and a long beard. Without it he loses all his magic power. And what is theology if not ancient magic in a new form? What matters is not what he says, but how he says it. He must speak in a singsong that puts you to sleep; he must be a hypnotist.

I have often wondered how it is possible for Reform Judaism still to continue existing. I am speaking of Jewish "Protestantism" because I am talking with Jews. I could put the same question to other people concerning their faiths. There is only one difference: with other nations the religious element plays a minor role.

The Protestants would, surely, have long ago given up the Christian faith had they not been detained by the worry about the morale and stability of the state. For other nations religion is often merely a shield against social dissatisfaction. Their motto is "the throne and the altar," and altars and finances are usually closely related. Yet, even in those cases we begin to see a kind of rebellion against the sobriety and the prosaic aspects of their observances. In England the High Church prevails, i.e. that form of Protestantism that is closest to Catholicism in dogma and its rituals, while in America Protestantism is experiencing a severe crisis.

The most astounding phenomenon, however, is the Reform Synagogue. From time to time I encounter Reform rabbis, and I always wonder: Can this smoothly shaven, ordinary-looking man possibly be a theologian? Is it possible that Jews can face a young man looking like a stockbroker or, at best, a bank president, rising up on a Sabbath, a Sunday or a Friday night to deliver a sermon and continue to listen to him?

It was once general knowledge that a rabbi was a scholar, studying Torah day and night, constantly at prayer, living an ascetic, modest life. Yet, even at a time when all Jews wore caftans and skullcaps, the rabbi was set apart in dress from everyone else. And what did the rabbi actually do? He did not preach, he did not give any sermons, he did not perform any dances on a heavenly tightrope. He merely interpreted the law. Since Jews had little respect for sermonizers, that was the job of a preacher. And the preachers were regarded with a bit of irony and a good bit of tacit scorn. The true rabbi, the real guide, was not an orator, or a preacher or a talker. He did bring them the Torah, but this was telling it, not talking about it. He transmitted high learning and thinking in a few compact words. And the reason that the great scholars and thinkers reacted so negatively to Hasidic rabbis was that they talked too much. They talked more than they thought; they preached more than they studied. All this is gone. Perhaps it still exists somewhere, in the hinterlands of Poland, of Lithuania, of Hungary or in the poorer sections of New York. But life has pushed them aside and has left them stranded.

The rabbi has disappeared, and it is the theologian who has remained. One of America's greatest theologians has written a book entitled *The Jewish Theology*. I read it because I was curious to see how anyone could fashion a systematic theology out of the grandiose chaos that is Judaism. And I saw what I had expected to see: a dry schematic retelling of an epic. Because what is Judaism if not an epic? With all of its dogma, all of its laws, all of the commandments one must follow, and all of the transgressions one must abstain from, it is still only a song of yearning, an epic of a wandering nation being led in mysterious ways, always looking backward, yet always wandering toward the future.

It is the law that forges the rhythmic structure of the epic. The harsher the law, the more forceful its rhythm. But then comes someone who is deprived of all poetic feeling and upsets the rhythm, retelling the epic in his own fashion, in his own language, producing an unbelievable prose. This is what Geiger and Haldheim and all the reformers have done. They have taken the poetry out of Judaism and have made of it a theology. This is very easy. What is difficult is being a poet, a singer who will render an ancient song in the same tone, with the same feeling as it was sung thousands of years ago. Usually, such a singer is blind, and this endows him with pathos and with power. But in order to tell, or retell, the content of a poem you need to be nothing more than tone-deaf and pretentious. The religious artist becomes a religious acrobat. The guardian of the Jewish spirit and Jewish ardor becomes a Jewish theologian, a rabbi, a "sky pilot."

Once you are standing on the tightrope, all tricks are permitted, and you can juggle things as you want; no one takes it seriously. Yet the higher the acrobat climbs, the stronger becomes the pull of the earth, of simple, matter-of-fact reality. And, sooner or later, the rope will snap. Jewish "theology" is facing a severe crisis, and it does not know it. It is unaware of it because it has lost the element of profound religious faith. It has become a profession, no longer a call to service.

Is it any wonder, then, that people are beginning to back away from this homey, self-satisfied, word-saturated theology? This holds true for both factions, both extremes. The intellectuals, the youth, are losing all interest in Jewish spiritual life, while those who are deeply interested are joining the fanatics, the zealots, the Jewish clerics. The left is aspiring to total freedom, while the right is adhering to an iron-cast submission, to pathos, to a burning fanaticism. And between the two extremes is a gray, matter-of-fact theology. Both extremes are very much in earnest, while those in between are engaged in a tightrope dance, a sky-pilot game. And it is the earnest ones who always prevail.

The "Yesterday Jews" and the "Tomorrow Jews"

Years ago Max Nordau coined the terms "also-Jews" and "stomach-Jews." Into the first category fall Jews who are Germans, Frenchmen, Englishmen, and "also-Jews." Into the second category fall Jews whose link to Judaism is through the kitchen. In his time these terms hade a great impact and were used by the Zionists as a propaganda tool in the service of Jewish nationalism. But all the terms which Nordau coined, like "conventional lies," "degeneration," "the end of a centuries-old culture," etc., turned out to be words of the hour and for the hour, and have not remained among the treasured Jewish sayings.

The things that Nordau denounced are now praised. What he considered signs of a downfall are now considered signs of an ascent, and by the very same people who had accepted Nordau's national-political program, the very Zionists who have become less maximalist in their demands, less exacting, who have, indeed, become very, very conciliatory. Let a man be whatever he wants to be, as long as he is also a Jew, and he is a good Jew if he donates a few dollars for Palestine. And when an "also-Jew" is an outspoken, or, more importantly, a wealthy supporter of Palestine, then he is elevated to leadership status.

On the other side are the "Judaism Jews" who night and day preach *kashrut* in a literal or an allegorical form of "stomach Judaism." Or, differently interpreted, those who promote a "Jewish ethos," "Bible," "religious education," etc. What yesterday weighed lightly on the scale of values, now weighs heavily, and vice versa. Were Nordau alive today and able to view American Judaism, the Judaism that left one ghetto and is now moving toward another, he would certainly revise his terse formulations and search for new, more appropriate ones. He would only have to read a few issues of the Jewish magazines written in English for the Jewish intelligentsia; he would only have to attend a few banquets hosted, from time to time, by representatives of the Jewish intelligentsia, and he would hear and see a new form of Judaism, which is, perhaps, in an even worse, more unnatural state, than the "also" and the "stomach" Judaism. Because those were, in the final analysis, grounded in reality. The German Jews who were Germans for 23 hours a day and Jews for one hour, or the Jews who acknowledged their Judaism only on Friday nights over their gefilte fish: they lived in a solid, firmly settled community; they stood with both feet on the ground; they carried on an old tradition; they worked and produced goods, both material and spiritual; they lived the lives of their time, taking part in shaping history, every Jew in his own field: banking, politics, art, and scholarship; they achieved something, inscribing their names upon the pages of history. And if they were "also-Jews," this was often because they felt instinctively that they had some "mission" to fulfill in the world, that they were called upon to accomplish a task.

The German Jewish liberals, the socialist leaders, the "Jewish press," who for half a century struggled on in Germany; the French Jews who fought for democracy and a freer society; the Jewish artists and writers who contributed their Jewish temperament and their intellectual acuity to universal thought; they have not lived in vain. It is still a moot question as to who has been more loyal to the Jewish spirit: those who have labored and sown seed in "foreign fields" or those who have stopped any progress and have called for a retreat. It was in Germany, in the assimilated circles, that a sort of a national renaissance, a desire for a more profound, more noble Jewish nationalism, came into being. It did so out of a feeling that those assimilated German Jews had accomplished something, had done their duty for their time and society. One accomplishment leads to another, and their developmental process led from the universal humanity to Jewish humanity.

There is now a third group of Jews, one with a new orientation, who are neither nationally committed nor assimilated, who have broken away from the old, complex Jewish world and have not even tried to become part of their new general community. These are Jews who have forgotten the old but have not learned anything new, who have merely distanced themselves from their past but have not associated themselves with anything else. This is an intelligentsia that remains outside of all intellectual life, negating all its movements, refusing to join any of them, rather than allowing itself to feel the lure of vital participation.

What has the Jewish intelligentsia, except for a few German and Russian Jewish immigrants, contributed to general American culture up to now? No member of the "Americanized" generation, whose mother tongue is English, has contributed anything to American culture. Except for one or two writers there is not one personality, no leading figure in any field, not even in finance, that can stand comparison to German or French Jewish leaders.

The reason for this is understandable. America is a young country, and its Jewish community is also young. But this is merely an excuse, an explanation; it does not change the fact. It also does not answer the question: Why have Jews become weary so soon, why did they so quickly lose their spiritual bearing? I have listened to their speeches, and their main motif is: What will happen tomorrow? What will become of Judaism? You hear only "We were...," and there follows a flood of flowery descriptions of all that "we" have been: We were heroes, preachers of peace, we have brought God into the world.... This is followed by another flood of words about what "we want to be, we must be...."

Every time I hear these speeches, I remember I. L. Gordon's poem "We were slaves — and what are we now?" You may change the first line and replace slaves with heroes, or whatever honorific epithet you choose, but the question still remains: "And what are we now?" We were, we will be, yes. But what about now? What do the nice, young people know about what yesterday's Judaism was really like? And how can they know what it will be like tomorrow? Let us hope that all will be well, but the issue is today. Their fathers have done their work, and their children will do theirs; but what about these who are children of their fathers and not yet fathers of their children? Who are they, themselves, and what is their place in life, in Jewish or in general life?

They have only two choices. If they want a great, autonomous Judaism, then it is their duty to create it today, by their own efforts. The field is wide open: Young people can go to Palestine and work there, like the *halutzim* from Germany or Austria, and spend their energies and enthusiasm on historical work in a historically creative time. Or, if Palestine is too remote for them, let them come closer to the Jewish masses in America, who have still remained a part of their national community. Let them learn the language of the Jewish people, speak it, read its literature; let them support the Jewish people spiritually and materially and embrace them with sincere affection.

But if they can no longer hear the voice of "yesterday," let them be creative in their new environment, tear down the walls that may stand in their way, and bring their Jewish impetus and fire into their American life, the same fire that Jews have carried with them into all of their exiles. Let others worry about tomorrow. Maybe the old nursery rhyme is right: "Tomorrow, tomorrow, not today, that is what all lazy people say." What sense does it make for you to worry about tomorrow? The future of American Jewry will be the result of what you do today. Your present-day actions will determine your tomorrow. You can be sure that the Maccabees, who had raised the Menorah as a symbol of national liberation, did not ask themselves: What will happen to the Jews tomorrow when the Hellenists win? They did not wait, they did not surrender, but rather they kept on fighting for the present day. If one engages in a fight with Antiochus and the Hellenists, one does not fight them with promissory notes for tomorrow, but with the determination to win the present-day battle. One must light the Menorah every day, not as a decoration, or an ornament, but as an "eternal light" endowed with sanctity.

It is an either/or stand: Either be a Jew, with all that this entails, or become assimilated in a meaningful, purposeful way. Either choice is a commitment to the realization of one's aspirations and will work to ensure the continual brightness of the Menorah lights. It is the half-and-half stance, the flowery rhetoric of celebrating the past and making demands of the future, that will deplete the oil in the cruse and will extinguish the Menorah lights even before they are slated to flicker out.

The Spirit of Our Time

In one of his profound, thoughtful novels, the Spanish writer Pio Boroja presents us with a very interesting scene from the Paris Commune. Barricades have closed off all the main streets, while enthusiastic workers, bedecked with red ribbons, are waving rifles and shooting at random. Thunderous noise and the smell of powder fill the air. Somewhere on a side street next to a barricade, stands an old, gray-haired, insignificant looking man, except for his big, veiled, yet observant eyes. He, too, is holding a rifle, but he is not shooting; he is thinking. A group of workers and a few bourgeois intellectuals surround him, looking up to him, waiting for him to speak. And the old man says, almost to himself: "All this is quite useless; nothing will come of it. What is needed is for a small elite group to acquire power, dictatorial power, hold it for 50 years, and use it to educate, educate, educate."

The old man was the famous French revolutionary, the spiritual father of Bolshevism, Louis Auguste Blanqui. Pio Boroja may have added a few colorful touches, but, however presented or described, this is a historic fact. This was Blanqui's final, basic thought, and it is the thought of all social reformers and of all societal leaders. This was even the basic idea of the Bolsheviks. The mistake of politicians — a mistake that has been enacted in its most classic form by Blanqui's disciples, the Bolsheviks — is the very fact of being politicians. They cannot renounce political methods, i.e. force, power, coercion. They do want a spiritual renewal, but they go after it with bayonets. They want to educate by force and coercion.

Educators who teach individuals long ago understood that the way of the spirit cannot be pursued in a land where force holds sway. Modern education proceeds by encouraging a slow growth, allowing a ripening process to occur, engaging in ongoing discussions and providing examples of good living. The true teacher is the one who lives according to his teaching. The spirit must be a manifest vital force.

Those aiming to educate society as a whole have not undertaken the approach used successfully for educating individuals. It is too difficult a task, one that demands great talent and a degree of mental energy, qualities which are not readily available. Their intentions are often very good, but they use the wrong method. They try to reach the spirit by way of political indoctrination. And this leads to a new spiritual corruption. Blanqui was a shining phenomenon, but Blanquism is dark, brutal and evil.

Spirit versus politics: this has been, in a certain sense, albeit often unconsciously, the Jewish position throughout world history. The Jewish people were able to withstand the pressure, the terrible load of hatred and persecution, because they created for themselves their own spiritual atmosphere, and, even more, because they never used force to oppose a political system; that is, except for the times when Jews in Hellenistic Egypt, Arabia and Persia tried it, with very sad results: they were physically suppressed and annihilated.

Even today Jews instinctively follow the old way. Left to themselves the Jews are the least politically active people among the surrounding groups. But if they are not left alone, then they find themselves forced to adopt the generally prevailing political method. They must go along, and in so doing they must deny their own identity.

In their struggle for national existence and against anti-Semitism, Jewish communal leaders have used the wrong approach to the whole problem, both in its positive and its negative aspects. Political action has to keep in step with cultural developments, because political organization follows the more important formation of spiritual credos.

At this point I am going to limit myself to considering just one aspect of the entire, broad range of Jewish problems; namely, the problems facing American Jewry. And this problem does exist, neither America nor the Jews can deny it, and it is becoming more acute with every passing day. It is not talked about too often, nor too loudly, partly because Anglo-Saxons are by nature more inclined to conceal their true feelings, to control their emotions, and partly because Americans want to adhere — if not always in deed, at least in speech — to their old, fundamental principles. But mostly this is because Jews themselves are trying hard to minimize and play down the problem. "One must always think but never talk about it," Gambetta instructed Frenchmen after the disaster of 1870, at the inception of the Revanche movement. But it does not work. The French have tried hard for 40 years "not to talk about it," but, hating the Germans, they have always thought about it. And, in the end, thought led to action. The long silence still deepened, and, therefore, sharpened their hatred. And it would have been better for France, and for the whole world, if, during these 40 years, Frenchmen had talked more and thought less, if they had talked it over and arrived at a resolution. It is a pity that Freud's theory of the traumatic effects of undischarged emotions was still unknown, for it might have played a significant role in European history, and also possibly a healing one.

To refuse to acknowledge anti-Semitism, in whatever form it may manifest itself in America, is an old German-Jewish ostrich policy. The more one talks about it, the better; better for us and better for the country. The only question is: How do we talk? Shall we complain, thunder, vituperate, accuse everyone who criticizes Jews of being anti-Semitic? Shall we lump together the pogrom-advocates with the "a-Semites," those who do not hate Jews but simply want to keep their distance?

It is, once again, the old, old-fashioned struggle, such as took place in Russia and all of Eastern Europe, where the method of fighting for Judaism meant a fight for survival, for civil rights, for the right to live where one chooses, the right to study and to ascend. The anti-Semites employed, to use a military phrase, a frontal attack on all of Jewry, and the defense had to respond in kind. Jews had to close ranks in resisting a hostile society. The main thing was to prevail; the less self-analysis the better. Self-criticism weakens one's determination, renders one too considerate and too discerning.

There is no justification for employing such a method in America, nor does it have any strategic value. No one here is staging any frontal attacks on Jews. No one, not even the new anti-Semites, even if they may think it, are talking about limiting Jewish civil rights. This stage of anti-Semitism is being phased out throughout the world, while in America it would yet have to begin. The conflict between Jews and America is neither a political nor an economic one; it is a psychological conflict between two temperaments, two world views, two different approaches to life. The American is calm, self-assured, more moralistic than intellectual, and young, at times too youthful. A professor at Columbia University has stated that the mental development of the average American stops at the level of a

13- to 14-year-old. This, of course, may hold true for many other peoples as well, it is only that it manifests itself more prominently in America than elsewhere. The American is uncomplicated; he likes clear formulas and brief, easily understandable speeches. He is not so much anti-intellectual as anti-philosophical. He has great respect for the past, but the past presents itself to him in a simplified form.

The most typical representative of the American mind at its highest development is Woodrow Wilson. And he is the most single-minded, "one-way" follower of all of the spiritual leaders of modern times. He is a single-minded, one-tone proponent, with all its good and bad consequences. There is no other country in the world where a slogan can acquire such a hold on the minds of its people than America. One can accomplish everything overnight — the best and the worst. Such are the reactions of an impulsive people. Prohibition was enacted in an instant and was repealed a minute later.

It is this emotional impulsiveness and intellectual orientation that the Jewish intellect and character are facing. Opposition here does not express itself in hostile attacks, in overpowering one's opponent, and in excluding him, but rather it aims at drawing him into its orbit, the way different metals are melted together and fused into a new one. In what way do we, as Jews, depart from this "Americanism"? We oppose their intellectual calm with disquiet, with our searching, stormy spirit; we oppose their matter-of-fact rootedness in their home-soil by being eternal strangers. In a world where everything is wonderfully new and simple, we are old and complex, Jews being the most complex people on the face of God's earth. This is why Jewish thought, at its highest level, is so difficult to understand. Someone else's simple thought becomes so convoluted as it enters the Jewish thought process that it is often difficult to follow.

Compare Spinoza with his mentor Descartes, Kant with his teacher Shlomo Maimon, Hermann Cohen with Georg Simmel. The non-Jewish thinkers each put forth his system, representing his particular view of the world. The Jewish thinkers incorporated some of these ideas into a wide web of universal motives. Wherever the Jew entered a country's life, that country became richer, financially and intellectually. Richer, but also more amorphous, and this is one of the great faults for which the cultural world cannot forgive us. We are destroying the completeness; we are challenging the acceptance of the predominant way of life. We face the dictum "This is the way things are," and we counter it with "Yes, but this is the way they should be," thus disturbing the societal equilibrium. We often play the role of Mephistopheles, who can never say: "Yes, let it stay this way, this is good." We are being driven by unfortunate creative urges. And, impatient people are often not the most pleasant of neighbors. They are always in a rush; they lack moderation, be it in sorrow or in joy. Impatient people lack manners, because manners require time and restraint, and restraint is based on moderation, on graciousness.

In the Old World, i.e. in Russia and in Poland, we had no need for manners, for no one demanded them of us. But America does demand them from us and will not overlook any tactless utterances, any false steps. As Jews and Gentiles in America are beginning to interact to a greater extent and more closely, both our faults and our merits are being more prominently displayed. But human nature tends to magnify failings and play down the merits. Thus, the deeper we penetrate into the American intellectual community, the more isolated we find ourselves.

I do not know whether we shall ever manage to get rid of the Jewish problem. We shall, certainly, not do so as long as we encapsulate ourselves in our old, inherited ways. And we cannot expect America to be an exception, a historic oxymoron: a country with many Jews and without a Jewish problem. But since there is a Jewish problem, let it at least be a worthwhile one; let Jews at least use all the opportunities to pull themselves up to the highest rung of the ladder they are able to reach; let the American period of Jewish history be a second, and an improved, version of the Spanish Jewish period, the greatest and most beautiful period in Jewish history, a period when the Jewish will and Jewish spirit blended into the surrounding culture of its time. We must give America the things that its founding race could not give it: colorfulness and diversity. And we must take from America what our history has denied us: security and moderation. In other words, we must consciously reeducate ourselves in order to be able to achieve the greatest self-realization. Jewish political life in America, therefore, must not be merely "politics," but a great spiritual effort. It must include self-criticism, it must be a re-evaluation of all of our values, and it must be a new fusion of all of our treasures

Some may wish to call it assimilation, but this term has lost its terror, at least here in America; it cannot deter us anymore. It is not assimilation that poses a danger to Judaism — the Spanish Jews were also assimilated — but forsaking our origins, an abandonment of our Jewish continuity. Such an abandonment is not assimilation; it is, rather, merely a hiding in the basement, and there is no room in America for this kind of assimilation. Assimilation is a mutual process. It is a give and take, and such an assimilation is possible, even necessary, in America. This is the only way for American Jewry as well as for America. The spirit of our times demands a cultural interpenetration, and the faith that neither America nor Judaism must lose something in the bargain.

A Bundle of Keys

I once heard a story about the old city of Cracow. In that legend-steeped city there was a street named after Emperor Joseph the First, the Enlightened One. I do not know its present name, but today, as of old, it is the most Jewish street in the Jewish section of Cracow.

It is a medieval street, narrow, flanked by tall houses, with synagogues and schools on every corner. There was a custom observed by the community of Cracow: when someone lost something, he notified the sexton who then walked along the streets, mostly along Joseph street, announcing the loss. The older inhabitants of Cracow still remember how the old sexton (so old that no one, including the sexton himself, could tell his age) would call out the lost item in his weak, trembling voice. And they recall how he had once walked along Joseph street announcing: "A Jewish woman…fell from the fourth floor window…a bundle of keys…" And one was left in doubt whether a woman had fallen out of the window or just a bundle of keys. Yet, clearly, a bundle of Jewish keys had been lost and needed to be found.

We are still searching for it. Because among the various keys that open up drawers and cupboard, jewelry boxes and closets filled with fancy raiment, there is also a key that unlocks the main gate. It is the oldest and most important key of all, disguised by its beautiful ornamentation, and it cannot be duplicated. It is this key that has been lost. It is this key that the Jewish woman who fell from the fourth floor was looking for with all her might. And it is the loss of this key that the old sexton was proclaiming as he walked along the Joseph Street.

And so we go on searching...

I will admit that the analogy is a bit far-fetched, resulting from an association of words. The story of a sexton of Cracow announcing the loss of a bundle of keys came to mind as I was reading A. M. Gershenzon's *The Key to Faith*. But, for all that, it is not a mere verbal association, and even less a play on words. Because the story is a parable of the idiosyncratic, meandering mode of Jewish thought.

Somewhere, long ago, a bundle of keys fell from on high, and among them was also the key to the gate that leads to truth, guarding that which is hidden, which is the Holy of Holies. No one knows which of the keys opens this gate, and no one knows who lost it. Yet the search for the right key has been going on almost from the beginning of Jewish thought, from the very time that it lost its iron-cast, hard-edged uniformity.

Each of the seekers turns to the best locksmiths of his time. Philo turned to the Greeks. They were marvelously creative in all areas, except one: They were unable to find a place to stand. "Give me a place to stand and I will move the earth," Archimedes claimed. It may be that he would have been able to do so, but in the "give me a place to stand" lay his weakness and his limitation. It was the limitation of Greek thought. Philo sought to open the gate to Judaism with a Greek key, with logic, with science, with clear, rational thought. It did not work. Trying the best of all the keys, the Platonic one, he set out to explain God, to understand Him, and ended by using Biblical chapter and verse to interpret Plato's philosophy of the supremacy of the Idea and using beautiful Greek phraseology to interpret the Biblical text. Philo was the first of the interpreters.

Next came the Rambam, trying out the Arabic key; he called it Aristotle, Aristo, but it was actually Eastern, Arabic thought. A better key than the Greek one, yet still not the right one. Once again it was a system; once again there was explanation and justification. Maimonides opened up one gate after another — the moral, the national and the logical — but he could do no more than expound. "The rule of precepts" constituted the limit of the Rambam's thought. And so the sexton was again walking the streets announcing the loss of a key.

Spinoza was the next to respond. He came equipped with keys to the entire Western world: the precise scholastic Medieval thought and verbal hairsplitting, as well as the new European Cartesian method of mathematical proof. And he became embroiled in contradictions. In his *Theologico-Political Treatise* he spoke as a rationalist, a historical critic, bent on destroying all of the partitions. After that he leapt over the partition erected by critical reason and became a mystic, rising to the highest rung of human reasoning and abstraction. And in the end he arrived at the "what is, is." There is nothing more, nothing else. It is the basic Jewish thought process, only without the ancient Jewish ladder that leads up to it. Just like the golden ladder in the famous picture by Sir Edward Burne-Jones; this Jewish ladder is suspended in midair.

Later on there followed, one after the other, Nachman Krochmal, Samuel Luzzatto, Hermann Cohen. Each one of them sought to find the key and each one borrowed it from others, from the gate openers of the non-Jewish world. Krochmal borrowed the key from Hegel, Luzzatto from the Italian mystics, Cohen from Kant.

And the gate still remained closed.

A. M. Gershenzon also tried. He borrowed the key from the Russians, from the Slavophiles of the 1860s, from Dostoevsky. This is the most remarkable of all the keys. The East claimed that the key to the Divine gate was contained in the telling of stories; the Western world posited that it was contained in reason; and the Russians added a new claim: the key to God lies in suffering. Man is torn, he is a particle plucked off of the totality of being, and therein lies his "original sin." From this he suffers. It is man's destiny to suffer; his aim in life is to immerse himself in the wholeness of being, to free himself from himself, to throw himself on God's mercy, to abdicate his free will, to become a mere wave ruled by the ocean.

It is this motif that Gershenzon has brought into his meditation about Judaism. He asks: What is faith? Which is the key to religion? And he answers: The essence of faith, the key to religion, is the willingness to modify one's life according to the correct concept of how human beings should conduct themselves. The way of life — the way to God — is strewn with obstacles and barriers. They must be overcome; they must be stormed. There are, he says, constant "explosions" as will confronts will — the will of man confronting the will of God. The final, the highest rung, the ultimate concept is, therefore "the fusion of the universal and the human, the unity of man and God."

Is this a Jewish concept? No. Spinoza was much more Jewish when he denied the existence of human will, when he altogether removed the will motif from philosophy and religion. Can there be two wills? How can man, the "worthless insect," have a will of his own that can face up to the will of the universe? Is there, therefore, something within me directing my will? And this "something" is still the final mystery.

Gershenzon was not a deep enough thinker to pose these questions. And no one expected sharp analysis from him, just as no one expects a new Russian philosophy. Russian thought is born of and filled with suffering, and sometimes it is also tinged with hysteria.

The "key" was not found in Alexandria, nor in Cracow, Amsterdam or Berlin. And it would have been futile to look for it in Moscow. It is possible that it will never be found, not even in Jerusalem. Or, who knows, perhaps at a later time, when the Jew will again come home, when he will once again settle in the Sinai, the key may again be found in the burning thornbush, if it has not yet been consumed by the fire.

In the meantime, the old sexton still walks all the streets in the town, walks the old narrow, synagogue-flanked streets, and calls out in his old, trembling voice, "A key has been lost!" A pathetic figure.

The Gaon of Neswicz: Shlomo Maimon

There are names which form a part of our consciousness, which accompany us like loyal friends wherever we go, which resound within us like bells, awakening, cheering and exhorting us. The number of these ringing bells is not large; as changing times silence some of them, they are melted down and re-cast. The bell of Aristotle resounded continuously throughout the entire cultured world for almost a thousand years. From Samarkand, where the great Arabic thinker Ibn Sina lived, to Córdoba, Spain, where Ibn Rashid and Rambam were born, from Rome to Paris and to the big island of Ireland: In every place Aristotle was the teacher, leader, guide and center of all debates. When the bell of Aristotle lost its resonance, the bell of Plato began to make itself heard, and its metallic peal has not yet stopped resounding in ours ears.

Other names have emerged and produced other reverberations in Western culture, and the name with the strongest resonance is that of Kant. Wherever you go, wherever you turn, you will hear his name. If you want to fashion a conceptual framework within which to view the world, you will have first to come to grips with Kant, with the slight, short university professor from Königsberg, where he lived modestly in near poverty without ever leaving his small city. There are few other such names — very few. Some of them cause us to stand transfixed in horror and amazement as we gaze at the embodiment of human tyranny and despotism, and others make us bow our heads in humility before the holiness, greatness, grace and benevolence of genius.

I do not know how these differences come about. I will not even try to tackle this problem. Many psychologists and students of human nature have undertaken to answer this question, and no one has, as yet, succeeded. What do we actually know about the mystery which we call the human personality? What key will unlock our comprehension of what it is that distinguishes one human being from the next? How does it happen that, of two children growing up in one family, buds on the same twig, sharing the same mother and father, one will grow into a normal, average, simple person while the other will turn out to be an extraordinary personality?

But right now another question occupies my thoughts — a question that is just as difficult to answer as the one concerning the essence of genius — and that is the question of the sages: the *geonim*. This is a purely Jewish question, and therefore a complex and multifaceted one. Why do we, Jews, have so few geniuses and so many *geonim*? Too few geniuses, considering the length of our historical existence; too many *geonim*, considering our numerical strength. It is, indeed, a very characteristic trait of Jewish life that wherever you look you can find a multitude of highly talented, extremely able, penetratingly clever, far-sighted people, their heads filled with knowledge, their brains as sharp as razor blades, their intellects endowed with the strength of loading cranes, smoothly ferrying heavy loads through the air.

Names come to mind, names out of olden times, of wise Talmudists who produced analyses of such penetrating acuity as to remain nearly unmatched by ensuing generations of *geonim* — Rabbi Saadia, the Rambam and Rashi. Then there are learned men like Rabbi Yom Tov Lipman Heller, the Rashbam, and, closer to our times, the Gaon of Vilna and the Baal Haturia, as well as some more recent ones. A gallery of spiritual ancestors unlike any other in the world; and yet, when contrasted with the ancestral galleries of other nations, ours appear rather outlandish, alien and exotic. The Czech novelist Max Brod once tried to illustrate the difference between a *gaon* and a man of genius by way of the personalities of the Danish astronomer Tycho Brahe and his disciple, the German Johannes Kepler. Brahe was the more perceptive, more able and more imaginative of the two; he was in his way a *gaon*. But Kepler, the more modest, quiet and naive personality, was a genius. Brahe comprehended, while Kepler created; and genius, in the final analysis, is creativity. The *gaon*, however, does not create; the *gaon* is not naive. The *gaon* is acutely perceptive, keenly intelligent. He has everything needed to achieve greatness except the ability to face the state of nonbeing, to wrestle with chaos, and to emerge with an ordered formulation. And this may have been the barrier in the path of Jewish sages: They feared chaos and lacked the courage to be creative.

These random thoughts were aroused while I read a remarkable book, a book out of the past and yet as fresh as if it had been written the other day: the autobiography of Shlomo Maimon. As I was leafing through the excellent Yiddish translations of the German original which I read many years ago, my eye was caught by the picture of Shlomo Maimon, who was born in 1754 in Neswicz and died in 1800 in Silesia at the house of his patron, the Graf von Karlkroit. Maimon was dressed in the garb of the 18th century, with a braid dropping onto his collar, his clean-shaven face expressing a keen intelligence, and bearing a strong resemblance to Immanuel Kant. As I looked at his picture, Shlomo Maimon the man began to come alive for me: the nomad of old Poland, the Gaon of Neswicz, filled with wisdom and a search for knowledge, the teacher, the thinker, the unworldly student; a lonely man and a misunderstood one.

I picture him striding through his small town, shabbily dressed in a tattered coat, and wearing old worn-out boots. He is on his way to the preacher to study Kabbalah, a study which keeps him up late into the night, as long as the candle lasts, preventing him from going to sleep, to the utter despair of the poor preacher's young wife. I picture him coming home and having his ears boxed by his mean mother-in-law and cursed by his miserable teen-age wife. And I see him later on, stealthily creeping under his mother-in-law's bed, pinching her black and blue, and scaring her half to death in the process. And then I see him walking with a friend who is as poor and unworldly as himself, both still in their teens and already married and fathers of children. And as they walk across the fields they hold philosophical discussions about God and the world: Maimon the thinker and his friend, Lapidot the poet. And later on we find him in the abandoned castle of a Polish nobleman, chalk in hand, copying the old Gobelin tapestries. And still later, there he is walking along the streets of the provincial town of Königsberg, or petit bourgeois Berlin, or Hamburg, ever famished, lonely, harassed, profoundly unhappy.

He knows everyone, including Mendelssohn, the good-natured *Maskil*, one of the enlightened, but Mendelssohn is afraid of Maimon's acuity. Maimon is too much of a *geonic* thinker for him. Mendelssohn is an interpreter, a mere mediator between Judaism and German culture. He speaks moderately, does not transcend accepted norms, whereas Maimon breaks down the norms, cutting through them with a flawlessly sharp blade. He is a pathfinder among towering mountains. He understands the Rambam and Kant and the exact sciences thoroughly and deeply, so much so that he transcends all their tenets. His criticism is so refined that even the genius Kant can no longer follow him, let alone the more limited Mendelssohn. Maimon writes books in Hebrew, and no one is willing to print them. He writes, in German, an analysis of Kantian philosophy, an outline of a new system of logic, and other books, but only a few read them, as they are too difficult, too profound, and they contain too few constructive elements.

Maimon dies young, and soon his name fades into near oblivion; he remains a shadow, a legend, no longer a spiritual reality. From time to time one scholar or another will recall him, and modern logicians have quoted him in some rarefied dissertations on logic, destined to be read only by a few learned specialists in the field. But even there he is remembered as one who strove for knowledge and who stimulated philosophical thought, but one who did not pursue it to its conclusion.

His face bore a resemblance to Kant's, but he was not a man cast in the Kantian mold. He was a sage but not a genius. From youth on he loved to paint, and had he lived under different circumstances, he himself felt he might have become a great painter, but one whose work would comprise only sketches, drafts, beginnings rather than finished, completed canvases. He saw an image and he could draw the outlines, but he was not able to flesh them out, nor did he have the patience for it. This meant that he lacked interest in the process of formulation, was devoid of the urge to shape and to form, and therefore lacked creativity.

Had he been born a few hundred years earlier, Shlomo Maimon would surely have been a second Ibn Ezra, a great illuminator of thought. Had he been born into the European atmosphere of the 19th century, his writing would have been more sorrowful and fanciful, more paradoxical than reasoned. But born late into the 18th century, at the onset of a great cultural struggle and the development of new ideas, Maimon could not find a place for himself, neither in German culture which was at the beginning of its formation, nor Jewish culture which was beginning its process of disintegration. Wandering from place to place — both geographically and in his heart and soul — he was indeed homeless.

It seems to me that Judaism is entering a new spiritual epoch, characterized by a return to a more naive outlook on the world. A current of fresh air can be felt, an urge to be creative, and the Jewish *gaon* is slowly disappearing. We still do not have any geniuses, except for Einstein, nor do we really have a spiritual climate which produces geniuses; but neither do we have any more *geonim*. In the meantime, we are predominantly average; but it is better this way. It is a liberation which can lead to a renewal. Our *geonim* are already becoming part of our history. And there is no doubt that next to the Gaon of Vilna, enshrined in the gallery of our great remarkable ancestors, the portrait of the last of the *geonim*, the Gaon of Neswicz, Shlomo Maimon will hang.

Nachman Syrkin: 1868–1924

It was a summer afternoon and my friend Nachman Syrkin and I were walking up and down the marble hallways of the New York Public Library, engaged in one of our perennial discussions. Our meeting there was not a rare occasion for the library was his home. Winter and summer would find Syrkin sitting in the large reading room surrounded by books. There were thin and thick ones, old and new, profound books and more lighthearted ones, those that challenged the mind as well as those that responded to the yearnings of the heart. And when he was not sitting and reading, he would be promenading along the wide, almost cloistral hallways, thinking, and, at times, smiling at his own thoughts.

On that summer afternoon I was in a mood to talk, and even more to listen, to exchange ideas with someone dedicated to the process of thinking, with a friend who felt the importance, the necessity, the driving force of spiritual life. And I knew that it would be difficult to find a better companion than Nachman Syrkin for such an exchange of ideas, for venturing into uncharted, infinite, "universal" spiritual quests. There are very few people who lead a life of the spirit, i.e. whose main interest in life is focused on "spirituality," on questions unrelated to their personal daily existence, who have become absorbed into the world of pure thoughts — people who lead a life of abstraction. Only an exceptional person can attain such a level, can stand high above the multitude. At Schiller's funeral Goethe delivered a brief eulogy. And the best, the highest tribute that the poet paid his follow poet and friend was: "Schiller's life was one of an ongoing spiritual labor." And this is truly the highest eulogy one can offer a person.

To be involved in an ongoing spiritual labor means to remain forever young. The only part of us that can grow more complex and more vigorous with the passage of years is the mind. Like aging wine, it can grow more piquant, more intoxicating. I have often thought about Syrkin's "youthfulness." His gray hair and stooped posture were made incongruous by the flaming utterances of a naive enthusiast, utterances of a man to whom it was still of great importance to achieve his own view of the world, to arrive at his own concept of life and of how to live it.

Not long ago, following a long conversation about everything in the world, about various contemporary ideas and movements, about science and philosophy, and mainly about Judaism, I could not resist asking Dr. Syrkin: "How old are you, actually?" "I am 56-years-old," Syrkin answered, smiling at me, and his twinkling eyes harbored none of the sadness which one usually sees in the eyes of those whom one reminds of their age. It was as if he had said "I am 25-years-old." And I found myself at that moment unable to associate the number 56 with old age and would have been neither astounded nor shocked if someone just then would have come up to Syrkin and said to him, as one did 30 years ago in Berlin: "Nu, what are you up to, Nachke?" And he would certainly not have considered it out of place. He remained the eternally young "Nachman Syrkin," the Berlin student who stormed and ranted. The gray hair was merely an accident, a joke, and he himself considered it as such: "Oh well," he might have said, "who cares what that silly hair is doing."

I remembered something Ussishkin said at the Carlsbad Congress. He was talking about the opposition, about the "youth" which gets excited and wants to turn the world upside down, and in his dry, humorous way he said to me: "Try to get something done when even fifty-year-olds still see themselves as 'the youth.'" And once again, this was one of the highest compliments for our generation. The body ages, but not the spirit. The issues of concern are so complex and so great, life is so gripping, the creative urge is so strong, that one does not pay attention to one's growing physical limitations and need for rest. And all of us hear the resonance of the great, beautiful and heroic saying of Rabbi Nachman of Bratslav: "It is forbidden to grow old!" We may not grow old because we cannot afford the luxury, because a great commandment has been placed upon our shoulders, and we must carry it to fulfillment. Nachman Syrkin followed the injunction of the greater Nachman faithfully and enthusiastically. He did not grow old.

A few weeks after being with Syrkin at a lively gathering I was to see him in quite another setting, a small room at Mount Sinai Hospital. I had difficulty believing the news that had reached me: "Syrkin is sick; Syrkin is dying." Syrkin and death: it seemed a truly incongruous notion. When I entered the narrow hospital room and saw Nachman Syrkin on his deathbed, I felt a veil descending in front of my eyes and was gripped by a terrible, heart-breaking, strangling sadness. It was caused not only by the sight of death or of a dying person, not only by the awareness that a friend was departing from life, but by something more, something deeper. I was overpowered by doubt of the worth of everything that I valued so highly and loved so dearly, of the worth of thought and of spirituality, and by the fear that all human values acquire a sameness in the face of death.

But a moment later the veil lifted and doubt disappeared. Syrkin himself helped me. The dying, suffering man consoled and lifted the spirit of one who had come to pay a sick room visit, who had come to bid his friend farewell. He spurned the usual, the so human assurances of comfort and hope. With a strong wave of his hand he swept aside my initial attempt to express my hope for his recovery. "One may not, one must not, mouth banalities in the face of death," he said in his fading voice. And suddenly everything changed. Once again two friends, two spiritually close people, were talking together. And, once again, the eternally living thought spun its golden web playfully, swinging from one side of the web to the other. "A Socratic scene," said one of those present, enraptured by the tragic, consoling beauty of our friend's fervor. We talked about all that was so dear to him, so essential throughout his whole life, for which his soul had so deeply thirsted: Jews and Judaism. Judaism to him was not merely a matter of national identity, not just the history of a people struggling for its rights, nor was it a problem to be resolved politically. He saw Judaism as something much deeper, more beautiful and more encompassing. He saw it as a phenomenon of world-historical scope, as a picture within a gigantic frame, as a time-transcending idea.

Being an abstract thinker, he viewed Judaism as an abstraction, a concept. Spiritual Judaism was much more important to him than the historic data of Jewish life, and it was this view that drove him to an often fanatical optimism which underlied his utopian dreams. He saw Judaism as the ancient Greeks had imagined the legendary figure of Prometheus, a fettered giant, striving to liberate the world, and who, in the end, succeeded. He was tortured by ravens picking at his liver and by lightening and storms which assailed him. His gigantic suffering paid tribute to his gigantic pursuit.

Realistic thinkers among us have often smiled at Syrkin's enthusiasm and his idiosyncratic approach to events and to problems. We often did not know why he was taking a given position, what was the reason of an endorsement or a sharp rejection (and only those capable of strong love are capable of fierce rejection, since this, too, is a fiery response to given stimuli). But even Syrkin's devoted *Poalei Tsion* comrades were often unable to follow his train of thought, his glorification of warfare, his utopian-hued socialism, his strange views on Bolshevism, his intense dislike of Yiddish, and his flaming love for Hebrew. And I can well imagine the many times he must have greatly embarrassed his *Poalei Tsion* friends, just as he has often evoked a sense of wonderment in the general public and even in his closest literary friends and coworkers. But all the contradictions, all the lack of clarity in Syrkin's literary and political work, stem from one source: his passionate devotion to abstraction. He viewed the entire world as a battlefield of ideas, with corporeal reality pitted against the reality of pure spirit. And once Syrkin espoused an idea, his adherence to it was as limitless as the idea itself. And when he hated something, he hated it to the ultimate degree. It was the idea he hated, often forgetting that ideas assume bodily shapes, that they always originate in the minds of imperfect, mortal human beings.

On his deathbed, as his physical life was waning, he returned to the source of all being, and he felt its pure coolness, its eternity. He perceived the true wellspring of his life. And so did I. The half-hour I spent at Nachman Syrkin's bedside made me see more clearly than ever before that the only, the one and only meaningful life is the life of the spirit. He was illuminated by inner beauty, the beauty of invincible truth, of eternal life. Whatever it may be, however we may want to call it, what matters is that the essence continues…somewhere.

We talked about the mystery of "One," of the great unity which surrounds us like an ocean. We talked about God and Judaism. And suddenly Syrkin shook his head a bit and said with a smile: "A small muscle of the heart wants to overturn the world." But soon he added: "A million muscles of the heart really can overturn the world." He retained his faith, his will to believe, up to his last breath.

◆   ◆   ◆

These moments held me captive for a long time, and even now I am not quite free of the vision. I look at people on the street and think of the man who on his deathbed was wrestling with God. He was neither struggling for his life, nor for his physical existence, but rather for something that he had been searching for all of his life in metaphysical abstractions. He was struggling for a glimpse of the mystery of life as he was coming ever closer to the only, the final reality. At such moments daily life around me tends to appear noisy, colorless, empty. But then the veil lifts once again, and I see life as containing beauty and dignity, as filled with sanctity, with seeking, and with yearning. I see it as a struggle and a journey, the eternal journey to its source. And I feel how blessed it is to be granted as harmonious a death as was granted to Nachman Syrkin.

Together

A few days ago, when I answered the phone, I heard the following: "You know, there is a beautiful week ahead of us, a week filled with awe, when stories are told about the rabbi of Berditchev…and as Franz Werfel says…and as once happened to Rabbi Karliner…" I did not need to ask who was calling. I knew the voice, and I knew that I could expect to hear this outpouring of joy and exultation at the eve of each holiday, each Jewish holiday.

The voice is always filled with joy and exultation. At Passover: "You know, liberation." At Shavuot: "The Torah and The Song of Songs. What better gift could one have given the people, the world, than such a revolutionary document?" Succoth, Purim, the Fast of Gedaliah — there is no holiday or fast which does not fill him with enthusiasm, with a sense of beauty and sweetness. Thus I understood, without any explanations, that his call was brought on by the impending festival of Hanukkah.

It was somewhat difficult to conduct a high-spirited conversation about Hanukkah on the phone, and I really wanted to talk some more. I found myself wondering: This is a modern, educated, mature man, with a European cultural background, not even a committed Jewish nationalist for whom the Hanukkah motif might be a tool for political agitation. Why does this New York resident respond with such enthusiasm to this historic event, especially since the Hasmonean chronicle is nothing more than a historical romance woven around quite a small event. And so I invited "the voice" to come and see me. "Let us discuss this matter in person," I said.

My avid holiday-observing friend came and talked with shining eyes. I saw the deep spiritual joy that came to life within him every time he "recalled" Hanukkah, the poetry of the candlelighting. This led him, in some convoluted way, to the mystical teaching that Jewish souls are like lights, illuminating everything, spreading light throughout the universe.

I listened to this oration, filled with strange connections and allusions, stretching from the Midrashic and Hasidic legends to anthropology, Dostoevsky and much more. Finally he came to a stop, needing to catch his breath. And then, for the first time in all the years that I have known him, I asked him: "Tell me, my friend, do you believe in all that you are saying? Look, we are both made of the same dough; we attended the same schools, went through the same experiences and misfortunes; we have lowered our cup into the same well; and I am convinced that essentially you think as I do. Why, then, do you let yourself be swamped by a flood of words and lyricisms; why are you placing yourself so fully into the power of ancient images and sentiments? People tell me that you are getting more and more old-fashioned, that you appear to be following after Dr. Nathan Birnbaum, who changed from an evolutionist to a secretary of the *Agudat Yisrael,* and became a fanatical adherent of Orthodox Judaism.

"Do explain to me, Count Ehringer, this split in nature. I understand when observant Jews speak as emotionally about Hanukkah as you just did. For Zionists, who know almost nothing about the festival of Hanukkah except, perhaps, the name of the Maccabees, it represents little more than flag-waving and slogans. But you are a bystander; you avoid synagogue involvement; you are apolitical; you want to go your own way in life as well as in thought. Where does your elation come from?

"Let us leave aside the mysticism and the imagery. It is, indeed, a beautiful legend, the legend of lights. But you know yourself that it has no connection at all with historic reality. You know as well as I do that underlying the legend is the struggle of a religious sect against Hellenism, against the new, broad culture that was spreading over Asia. Mattathias and his sons have dammed up the flow of history, that is, the spread of universal cultural thought. And, as is usually the case, they proceeded to depict their enemies, the Hellenists, in the blackest of colors, branding them forever as traitors and despoilers of their people. It is, of course, unimportant what truly took place; what is important is how the people have dealt with it. All history values its legends and symbols, if only because without this admixture we would merely be left with bones, stones and names. But it is the content of a legend that determines the esteem in which it is held. The survival of a symbol depends on its ability to shed light on, and to energize the present. Is this symbol doing this for you?"

My friend thought for a long time, much longer than was his wont. And then he replied. Omitting much of his oratorical flourishes, here is the gist of his answer. "You are, perhaps, essentially right. History did not take place the way it is written down in books, and what we are told is not necessarily true. And when you ask me point blank: Do you believe in it? Then my point blank answer must be: No. I also know, since you and I have read the same books, that Hanukkah is a legend wrapped around a legend, or, rather, a web of legends that are quite unrelated to one another. It may be that it was the Menorah symbol, which goes back to the beginning of Judaism, that was spun out into the Hanukkah cycle: Mattathias, the Maccabees, the cruse of oil, the war against Antiochus — these are episodes of national history, or, perhaps, romances, just like the French legend of Roland, the Spanish one of Cid Campeador, etc., etc.

"Everything is possible, but this has nothing to do with the festival of Hanukkah, with my Hanukkah. Just as it does not matter at all to me what the origin of the Passover legend may be, or whether Purim was an old Persian carnival, or whatever may really have happened. Historical beginnings and psychological reality are two quite different elements, two different aspects of life. You want to know why I grow so enthusiastic at the approach of a holiday? Why the light of the first Hanukkah candle kindles a light in my soul? Why? I will tell you: it is the substance, or, as we would now say, the principle of togetherness. You yourself and the whole intelligentsia have often bemoaned the fact that you, that we, are all lonely.

"The problem of loneliness, of alienation, is an old one, as old as culture, as old as man's state of consciousness. It came to the fore, became acute, in the last thirty to forty years. Do you remember Gerhard Hauptman's drama *Lonely People*? This drama was, as it were, the first thrust, the prelude to naturalism, or psychologism, in German literature. The intellectual was heard sighing: I am lonely. The people belong to various organizations, clerical, military, political. The intellectual is on his own. And as time goes on, the loneliness grows deeper. Do you know why some intellectuals respond to extremist movements, to communism and to fascism? Because they preach and demand: Become one with the masses! And this offers an escape from oneself.

"Take the latest, the newest philosophical system, the one that is so popular, at least in the highest intellectual circles, that of the philosopher Martin Heidegger. His basic motif is that philosophy, that is to say, thought, which means conscious psychological life, is ruled by the fear of nothingness. Man seeks to escape negation and searches for affirmation; he wants and needs to build, and to do it together with others. This is, in essence, nothing but escape from loneliness. And of all the lonely ones, the Jewish intellectual is, perhaps, the loneliest. He has nothing, neither a real home nor a community of his own. He cannot immerse himself into the masses and become part of them because he is not accepted. And I feel this loneliness. I cannot join any group because none of them are authentic. There is not a single group that sees itself as having emerged from the genuine flow of history. The extreme nationalists, especially the Yiddish-speaking ones, affirm the traditional version of history, while the communists reject all historical claims. Between the two of them is the group of mediocre, gray, passionless people whose lives are filled with boredom. Were it not for the tragedies that afflict the Jews from time to time, our stagnant pool would have been covered with miasma.

"But I cannot be alone. I am yearning for a togetherness, which is more than a collective, more than an assembly, a togetherness which includes an element of ingathering, of spirituality, of religious fervor. This is what I am looking for in the legends, the festivals, and the symbols. When I light the first Hanukkah candle I know that this is a moment I can share with others. I know that at this hour (never mind the different time zones) the candle is piercing the darkness in the small cities of Poland and Lithuania, in Morocco, in Jerusalem, in Australia and in all the places where Jews are living. The light flickers around the world. Tomorrow two candles will be lit, then three, and so on until the last day of Hanukkah.

"This, then, is what gives the symbol its ennobling, heart-warming glow. Yes, heart-warming, because our life has grown cold, as cold as a corpse. Shall I go on explaining and analyzing? I am ready if you are."

But I was not ready for more. I saw before me a new phenomenon: a modern Jew who deals with the tragedy of his time in his own, Jewish, ardently passionate way. I saw before me the burgeoning of a new symbol: togetherness. And this was enough for now. Other aspects, the individual and his experiences, these, for the moment, were too much for me, too deep and too difficult. This conversation left me enriched and burdened with thought. My friend, for his part, left in a lighter mood, having unburdened himself in confession.

David Lubin

I have just read the most wondrous novel. It tells the story of a Polish Jew, born in 1849 in the god-forsaken Galician village of Klodova, who was brought to America as a small child. He grew up in New York's Lower East Side, then wandered about America, doing various jobs in Massachusetts, panning for gold in Arizona, fighting with Indians, and making friends with some of the wildest, most ruthless adventurers of that legendary time when America was being re-discovered. He then opened a department store in Sacramento, California, and ended his life as the founder of the world-renowned International Institute of Agriculture in Rome. What is most wonderful about this story is that it is not a novel but a biography of the Sacramento Weinstock-Lubin Department Store co-owner David Lubin, whom many of us had known personally.

H. G Wells had once shown an interest in Lubin and had thought of making him the protagonist of one of his novels. It is a pity he didn't do it. Or, maybe, it is just as well. Wells could not have written a better, truer book than the unpretentious biography written by David Lubin's secretary, Olivia Rossetti Agresti. Furthermore, Wells surely could not have done justice to Lubin because he was an alien figure to him; he could not have established a connection with him. There was a wall separating Wells from Lubin, and the wall was Judaism. Wells did not dislike Jews as individuals, but he reacted negatively to Judaism, he felt hostile towards its ideas and essence. David Lubin, however, became what he did only because he was a Jew.

◆   ◆   ◆

There is much talk about Judaism and the Jewish spirit. The discussions vary in depth and range, but only rarely do people ask the basic question: What, actually, is the Jewish spirit and how does it manifest itself? Torah, Prophets, Ethics...how well do Jews follow their own teachings? We look at Jewish peddlers, merchants, insurance agents, vaudeville actors and theater critics, and we ask ourselves: How do they represent the spirit of Isaiah and of Amos? Are they any better, more ethical, than countless non-Jewish Toms, Johns and Mikes? Is there really such a great difference between them? From time to time, of course, there do appear remarkable Jewish figures, such as a Lasalle, a Marx, who shake up the world, whose words ignite fires, who exert leadership. But are they not matched by non-Jewish firebrands and world-shakers? Weren't Lasalle and Marx, in the final analysis, disciples of Hegel? And what was particularly Jewish about them?

But here emerges among us a Jew, a simple merchant, a barely educated man from the Lower East Side, who is not even very well-to-do, a Jew who feels the ancient, burning, unslakable thirst for justice, for righteousness, for true charity. He does not merely thirst for it, he also has the drive to act on it, the will and the ability to build and to organize. David Lubin, a Sacramento department store owner, becomes the spokesman for the American farmer, a caretaker of the soil, not just of American soil, but of the soil of the entire earth.

The most prominent economists and social reformers had been unable to achieve an internationalization of agricultural interests, and it was left to a transplanted Polish Jew to accomplish this task. Small wonder, perhaps, because a Jew is the only one who thinks and feels internationally. The Jew is a citizen of the world, the true cosmopolitan, in the best sense of the word. This is perhaps the only significant thing that the Jew has contributed to universal culture — neither science nor the arts, but rather a sense of interconnectedness of values. The Jew had brought forth the concept of togetherness, the world's desire for unity. Philo of Alexandria already understood this, since his concept of God was nothing more than the core of all existence, the geometrical center from which all aspirations were radiating. And where is there a better, deeper, and purer God-concept than the Talmudic one of Omnipresence? There is a center, and from the center spread out waves which then return to it. This is the essence of Judaism, the philosophic expression of the ethical formula: Treat others as you treat yourself.

Such a worldview cannot be confined to a framework of national interest. Nations, people and all that derive from them are good things, but they are only the means and not the end or the purpose; they are a passage and not a final destination.

Only rarely does this Jewish spark burst into flame. And when it starts to happen it is often extinguished by the Jews themselves, since the mores of their surrounding culture are too alluring, and the Jews become too eager to adapt. But if and when the spark does catch fire, it is inextinguishable. It has proven to be quite powerful, and has prevailed in world history. It prevails today, too, wherever it alights. David Lubin's example bears this out. For a time he was considered a modern fabulist, a "crank." How could it have been otherwise? A Jewish merchant begins to preach about creating an international organization of agriculture. People only laugh. What connection does a Jew have to working the soil? What have the American farmer and the Russian muzhik in common with a Sacramento department store owner? Lubin had no certificates or diplomas, and he did not even use scientifically correct terms. His spoken and written vocabulary was a mixture of Lower East Side and Arizona-cowboy English. His arguments, moreover, were based on startling sources: a spoonful of Spencer, a serving of Emerson, and overflowing cups of the Bible. The Bible was the source of his enthusiasm, and when he addressed audiences he interspersed passages from Isaiah and parables from the Bible amid his wild west cowboy stories. He simply spoke his mind and carried his listeners with him.

Nowadays the Bible does not exercise the same power because it is read, if at all, as a piece of literature. But when you hear someone read a chapter from Isaiah with conviction, the ancient word for justice and a phrase like "just measures and a just scale" — which had become rather commonplace through overuse throughout the ages — acquire a new, hypnotic sound. Thus, when David Lubin recited those well-known words to Victor Emanuel, King of Italy, and assembled European diplomats and ambassadors, the eminent listeners felt, to their own astonishment, that they were hearing them for the first time and fell under their spell.

One of the most interesting events Olivia Agresti recounts in her book is the encounter between David Lubin and the Italian Minister Luigi Luzzatti. This meeting had been of decisive importance to Lubin, since without Luzzatti's approval he would not have been able to carry through his program. I can visualize this remarkable meeting between the Polish-American Jew and the Italian Jew, and their experience of mutual kinship. Luzzatti was dubbed in Italy "the prophet," and the proud, realistic, power-hungry Romans had smiled a bit derisively at the naive, prophetic idealism of the old Luzzatti. Luzzatti, in turn, conducted his life in a completely "correct" way. He was an economist, a professor, a successful financier, a clever, moderate politician, a thoroughly cultured man, a State Counselor for life, twice a Prime Minister and a brilliant orator — but underneath all of that was the Jew. His politics followed a Jewish, international orientation, pressing for justice, righteousness, equality and ethical standards in international dealings. Luzzatti, therefore, had understood his brother from Sacramento, and the two Jews decided to found an international association of the toilers of the earth. Luzzatti proceeded to recommend Lubin to the Italian King, and the International Institute for Agriculture, the first attempt to conduct a constructive, universal farming policy, had come into being.

As a young reporter stationed in Florence, I still remember admiring the beautiful structure, located in the new section of Rome, on the other side of the Tiber. And even though I lacked both knowledge and interest in matters of agriculture, I felt that here is being created a universal policy which may be more significant than all the political machinations being hotly discussed by journalists in the cafe Ariana, or, perhaps, even in the Italian parliament. What I didn't know then was that David Lubin had created this enterprise to carry out the teachings of Judaism.

In 1918, just before his death, David Lubin put his spiritual testament into a letter. His path, he said, had been to study "the way of life commanded to the people Israel, especially the teachings of the Prophets, and to pursue them in order to establish justice and an equitable dealing among the nations — a process usually called democracy. 'Israel' contains all the forces of democracy, and it will be victorious. Maybe not in our time, but in the days to come. We believe in it, as we believe that God is the God of justice." This is a voice of ancient Israel, which, one would think, would already be silenced, but which yet suddenly arises out of the depth with such an elemental force that the walls of Jericho come tumbling down.

Lubin was, however, a very national internationalist, who propagated world unity while being quite proud of his roots. He was a spokesman for the peasants, and he interspersed his arguments with farmers and diplomats about wheat prices and tariffs with quotes from the Rambam. No wonder that his audience, whether a farmer from Tennessee or the Russian Minister of Agriculture, was surprised. Surely each of them had met with Jews in their life, but such a Jew they had never seen, could not even imagine his existence. For the first time they came in contact with the fiery source of Judaism, and it warmed their hearts.

In his introduction to Lubin's biography, the noted American historian William Roscoe Thayer sums up his impression from an interview with Lubin: "I left him with the conviction that I had listened for two hours to a Jewish prophet…"

— a Jewish prophet who addressed the larger world. But where is the Jewish prophet who will address the Jews? I, too, believe that Israel is a universal force, and that its great day is still to come. But if Israel is a tool of history, then every generation must cleanse and hone and reshape that tool to work on the gigantic task of bringing about universal justice and righteousness, a task calling for our dedicated efforts.

A Budapest Dreyfusiade

The judge in Budapest is reading out the name of the accused: "Hatvany Lajos, Baron!" The man so addressed is about 45 years old, pale and nervous, his fine features and thoughtful countenance proclaiming him to be an intellectual, an aristocrat. Born to wealth, his father a baron of the Holy Crown of Saint Stephen, a member of the old Hungarian circle of magnates, Hatvany Lajos, or, as he was called in Berlin and in Vienna, Ludwig, Baron of Hatvany, was a sharp, scholarly critic and a first-class stylist.

It was about twenty years ago that the German literary world was taken by surprise by a book with the strange name: *The Knowledge of Things that are Not Worth Knowing.* It is a book that leads the thoughts of Nietzsche to their logical conclusion; a book that, with a knife-like sharpness, dissects the mentality of European cultural life and exposes its basic failings.

Vienna and Berlin listened to the voice of the new Hungarian writer, and soon other books issued from his pen, as well as essays and articles, in German and Hungarian, written in the remarkable, expressive, colorful style of Budapest. Budapest does have its own style. "You think you are writing in German," a German writer once said to Herzl, "but you are mistaken. You are writing in Viennese-Budapest French."

This may be so, but this same style was so beautiful, so sonorous and cultured, that all Germany was fascinated by it. Herzl, Nordau, and Hevesi were all German writers who had come from Budapest and had brought into German litera-

117

ture their Hungarian-Jewish idiosyncrasies. Their gentle, skeptic, sentimental yet clever style had gained them citizenship rights in Germany. They were all Jews, Hungarian Jews of German culture, and, therefore, cosmopolitans, whose fusion of lifestyles made their writing complex, refined and beautiful.

Hungary is a strange land, a land of Mongols yet an ultra-European state. It is a land of peasants who have remained just as primitive as their forefathers, the Huns, who had arrived on small horses, armed with bows and arrows, with blood-lust shining out of their Tatar eyes, consuming the raw horse meat that had been warmed beneath their saddles. Having captured European nations, the Magyars forced the vanquished to provide them with culture. The Slovak Kossuth had staged a revolution for them; the Serb Petofi, or, in his true name, Petrovich, had written their best lyrics; the Slovak Kalman Miksa had given them the novel, etc., etc. But the ones who had served them best and most loyally were the Jews. The Jews furnished them with finances and developed their press and literature. When the world talks about Hungarian playwrights, they talk about Molnar and Lengyel, both Jews. And when Hungary boasts of its painters, it is, once again, the Jew Laszlo who heads the line.

The Jews disguise themselves; they change their names: Klein becomes Kish, Gold becomes Arany, Poltak turns into Lengyel. Each of them had sacrificed his name, his personality, his roots to Magyarism; each had made a gift of them to Hungary. The Hungarians smilingly accepted the gift, and, as had the Tatars when they ruled all of Eastern Europe, rewarded them with the whip.

"Hatvany Lajos, Baron," the voice of the judge breaks into the musings of the accused, "is it true that seven years ago you wrote a book and an article attacking the current government, the regime of the reigning Admiral Horthy?" Hatvany nods: "Yes I have done so, just as many other Hungarian patriots did. I have fought for freedom, for democracy, for the ideals of Lajos Kossuth and Franz Deak, the great leaders of Hungarian liberation. But I have also written a book called *The Wounded Land*, accusing Europe of the wrong it had done to Hungary by robbing it of its provinces and by the unjust peace. I have demanded a revision of the peace accord; I have called on Europe to undo the wrongs inflicted on Hungary."

"Well, well. Why did you voluntarily come back to Budapest, why did you leave Vienna and come back to face a Hungarian court?"

"Why? Because I am a Hungarian. I was born and raised here. My father was a Hungarian industrial magnate, my language is Hungarian, my soil is the soil of the Magyars. I believe in the Hungarian people and in its justice. It is true that my friends Oscar Josi and others warned me, but the aide to Prime Minister

Count Bethlen assured me that the Hungarian court would treat me with the same clemency as it treated the money forger Furst Windishgrets, as it treats the murderers who organize under the name Awakening Magyars. And I have trusted the politicians of my fatherland. I was homesick abroad; I cannot live without breathing the air of Hungary. As the old Hungarian motto says: 'There is no life outside of Hungary, and if there is life, it is not as sweet.'"

The judge hardly listens to these words and, after a few desultory questions, asks the central one: "Hatvany Lajos, Baron, you say that you are a Hungarian, a Magyar, fine. But is it not a fact that you are a Jew?"

The accused grows even paler and begins to stammer: "Yes, of course...I mean I come from a Jewish family, but what does this matter? I have nothing to do with Judaism, and in any case, a Jew is still a Magyar."

The Judge interrupts him: "Enough, I do not argue with Jews. I do not want to listen to speeches by a Jew. And I pronounce my verdict: seven years of imprisonment with hard labor and a fine of $500,000. And I say: Long live Hungarian justice!"

The session comes to an end, the accused is led to prison and Hungarian "justice" has triumphed.

The dictator Horthy is smiling contentedly, and Count Bethlen is rubbing his hands in glee. The state has acquired nearly half a million dollars of Jewish money. The intelligentsia of Vienna and Berlin, of France and of Holland, will scream about judicial miscarriage, but what does this matter? Who pays attention to such protests today? Did the whole world not protest against the Sacco and Vanzetti trial, while America paid no heed? A new Dreyfus case? So what? Who is afraid of words? The time has passed when the words of a Zola or an Anatole France could have an effect. Human rights, Jewish rights — bah! These are just phrases. This is the way we Magyars are: anti-Semites, abolishers of rights, barbaric. And what are they going to do about it? This is what we are, and we couldn't care less about the world. Will England and America refuse to grant us loans? They will yield to the persuasion of good guarantees and high interest rates. No one will do us any harm if we imprison, or even kill off, all the Jews. The foolish Jew trusted in my good will, Count Bethlen might say, and who is to blame for his losing his sense of reality? As the Anglo-Saxons say, "All is fair in love and business," especially when one deals in hate. The Hungarian liberal press is protesting; they are writing that the Hatvany trial is one of race hatred and suppression. Let the Jewish journalists have their say; let them yelp. We will get them too. Thanks to Saint Stephen there are enough judges in Hungary.

Bethlen chuckles over his last pronouncement, and the echo comes back: There are enough judges in Hungary! Only one man is astounded, only one man is hurt, the Jewish intellectual Hatvany. And the thought occurs to him, perhaps for the first time in his life, that there are also "loves which do not deserve to be loved." In his dark prison cell he sees the light of truth, the truth propounded by Antisthenes the Cynic: "What is so great about a fatherland? The insect is also a native, and the worm is also a citizen." And the old Jewish thought illuminates his mind: One must not go against reason; one must not allow sentiment, yearning, pleasure to lead one into making peace with injustice, into shaking hands with the hangman. One must not!

The Magyar-European baron and essayist had forgotten this commandment and is paying the prize for it. And the Tatar is laughing.

Zionism and the
Land of Israel

Theodore Herzl

At times the thought strikes me: Perhaps he is nothing more than a dream, a figment of our imagination…And the more time passes, the further away he recedes from his contemporaries and from generations yet to come, and the more insistently people will ask: "Did he really exist? Had he once been a human being, like the rest of us? Had he too, walked along the same difficult, dusty, uncertain, path of life, or is he a myth which emerged out of centuries of Jewish longing and striving?"

We Jews of today are blessed with very little colorful, poetic imagination. Many years have already passed since Theodore Herzl's death, yet no one, not a single Jewish artist, has come forth to capture the essence of this man of rare beauty, this dreamer, who was himself a dream, one of the great "historic" figures that the Jewish people has produced.

The term "historic" is not one we ought to use to describe how men lived and what they have accomplished since not everything that happens in the course of our individual daily lives or in the course of national existence is of historic significance. Events which reoccur throughout the ages as part of normal life do not constitute history. History begins at the point when a new element starts to modify the lifecycle of its time, slowing down for a while the inexorable rotations, feeding it new impulses and pushing it into new directions. And this element of extraordinariness, of uniqueness, is also the characteristic trait of a historic personality, a personality without any forerunners and without any possible successors. Thus, one can be a skillful politician, a clever, accomplished statesman and still not become a historical personality. The reverse is also true. One can commit mistake after mistake, stumble along the way, yet still remain forever enshrined in the memory of man.

Napoleon once asked, "What is a great name?" and answered it himself. "It is a ringing sound — laws, institutions, monuments, whole nations may be destroyed and vanish forever from the face of the earth, but the ringing sound remains and reverberates in the human consciousness for generations to come." And what brings forth such a sound? The extraordinary, the new, the things that appeal to man's imagination. Napoleon himself is the best example. What of all the things that he wrought has survived him? Men of not more than average stature, politicians such as Metternich and Lord Castlereagh, have, with one stroke of the pen, abolished all that Napoleon worked for all his life. All the blood he spilled and caused to be spilled in various parts of the world were spilled in vain. All his dreams were dreamed in vain; nothing survived, except a shadow, a legend, a name, a ringing sound — and that is history.

And so we ask: What is it that Theodore Herzl actually achieved? In what lies his greatness? Did he propound anything that others before him had not thought through, had not talked about and not acted on? No. Let us take *Der Judenstaat* for example. Years earlier, Dr. Pinsker had expounded this idea so clearly and intelligently as to defy any improvement. Baron de Rothschild had not only thought through the practical aspects of colonizing *Eretz Yisrael* but had already begun to realize his plan. Baron de Hirsch had created the same experiment in Argentina. The entire ideology of modern Zionism was in existence years before Herzl. Moses Hess had laid its philosophical foundation; Disraeli had created the poetic image of the old-new Jewish spirit, of Judaism having come back to life; the *Hovevei Tsion* had shown the way to idealistic, practical, political activism.

Everything had been in readiness, the entire structure of Zionism had been erected, from its foundation to the very rooftop by the time Herzl arrived on the scene. In the age-old memory of the Jewish people were stored all its experiences, all its hope and despair, along with the deep, bone-weary conviction that "…there is nothing new under the sun…." Therefore, to bring a new concept into Jewish life seemed utterly absurd. How could anyone venture on saying anything at all since everything had been said already? Every Jew was condemned to carry on his own shoulders the heavy load of thousands of years of Jewish life. Everything had been tried and nothing had prevailed; one had walked down a multitude of roads and none had led to the desired goal, nothing had been accomplished. And so one came to believe that all avenues had been exhausted, that all gates would remain closed.

And suddenly there appeared a man unburdened by memory, a man who looked at Jewish life in quite a new way. He did not see a people full of years and bitter experiences, a people weighted down by tombs and gravestones. Instead, he saw the Jewish people as a young, fresh, new people, a people which was only just beginning to live, to dream, to hope. Throughout the course of its existence, mankind has been grappling with basic questions, questions that are as old as the world, as old as mankind itself, but very few people have had the courage to pursue these questions to their very depth — the eternal questions about life and death, about God and man, about the incomprehensible mysteries of existence and impenetrable mazes of our own nature. Only occasionally will someone come along with the courage to approach these questions anew, to transform them into his own, personal, acute experiences.

Herzl approached the "Jewish problem" as a new phenomenon. He did not begin to study old books and manuscripts, nor did he seek to find out what was said, tried and done in more recent time, and therein lay his good fortune and the root of his historical genius.

Conjure up a picture of a young man growing up in cosmopolitan Vienna where intellectual alertness lived cheek by jowl with sentimentality, an essayist writing in a light, smiling, slightly ironic style, an author of a few, not very profound nor very dramatic comedies. Imagine an elegant young man with the legendary beauty of an oriental prince, a European to his fingertips, living in Paris as a correspondent for the Viennese paper *Neue Freie Presse*. Steeped in the maelstrom of Paris life, he is far removed from all national aspirations, is altogether apolitical, temperamentally predisposed to keep aloof from social consciousness and social pathos. And this man, whose outlook on life had been shaped in an environment devoid of Jewishness, but who had still retained in the depth of his soul a few childhood memories of a Jewish home, this young man suddenly turns his attention to the Jewish question. It was the Dreyfus affair that reminded him he was a Jew. Well, that was not surprising; everyone's attention was aroused by the Dreyfus affair. Everyone was stirred up by it, all of France, all of Europe, all of the civilized world. Many expressed their indignation against militarism, the reactionary forces of society, anti-Semitism. But scarcely anyone, even among the Jews, either looked at the Dreyfus affair as an essentially Jewish problem, or saw it from the point of view of Jewish nationalism.

To perceive any relevant connection between the fate of a Jewish captain in the French army and the course of Jewish history was, obviously, far-fetched, yet that was the entirely unexpected impact the Dreyfus affair had on Herzl. He found himself face to face with the Jewish problem and confronted it; seeing it as if for the first time, he mustered the strength and the courage to think it through to its resolution. And the resolution he arrived at was Zionism. It is true that all the raw material had been readied and all the tools were at hand, but the design created by Herzl did not previously exist. It is the same thing that happens in the creation of a work of art. When Rodin created the "Burgers of Calais," "The Thinker," or "The Hand of God," the marble obviously was there already, as were the models he used, and even the ideas underlying his works were not new. Each of these elements already existed. But they existed independently of each other until the artist used his perception, his personality, his soul, to weld the separate units into a new organism. The material was not novel, nor were the ideas. It was Rodin himself who was the new, creative element. He was unique; no one before him had looked at things the way he looked at them, and no one will look at them in that same way again, because each of us constitutes a world of our own, a world that does not reoccur and that cannot be reproduced, moving at its own pace, following its own beat. But a great human being, a genius, has the power to transmit his own beat to those around him; he has the power to put his stamp on his times.

It was said that Herzl's greatness consisted of his organizing the Zionist Congresses, founding a bank, creating an international Jewish organization. But are these really such great achievements? Did one have to wait for hundreds, for thousands of years to arrive at such ideas? Who did not understand, did not know that these things were needed, long dictated by simple common sense? And take Herzl's political formulation of Zionism; is this, truly, an original idea? What Jew, sweltering behind the stove in the cubby-hole he used as his study, had not long before Herzl arrived at the conclusion that it would be a good idea to buy *Eretz Yisrael* from the Turks, "…if only Rothschild would be willing."

But under Herzl's hands everything was transformed into new patterns, became a brand new discovery, caused a revolution in Jewish life. All of a sudden, overnight, the Viennese writer became the leader, the guiding light of generations, the redeemer, even the Messiah. All of Jewry felt at once that this was "a man of providence," that a new chapter of Jewish history had begun. Nobody knew why this was happening, no one understood the phenomenon, and up to this day no one has been able to reason it out. Why do we become enthused, charmed, drunk with joy before a work of art? Why do we feel that we are becoming enriched, better, deeper, younger, more beautiful when we contemplate a *chef d'oeuvre*? It is a mystery that cannot be elucidated.

Herzl rejuvenated the Jewish people, took thousands of years off its back, and removed accretions deposited by the ages, accretions of experience. He moved the Jewish people out of the shadows of the past and brought them back into the sunlight, exposing them to the warming rays of life. And all of us feel it, whether we are Zionists or anti-Zionists; we feel that as Jews we have become younger and fresher, healthier and more naïve. We feel that we are not, as yet, a dead body, nor dried bone, that there is still hope for a new life; the dream and the yearning have been returned to us. Because Herzl lived, because Herzl hoped and dreamed, and because he looked at Jewish life with bright, fresh eyes, we, too, are able to view it anew.

As a man, Herzl was the personification of a work of art. He was a figure straight out of our dreams, a hero stepped out of a legend, a legend of ancient times. Nowadays we are used to men of smaller stature, and we hardly recall the attributes of a true leader. Past generations had their visions of what a leader should be; a man who ruled his people had to be perfect in all respects, and so is he depicted in ancient legends. The king is described as the best, the most handsome, and the most accomplished of all, "head and shoulders above, greater than the entire people…." Now it may well be that in reality they were not quite as superhuman. For instance, scholars say that Alexander the Great of Macedonia was short, and that his features were less than handsome, but human imagination refused to take account of reality, and ancient statues depicted Alexander as a handsome young hero, tall, broad-shouldered and without a blemish.

Herzl, however, had indeed been endowed with all the attributes that legends bestow on their heroes. If modern times have produced any man who could be termed a man of "regal" stature, that man was surely Herzl, a man with the bearing of a merchant prince and the aura of a Saladin, and therein lay his good fortune and ours. The world beheld for the first time a Jew who was stunningly handsome, whose pronouncements left no room for doubt, who did not call forth any ironic responses. Imagine, for a moment, Achad Ha'am as the head of the Jewish people, a "Ghetto Jew" straight out of literature: small, weak, pensive, with melancholy eyes and the high Jewish forehead. He does not impress anyone, he does not fire up our imagination. He is the personification of thought, of logic, of reason, but reason calls forth reasoning, and thoughts evoke controversy. But against beauty, against a shining determination, against a primitive, naively wholesome, fresh, strong faith, against a wondrous tale, what can prevail against all of that? Captivated by the form, one forgets to scrutinize the substance.

Good fortune also shone on Herzl himself. He came upon his life's work in the vigor and beauty of his youth, and he was called away from life, still in the beauty of his prime years. His good fortune spared him the prosaic process of aging, spared him the sobering awakening. He came upon us as a legend, he departed as a legend...and a legend he has remained.

What will become of his work? Who can tell? In any case it won't be the realization of Herzl's dreams, since reality is more trite than dreams. But that is not important. As Napoleon said, "the ringing sound remains and reverberates in the human consciousness for generations to come." The sound, the legend, the beauty, the personality of Herzl, these are more important than anything that he himself wrought. Our lives and those of generations after us have been made richer and more beautiful because Herzl lived. He was the only beautiful Jew of our times, the great modern Jewish work of art perfected in our era.

The Eternal Sacrifice

A recent news item has assumed an emotional, even sensational character: The son of the most prominent Jew of our time, the heir to a name that Jewish history places next to Nehemiah, to Judah Maccabee and to Bar Kochba, Hans Herzl, the only son of Theodore Herzl, has converted to Catholicism. It can be viewed as a tragic event, as a surprising happening to be aired in newspapers and discussed in flowery language, but it cannot be viewed as incomprehensible.

It is not the first and, surely, not the last time that the Catholic Church has attracted weak, despairing people, people who want to lay down the burden of their personality, their free will, and surrender to an alien, a collective, a mystical will. The old Spanish Rabbi Abner of Burgos, who became Pablo of Burgos, a fanatic Catholic and a scourge of Israel, surely did not convert for the sake of material gain. The glitter of the Catholic Church blinded him, the incense intoxicated him. They lured him away from the stern, strong Judaism, from its perception of life built on a foundation of individual responsibility, to a worldview that erases individual responsibility and lifts the burden of life off his shoulders. It is, truly, "hard to be a Jew," not only because one must suffer for it, but also because the Jew stands alone in the world. All the ways are open to him; he may enter all the gates, except the last one. He has access to all the commandments that God has imposed on him, but the gate to the personal God that is the foundation of Judaism, the "Thou" that binds man to God, that gate is closed to him. And yet, this is just what man is yearning for, this is the gate on which he is knocking.

129

The Catholic Church has opened this gate as well, and has done so mainly by exalting ritual. If you observe it, everything is possible. The Church's main tenet is a spiritual authority that unites people and nations into a universal unity, with one sole center — Rome. This is Catholicism's eternal dream. This is what has so strongly attracted romantics and people with imagination, from Dante to Cardinal Newman, from the German Neo-Catholics to the Russian philosopher Solovayev, who preached the Caesar-Popism, the unification of the Christian world under the leadership of the Pope.

One can well imagine how a man like Hans Herzl came to embrace Catholicism. Just because he was a Herzl, just because he was an "orphan of Zionism," as it were, an orphan of the Jewish people, he felt, perhaps more sharply than the rest of us, the chasm that lies between Judaism as a religion and Judaism as a political, national institution. What meaning did Judaism have for him? What did he know about it? In his father's house he heard talk about a *Juden Staat*, a state to be built, with old, crumbling material. Theodore Herzl was an intuitive Jew, a political Jew, but not a Judaic Jew, and this may have been true for most of the older Zionists. For them Judaism, itself, was a heritage, that had lost its spiritual value, which was, in the best case, an addition to the political ideal, but of no intrinsic value. What did Herzl know about Judaism? His *Alt Neuland* is the best demonstration of the extent of his knowledge. Achad Ha'am was right in his attack on the weakest point of Herzl's idea, pointing out that he may, perhaps, represent the Newland, but the Oldland had totally evaded him.

Herzl looked at Judaism and at the historic evolvement of the Jewish people the way Nietzsche had looked at present-day mankind, as a step, as a condition one must overcome. Herzl gave no thought to things as they were, only to the way they ought to be. And Hans Herzl had grown up in a Viennese atmosphere where Hoffmanstahl vied with Schnitzler, and the *Neue Freie Presse* realism contended with Palestinian dreams. And when, after his father's death, he came to England as the "heir," instead of a warm, soul-satisfying Jewish atmosphere, he found the same split: the English rooted to the practical and realistic and the Jews talking idealistically about Palestine. Can we truly wonder at Hans Herzl's being overcome by feelings of emptiness and dissatisfaction and seeking for another solace, finding it at Stephensdome?

He had, of course, another choice. He could have gone to Palestine, becoming a worker in the fields that his father had readied, a simple laborer, who finds meaning and consolation in his work. But he could not do it, because he was the son of Theodore Herzl — too small to live up to his name, but too grand to lead a simple, ordinary life. And this is, perhaps, the most tragic, the most human, all-too-human aspect of the step taken by Hans Herzl. It is a tragedy shared by all children who are heirs to a great name, and the greater the name, the harder it is for those who inherit it. Because the life of any extraordinary person is an extraordinary event, being the end result of a long process of human development, there is, therefore, only one way available to those who follow him, the descent from the summit.

For ordinary people, fatherhood is a condition that requires sacrifices. The father makes sacrifices in order to enable the child to develop, and his only hope is that the child will be able to surpass him, rising higher and higher on the ladder of achievement, each generation reaching a new rung. In primitive societies the father lost his usefulness when the son grew up, and the weakened, old parent bowed down before the strength of youth. But when the father, himself, has already attained the highest possible rung of human development, what then? Then the process is reversed, and the child becomes the sacrifice, and the *akedah*, Isaac's ancient tragedy, is reenacted.

Abraham was the stronger one, he was the creative mind, the driving force of history. He was the Father, the origin; all further events were mere developments, weaker reflections of the initial momentum, of the *ur*-passion, of the *ur*-force. Abraham said everything that could be said, and neither Isaac nor Jacob had anything to add to it. They could only repeat, protect the fire that they had inherited; they were the sacrificial offerings on the altar of Abraham's greatness.

What do we know about the children of great personalities? History does not tell us much, except in passing, offering us occasional hints. And the greatest minds seem not to have had any children at all. Plato may have had some children, but who knows about them? Or who has heard of the children of Aristotle, or of Galileo's son? It is almost impossible to imagine a child of Leonardo da Vinci, of Raphael, of Spinoza or of Kant. They had the good taste, or rather, the instinct, not to leave any heirs. And what became of the children that Rousseau fathered? He placed them in an orphanage. Goethe left a son, a living sacrifice. One can still imagine young Napoleon, the "Eaglet," as an heir of Napoleon the Great. But the young eaglet did not have the wings of the old eagle, even though he had, or rather, he could have had, a substantial inheritance. It was Napoleon III who was no eagle at all, who became Emperor of France on the strength of his name. What about Goethe's son Augustus? What did he inherit from his father? Had he been any closer to him than all those who surrounded Goethe? On the contrary, though his father's blood was flowing in his veins he was kept at a greater distance from him than all others. And we have a living example in Tolstoy. Who are Tolstoy's heirs? His children? What do they know about their father besides a few anecdotes? What do they remember of him besides things that might be better not remembered, that diminish the stature of the unique personality that had risen above all others? The children of great men stand like strangers around the gravestones of their fathers, feeling rejected, envious and bitterly angry. Though they are not close to these parents, they also do not have sufficient distance from paternal greatness, and are, therefore, unable to understand it.

In the history of mathematics, there is a very charismatic, a very humanly touching episode. It is a contest between father and son for eminence. About 200 years ago, there lived in Switzerland a family by the name of Bernoulli, which was remarkable for the fact that a talent for mathematics was transmitted from father to son. Each generation surpassed the one previous, until the talent reached its apex in the achievement of Daniel Bernoulli. A son was born to him, who, from early childhood, began to exhibit extraordinary ability. The father displayed great pride in his small son, but when the boy grew up and began to show signs of becoming an outstanding mathematician, the father became jealous. It so happened that the father was once working on a mathematical problem that he was unable to solve and kept this from his son. But the young Bernoulli became aware of it and with his sharp, young mind solved the problem in no time, proudly and joyfully bringing the solution to his father. But the father was unable to share his enjoyment. Envy, the fear of being overshadowed by the young man's great talent, overcame his paternal devotion, and he drove his son out of his house. The father refused to sacrifice himself for the sake of his child. Maybe this is the instinct that drives great personalities, thinkers, explorers, artists, to remain alone, not to have families. Or maybe it is nature's profound respect for great achievement, that stops the growing process and limits the intellectual development of the children of the great ones. Such is life — it requires a sacrifice. If it is not the father it must be the son. And if Isaac is the son, then he must go to the sacrificial altar.

Chaim Weizman

Fate. Destiny. Chance. Three words expressing the same idea, the idea that there are things beyond our understanding, things which defy rationality, which exist according to the inherent laws of their nature rather than according to any of our established causal laws. And what applies to things applies as well to human beings. The impact of an unexpected meeting can be disconcerting or uplifting; can erect a wall or lay open a path; can lead or mislead you; can pose a puzzle. You ask yourself: Why does this man affect me this way, what is his aim, and what is his secret? How has he acquired such power over my volition? What gives him the right to determine my fate? You cannot find an answer. You weigh and measure all the factors, but they do not add up, for despite his errors and problems his side of the scale heavily outweighs them.

I do not want to engage here in a far-reaching analysis or quote historical parallels, since, according to the clever Frenchman Voltaire, examples do not help, and comparisons lack spice. So here is our puzzle: Weizman. He is not a mythical figure, nor is he a mystical one, arriving from far away, such as David Reuveni, the "prince of the black lands," or David Alroy, robed in the splendor of a pseudo-Messiah, or even Herzl, the first and unique one among us. We all know Weizman, and at the Congress his comrades knew him all too well. In America, in South Africa, or on New York's Lower East Side, he may appear as The Leader, as the modern-day Nehemiah. They have the necessary distance for this view of him; he is a stranger to them, and they see him as Dr. Chaim Weizman. But we, at the Congress, saw him as one of us.

Almost every one of the delegates, especially the older ones, remembers the student from Bern, the assistant professor from Geneva, the member of the opposition, the westernized intellectual with his own dry sense of humor. To them he is simply Chaim. And yet, even to them he is a man of destiny. Even his opponents lack the serious determination, the true will, to remove him from his position, to take the reins of leadership out of his hands.

An impressionist, a political columnist, an amateur — these were the things said about him, both publicly and privately, in the hallways of the Congress. Greenbaum, Soloveitchik and Jabotinsky all sharpened their knives or pointed their arrows, but when it came to committing the deed, the knife and the arrow changed to mere toys in their hands. "Why do you make these gestures, what need do you have for these tricks?" I asked more than once my friends in the opposition. "You know quite well that Weizman's time has passed, that he lacks his former popularity, that he has dissipated his strength and has gone over to the 'notables,' as Greenbaum likes to call them. Even in Palestine he has handed over the reins to someone of greater strength. You know that he is not a leader, but one who is being led. So what are you doing? Gird your loins and take over the leadership yourself!" I was arguing with them not because I really wanted them to take over the leadership — I have even less faith in their ability to lead than I have in Weizman's — nor was I seriously suggesting that it was time for Weizman to put down the reins which he is now holding so loosely. I was merely interested in the psychological aspect: Why do they not want to take the decisive step? Why do they lack the courage to act?

Their answer, in typically Jewish fashion, was a question: "Why and for what purpose shall we do this? He is the one who has cooked up this mess, so let him now deal with it. In two more years we will, God willing, be through with him, so why act now?" They may not have known themselves what a compliment they were paying their opponent, what a testimony they were giving to Weizman.

Leaders. Do they truly exist? It is said that Lenin and Mussolini exerted leadership, but how did they lead? They were going with the stream, believing that they were going against it. Lenin joined the masses, following their instincts, and Mussolini did the bidding of the haute bourgeoisie. Leadership is an illusion and a mirage, especially when it comes to the problems Jews are facing in their aim of restoring *Eretz Yisrael*. What is it that we really need? We have a land, we have a people, we even have the will — all we need to reach our goal is time. We need time to evolve social and moral values; we need time for growth.

While others require spatial bridges, bridges leading from one mountain to another or spanning abysses, we need bridges of time, as well as the leadership to help us create those bridges. And it is Dr. Weizman's uncanny ability to build these bridges which has led him from a somewhat haphazardly acquired leadership to becoming the "man of fate." The man who can wait, who has the courage to be inconsistent, a man of varying moods, who follows the byways and zigzags of life. One way today, another way tomorrow — what of it? Illogical, contradictory — so be it. Is life logical? And has Jewish history, up to now, followed a path as straight as a violin string? Dr. Weizman's greatest strength, however, consists in being a genuinely Jewish personality combining whim and reason, moodiness and steadfastness, wit and skepticism, and an unreasoning faith. At times he manifests some Hasidic traits: enthusiastic at one moment, and raising a skeptical eyebrow the next, a friendly smile followed by a contemptuous one, a contempt that includes all of mankind. He is a synthesis of all of Russian Jewry, not having a single drop of Western blood in his veins. Even though he is a European who lectures in Geneva, an English professor far removed from his native Motol, from Pinsk and from Vilna, he is yet more Jewish, a more home spun Russian Jew, than all these national politicians in Warsaw, or than the ultra-Zionists like Jabotinsky who want to Garibaldize Jewish life.

Weizman's opponents impose ready-made concepts and formulae on Jewish reality, but life is not so amenable to being forced into molds. It yields when you follow its lead, but turns hard as granite when faced with an imposition. Weizman does not want to impose; he does not want to dominate; he does not want to introduce new motives into the Jewish soul. He is a connecting link, a bridge which gradually leads from one span of time to the next. And building for eternity can only be done gradually. He is a connecting bridge between the West and the East, where the East prevails. This is Weizman's secret, this is his meaning, and this is his destiny.

Fifty years ago there lived, right here in Basel, a solitary man, a rebel, and he lanced into the world the words: "And life says: Do not follow me, not me, only yourself, only yourself." Nietzsche dreamed an unhappy dream; he thought that he had heard the voice of life, but it was his own voice protesting against life that he had heard. Because life does not heed any will except its own. It will not follow any path except the one which fights its way through mountains and across boulders, out of the abyss and into the plains. All protests against it are made in vain. Nietzsche wanted to bypass the bridge and leap over the abyss, but the roaring waves claimed him. We Jews, however, do not have the right to take risks. We must follow the bridge until we come to the mountain, wherever it may be.

The Akiba Smile

On my way to the office this morning I was stopped in the middle of the street by an old man with a splendid white beard, a halting step and a deeply wrinkled face — signs of age rarely seen in our country today. A big smile illuminated his furrowed face. "You see," he said, "the day has come, and you are ready to recite Lamentations!"

I had never seen this old Jew before, but I did not need to ask what he meant, or what day he was talking about. I understood that he was talking about the day in Zürich when the Jewish clock struck one, when the Jewish Agency had its first, festive occasion. So instead of asking what he meant, I asked the old man where he came from and he told me that he had escaped from Proskurov, one of the few who had managed to save themselves. This was enough; it was all I needed to know. The reason for the joy and the smile became clear. And I also knew that this was, perhaps, the one day of his life when he was no longer beset by feelings of sorrow and rootlessness, the first time after so many years that he could smile again.

From far away, beautifully sounding words had reached the old Jew from Proskurov, words uttered by Oscar Wasserman, the German representative of the Jewish Agency: "We already have the land of Israel, even if we do not yet have the state of Israel." And this, in itself, is already a step forward, an achievement great enough to illuminate the countenances of the Socialist leader of France, Léon Blum, and the German financial magnate, Oscar Wasserman, with the same smile that illuminated the face of the old Jew from Proskurov who is spending his last days with his American "all-rightnik" children — the ancient smile of Akiba ben Joseph.

The Midrash tells us about Rabbis Gamaliel, Eliezer Ibn Ezra, Joshua and Akiba walking along the streets of Rome. The city of mighty rulers was vibrant with power, citizens were enjoying the display of wealth, and the tumult could be heard 120 miles away. Three of the sages wept, but Akiba smiled a joyous smile. His friends said to him: "Akiba, we weep, and you smile. We weep because all goes well with them, because they enjoy so much wealth and we live among ruins. The House of God is destroyed, and wild beasts are roaming through it." Rabbi Akiba answered: "I am smiling because they are incurring God's anger, and I wonder what will befall them when they come to feel his will."

There was another time when the four of them walked together. This time was in Jerusalem, on the Temple Mount, when they saw a fox coming out of the Holy of Holies. The three Sages wept, and Akiba smiled. "Why are you smiling again, Akiba?" they asked, and Akiba answered, "There are two prophesies — one by Uriah, a prophesy of destruction, and the other by Zechariah, which says: 'Men and women, full of years, will be strolling through the streets of Jerusalem leaning on their canes, and children will be playing on the streets of Jerusalem.' I am rejoicing, knowing that since the prophesy of Uriah has been fulfilled, the prophesy of Zechariah must also come true!" And his friends responded: "You have comforted us, Akiba."

Every time I look into Jewish eyes, I search for the old, heroic, Akiba smile. Is it still shining? Is hope still alive? On the street of New York it had beamed at me so warmly out of the eyes of the old Jew, and I had not wanted to spoil his gladness, even though I could not fully share his joy and his faith.

And yet, why not? We are, actually, following a well-trodden historical path, taken by all movements and all dreams. In the beginning youth carries the banner. Then the initial enthusiasm is followed by a cooling off and by division. The many grow tired and lag behind on the trail. Only a few of the elders and the spiritual elite keep on pushing forward. And this holds true for Zionism as well. A mass movement? I do not see it. Not yet, or, perhaps, not any more. The people, the broad masses, have grown tired; the path is too steep and the demands on their commitment too great. They cannot focus on just one goal, especially on one so distant. Gradually a cooling off sets in. And the movement that in the preceding years had gripped the majority of Jews throughout the world, becoming almost the center of all of Jewish life, has again become a movement of the few.

This is the fate of all great movements, even of Socialism. There, too, the great masses are becoming indifferent, and when they experience some small successes along the way, they grow satisfied and want nothing more. Were if not for the intelligentsia, and for the determined faith of the elite, Socialism would long ago have lost its vitality. This trend holds especially true for a movement like Zionism, which is comprised of adherents who pursue very different ends. Some Zionists are looking for the salvation of the Jewish people, while others are looking for universal redemption. Small wonder, then, that the majority has grown tired, for the burden of hope is too heavy. Just as Bontshe the Silent was astounded and frightened when he was shown the glittering palaces of heaven. "All this for me?" he stammered. His aspirations had never extended beyond a fresh roll with butter.

It was difficult to wean oneself from the illusion that Zionism is a mass movement, difficult even for those of us who have long known and felt it to be an illusion. The difficulty was not caused by our faith in the people, it was simply the old Jewish superstition, or, if you will, the old Jewish pride, that every Jew is a prince. I once heard an old Jewish song that is so characteristic of today's general Jewish mood. A storekeeper, one of a hundred storekeepers on a street, sits in his store and waits for a customer. And he thinks:

> A Jewish government, my friends,
> How lovely to imagine this.
> A kingdom made up of sages?
> A kingdom made up of kings?

But this daydream does not last long. A customer appears who wants a penny's worth of herring, and that's all he wants. Thus kings and wise men make way for a customer buying a penny's worth of herring from one of the street vendors, which earns him the hostility and envy of the other 99 vendors. But if the masses do not uphold Zionism, then who does? Who remains to give the matter further thought? The storekeeper cannot do it, nor can the worker. On the Jewish street herring is of prime importance.

The real function of the Jewish Agency should be to assemble the finest among our people, those who yearn for a kingdom of the sages, a kingdom where every one can be a prince. The Zionists, driven both by necessity and by ambition, have lowered their standards, and have almost reached the level of "herring-ism." They had to turn, therefore, to the Agency and renounce their hegemony and their historical role within the Jewish world. They had to free themselves from the concept of a mass movement in order to save Zionism from spiritual decay. That would have been the final destruction of the Zionist idea. Foxes running around in the Holy of Holies are not a danger as long as the smile of Akiba is still with us, as well as his readiness for self-sacrifice. Jewish history circled around this smile in the days of yore, and it is still doing so today.

The Wider Circle

I am frequently asked — and I often ask myself — why Palestine? What is it that attracts my interest to a land that I have never seen, such a faraway, alien, Oriental land? And what is it that leads people who are little concerned with the general national and cultural problems of Judaism to this most nationalistic of all solutions?

One used to say in Bundist or in *galut*-nationalistic circles that Zionism was an assimilationist movement, that a Zionist was an assimilator. This has always been the accusation, and today more than ever. Yet history has proven that the Zionists were, really, the only enduring nationalists. The Bundists crumbled under Bolshevik pressure, and so have the Socialists and the Populists. The only ones to have withstood both pressure and temptation, to have clung with all their might to the national idea, were the Zionists.

It is easy to be a nationalist in Poland, where government policies force one into it, where even socialism is saturated with a narrow-minded, sinister nationalism. And in Russia, where nationalism is an anti-government movement, it makes sense for Zionism to demonstrate its vitality. But what accounts for the yearning for Palestine in America? What logical or moral reasons can we offer? I hear this harsh and earnest question almost daily, and it leads us to a broader analysis. For instance, does the urge for Palestine have other roots than Zionism? If so, what might that mean? Zionism is a movement that crystallized too early into a party. Zionism is a system that is, in actuality, not organically connected to

Palestine, as proven by the currency of "territorialism." The error of this idea was not its practical impossibility, nor its political impossibility, but its too logical pursuit of Zionist thought. It is not correct that Jews could not have obtained a territory if they had really wanted it. The Hungarian project was really not such a bad one, and even if Hungary had been unwilling, one could have found another opportunity. If the Jewish problem could really have been solved through an autonomous Jewish territory somewhere, would the means to attain it not have been found?

A little more autonomy, a little less — one could have bargained and arrived at a settlement. But the Jews decried it, waving their arms and rejecting territorialism. They had rejected the logical aspect of nationalism, but had become more deeply attached to its emotional, mystic side. And the result was…Palestine. Its appeal rests partly on everyday, Bundist territorialism, on a philosophy of Jewish history reduced to its commonplace, assimilated form. Its logical formula states: "Every people has its land; the Jews are a people, therefore they must have a land." It is, furthermore, a view of history that follows the pattern of anti-Semitism: "Why do the Jews suffer? Why are they being treated with hostility? Because they are aliens. Why are they aliens? Because they have no homeland." Ergo, we must obtain a homeland.

It is a simple philosophy, a theory based on unsubstantiated premises and questionable conclusions. How does one get from the need for a home to Palestine? Where is the logical bridge? The doctrinaire Zionist has no answer. Something has forced him to include Palestine in his formula; he does not know himself how and why. Perhaps because the movement had its origin in the concept of Zion, and he has become enslaved by the word? Or is it because Palestine, nationalism and the land-philosophy are merely a refinement, a modernization of an old, mystical concept? Is it perhaps because Zionism is not a political but a psychological, a spiritual movement?

Logic and rationalism say: No, this is not the way; this is no answer to anti-Semitism. How can it help Jews outside of *Eretz Yisrael* if a group of Jews settles in Palestine? The idea that sending Jewish ambassadors to Germany and Poland will induce these countries to treat their own Jewish citizens with more respect is simply absurd. America proves this best. Japan is a great, powerful country, and America hates it, subjecting the Japanese to various exclusive regulations. And the Japanese do not even have the privilege of protesting and appealing to human rights since, as they say, "No one is asking them to leave Japan to come here. After all, they have their own home."

If anti-Semitism has root causes, they are deeply social and religious, i.e. psychological, ones and cannot be eradicated by political means. And it is altogether erroneous to assert that Jews are being hated because they do not have a land. The hatred has nothing to do with the Jews, but with those who hate them. Anti-Semitism is not a Jewish problem but a universal one, and Jews cannot solve it.

Furthermore, it is argued, a people *must* have a land? Must? Why? What they are really saying is: It is commendable to till the land, but not to be intellectual, to be *Luftjuden*. Fine, but if the Jews really wanted to they could be normal people, tilling the land even in the Diaspora. There is room for them in Siberia, Argentina, Canada, and Texas, but the will is lacking.

No matter from which angle you approach it, the logic formula cannot stand up to criticism. And this goes also for the official, accepted version of Zionism. Therefore, when I or others who share my views are asked: Are you a Zionist? The answer is: "No, not according to the demands of the official Zionist theory." But Palestine has nothing to do with this theory. It is a mystical urge and it requires no justification. One can lead quite an assimilated life, and yet, as long as one feels any ties to Jewish life, one is likely to have a warm, deep feeling for Palestine. For some it is a longing for the "heavenly Jerusalem," for some it is the core and the meaning of life, and for yet others it is a key to the history of the Jewish people. One can tell oneself: Judaism is neither an accident nor an exercise in stubbornness, but rather a historical necessity. One does not have to be a believer and talk about God in order to arrive at such a concept.

Jews may have once been simply a people that, by misfortune or due to its own weakness, lost its independence, as happened to many others. But history turned it into a universal symbol, into a spiritual force, and the spiritual force is now growing weaker. We are losing our identity; we are in the terrifying process of disintegration. And in order to save Judaism, in order to escape the responsibility for its collapse, we must return to its roots. Judaism has begun its historic journey in Palestine, and there it must return to end it.

One can, however, take a more optimistic view. Judaism has never made itself felt in as many places as it does now. Anti-Semitism has grown stronger because we have grown stronger, wealthier, greater. And we are now aiming to play a greater role in history. For the first time in many years we have begun to design a new path, a path our forefathers could not have dreamt of. The East is waiting for us. We have given all our strength to the West, have offered it as a gift. Now it is time to turn to new possibilities, to a new way, even — dare I say it? — to a new role in world history.

There are many different paths, both continuous and broken, yet they all lead to Zion. The political party is not Zionism's only, nor its best, recourse. And if this be so, then it is necessary to lengthen and to widen the path to *Eretz Yisrael*, so that the movement toward Palestine can involve the whole Jewish people, with the Zionist organization being merely a link in the chain and not the entire chain. Those who are working on rebuilding Palestine must take this into account. They must widen the circle.

The Land Phoenix

At times of great anxiety, at times when misery overtakes us, when our hearts are filled with sorrow, we heap ashes on our head. It is an old custom, a primitive one, rooted in the depths of history. And it is this very fact, the very primitiveness of this gesture, which makes it a symbolic act. And ancient symbols have the power to elicit new interpretations from succeeding generations, to demand that they invest it with new meaning. But whatever new interpretation it may receive, the symbol reflects age-old experiences, and it does not die.

Ashes on our heads. It would seem that the Jews are the only cultured nation still to remember this custom. The ash symbol is so much a part of every aspect of Jewish life that one might almost consider it an essential Jewish trait. The well-known Russian Jewish writer Gershenzon once tried, in a remarkable booklet, to grasp the essence of the poetry of Pushkin, and he found it in the word "flame." Flame, fire, ashes express the way this greatest of Russian poets and thinkers (and, according to Gershenzon, perhaps the greatest of all the poets of modern times) related to God and the cosmos. Everyone finds what he is seeking, and everyone hears in the voice of another the echo of his own. Thus Gershenzon, the idiosyncratic Jew, sought and found in the work of the poet he so dearly loved — yes, flame and fire. And he did so because the fire symbol is an essential part of every Jew — if he is true to himself, if he is rooted.

After the fire come the ashes, and then a return to the fire, just as the legendary Phoenix is consumed by the flames and must be so consumed in order to regain its youth. Its name shows this to be an Eastern legend, a Phoenician symbol, akin to the Jewish psyche, illuminating Jewish history. Why? Because history is nothing more than one generation succeeding another, an unceasing burial procession. People are buried in the ground, cities disappear under layers of sand, cultures are covered up by mountains of cinder. And going back further, into pre-historical and, perhaps, pre-human times, there is earth torn asunder, continents displaced, swallowed up, forgotten. And in all the deserts there are cities buried in the sand. The feet of the living step on forgotten graves. Sand covers up and devours all things; the buried cities do not come to life again. Each restoration is, at the very best, merely an archaeological one, and any lost treasures that may be found end up on museum shelves.

I do not know why and how this has come about, and no amount of speculation can solve this mystery. And it is a mystery, the mystery of Jewish history, the mystery of fire and of ash. There is searching going on in *Eretz Yisrael*; spades are being pushed in deeply and the earth is yielding up what has been long forgotten. And now an American expedition has found, 13 miles from Hebron, traces of ancient *Eretz Yisrael*: the cities near Tel Beit Muzrim, which was once called Kiryat Sefer. Ten cities were discovered, one atop another, separated from each other by layers of ash. Ten layers of ash until they reached Kiryat Sefer; and Kiryat Sefer, too, no longer exists, except in name, as a historical symbol.

All this takes us far, far back in time, to when there were as yet no Jews, a time when Palestine was still unnamed, but when the process had already begun, the process of being consumed and being reborn, the Phoenix process. At that time Palestine was still an unknown spot on the face of the earth, surrounded by flourishing states. There was the Hittite kingdom, with a developed culture, full of power and aspirations, and all that remains of it is some stone masonry in the village of Bajezki. There were the great kingdoms of Mitaun and Art Neharim, and they have vanished — the peoples have died, the monuments have fallen and crumbled, and dust covers all. But a city next to Hebron burned down, and upon its ashes arose a second city, and when that one went up in flames and was buried under ashes a third one was built on that layer....ten cities in all, one following the other, until Kiryat Sefer was uncovered. And Kiryat Sefer survives, not in stone and not in bricks, but in the mind, and that is the most important, because ideas do not die.

Ashes on our heads — this is the mood among many Jews who, not long ago, only last year, were singing Hosannas. The skies are clouded; the air is full of sorrow. Wherever one looks there are fires, forest fires which are spreading. Jewish homes are burning in Romania, hatred flickers up in all corners of the world, and ashes fall upon our hopes, gray ashes fall upon our highest, final hope: Palestine. And in moments of sorrow I sometimes wonder and ask myself: What is the use of continued struggle and of hope? To what purpose do we pursue the eternal illusion which leads us to bitter disappointment? And I perceive, here and there, a cooling off or an indifference, which is even worse than disappointment. I see the beginning of another struggle against Jewish hope and the Jewish spirit, and I see all the old slogans being revived. "Zionism is dragging Jews back into the Ghetto…Zionism is a utopia, and a noxious one at that…." And others say regretfully: "We advocated it, believed in it, had hope, but bitter experience has taught us to face the truth." And on all sides we are being reminded of Goethe's dictum: "You must renounce!" One must renounce, one must submit oneself to the decree of history and that of life, because life does decree: ashes to ashes, dust to dust, and once something has died it can never come to life again.

Logical arguments, perhaps; rational ones, to be sure. But then it was neither logical nor rational to persist in building city after city upon the ashes of those that preceded them. It would have been altogether logical and rational for Jews to have capitulated the moment they had lost what was most essential to them: their land, their power, their independence. The situation then was as hopeless as it is today, and it was as irrational to persist as it is now. But Jews refused to submit to the power of facts. One of Hegel's famous utterances is: "If the facts do not conform to your theory, too bad for the facts!" And if this paradox can be said to have any validity at all, it can be found in Jewish history. Not to submit to actuality, but to subjugate it; not to be stopped by the mountain in our path because "the law is mightier than the mountain," which means that the law, the thought, the idea, must become one with our will, and we must burrow through the mountain. The mountain submits to the force of the spirit, and thus, instead of being stopped by the barrier, we overcome it.

And perhaps this is the ultimate essence and the deepest historical meaning of the entire Zionist idea: the struggle between the law and the mountain, between spirit and reality, between creative idealism and barren rationalism. Ashes upon ashes; ten layers until Kiryat Sefer. And perhaps new ashes will fall, in ten more layers, until we reach a new Kiryat Sefer, the city of the book, of the spirit, of living ideas. The Phoenix is subject to its own law, and it must follow it.

Shalom

The night has passed — a hot, sleepless night. How can one sleep when one is crossing the Sinai Desert? How can slumber overtake you while you are looking out at the ocean of sand shimmering in the light of the white, silvery moon? And yet, a desert is merely miles and miles of sand, nothing more. I have journeyed over deserts and have soon become weary of the sight, as I get weary of looking at the ocean, at anything that is unchanging, that merely exists. But this journey found me unable to tear myself away from the sight, unable to close an eye until overcome by sheer bodily exhaustion.

I am not prone to sentimentality, and furthermore decided from the outset to eschew enthusiasm, Biblical ecstasy, and the blandishments of history. I decided that I needed to maintain a cool head, a detached eye, to perceive things as they are and not as the colored lens of imagination may present them. But to no avail. You make a decision, but something in you overpowers it, demands its rights, the right to be carried away by enchantment, to be inspired. Thinking coolly, I had to ask myself: What meaning does the Sinai Desert have for me? I have outlived the faith of my childhood, and everyone knows that the Biblical story is merely a beautiful legend. Sinai is an old volcano that gave rise to eternally new stories, added on to each other, interwoven and re-worded; this is common knowledge, attested to by all scholars. Read Sir James Frazer's *The Golden Bough* and you will find there many legends on the same theme as the Sinai one. And still...and yet...

Here I am crossing the Sinai Desert and having difficulty coming to grips with the knowledge that I, a man from the faraway north, a man who has derided Mount Sinai and been a disdainful heir of its legacy, that I was now following the way of those who made the first journey. The Fathers, the Founders, with their staffs and their packs, their sheep and their cows, old and young, full of hope and of despair, falling down and arising again, thus they had come across the desert. Taking the same road I was taking now, from Egypt to Canaan, from the Nile to the Jordan, from the plains to the mountains, they had journeyed into world history.

Of what import is Sinai to me, and why does it attract me so much? Was my soul also at the foot of the mountain when it erupted in thunder and lightning? Am I among those who had pledged loyalty forever, through all generations, to the end of time? For years my answer had been "no" — we have had enough of Sinai, we are a part of today and of tomorrow. And then came the doubt. Today and tomorrow, fine, but what of yesterday? The future is an unknown, it is not a part of me, nor will I be a part of the future. But I am a part of the past, I belong to it and it belongs to me — the yesterdays and the days before and further back, much, much further, up to the time when man lighted his way with the use of tallow. And with each passing day the pull of the past becomes stronger, and, before long, it will altogether have become an integral part of me; it will, instead, be the present that will seem shadowy.

Is this a mood brought on by the Sinai Desert? Is this a mirage? Am I going to be turned into a silhouette, just like the silhouettes of the camels I see in the distance, black figures kneeling beneath the silvery light? I watch them go on their way, to their place in world history, shadows wandering from place to place, from the plains to the mountains, from watering place to watering place, and in their midst the terrifying mystery of the burning, fiery thornbush.

Day is breaking; we have left the desert and entered Palestine without my being aware of it, though I had passionately wanted to know the moment of entry. We now see the mountains on the horizon; and small stations dot the road. Hebrew inscriptions, green fields, vineyards…the colonies. I look more closely and make out the words *Rehovot* and *Bar Yaakov*. I read and read, yet I don't feel the impact. The desert night had been too austere, too grandiose and uplifting, so now I cannot trust my eyes. This is it? This is *Eretz Yisrael*? And suddenly I hear, wafting up from one of the stations, the voice of a young girl, a voice bringing forth sweet, dewy-fresh silvery tones. The young girl is standing at the station, waving a small brown hand at someone just arriving, and saying *shalom* with such a soft, tender inflection as I have never heard it said before. The word falls on my ears as a dewdrop falls on thirsty ground; it refreshes me, it arouses me from the night.

Shalom! I have heard this word a thousand times, from the *shalom aleichem* with which one Jew greets another, to the *shalom aleichem* addressed to the ministering angels, the great mystical song with which the Jew greets the world. And the word always sounded very harsh in my ears, whether pronounced *sholem* as in western Russia, or *shalem* as in Lithuania, or even *shalom* as the Sephardim say it; it always had a down-to-earth, everyday, prosaic ring to it. Now I heard and felt, for the first time, the melodic quality of the word, its inner glow, and its contained music, as it saturated the early morning air of *Eretz Yisrael* with its moisture, mildness and utter naturalness. And it seemed as if this greeting was meant for me, just as if my old mother were rejoicing over my homecoming, offering me her first quiet, tearfully joyous welcome. I found myself responding in a tremulous, unsteady voice: "*Shalom, shalom* to you, land of my cradle, *shalom Eretz Yisrael.*" This was Shulamit coming to meet me in the fields of Judea, enchanting me with her voice which found its way into the depth of my soul and implanted joy within me. I thank you, you unknown young brown Shulamit for your *shalom*-greeting, and I thank you, Mother *Eretz Yisrael*, for the deep joy that I am experiencing.

I feel invigorated and ready for anything, for whatever realities I shall find in the hills, valleys and towns of Palestine. Whatever disappointments may be awaiting me, they will be deflected by my protective shield. *Shalom…*a feeling of peace and restfulness has descended upon me, of stillness and quietude, and I am able to understand the great holy man Rabbi Nachman of Bratslav, whose pilgrimage to *Eretz Yisrael* had cost him a great deal of effort and self-sacrifice, yet who returned to his small Ukrainian town after a sojourn of only a few days. This had been enough for him; he brought greetings to his mother and received her blessing. Everything else, all further things…. Is one night in *Eretz Yisrael* not sufficient for one's entire lifetime? Am I becoming sentimental? Perhaps, but even if it be so, I do not mind, am not embarrassed, because….*shalom.*

The Night of Canaan

A day in Jerusalem. The entire day I walked along the hard, gray-stoned streets of Jerusalem, along the old and the new. I went everywhere, to all the old graves, gravestones and monuments out of a past so far removed and yet so close to us. I walked without any plan, not as a tourist bent on seeing the sights but as one who belongs here, who dwells here, a native returning home after a sojourn abroad.

This sojourn abroad does stretch over a couple of thousand years, but of what import is that? There are places where one day stretches out like a thousand years and a thousand years pass like a day. Time is naught but a coffer filled with lived experiences, and among these coffers are magic ones and such a magic coffer is *Eretz Yisrael*, is Jerusalem. It covers only a small area, but it houses a world where the past merges with the present and...yes, with the future as well. They unite and are welded into a deep, infinite longing.

I walked from early morning until well in the evening. I climbed among the ruins of the Tower of David under the burning midday sun, and afterwards I followed in the footsteps of the old guards atop the walls of Jerusalem, the walls which surround the City, that is, a section of the Old City, old Jerusalem, a remnant of times gone by. Atop this same wall, or, if not the very same one then one rebuilt from the same stones, on this same wall the guards were patrolling the City at the time of Isaiah, calling out to each other: "Watchman, what of the night?"

Following their footsteps, I see the Mount of Olives before me, and Emek Yehoshaphat stretching below me, with the grave of Zachariah and the Yad Absalom, and I see the Temple Mount with the minaret. Wherever I look, wherever I turn, I meet history — unfathomable because it is too close to us, mysterious because its scope is so gigantic and our perspective so limited. I walked the entire day and in the evening returned to my room located close to the border of the Old City, opposite the Tower of David. A couple of young people had accompanied me but we did not talk a great deal. I could not discuss the fine points of history or archeology with them because they knew too little about it, and just to talk, discourse about anything on earth, as Jews are wont to do, that is something that Jerusalem does not allow; she is a stern mistress and demands respect. But they sang a song for me, or rather *the* song that is being sung in all of *Eretz Yisrael*. The words by a poet from Lodz have been set to music by someone in *Eretz Yisrael*, a simple Arab melody permeated with a Jewish sigh. I don't know whether I am remembering the first few lines correctly, but it does not really matter if one word takes the place of another; it is the resonance that matters, the point and the counterpoint:

> Beautiful are the nights of Canaan,
> They are cool and clear.
> Out of their silence arises a song
> And my soul responds with a song of its own.

The bittersweet melody with its dramatic, eastern cadences entered my room and became part of the night.

It grew late, my guests departed, and I remained alone with the silvery moonlit night; the night of Canaan riveted me to my window that looked out on Jerusalem, on a majestic, unique view. Before me lay the core of Jerusalem: the Mount of Olives, Mount Scopus and the massive gray-blue dome of the Mosque of Sharif on the Mount where the Temple had stood. The night was cool and clear. The sky was covered with stars the size of diamonds and of a blueness which we, in the West and the North, cannot even imagine. In our prosaic world we have stars and we have stones, we have heaven and we have ruins. Ruins? There are no ruins in Jerusalem. There are ruins in Egypt, there are ruins in Rome: the Forum Romanum, the ancient monuments, the colonnades, fountains, all remnants from the past. In Jerusalem there are no ruins; there is life that has become frozen for a time, there is a continuity that has not been destroyed.

Jerusalem has claimed me totally. From midnight until dawn, I sat at the open window unable to tear myself away from the unchanging view, the white stones of the Mount of Olives, the gray outlines of the Judean Hills, the domes and roofs of Old Jerusalem. From time to time a question clamored for attention: What is it that you are seeing here? What is it that you are seeking here? And the answer came from deep within me: I am seeking that which every man must find once in his lifetime. Call it "revelation," ecstasy or self-discovery; it matters not what we call it. We find ourselves immersed into holy water, and we emerge cleansed.

Why is it happening only here? Is this, once again, the House of God? Is it God I have been struggling with all night? I say, "Sure, God exists, but why just in this land and in no other? Why are the stones of the Temple Mount more mystery-laden than other stones, in other places, on other mounts? Because...Must there always be a "because?" Must I explain everything to myself? Suppose, for a moment, that I were not a Jew, that the sweetness and the harshness of Judaism had not been imparted to me with my mother's milk, that Father Abraham and all the Mothers had not been holding vigil at my cradle. Would Jerusalem still be such a wellspring of inspiration, such an evocation of eternity? Is the mystery truly here and only here, or is it here because it is within me? And I had to smile at my own naiveté. What foolish "what-ifs" and conjectures. How can one even pose such perplexing questions?

Were I not a Jew, if the last 2000 years had passed without leaving any imprint, if Judaism had not existed, nor Europe, nor Christianity, if we were not who we are, then Jerusalem might well have been no more than a small Oriental mountain town, with crooked streets and old graves. Just as in the old conjecture: If Cleopatra's nose had been just a little bit longer or a little bit shorter, there might have been no Europe, and the plains of America might still be the pasture of Buffalo herds, populated by Red Indians. All the "ifs" and "would have beens" are devoid of meaning, for only the "this is the way it is" counts. This is the way we are, and because I am who I am, an heir and a descendent, therefore I see Jerusalem this way; and by perceiving it this way, I make it a reality.

The night of Canaan was beautiful simply because this is Canaan, an ancient land enmeshed in a silk- and gold-threaded net of memories, because it is sanctified land. Do you recall the poem by Bialik that starts: "One hears tell that there is love in the world. What is love?" My question to myself was: One hears tell that somewhere there exists holiness, that there is something that one can call sanctified. What is holiness, what is sanctity? The answer came out of the night of Canaan: There is sanctity and there is holiness, not because just a few steps away from my window seat young bullocks were once sacrificed on the altar, and not because Isaiah, the Prophet, may have stood on exactly the same spot I am standing now, nor because on the mountain facing me Jesus of Nazareth prayed for the last time in the Garden of Gethsemane, and not because of any number of other historical events. This land is holy because human souls have poured their yearnings into its streams as in no other part of the earth, and because below the surface of the earth their springs are still running.

Cold is the night of Canaan, clear and pure, and you feel a great weight lifted off your shoulders, the weight of all the words and precepts accumulated in the course of your life, and you feel free again and pure, pure as the night and as serene.

The night passed, and with the dawn came the return to reality, and the memory of the song filled me with apprehension. I was, after all, a "public servant," deputized to observe and explore the doings of the day, the down-to-earth, prosaic life in *Eretz Yisrael*. Was I going to be misled by the night, held spellbound by its mystery? And yet, have I really made this long, long journey across the oceans to obtain statistical data? Has anybody ever come to Jerusalem with this aim in mind? Does not everyone, whoever he may be, journey to the depth of Emek Yehoshaphat in the hope of undergoing a resurrection, each one in his own way? Is not all of Zionism a call out of the depths, a call from the depths, an appeal to the depths, because life is flat and without meaning?

An entire night I had called from the depths, out of the depths, pleading: Answer me! Give me an answer, you fathomless depths of Jerusalem! And their answer came softly, so very softly. It is a secret between my soul and the valley of Yehoshaphat.

Israel: Old and New

Yesterday I was fully informed. I knew exactly how many dunams are at the disposal of each colony, how they came into being and what is the founding credo of each of them. I knew their economic situation as well as their differentiation into various categories: colonies, moshavim, kibbutzim. I was surrounded by *Keren Hayesod* brochures and by books on Palestine. I had lengthy conversations with experts or, at any rate, according to some skeptical heretics, with some professional administrators.

Yesterday I knew everything. And not only yesterday but quite a while back, before I had ever seen *Eretz Yisrael*. Yet, today I have forgotten almost all of it. I have put all the documents and all the statistics aside, and I have let reality tell me its story and show me its face. And what I heard and saw erased all this acquired data from my mind.

Day after day, from early morning to nightfall, I was being driven by car over the rocky roads of *Eretz Yisrael*. From colony to colony, from the old settlements along the Mediterranean shore — Petach Tikva, Rishon Le Zion, Rehovot, or the Emek — to the new settlements and still further up to the borders of Palestine, to the outposts of the future, the colonies around Tiberias and Haifa. I wanted to banish all romantic notions, to separate reality from legend or history (which of course is one and the same). I wanted to see only facts, facts and concrete reality. This is what I wanted, but history followed my every step and spread its veil over the dry truth.

154

We have been told so much about the miracles and wonders taking place in the new, the brand new *Eretz Yisrael*. The halutzim and the kibbutzim and the new crops of the Emek have been presented to us with such enthusiasm, such pathos, and in such flowery language. They were hailed not just as tillers of the land and builders of a nation, but their task was claimed to be greater and more important. They were the builders of a new social order. As these pioneers were breaking up the stones on the roads of *Eretz Yisrael*, they were breaking up the chains of the old world, chopping up their ideals, and pulverizing the old ideas. They were laying the foundation for the Kingdom of Heaven.

The old settlements? Brought to life by the sweat of the Jewish intellectuals and the money of Baron de Rothschild, these colonies have lost their glamour in the eyes of Diaspora Jewry. Old versus new, and the new prevails. But I felt drawn to the old. Just because it is a bit older it has had time to strike roots in *Eretz Yisrael*, to adapt itself to the land, to its old-new style. Thus I went first to the pioneer colony whose name had already entered history: Rishon le Tsion, meaning the first of, or to, or for Zion. The first brick in the pyramid.

We leave Tel Aviv on a summer morning. The landscape differs from the one you pass on the way to Jerusalem. It is less majestic, softer. We see green fields, orange, fig and almond trees, and sheaves of corn with the golden yellow ears awaiting the reapers. Arab women are working in the fields, while the men are walking around, leisurely looking on and talking to each other. From time to time we meet a wagon, a car or a caravan of camels laden with bags. They proceed calmly, silently, at a measured pace; it is a life rooted in the soil and in its ways. And then we come to a highway, a broad, much traveled, smoothed-down road, bordered by trees and with green fields stretching out on either side. The stern, harsh Palestinian earth had been softened by human toil.

We pass some houses with red roofs and yellow walls, red and yellow against a blue-green background. We see some strange looking figures out in the fields. Arab-looking and yet not Arabs. It is a Yemenite colony. They speak Arabic, dress like Arabs, their sunburned skin is dark, but their thin narrow faces and their long grizzled sideburns proclaim their Jewishness, tell of their suffering, their struggle and their joy at reaching *Eretz Yisrael*.

Upon meeting Middle Eastern Jews such as Yemenites, Bukharans and Moroccans, whether in their various quarters in Jerusalem or in the colonies, it strikes me that they may be the only ones who feel truly happy, truly at home in *Eretz Yisrael*. They have no problems, they have had to undergo almost no changes. It is the same East, the same old, familiar way of life. They have even retained their way of dressing: the colorful pants and tunics, the overshoes that the Bukharans wear even on the hottest days, as they have done in Tashkent and in Samarkand, seemingly oblivious to the change of place. But happiest of all are the Yemenites, living as they do among Arabs, the same Arabs as in Yemen, but feeling free, safe and at home. In the vineyards of the Yemenite colony, young Yemenites are singing Arabic melodies, a bittersweet music, that can be heard and, perhaps, enjoyed only in the East.

We pass the Yemenite settlement and soon come to a nice, clean, well-kept village, or maybe I should call it a townlet. We are in Rishon, a community of 1500 inhabitants, a Jewish townlet and yet so quiet, so calm, almost as if no one lived there, certainly no Jews. "Where are they all?" I ask a man standing in front of a small shop. "They are in the orchards." "They" meant the young people of the colony, the heirs who were now reaping what their elders had planted 44 years ago. We drive to the *yekev*, the wine cellars, and this biblical appellation evokes childhood memories. "From the fields and from the wine cellars..." our rabbi had intoned. I had not quite understood what a wine cellar was, but "cellar" evoked a feeling of cold and of age and "wine" made me think of the liquor store, with its sharp smell of spirits, the sight of red noses and of people plunking down money, an alien, drunken world. And yet, the *yekev* figured in the Bible together with oranges, pomegranates, myrtles and cedars with their ancient, sweet, spicy scent. But here a present-day wine cellar is pointed out to us: a spread out building, with an aroma of freshly bottled wine wafting towards us, of wine mixed with the hot sun.

Soon the small group of my travel companions and I are sitting with members of the administration in a bright office drinking a peculiar Palestinian champagne, served in finely cut, shining glasses. And we exchange stories about Jews. They want to hear about American Jews and I want to hear about *Eretz Yisrael*. I soon forget where I am. It seems to me that I am sitting in a Russian town, with Russian-Jewish intellectuals of the good old school, idealists of our pre-flood time, in an atmosphere of refined Russian-Jewish culture. Just looking at the administrator, H. Mayerovitch, with his graying curly hair and his Anski-like features, transports you into the time of the Bilu legend, makes you see its embodiment. His silvery-white hair may betray his age, but his eyes have maintained the bright blue of youth.

The Anski-leader is talking. Simply, smilingly, he tells about the long years of struggling and of suffering. They have endured for forty-four years. They have survived the Turks and the War; they have gone through the highs of enthusiasm and the lows of disappointments; they have endured it all and have brought Rishon to its current state. It is true, of course, that the Baron helped with his money. But how could the money of the Parisian nobles give the young idealists that for which all youth yearns? They could have returned to Russia or gone to America to achieve a good life for themselves. It would have been easy for them, the world was still open and accessible, but they had not gone. They were determined to stay here, among the hostile Arabs, beneath the fiery sun, smarting under the indignity of having to accept the Baron's charity, putting up with all of this in order to achieve their goal. And now they have their orchards and palm-lined avenues, they feel secure and at home. The settlers were obviously content with themselves, the world, and *Eretz Yisrael*. And this is at the root of their flourishing. We say goodbye to the administration and are taken on a tour of the wine cellars. We walk the long corridors, look into the complex, imposing mechanism, bathed in the aroma of old and new wine, and leave in a cheerful, slightly intoxicated mood.

We go from colony to colony. Here is Zikhron Yaakov, the beautiful. There, Rehovot, the spacious, and after that is Ness Tsiona, a small village, and everywhere you feel a rootedness, a sense of at-homeness. They do not boast of their achievements anymore, nor do they show off the results of their toil. The pioneering phase is over. Now they are living and are not ashamed of their being well-off, of their having nice homes. (The main street of Rehovot is dubbed the millionaire's street.) They are not ashamed to live almost like landlords.

At present, young and old are in the orchards picking grapes. On the streets and in the houses one sees only children and the aged, all looking healthy and well. In the main hotel of Rehovot, I am served a homestyle meal at which I am joined by one of the oldest settlers, one of the pioneers of the *Eretz Yisrael* colonization. A man of vigorous bearing, with silvery white hair and black eyes sparkling with youthful fire, whose ancestral lineage, I am told, goes back to King David. I ask him to show me his genealogy, but he does not want to. "I will show it to you some other time. Today I want to tell you of other things I am proud of." And he tells me of laboring forty years in Palestine, of the romance of the beginning, of illusions, of struggles and of young Russian-Jewish intellectuals cast away among the Bedouins, of homesickness and of doubts, of toil and achievements. And I lose all interest in his genealogy; his second source of pride is much more impressive.

And the children! I don't think that I have ever seen such beautiful, graceful children as in the colonies of *Eretz Yisrael*, especially in Rehovot. They are like sunflowers ripening beneath the far-flung blue sky covering the spacious colony.

Next comes Ness Tsiona, a much simpler, more modest village. The roads are covered with sand reaching up to your knees. The houses seem more like those in a small Russian town than towns in the East. Even the Arabs, who are selling vegetables in the street, look more like Ukrainian peasants than like Orientals. The atmosphere reminds me of my childhood. We enter the house of an old colonist. He is away at Safed. On the table are books and magazines, the shelves are stacked with books, and the familiar atmosphere of a studious man prevails in the house. A young girl takes me across the street to the colonist's daughter who was born in *Eretz Yisrael* and brought up in Ness Tsiona. Sunburned, slender, moving with eastern grace, she greets her guest with a smile. And then I find a member of the third generation clamoring for my attention. The three-year-old daughter of my hostess settles on my lap, smiles, laughs and demands, "Uncle, give me the parasol," thus teaching me its Hebrew name. This third generation knows only its own land, its mountains and its language. At that moment I found myself envying Leyele, the colonist's granddaughter, and her gracious mother, for the simplicity and clarity of their life, at least for the time being. But then, do not all of us live our lives "for the time being?"

I leave Ness Tsiona. On the highway, where Ness Tsiona ends, a new settlement is starting, a new layer is being added. Wooden huts, still unfinished barracks, with young girls and boys working on their completion — a new type of human being, and a new type of Jewish worker. This is the beginning of an indoctrination into kibbutz life. They will work for the colonists until they are ready to manage on their own, as a kibbutz. While Ness Tsiona retains a familiar, homey atmosphere, the new barracks settlement represents a new romanticism, filled with vague ideas and social visions. Ness Tsiona exudes the calm of a thorough adjustment and rootedness, while the young settlement is in the process of searching for its way of life. It is a junction of two cultural strata: European culture meeting up with its rebellious youth; old Jewish culture facing its new generation.

Among Old Friends

We had not seen each other for eighteen years. In 1908 he was living in a small town in the Ukraine. He was an intellectual, a bit of a teacher, a bit of a preacher and, at times, also an accountant, but most of all he was a man of leisure. His greatest pleasure was talking about Zionism and about *Eretz Yisrael*. Smolianski would be his hors d'oeuvre, Achad Ha'am his entree and Berdyczewski would be served as dessert.

I recall a summer night eighteen years ago. It was a starry night; a group of us were sitting on the terrace drinking tea with preserves and talking, each one about his own dreams, his own desires. He was talking about Zion. He truly felt it, the "love of Zion," felt it sincerely and honestly, the way one loves one's mother, one's child. Most of those present belonged to "the other camp," Bundists and socialists of various hues, and they laughed at him. They were naive, provincial semi-intellectuals, filled with abiding faith and enthusiasm and a complete intolerance for dissenting opinions. The Bundists would declare: "Zion, Zion — the little bird, the hope — what empty dreams, what foolish illusions! The reality is here, and the ideal and the future. Open up your eyes, you idiot, and see!" The Ukrainian night had smiled tenderly, encompassing us in its silvery rays, and I felt compassion for my poor friend with his far-flung, flowery, utopian dreams.

Eighteen years have passed. The old terrace in the small Ukrainian town has crumbled away. All the dreams of "here" have been crushed. The entire "real world" has been destroyed. Of those who had been sitting on the terrace that night most are eking out a living in various European capitals, and have no hope left. Only he, the most utopian of us all, stood with both feet planted in the soil.

Another summer night and, again, a clear star-filled sky, and a terrace-like entrance into the house. But this is no longer the Ukraine, it is *Eretz Yisrael*. We are not in a small city anymore, but in a moshav, a village in the Emek, in Nahalal. He had struggled to get here. He had already been in *Eretz Yisrael* for thirteen or fourteen years. He had not waited for the Balfour Declaration, but set out with wife and child, relying on God's mercy. And, with God's help, he weathered all the calamities, the war, the bitter, hard times, and is now a settler in Nahalal.

I arrived in Nahalal at about eight o'clock at night. It was dark, a total darkness, and only the stars were shining. And it was quiet. The village was already asleep. Only here and there a small light was flickering. Stillness prevailed, not a sound was heard. The earth was tired and so was man. The adjacent huts, or barracks, seemed to be leaning on each other for support. In one of those huts someone was waiting for me; eighteen years of my life were waiting for me.

Poverty. More than poverty. Destitution is imprinted on all the ill-matched boards and has seeped into the earthen floor. It is spread over the rough-hewn wooden table, it has put its stamp on the face of the people sitting on the benches: his, hers and their children's. They are all burned by the sun, barefoot, and the faces of the parents are deeply creased. In the beginning they address me in Hebrew, the parents speaking with the familiar Russian Yiddish accent, with just a bit of Sephardi admixture. The children speak a pure, resonant Hebrew, but it alienates me. It is not part of the eighteen years, of the Ukrainian night, of my terrace memories. And we soon switch to Yiddish. The old sounds spread their warmth, and I soon feel at home with them again. "*Nu*, what are you doing now in Nahalal?" "What should we be doing? Everything would be fine except for the livelihood, the livelihood." And now, each and everyone present, each in his own fashion, begins to relate that the fields are as hard and as difficult as is Jewish life, that the need is great, and that times are hard and bitter. They talk of very, very concrete things, of harvests and cows, of spraying the fields, of oranges and olive trees, of the cooperative, of work and working conditions.

At around eleven o'clock the oldest son comes in straight from work, without taking time to clean up. Having greeted me, he starts talking at length about a cow. Soon the entire family is engaged in a lively dispute about the respective merits of the Dutch versus the Damascus cows. I am soon forgotten. They talk in Hebrew, the parents still haltingly, the young as naturally as if this were the only language in the world. I try to enter into the discussion about cows, but unsuccessfully. While visiting Hertzelia and some other old colonies, I had been shown both Damascus and Dutch cows and had been told about their distinguishing qualities, but I had not really understood. I come forth with some meaningless generalities about the Damascus cow, and everyone smiles. Then the 10-year-old who speaks Hebrew like a king breaks out in laughter: "Uncle really doesn't know anything about the Damascus cow." The child laughs and everyone joins in, myself included, but there is an element of sadness in their laughter because the entire discussion was a purely theoretical one. It seems that they do not have any cow, or, if they do, it is certainly not a Damascus one, or perhaps it is a Damascus and not a Dutch one. I am quite confused about it. But one thing is clear; whatever the cow may be, it does not give enough milk.

We are soon joined by a young girl. Slender as a gazelle, she walks with the swaying gait of the Mediterranean woman, even though she arrived from Russia only a couple of years ago. But the East has already put its stamp on her, tuning her like a violin string, endowing her with demure grace. She knew that a guest from afar had arrived, and she dressed for the occasion, even to the point of wearing stockings. And she felt, once again, "European." The oldest son stops talking about cows and leaves to wash up. "I must go home," the young girl says after awhile. "Wait a moment, I'll come with you," comes the voice of the eldest son who had been washing up in the yard, and she waits for him to escort her. Actually, her hut is only two steps away from where we are sitting; but when one is young, one likes very much to escort one's beloved, especially on such a night as in Nahalal.

The young people soon withdraw, the worn-out mother had fallen asleep in her seat, and there remains the two of us: the colonist of Nahalal and I. "Well, tell me truly, how are you doing here, are you content? Are you pleased with *Eretz Yisrael?* Is your dream fulfilled?" "Ah...it is a long story. Once, you know, I felt quite a somebody, a hero, a fighter, a builder. And today, you want to know how I feel today? Not a builder but a peasant. Just a kind of Jewish *muzhik*, as Spector once described a settler. Earlier there had been a choice: if not your land of birth then some other land. You could buy a ticket on some boat and sail to a new home. If not Russia, you could go even as far as America. The whole world was open to you. And it was this very choice that made *Eretz Yisrael* so alluring. Tribulations, we knew of the tribulations: poverty, hard work, burning sun, a desert where nothing grows. But now whatever we do, we do because we must. All other roads are closed. *Eretz Yisrael* has become a duty. And believe me, I feel it. You ask me how I am doing, what can I say? You have seen children, a wooden hut, a cow, up to my neck in work, and I barely make a living. Work is hard. You see these rocks, these mountains which surround us? The land is dry and stony, it demands the last ounces of your strength.

"Still, however hard things may be, we here in Nahalal enjoy a privileged position somehow. We are, as it were, the aristocracy of the Emek, since we are laboring in a danger-zone. It is a hard time, a bitter time. There is a crisis in the country, and our whole life is spent struggling for a piece of bread. But, if you are asking me whether I have any complaints or regrets, then come outside and see for yourself." We step out of the hut and walk silently along the "streets" between the huts and the small garden plots of Nahalal. The night is filled with aroma, and in the sky the stars are glittering like diamonds, like large glowing crystals suspended from a dark blue firmament. In response, it is the former Russian intellectual still inside the Nahalal settler who begins to recite, as if to himself, the lovely sad poem of Lermontov:

> As I start out on my way at night
> The road before me is rocky
> The desert listens to God
> And the stars are calling to each other.

"There you are," my friend continues, "a rocky road, the desert listens to God's voice, and the stars talk — here it is, night after night. When a day leaves me exhausted and despairing, burned out and embittered, I come out into the night and listen to the stars talking to each other." "You have become a poet, my friend." "One has to, because this is the secret of *Eretz Yisrael*, it is poetry. Impractical? Perhaps, but beautiful, so beautiful." "And what about the youth? What about those who have not read Lermontov, do they also see Israel as a poem in prose, or do they see it merely as prose?" "I do not know. One cannot tell. But one thing I can tell you, they are wonderful people, our children: better, more generous than you and I. They are so clear-eyed, so warm-hearted, and so self-possessed. Something is blossoming within them that we, the elders, cannot understand. They do not know what it is, they cannot articulate it. They do not have much book learning, but they do think. But, while our thoughts tend to reach out to wide horizons, their thoughts go deep, very deep, their dimension is depth, not breadth like ours. Something is being spun and woven here in the valley of the Emek, and someday we will see the fabric."

We part. He returns to his hut and I to my night accommodation in Nahalal's only "hotel." I cannot sleep that night. The stars bewitch me, and the words of my friend keep sleep at bay. What is it that is being spun here in this valley? Here, close to Nazareth, not far from the Sea of Kinneret? What is sprouting out of the stony, dry soil? A village? A Jewish village? A settlement, and nothing more? A cow, water for the fields, grapes and olive trees. Is that all? And if more, then what?

Throughout the night I am assailed by recollections of my talks with a variety of Jews in *Eretz Yisrael*. Among them was a rabbi from Poland, a fine, idealistic, gentle young man who bemoaned his fate. The Hasidim who followed him to *Eretz Yisrael* had grown tired and wanted to return to Poland. He was holding them back, he was making every effort to save their souls from damnation. For this purpose, he had come to Jerusalem to ask for support from the Zionist leadership, and he was waiting, like everyone else in *Eretz Yisrael*, for an answer from *Keren Hayesod*, which means, actually, from American Jewry. And it made him suffer. "Rabbi, it is incumbent to perform the sanctification of the Name, but tell me, is the Name being truly sanctified?" The young, black-bearded rabbi with the sad eyes answered only with a deep sigh. Is the Name being sanctified, the hidden, mystery-laden Name? Does the way to Him pass through Nahalal, the huts, the barns with the Damascus cows? We had lost Him amid noise and tumult. Will we perhaps rediscover Him in stillness?

Suddenly the stars are gone. All at once it is day. This sun announces its coming, sending out rays of heat with its first greeting. I walk out of my hotel. People are at work already, young men and women in the barns are covering their heads from the sun. The village comes to life, small children, barefoot, clean, neat, are on their way to school. You can hear their laughter, their melodious Hebrew. I am seized with a desire to work with the workers in the barn, the workers in the fields, with all those who are moving about absorbed in the task of making the best of the primitive tools at their disposal, who are shouldering a burden and a responsibility. "What can I do? How can I help you?" I ask my friend of old. "Help me to put the bags of grain on the wagon. I have to take them to the mill," he answers with a smile. And soon both of us are on the way to the mill, on the road to Nazareth. We pass a hill topped by a white gravestone — a memory to my young brother's untimely death. I bow my head in a last farewell, and we go on toward the mill. We carry the bags into the black, antiquated Arab mill. The Arab bargains with us, and we arrive at an even deal. The wagon is much lighter now, and we are shaken and tossed around as we go on to Nazareth. Here our ways part. My friend returns to Nahalal, and I continue on my way. I want to see more, I am still not sated.

I crisscross the Emek, but am turned away from some places. There is an epidemic, typhus or something else, and I am unable to visit places I had wanted to see: Ein Herod, and Tel Yosef. But then I come to Degania, at the confluence of the Jordan and the Sea of Kinneret. It is surrounded by palms, and you are engulfed by the heat of the desert, by the desert atmosphere. The long, big white building is the kibbutz. Again it is the same picture. The young people work in shifts and women take turns taking care of the children. The leader of Degania appears to be home. He takes me around, shows me all the housekeeping arrangements, and explains the tenets of their operation. But I feel like an alien, maybe because I cannot feel at home in any commune, or maybe because I cannot help feeling that this is a mere experiment, that this has the flavor of a social science laboratory, that this is not real, simple, genuine, liberating life.

"How can you live so close together, always in each other's presence?" I ask my guide.

"It is very difficult," he confesses. "As we get older we want, of course, to have more of a personal life, to be a bit more on our own. We do want to live and not just to exist. At first we felt we were pioneers, we were shouldering the responsibility for all our people. Today, we just want to be what we are, we have had our fill of wandering and of pioneering, we do want to enjoy some of this world's pleasures too."

One after another the Degania settlers come to tell me of their yearning for a calmer life, without the communal bustle, and without the never-ending conversations and debates over politics, principles and problems. One tells me of an occurrence that took place in one of the kibbutzim. The old discussion about "politics," i.e. the procedures and tenets governing the kibbutz, had become so acrimonious as to make getting along almost impossible. A General Assembly was convened which adopted a decision of not talking about politics for the next six months. The Sabbath came, work was at a standstill, all the members of the kibbutz got together, and silence reigned; there was nothing to talk about. *Eretz Yisrael* consumes one so completely that one loses interest in anything that is not connected with the land. One of the comrades started out: "Well, we certainly did the right and smart thing when we decided not to talk about politics." A number of comrades sensing where this was heading stopped him from explaining why it was smart not to talk about politics. And silence reigned again. Until someone had the bright idea to start talking about the mule. And the comrades breathed a sigh of relief — a topic of conversation had been found, and they kept talking late into the night.

This episode undoubtedly has become embroidered in the telling, yet it is a very characteristic one. Communal life, constant close companionship, dries out a person's vital juices, deprives him of his depth. But *Eretz Yisrael* cannot afford this. It must have depth, or nothing. And depth requires solitude, being by your-self and with yourself.

Degania also echoes other general complaints, and again I hear, *Keren Haye-sod*, America." It troubles me. Are they, too, looking to America? Does the collec-tion box hold sway here as well as in New York and in Chicago? Are the new, the strong, the ultra-modern settlers also listening for the drop of the penny? The *pushkes* of London and New York and the *pushkes* of Rabbi Meir Belnos, aren't they essentially the same?

I continue my trip through the Emek. There is Balfouria, a prospering village, peopled by healthy-looking, earthy, bearded Jews. And Afulah, the most remark-able, American-looking town that I have yet seen. A town with a "plan," but without any meaning; with a purpose but without any aim; with streets and houses, but without people, a hook for a lantern which is not there. Workers walk around lugging stones. There is hammering, fixing, arranging, but no one knows to what end, what is the sense and meaning of all this activity?

I turn around and come to Safed. And there, in close proximity to Rabbi Simon ben Yochai and to the Kabbalah, I spend three solitary days in my room, sick. I am the only guest in a clean, good hotel. Three days in a row I read the Pentateuch. I read about the Exodus and the wandering in the desert — the won-drous tales of how the Jews came to *Eretz Yisrael* and how they took it over. And as I keep on reading the Biblical account, it all at once becomes so lucid and so very humanly close. Why should there by legends? It is all so natural, so self-evi-dent. Only this way, only the way the Bible tells it, could the Jews have been able to carry out their yearning, to settle as a people in a land by establishing borders, protective walls, by becoming powerful. Through forty years of wandering through the desert, through struggle after struggle — then as now, now as then.

The desert, the greatest secret of Jewish history. And *tzimtzum* — divine con-traction — is the key to it. To magnify the small, the physically insignificant, to allot to it a dominant role in the affairs of the world, while ignoring the large, the spread-out, the obvious forces, is this not the purport of Judaism? Or is this, per-haps, the spirit of Safed talking to me, the spirit of mysticism?

I do not know. I am tired. The story of how the Jews have wandered and reached their destination consoles me, strengthens me, and Safed concludes what Jerusalem had begun. But Safed also likes allusions; it only intimates, it will not elucidate the final, clear truth. Does it really know the answer? Could the cave of Rabbi Simenon shed some light? But I am tired. I do not want to go into the cave. I will wait.

The Stone

This is my second time at the Wall, at the only wall that Jews can lean against. Such a thing could only happen to the most remarkable of all peoples: to lose all ties with their soil, to lose all the strength and simplicity that such ties provide, and to transform their narrow but secure, reality-based life into a broader, out-ward-reaching, rainbow colored unreal world of possibilities; to lose everything except for a wall, the "Western Wall." It is the only thing that is beyond any doubt. All other memorabilia, and even ruins, are, after all, more a testimony to our imagination than to historical truth.

We do know how the various gravesites and monuments have acquired their fame — due to Arab imagination or to Jewish dreams. One fine morning a saintly rabbi arises and announces that a dream sent from heaven has shown him where one of the Tannaim was buried, and then another, and the Jews believed him. The local Arabs, on the other hand, guided by child-like fantasies or, per-haps, by shrewd calculation, put forth their own historic geography of *Eretz Yis-rael.* Up to this day, Arabs can show you the spot where Noah's Ark landed, creating a hole in the top of Mount Ararat. And there are, surely, many Jews who have not the slightest doubt about it.

Only one monument is safe, is independent of all imagination — The Wall. A wall which stands upon a foundation. What more do we actually need? It is not yet a house, but still an accomplished beginning; one needs only to go on build-ing upon the same foundation.

166

I am again at the Wall. The first time was late at night, a few hours after my arrival in Jerusalem. I entered the Old City through a narrow ascending lane, climbing step by step through the dark, hushed, almost spellbound city. The Old City was asleep. The houses were darker and more secretive than in the daytime. On all sides there were gaping holes, like gravesites, like open jaws. And there were small stores, meat markets, monasteries, smithies, mills with camels turning the wheels that grind the flour for Jerusalem. And in between them all, between the basements and the turrets, the most singular structure in the world — an empty grave. A grave which has always been empty, an impossible grave, an impossible idea, the grave of "The Master" — of Yehoshua.

I proceeded further, deeper into the city, still climbing, step by step. My steps resounded in the still of the night; there was no other sound. And suddenly the path came to an end. I stood in a small narrow lane, a few steps away from the Kotel. I was all alone at the Wall, waiting. I waited for it to speak to me. It kept silent, and silence reigned within me. The granite stones lie heavily and powerfully one atop the other, square blocks with a stone surface. The uppermost ones were smooth and polished, the lower ones rough and worn. Generations have touched and kissed them and drenched them with their tears — salty, bitter, demanding tears. I had heard that people weep at the Kotel. Not only pious Jews, who do it out of duty, performing a commandment, but even those who have lost the innocence of faith. I heard tell of an American Jew, the editor of a newspaper that had very little connection with the Jewish faith and with the Kotel, a Jew who was officially a socialist, who broke down in tears when he came close to the Kotel. And there I stood; I who had, it seems to me, a much closer connection to the whole matter. Yet I did not feel anything, was as cold as the stone, and as hard. And we faced each other, the stone and I, asking ourselves: From whence spring the tears? And why should one weep? The Wall was still alive; it was standing firmly. It waits. It has time and fortitude. Why weep?

And here I am on the way to the Wall again. This time I am retracing the same steps in the daylight. Now the narrow streets are full of life and noise. Yet this does not make them less fantastic; perhaps they are even more so. A variety of people are on their way to morning services. Yemenite Jews who look like Arabs, like Bedouins with graying bushy sidelocks. Bukharan Jews and Jewesses in long robes and shoes protected by snow boots, as the Tatars are wont to wear. There are Sephardim in red fezzes and Polish and Hungarian Jews in fur hats; there are tourists and young Russian men and women talking half Russian and half Hebrew; and all of us are going to the Wall.

There we are at the narrow street, and it is lined with beggars, beggars of a kind that Europe could not even imagine. These beggars seem to belong to an order, to a sect with its own secret code and insignia. Such ugliness, such poverty, such physical abnormalities could not have been wrought by nature. They are artificially produced. No illness goes underrepresented; no misery fails to parade itself and to feel perfectly at home there. They are with us all along the street that leads up to the Wall, and right up to the Wall itself.

And there, there I view what I have so often seen depicted and described: Jews from all corners of the world standing at the Wall and praying. One of them, broad-shouldered, his solid form bedecked in a multi-colored robe, feels very much at home. He is a Hungarian who lives in the Old City. He holds the prayerbook, but he does not look at it; he knows it all by heart. He exchanges some daily news with a few bystanders and then goes up to a stone, which is clearly *his* stone, leans close to it, and murmurs a few prayers. Next to him stands a Sephardi, a simple workman, who prays aloud, but whose diction is difficult to understand. Who knows where he comes from, perhaps from Persia or from Morocco. He does not let go of the stone, he presses his forehead against it, and he talks and talks....

Jewish women, both old and young, are sitting on the benches and weeping. Among them are some very stylishly dressed American tourists. I cannot understand what they are saying because their words are drowned in tears, but the few words which emerge from the flood are words of old familiar prayers. They do not talk to the Wall anymore; their pleas are directed at the cracks between the stones, as through a curtain. Because there, there behind the stones, what is there? Is this where "It" is?

Once again, I remain cold, even colder than the first time. I cannot stroke the stone and kiss it, as does a young Jew with a blond little beard and such awe-struck eyes, most likely one of the new Polish *olim*. There is nothing that I need to tell, to confide to the Wall. We face each other again, the petrified reality and the will to resist petrifaction. asking ourselves: Will our paths ever meet? We part again. The Wall remains the guardian of treasured memories, and I, I direct my steps to the treasure itself, I go to the Temple Mount, to the spot where the Sanctuary stood. From the curtain to the center.

There is a profusion of gates leading to the Al Haram El Sharif, as the Arabs call the Temple Mount. But for the "infidels," for Jews and Christians, there is only one entrance, at designated hours, from 8:30 to 11:30 AM, except on Fridays. What a historic irony! All the honor, all the sanctity is derived from us and yet we are merely tolerated guests. Even the Christians have closer ties to the

Mount than the Mohammedans. It was on the mountain facing the Temple Mount that the entire Christian spiritual history was enacted. This is their source. Should you take the Temple Mount away from us, we still have the Sinai, but what else do they have? And then come the Arabs who have neither sown nor reaped, who have altogether no ties to Jerusalem, and they bar the entrance, holding the key to the treasure.

Fifteen piasters, a ticket, a malevolent look from a beturbaned Arab, and the "curtain" lifts, revealing a stage where the greatest scene in world history took place. A mountain which has been flattened at the top, leaving it in a cube-like shape. White steps lead up to it, bordered by arcades of graceful, slim columns of bluish-white marble. Tradition tells us they were part of the Temple, not of Solomon's Temple, of course, since not a stone of it has remained, but of the Second Temple. A few more steps, and in the center of the plateau is the Mosque of Omar, the most beautiful, the most wonderful Moslem sanctuary in the world, except perhaps for the Hagia Sofia in Constantinople (I am still in doubt as to which of the two is a more beautiful architectural work of art.) It is a blue marvel. The mosaics are in blue, gold, pink, white and reddish marble. And in the middle of the Mosque a stone, a large rock, gray and bare. Two curtains surround it. The first one, a bronze one, winds around the stone itself; the second one, made of metal and wood, is placed behind the first one — a two-fold guardian.

The reason for this is understandable. The stone is the greatest treasure the world possesses, it is the stone which was the beginning and which has been the foundation of the entire structure that we call the history of the world. It is the Foundation Stone. I could have touched it through the opening in the metal curtains, and I must confess, that had it not been for the presence of the black-robed, white-turbaned Arab guide, I would have done as did the young Jew at the Wall, I would have kissed the rock and bowed my head before its eternal grayness.

Here is where it all began. With Abraham's first gesture of submission: Here I am, God, I am Yours. You can do with me what you will, until the last moan of the perishing Jewish people. Sinai then, still the desert, still prehistoric. Today, Mount Moriah is distant history, the first rift, the first crisis in human consciousness. Mount Moriah, the most tragic mountain in the world, and the most Jewish.

An old Greek legend that I like very much comes to mind. A man roamed the world in search of sweet, liberating laughter. He lost it in the cave of Trofanus, the cave of sorrow and pain, and found it in the cave of Delos, where he had seen "The Mother," a representation of the mother of Apollo, a representation that turned out to be merely a piece of wood. He burst out laughing because a feeling of joy inundated his soul. In standing before the foundation, before the formless beginning of all beginnings, I too experienced a liberating joy.

During my stay in Jerusalem, an old Zionist leader told me with an impish smile: "We are merely leasing the Temple Mount to the Moslems, they are our caretakers." And I have faith in his words, and it seems to me that the Moslems, themselves, believe it too. They have boarded up the *Shar Hazahav,* the Golden Gate which leads from the Temple to the Mount of Olives because they believe that the Messiah will enter through that gate and with him all those who will be resurrected. They believe, and they are afraid. Because they know that what must be will be, sooner or later. *Bismilla*...in the name of God.

In Jerusalem:
Among Grey Stones
and Eternities

Friday was a week since my arrival in Jerusalem and, again, a day without water. The second time in a week. It is not so terribly hot in Jerusalem, surely not hotter than in New York at this time, but water is scarce. The water inspectors are getting ready for a hotter week to come and for a drought, and they are rationing water. You turn on the faucet — not a drop. One gets uneasy, "How does one manage to wash up here?" I try to be good-natured about it, but my voice evidently carries a note of dissatisfaction which reaches my mother's ear. "Wait a minute, my child," she consoles me, "have a little patience. Water will come soon." She feels apologetic for the lack of water in the city and rises to its defense, "Is Jerusalem to blame for this?" And father adds, "You think we don't have any water here? There is enough, more than enough, one only has to dig for it, yet we suffer. Jewish engineers have, more than once, undertaken to produce water for Jerusalem. Only a few months ago, a group of German-Jewish engineers had formed a water conservation company. They had presented the government with a plan to bring water into the city and to set up a system of water pipes. The government turned them down, claiming that they would do the work themselves, but in a way to make water available to all the surroundings of Jerusalem as well, which means the Arab villages, and this will take quite a few years, and in the meantime we...."

"In the meantime," mother takes up the defense, "there are still wellsprings and water-bottles, and Yehuda, the carrier, will soon bring water and one really must not complain. The Jews in the desert lived through worse times and God sustained them." Her voice is filled with such supplication, with such a plea for Mother Zion that I resign myself to the dryness and wait patiently for Yehuda the carrier.

I wait — what choice do I have? And soon I hear Yehuda's Oriental voice. "A jug of water, a jug of water!" A bent-over Jew, indistinguishable from an Arab, comes into view, with two heavy bottles on his shoulders. You can hear the splash of water as it is poured into dry jugs. The mood in the house lightens — "Water! Water!" It becomes a celebration. Margalit, the housemaid, as big as a thumb and as dried out as Jonah's gourd, comes in from the kitchen, beaming, and says in her peculiar Hebrew-Aramaic pronunciation, "water." I ask Margalit, "Where do you come from?" I know that she comes from Nineveh, but I want to hear it again; it doesn't happen every day of the week that one gets to talk to someone who comes from Nineveh. "From Nineveh, the city of Jonah, the prophet Jonah," beams Margalit, "the 'pearl' of Assyria." "You still remember him?" I ask. She does not understand and merely laughs. Nineveh, Jonah, monuments, legends, prophesies and magnificent epics — and the last epic is the bent-over pearl, Margalit in the kitchen.

I walk out into the street, go to the wells from which one ladles the water. There are lines of women, Jewish and Arab, with their vessels lined up next to them, with dippers made of tin, of wood and of clay. The sun is beginning to burn, but the women stand patiently and wait. "When will there be water?" "They say at two o'clock." The Jewish women sigh; it is Sabbath-eve, the children are home and there is not a drop of water in the kettle. They sigh and wait, the way one can wait only in oriental countries. And I remember the tragic words of Jeremiah, "Judah mourneth and the gates thereof languish; they bow down in black unto the ground; and the cry of Jerusalem is gone up. And their nobles send their lads for water. They come to the pits and find no water; their vessels return empty, they are ashamed and confounded, and they cover their heads." Jerusalem has been thirsting for ages, in the time of Jeremiah and in our time — a thirsty city and a patient one.

And a thirst arises in me, a thirst for Jerusalem and its suffering, Jerusalem and its unending pathos. I begin walking around Jerusalem. Soon there are three of us. One of my companions lives in Jerusalem, is in love with the city, with its every nook and cranny. He knows the city as one knows a beloved, sees all the details, yet as if through a veil. He perceives its hidden, mist-shrouded beauty, his imagination lends color and depth to grey stones and covers them with a golden haze spun out of poetry and legends. My second companion, a visitor like myself, is a doctor of philosophy, half-cynic, half-mystic, with a remarkable wealth of knowledge, a knowledge mostly of quite useless things. He collects Jewish folk-songs, writes poems, tells sophisticated Jewish jokes, yet is, at the same time, a bit of a Kabbalist — he knows the skies above as well as the streets of the town he was born in, and he endows them with mysteries and with piety, and he laughs at himself and at his mysticism.

"Let's walk around Jerusalem," I propose to my friends. "Yes, with the greatest of pleasure, but first let's make a stop at the tavern," says the doctor with a smile. I know already what he means. The "tavern" is the Cafe Wien, which opened in Jerusalem a little while ago. "So early?" I try to protest. Somehow I don't like starting my day in the Viennese fashion, in a cafe. Haven't I spent enough of my life in cafes, do I have to do it here too? "I have a rule," answers the doctor, "one must not tamper with tradition. And how is Jerusalem worse than Vienna?"

How, indeed. And we enter the coffee house. It is still early, but life here is already in full swing. The room is filled with tables, and Moshe, the waiter, is scurrying around to serve the customers. Voices are heard giving orders in Hebrew, in Russian, in German and Moshe replies to each request in the language in which it was given. I see an old friend, comfortably reclining on an old couch. A Hebraist by principle, but a Yiddishist by nature, he calls out in Yiddish, "Moshe, let's have a pot of coffee and some pastry." Moshe smiles and answers in Yiddish, "With the greatest of pleasure." He is hailed in all the languages as Moshe, with the accent always on the last syllable.

One group of intellectuals is playing chess, others talk politics, or are making plans for *Eretz Yisrael* and for the entire world. In the middle of the room are the German émigrés, recognizable from afar, huddling together, heads bent, absorbing with passionate intensity the contents of the *Züricher Zeitung* and *Die Neue Freie Presse*. They do not skip a line, comment on each sentence, but do so in a quiet, orderly way. They are looking, poor souls, for news from home, searching for a ray of light, of hope. Who knows, perhaps one can return already?

"These Germans," my Yiddishist friend complains half in jest, "they are always conducting post-mortems on their German papers. They are to be pitied, they are strangers even in their own home. They cannot assimilate to Jews." "Do you think that this is easy?" asks my mystically-minded friend, and suggests a game of chess. "But what about Judaism?" I ask. "It won't run away. The daughter of Zion is good-natured and likes to wait for her children, especially when she knows that they are sitting over a cup of coffee, playing chess." We play for a couple of hours and spend another hour watching others play, then resume our walk through the streets of Jerusalem.

◆   ◆   ◆

Walking in Jerusalem during the day is rather strenuous — the sun blazes, there is so little shade. The few trees which had provided shade had been cut down and the streets are paved with grey stones — hard and heavy ones, especially the streets in the new section of the town. We walk aimlessly through the new business section, which had been developed following the pogrom of 1929, when Jewish merchants moved out of the old city. Our Jerusalem resident assumes the role of a guide, and begins to point out and explain: "This is the house where Herzl stayed when he came to Jerusalem." "In this house?" And I see before me Herzl standing on the balcony of this two-story house, standing and looking out at the city of his dream, his history-making fantasy. I am trying to remember the Herzl I had known so well — the tall, handsome, proud man of regal bearing, with the wonderful brown eyes, eyes which had looked into the depths of a non-existing world. I want to recall the real Dr. Herzl, as I had known him, as I had seen him upon his return from *Eretz Yisrael* — but I can't. My memory produces only a blurred vision; his figure becomes interwoven with legendary figures from the past, assuming Biblical proportions, and I push this vision aside. I do not want to be caught up in dreams; I want reality.

Our guide resumes his explanations. "This is an old cloister, and this is a new house."

"Whose house is it?"

"It belongs to an Arab." And on each step new houses — white, beautiful, eastern-style houses.

"Whom do they belong to?"

"Jews live there, but it is an Arab house, it stands on Arab soil, the architecture and the style are Arabic." We come to Rehovia. New houses, small, gray-stoned ones. It is the new Jewish quarter where the Jewish intelligentsia and the semi-intellectuals live. I lack the courage to ask the next question, for fear that the answer will be the same — Arab owners, Arab architect.

"How did the Arabs acquire the necessary money and knowledge?"

"They got the money from the Jews, and as to knowledge, the Arabs have not remained at a standstill. Money stimulated their common-sense; they have been sending their young men to universities and have, by now, quite a sizable intelligentsia."

And here we are, in another remarkable street. Palaces, magnificent buildings — and, again, Arab and Christian, not Jewish. The new YMCA has a style all its own, one of stateliness and pride, expressed in an orientalized, Gothic architecture.

"Why don't Jews have a synagogue of comparable magnificence?" I ask my companion.

The doctor is the one who replies, "A temple, what for? There, take a look." And I see in the distance the massive, gigantic Dome of the Rock on the Temple Mount. "How can we build a synagogue in Jerusalem where there is a Temple Mount? Let there be, at least, a yearning for the "Jerusalem on High" and an open door for an ancient dream." And another proud building, the King David Hotel.

"Why call it King David and not *David Ha-Melech*?" I ask our guide.

"Because Jewish capitalists in England and in America have invested in it and Sir Wylie Cohen is president, and the director is a German Swiss who does not hire any Jewish staff and, altogether, does not love Jews too much. Do you understand?" I understand. How could there possibly be Jewish life without paradoxes and absurdity?

We go on from Rehovia down into town and up again to Talpiot, where the high-intelligentsia, with their pretensions and illusions, has woven its nest. We make a few visits. For a few hours we talk in Hebrew about weighty matters, and my friend, the doctor, grows tired. "Let's go back to the old city," he proposes. "Into the synagogue?" "Yes, to the old houses of worship and study." Once again we descend, and through winding, sloping streets, we arrive at the last vestige of Jewish coloration, at the old, holy city of Jerusalem. It is Sabbath-eve, and the Sabbath Queen sheds her glow over the wide stones of the narrow streets, labyrinths, hidden-away corners, forgotten generations. Each street houses a different world. A group of Jews in yellow robes and burnooses, with their trouser legs covering their boots, are talking, and I want to catch what they are saying; it sounds as if they are speaking Tataric to me. "These are Buhkars," explains our guide. In the next street children are playing, and I hear old Castilian rhymes coming out of the mouths of children playing hop-scotch on the cobbled streets. Georgian women, dressed like gypsies, Kurdish Jews and those from Yemen, Polish and Hungarian Jews — the whole world of the Jewish *galut*, thrown together but not mingling with each other, each corner preserving its own individuality, but all united in greeting the Queen, the Sabbath Queen. Old men greet us with *Shab-*

bat Shalom. Nowhere, it seems to me, have I seen so many handsome, impressive old men as in the alleys of Old Jerusalem. We follow them into the synagogues, but it is early. Just a few Jews wandering around, very much at home, having an argument. Young Jews are reading their prayer books as they sway back and forth, following the movements of their leader, a young man clad in white, shining gabardine. "Do you want to stay for *Maariv?*" asks the *shamus.* "Thank you, we have finished our prayers?" "Already?" is the skeptical and unfriendly sounding response.

We pursue further the sound of the Sabbath. "Let's go to the Kabbalists," proposes our guide. A few side streets and a few downward steps take us to an open door, and there, before my eyes, is the strangest sight I have ever seen. A small room, along the walls are benches, simple, unadorned ones, the seats covered with a red cloth, and atop the benches are standing ten white-haired and white-clad old men holding prayer books. They stand without making a move; even their lips are sealed. In the middle of the room stands a lectern and behind it an old man, his head covered with a *tallit,* standing in prayer. I can hardly discern a word, and I don't recognize any of the prayers. I hear only a long drawn-out sound, "Adonai...ai...ai." The *shamus* hands me a prayerbook. I stand close to the wall and am afraid to make a move. I would like to put on my glasses but hesitate doing so — not one of the old men is wearing glasses, so maybe Kabbalists are not allowed to wear glasses?

The prayer book is that of the Ari, printed in its special way, on each page "the Name," according to the Kabbalistic formula, with the letters going down: 4, 3, 2, 1, and up again, forming the shape of a goblet or of a tree with interlaced branches, a verbal architectonic of the mystery of the universe. The prayer book decrees: When you utter the word *Adonai,* you have to draw it out as long as your breath holds. And the *hazan* draws it out until he begins to gasp, until his breath gives out, and then he starts anew. But the old men remain silent. They read the prayerbook and only their eyes pray, their lips open only to say *amen.* Only one man is seated or, rather, semi-standing. He folds a prayerbook but he does not look at it, his eyes were closed, his lips sealed. Is he blind? Is he a holy mute? His face reflects a world which is closed to me. A soul which is locked in. Or perhaps there is a secret door which leads — leads where?

My mystically inclined friend answers my question when we leave the synagogue. "Thus is it written in the *Zohar:* 'In the hidden recesses of heaven there is a tabernacle wherein dwells the King of Heaven, blessed be His Name, and He unites us with the holy souls with the kisses of love. This is the kiss which unites the soul with the earth.' You see, there in that small room we have witnessed a great, rare, mystical event, the reunion of man with the essence of the world, the dissolution of matter, of physical man in the mystery of the cosmos. The blind Kabbalist is holding the key to the unknown, to the enigma of the universe." "Are you serious about this?" "I don't know. Don't ask. Let's go to Cafe Wien and prepare for the Sabbath."

Once again: chess, coffee, the *Züricher Zeitung* and Moshe. Night falls, and the streets are dark and quiet. "It is time to go to the Kotel," suggests my friend. And we return again to the old city. We descend, going down ancient steps, treading on soil covering the bones of generations, along streets dating back hundreds of years, down to the Wall. An English soldier scrutinizes us and greets us: "Good evening, gentlemen." Civilization draws near and recedes again — we are at the *Kotel*. It is pitch dark, and I feel hemmed in and uneasy. The Wall remains silent and so does my soul. I touch the Wall with my hand and I feel a piece of paper and I pull it out, then another and another, in each one of its crevices. Prayers from simple, poor worshipers, prosaic souls, down-to-earth people who have presented petitions dealing with their daily concerns, presented them to the august mystery. A butcher prays for his business, that his trade should prosper and that his rival should not take away his profits. A father pleads that his daughter should marry soon. Petitions — the Wall has become a post office. And I am beginning to wonder: Is it really necessary to struggle so hard for the petition wall, to shed blood, as in 1929, for the motto: "The Wall is our Wall?" Over there, the Kabbalists are immersed in silence. And where is Jewishness to be found — among the grey stones or in the silent depths?

And we walk again. Via Dolorosa, the way of suffering, the suffering that we human beings had to envision in order to free ourselves from the obligation to suffer ourselves. And more churches and more monuments. Our guide is in his element. He tells us about the stones and of the dust that covers it. Suddenly the narrow street opens up, and we have reached the Lions' Gate. Jerusalem stretches out before us, in all its spaciousness, under the star-studded firmament. The doctor stops, "Look, there is Sirius, silvery, blinking, and there is Ara, the altar, and there…Oh, let's stop talking about stones and history and legends. What is history, after all? Two thousand, four thousand, ten thousand years, and above us reign eternities." His voice takes on a dreamy intonation. "We must not look back at what has turned to dust. We must look up, turn our eyes upward; there lies the secret, there in the heavenly Jerusalem; there and in the silence of the blind Kabbalist in the small sanctuary."

Jerusalem was submerged in deep slumber when I returned home through the Shaarei Zedek. From the Shaarei Arayot, the Gate of the Lions, the gate of might,

to the Shaarei Zedek, the gate of benevolence, this is Jerusalem's mystical path —
for which it thirsts.

About the Wide
and the Narrow Road

This note, my last one on *Eretz Yisrael*, is being written aboard a small, graceful, shining Italian ship, riding the blue, sun-sparkling waves of the Mediterranean. We pass grain-rich islands and secluded, ivory-white shores; we pass islands bearing world-renowned names, wreathed in poems and legends. For Greece is unfolding before my eyes. My return trip follows the route of Odysseus, the wanderer, the restless seeker of rest. I am going home. Home. It was only a few short weeks ago that I was traveling in the opposite direction, toward *Eretz Yisrael*, trembling with the joy and the awe of homecoming. And now I am already returning, returning with an aching heart.

I take out the notes I made, thoughts and impressions I jotted down to be developed and fleshed out at a later time, and statistical data about the agriculture and industry and the economic development of *Eretz Yisrael*. But after one look I put them aside. I am, after all, a mere layman in the field of economics, and my notes and statistics are of little value. And even had I been better versed in, and more understanding of, these practical matters, what would my critical observations and my moralizing be worth? The economy is ruled by its own laws and processes, and Jews in *Eretz Yisrael* must make a living. No matter what means they use, the aim is bread on the table and clothes on their backs. Starved and exhausted as they are, they are grasping at any joy life can bring them this very moment, regardless of what the future may have in store.

I am leafing also through my notes on the several new colonies I visited and on the people I met along the way. The initial enthusiasm, the acclaim of the "new man" in the renewed land, has passed. Everyday life has not yet gained complete ascendancy, but the former holiday atmosphere is gone, and the second holiday, the final one, the celebration of the great redemption, is still far away. In the meantime we are in a *Hol Hamoed*, the intermediary period, and this is reflected in the people as well. The number of their wrinkles may vary and so may the individual nuances, but their main features are firmly drawn already.

Last night we sailed past Athens, and from afar there came to me the radiance emanating from the Acropolis. I remembered Renan and his famous "prayer," the prayer he had uttered upon "reaching the perfect beauty." He prays at the altar of beauty:

> Late do I arrive at the threshold of your mystery. I bring my repentance to your altar. I was going astray, without a guideline, until I found you. An over-powering tide pulls us towards a nameless chasm, and the name of the tide is oblivion. You are the true, the only divinity — an abyss. The tears of all the nations were shed on the altar of truth, the dreams of all thinking people contain a portion of truth. All things on earth are but a dream and an illusion. All gods pass, they are barred from eternity.

Thus did he pour out his heart, the old skeptic who had spent his life bent over the writings of the faith-rooted, God-enamored East, reading the books of a people and a land that had brought the yearning for God to mankind. From the dream of infinity to the smile of the finite, from the protest against morality, against the inexorable injunctions of life, to the joy of veering from the eternally male and subjecting oneself to the eternally feminine. This was the road that Renan and the generation that preceded us traveled. And we have been searching for the way back from the Acropolis to the Temple Mount, from the perfect statue to the unhewn marble, from the smile to the burning passion, and to the passionate yearning of drawing nearer to the unfathomable.

It was to escape nagging doubts that I had set out once again towards Jerusalem, to find there the yearning of my forefathers, to find the key that we had lost. "Not the God of philosophy do I seek, but the God of Abraham, Isaac and Jacob," had been the anguished cry of the passion-consumed Pascal. What I wanted to feel, sense, experience in Jerusalem was the affirmation of my connectedness, of being a link in a chain, of being a note in the songs passed from generation to generation. I sought a home for my homeless, lonely soul. I went to Jerusalem to visit my home and my roots — my flesh and blood ones — my father and my mother. And on the way a Midrash kept ringing in my ears, like a wondrous tune: God says to Jacob, "You have said that your portion lies in the land of the living — return to the land of your fathers, your father is waiting for you, your mother is waiting for you, I am awaiting you." And I thought, maybe this is addressed also to me: "I am awaiting you."

Whose fault is it that I am returning empty-handed? I have searched and I have failed to find it, I have listened and have failed to hear it, I have waited and my waiting was in vain. What is it I was searching for? There are two main streams of thought in Jewish life. One is represented by the teaching of the Rambam, the other by Rabbi Isaac Luria, or the Ari, who taught of divine expansion and contraction, the expansion into a growing stream, the contraction into a beam of light. The stream flows from mountain to mountain, becomes a sea and an ocean, yet remains encircled by shores, by limits. The light beam comes from unknown distances, comes from infinity, and loses itself in the cosmos. The Rambam says: The world is large and wide, and Jews must not confine and limit themselves, they must not hem themselves in. They must carry the word into all the corners of the world, into all the countries that they may enter, where they are still allowed to reside. It is the teaching of an expansive Jewish life, of Jews who are part of society, who are pillars of the historical structure. Opposite the Rambam is the teaching of the Ari: the cosmic concept of the *tzimtzum*, or self-limitation, of turning oneself into a universal force, of becoming the essence of all existence. To draw into oneself means also to live within certain spatial confines, to isolate oneself, to stay by oneself and to struggle with oneself until one has achieved a consciousness of the world which will burn like a torch, sending its beams out to spread light throughout the world.

This is the meaning and the historical mystery of *Eretz Yisrael*, its role in Jewish life and in the world — it is the land of the *tzimtzum*. Where the search for the essence is at the core of human thought, there form is excluded, because all representation is artificial configuration and because each such form is a denial of the infinity of all possible forms. The Acropolis is a finished work of art, while Mount Moriah remains unfinished. The Acropolis represents a completed realization, while Mount Moriah is still in the process of realizing itself; it can still grow.

This is a feeling shared by all of us who are living in a broad, vast world, especially now when the Acropolis-idea, the concept of Greek "perfection" is rapidly losing ground, when new values are being born in a world wracked with pain.

Now Jerusalem has the word once again; now is the time for all the spiritual forces accumulated by the Jewish people to draw together, to form a bundle of light beams; the time for the *tzimtzum* has come. And this means a higher spiritual creativity; this requires intellectual courage and moral pathos; this demands a Jewish commitment to further growth.

It truly was not a desire for literary material that made me dwell with so much love on the figures of the old believers, the "builders of Jerusalem." A source had opened up before me, a source of inspiration, of a life whose meaning reaches beyond our daily existence, of a life which transcends the understanding of our mundane reasoning. And if I have, here and there, with a word, a gesture, a wink of an eye, reacted critically to the work that goes on in *Eretz Yisrael*, believe me, my pen was guided by what was perhaps too great, too strong, a love. It is because I expect so much from the Jewish people that I am prone to disenchantment. It is because I sense its inherent spiritual strength that can reshape the world that its plot of land is too poor for me. Another colony, one more vineyard, one bank then another, and a new factory — and later, in perhaps fifty years time, *Eretz Yisrael* will be fifty-one percent Jewish, living in the shadow of dependence. And is this all? Is the entire meaning and purpose of the great Jewish tragedy merely a small Eastern republic?

Zionist leaders are calling "Israel" to account, and rightly so. What is the Jewish people doing to realize its dream? What happened to "Old and young, we shall go?" The men of power keep silent, the dejected masses keep sighing, and the building-up of *Eretz Yisrael* rests on the shoulders of those in between, a heavy burden when carried alone. But I have an even more challenging question: Where is the Jewish spirit? Of course it is difficult to build factories in a land devoid of steel and coal, but does one also need capital, mortgages and parties to create a *Weltanschauung*? Jewish intellectual luminaries, dispersed throughout the world, are the loneliest of the lonely, the truly orphaned ones. Why does the wave of longing not carry them to *Eretz Yisrael* to become the spiritual center that Achad Ha'am yearned for, but whose nature he was unable to define because he was still a disciple of the Rambam and not a follower of the Ari? But what is needed now is not a spiritual center, but a spiritual furnace where all the values shall be melted down, where all the problems shall be processed through the fire of passionate thought, and where the molten historical materials shall be cast into new forms.

Who can do this? You see, everyone is engrossed in the current interest of the day. Germany wants power, America wants wealth, France wants pleasure and the calm to enjoy it; only Russia is aflame with spiritual passion, a passion directed at engines and tractors. All of them have possessions which they must defend. We are the only ones without possessions and without expectations; we cannot look forward to attaining power, to being blessed with happiness, or even to be simply at rest. We possess only one thing: spiritual passion. Being the poorest we can be the freest, and being the weakest we are free from fear, since only the mighty and the rich are subject to fear. And *Eretz Yisrael* is like the Jewish people, a poor land and a rugged one, a land of solitary, brooding mountains, whose silence is filled with pathos. The caves and hidden crevices of *Eretz Yisrael* are filled with stillness and with *tzimtzum*. Its physical dimensions are so very limited, but its spiritual dimensions reach out into infinity.

Either the people are not yet mature enough for the land, or the land may have outlived the people. The connecting thread is breaking off. We are bringing in to *Eretz Yisrael* all the concepts which prevail in the world and all the drives to which men are subject: the drive for power, for wealth, for pleasure, all the concepts which are part of the "Acropolis idea." But we fail to give *Eretz Yisrael* the thing it needs most, a passion for spiritual exploration. And thus, the university that was established turned out to be a poor copy of a minor, small-town German university. A press comes into being and, at its best, proceeds to imitate the European and American press. And as to literature — seldom has the Jewish creative spirit been at such low ebb as it is now in *Eretz Yisrael*, busying itself with translating novels and producing mediocre writing. Divorced from its foundations, Jewish creativity has become ephemeral, and rarely have Jewish intellectuals been as lonely and as excluded from playing a role in the life of their society as they are in present-day *Eretz Yisrael*. The land that once was encircled by the wondrous threads spun by the great weavers of dreams is today ruled by those who produce threads for the manufacture of sturdy bags and shiny cloth.

Surely, it has always been like this, a repetition of the eternal tragedy of the Jewish people — the struggle of the few, of the elite, against the banality of life, the struggle of the beam of light against the broad prism that fractures it. The greatness and the beauty of *Eretz Yisrael*, however, lies in the supremacy of the light beam; the Jordan always retreated before the spirit. Can this miracle repeat itself once more?

Passing the Acropolis of Athens, I visualize once more the harsh mountains of Judea and I replace Renan's prayer with my own, that of a seeking, questioning man of today: Let all things that are on earth be a dream and an illusion and an eternal striving. May spiritual satisfaction never prevail on the mountains of Judea, and let the torches be relit that once enabled all Jews and all men to witness the emergence of new revelations of universal truth. Because these revelations extend into infinity, all flowing to the final source, to the final mystery. And may it come true.

The Religious Experience

Oedipus is Still Seeking

✦

"Me oun echon ti symbolon"
(Sophocles' Oedipus)

There goes the old, blind, guilty-innocent King Oedipus, wandering from place to place, seeking purification, seeking atonement for his sin. It had been committed in ignorance and without intention, this most serious violation of the basic laws of nature: causing his own mother to become the mother of his children. When Oedipus suddenly learns of his terrible deed, he flings the crown off his head, tears out his eyes, and wanders out into the world, an exile. And as his tragic wanderings come to an end, the poet Sophocles has him utter these words: *"Me oun echon ti symbolon"*: I have no guideposts, no arrow to show me the way. I have no symbol.

I do not know, nor does it really concern me, what Sophocles the poet intended to convey in this line, what meaning the word "symbol" had for him. There are volumes devoted to the interpretation of his words, yet, as Nietzsche once said: "The same text can bear a variety of interpretations; there is no one and only 'correct' interpretation." Great human figures are not captives of time or place. Oedipus lives on in each generation, in each land, always in one form or another, but always bearing the same tragic burden of guilt-innocence, the inner

187

rift of man who is always conscious of being guilty, even if he does not know how or why. And throughout the generations, Oedipus seeks his symbol.

What is the fundamental guilt of Oedipus? Not any particular action for which he is not responsible, since man, after all, is a kind of crossroads, an intersection of various paths which were neither planned nor laid out by him. Within him is the pressure of his bloodstream; around him countless lives, a tangle of fates, a web of deeds and motives. All of these come together and find their point of intersection in him, the individual, the unique one. How can he defend himself against them?

But then there awakens within him, after the event and therefore too late, a sense of his own, unique personality, and Oedipus experiences guilt. He asks himself: Why could I not, why was I not willing to reach into the depth of my being, to listen to my own voice, to my innermost self? Why did I not try to find within myself the road sign, the thread, the arrow, the symbol? Oedipus searches within himself for sanctification, the meaning of his life. It means little to him to be told: This is good, and this is bad; this you may do and this you may not. It is not enough. He wants to know why this is so and whether even those acts which are permitted should, perhaps, not be committed? How, though, can he find the answer? Within himself? He has no faith in himself, no trust. And rightly so. Who am "I" that I should dare it? Everyone must lean on somebody. And should one seek to disengage oneself from all support, to stand all alone in the world, "to place one's stake on nothing," as Max Stirner had fantasized, then one's solitude also turns into Oedipal despair. Because nothing springs from nothing; man was not born *ex nihilo*.

Professor Freud may say whatever he likes, and perhaps he is right in his analysis of faith, religion, the "great illusion." But being an expert on Oedipus, he should have known that the essence of religion, of faith, is not at all the "illusion," i.e. the concrete, substantive image, but rather the symbol. And must one then believe in a symbol? The explorers of ancient religions have more than once pointed out that neither the Egyptians nor the Greeks truly believed in their gods, just as the modern-day Hindu does not believe in the divinity of his cow. It was for them nothing more than an artistic, tangible expression of a deep, murky feeling of the coherence of the world. And like every finite expression of an infinite thought, so their symbols had to be naive and childlike, but at the same time dramatic, vital, full of sap from the old tree of history.

The older the tree, the more vital the symbol, and the more complex its content. Only when the tree begins to die, when the cohesion begins to loosen, does the symbol lose its meaning and wilt away. And it is at this point that Oedipus sets out on his wandering. And, in his wanderings and groping, he often reaches the stage of a theater, and the life-breathing symbol becomes transformed into play-acting, sporting a wig and a costume. Oedipus now walks on stilts.

If someone today were to take on the task of studying our contemporary religious beliefs, especially those of the Christian world, he would need to delve deeply, not into the content, the ideology of our time, but rather into its manifestations, into its symbolic expression. But scholars no longer know what to do with the old content. They are all in the same position as the Grand Inquisitor in Dostoyevsky's legend, who drove out the one in whom he so passionately believed, in whose name he built cathedrals and burned unbelievers on the stake. The Grand Inquisitor had lost the meaning of his own symbol; what remained were the outer husks, the theatrics and the painted canvas.

The thinkers among the scholars know this; the sensitive ones feel the emptiness. They are searching for new forms of expression, and, like Dr. Fosdick and others, they find it, they find the symbol, in dramatic plays. They introduce into their congregations Greek dances, Buddhist hymns and scenes from John Drinkwater's *Abraham Lincoln*. A whole new ritual has developed, collected in the book *Worship Through Drama*, by Rilis K. Alexander and Omar P. Goslin. Faith, art, artistry. The path is almost completed; the circle is about to close.

Each religion begins dramatically, but it must not remain so; it must become intimate, must progress from the public domain to the realm of the individual. Its beginning is drama, i.e. events, happenings. As it develops, it leads to symbolism, significance, meaning. And I often think that the uniqueness of Judaism, of its deeply rooted strength, lies in its religio-spiritual, and therefore universal, quality of transforming dramatic events into symbolic ones. Only the superficial observers or, rather, those who saw or were able to see only the surface, only the face that Judaism turns towards the outside world, could notice merely its historical element. I certainty do not wish to enter here into any theological disputations. It is not my department, and I could contribute nothing positive or even of thought-provoking interest. My interest in this matter lies more in its cultural-psychological or, more precisely, in its Jewish aspect.

There was a time, as can be seen in old Jewish neighborhoods even today, that Jewish ritual was centered not in public worship, not in the synagogue, but at home, in the intimacy between one's four walls. Suffering, persecution and necessity had forced Jews to infuse their religious life with greater spirituality, to conduct it in more intimate ways. In ancient times, Jewish religious life was permeated with dramatic manifestations: parades of the Kohanim and the Levites, the impressive ceremonials on the Temple Mount, the golden crown, the white vestments, the trumpets and the bells, the multitudes and the sacrifices — all this eye-pleasing, magnificent drama. And of the synagogue in Alexandria, Rabbi Yehuda tells us in the Talmud that no Jew has seen a more beautiful sight: a great basilica, colonnade after colonnade with golden chairs lining the walls.

The basilica has been destroyed, the columns are broken, the golden chairs melted down, and of Jewish life in Alexandria there remains almost no trace in history, just because it had been so dramatic, because it had been so beautiful. The Jew — perhaps the only one in history to do so — found the way to faith, removed its frills, and transfigured it into intimacy and symbolism. Such has been the entire, hard path of Jewish religious development: toward simplicity, toward less pomp, both structural and verbal. The main opponents of Jews and of Judaism, even when they are not outspoken anti-Semites, even when they intend to be objective scholars, view the ancient Jewish striving toward undramatic simplicity as plebeian, as aiming at the masses, the ordinary people, rather than at the elite. So argues, for example, Max Weber in the third volume of his famous and much praised work on religious sociology, entitled *On Ancient Judaism*. Perhaps it is so. But the categories also keep changing. The aristocracy of one time turns out to be very common, very plebeian, in another time and under other circumstances. And if Max Weber truly considers humility, sincerity and modesty to be plebeian, well, one cannot really measure the whole world with a Germanic measuring rod. At any rate, the Jews have never dramatized their poverty and humility as Saint Francis of Assisi dramatized his, nor have they been pretentious in the field of ethics. They regarded themselves as simple laborers, not as actors who create roles for themselves.

Yet Judaism is not static, and Jewish thought follows the general, universal process from simplicity and intimacy back to the drama, to artifice; from the supra-historical, universal symbolism to the purely historical, nationally conditioned concepts. It may be that I am too subjective, that I am idealizing the past and underestimating the present. But my memory contains the imprint of a different, a radically different Jewish mood than prevails today. There were no sermons, interpretations, dramatics or political or historical horizons, but rather a strong, deep pathos and much true symbolism. This was the norm for hundreds of generations, a line leading from the beginning of one generation to the next. Ancient words collectively created an idiosyncratic mood; not a historically reminiscent, nor a rationalistic one, but an abyss-deep, personal one, emanating from the very source of life.

But this, too, passes. The old spices lose their aroma, the "symbol drops out," and once again the old tragedy is reenacted. The old, blind Oedipus wanders — "in search of a symbol."

Paul

An old Christian legend called *The story of Paul and Thekla* tells of a young girl from the Anatolian city of Ikonia, today's Konia, who falls in love with the Apostle Paul and his faith. The legend describes how it came to pass: "Thekla set out walking on the road which led to Lystra and stopped at a crossroad to wait for Paul. After some time waiting and watching for him she finally saw Paul approaching, a man of short stature, bow-legged, snub-nosed and balding — and a man of great beauty. One moment he looked like a human being and the next like an angel."

A remarkable picture: a short, balding, bow-legged man, yet one endowed with the nobility and beauty of an angel. It is surely no wonder that this is the way the young girl saw the apostle. Women see things very differently when they are in love. What is interesting about the legend is its juxtaposition of ugliness and beauty, of being both bent and straight, vulgar and noble. Paul is a figure of contrasts. Everything about him is paradoxical: his life, his work, his death. And, more than anything else, the tremendous world-historical role he has played and is still playing up to today.

A short, bow-legged, poor Jew from Tarsus in Cilicia, the son of a weaver and himself also a weaver or a tent-maker. A Pharisee, a pupil of Rabbi Gamaliel, "a Hebrew of Hebrews" (as he called himself), becomes the founder, spiritual leader and dictator of world history. Being an inarticulate speaker, he nevertheless went from place to place on the road from Jerusalem to Rome, speaking, preaching, entering into debates on the new doctrine, the new revelation. Having but poor command of the Greek language, he still sent out letters to the well-spoken citizens of Corinth, Galatia, Colosse, etc. His letters met with interest, lit a spark, and evoked enthusiasm. Having a field of knowledge limited to Scripture, Commentaries, and the legalistic subtleties and hairsplitting of the Talmud, he addressed Athenians accustomed to clear, logical, philosophic disputations. And this ignorant man prevailed over the men of learning. A Jew whose every gesture testified to his being steeped in Judaism, and who, furthermore, had been a zealot ready to exterminate all transgressors, became Judaism's greatest enemy. Having entered life as Saul, he stepped into history as Paul.

His father taught him the art of weaving. And what is it a weaver does? He adds thread to thread and binds them together, unites separate strands into a complete pattern, fusing the weakest elements into a strong, resilient texture. Each single thread can be torn in two by a child, can be wafted away by a breeze. But the weaver comes and gathers the threads, binds one to the other and turns them into a yarn that none can tear. He weaves it into a robe that warms and protects; he weaves it into lovely ornamental rugs. And the finer the original threads, the stronger the woven texture. The strongest thread is a silken one, and the finest, most delicate thread is also silk.

Paul carried the art of weaving even further. He wove together threads which were even thinner than silk, weaker than the most delicate threads known to man: he wove spider webs, designed to catch living creatures, flies which fall into the sticky membranes and are sucked dry.

His forbears had been people of a different ilk: simple, naive, folksy people. What had his teacher been if not a whittler, carving history's old material? A whittler does not add anything; he only takes away. He cuts off everything that is superfluous, everything that does not fit into a reconstructed form. He cuts, he carves, he fits one piece of wood into another. And this was the task of the teacher. Had this not been the pursuit of the original, the historic Yeshua? He preached as his contemporaries and those before him had. They interpreted scripture and adapted it to their way of thinking. Some added and some subtracted. The historical Yeshua, however, wanted neither to add, nor to increase anything; he wanted to lift the yoke of commandments which had grown too heavy; he wanted to tear down the fence with which tradition had surrounded Judaism. Those following the "master," namely the disciples Simon — the Peter-to-be — Johanan, Jehuda, Mattathias and the others, were simple people, fishermen and small shopkeepers. They had no intention of overturning the world, not even the Jewish one. They were observing the law and were afraid of transgressing it. They were Jews who had their own master. At a time when everyone was talking about the Messiah, when everyone was awaiting him, when sect after sect came into being each with its own vision of the Messiah and its own Oriental fantasies, the disciples also formed a sect, with their own school of thought. The teachings of Shammai and the teachings of Hillel were now joined by the teaching of Yeshua. His followers, simple, ignorant people, not well versed in the fine points of doctrine, were content with a master who did not stress the importance of learning. It was a Jewish illusion, one of many.

Thus it was until the arrival from Cilicia of a Jew named Saul. Legend tells that his father came from Goshen and was one of those who had fled *Eretz Yisrael* after Johanan of Goshen had been unable to defend the last Jewish fort against Titus and was subjugated by the Romans. The son arrived in Jerusalem at a young age, bringing with him some knowledge of the gentile, Greek world. He could speak and write Greek, albeit imperfectly. His speech suffered from a poor accent and his writing from a limited command of grammar. His Greek was neither that of Euripides nor that of Plato, and as a result he was laughed at when preaching to the Athenians. But his Greek was good enough for Jerusalem since the Jews of Jerusalem were, after all, quite provincial. They did not venture out beyond their own region, and they disliked all foreign cultures. Hellenism and Romanism were to them symbols of suppression, foreign domination, and enslavement. Thus Saul's knowledge of Greece and the outside world, limited as it was, was more than sufficient for Jerusalem, especially since he was a Pharisee, a former student of Rabbi Gamaliel, and had sat at the feet of the sages. We do not know what kind of student he had been, but it is doubtful that he had been an accomplished one, or that he had a gift for scholarship. He lacked not only sagacity, not only the remarkable logical concentration of the great Talmudic scholars, but also the purely theoretical drive, the love of learning for the sake of learning. Developing thoughts into a scholarly system was not his vocation. Neither did the art of Midrash attract him. He lacked the needed feel for poetry and the love of confabulation. Saul was a man of action, an organizer. He needed to travel, to go about organizing, establishing, making waves. He loved the dramatic elements of life; he was a born actor, ready to play a role, whatever the role might be: that of a persecutor or of a persecuted one; the role of a defender or of an aggressor; the role of a Pharisee zealot or of an apostle of a new faith.

Saul threw himself into the task of combating the new sect of Nazarenes. They were a small, insignificant sect, of unsure, naive, unworldly men, calling themselves *evyonim*, the "poor ones." And so they were, in all respects. Had they been left alone they would surely have withered away and been forgotten. But it was not given to Saul to leave something alone; he had either to attack it or defend it. And when he attacked, it was with the full force of his dramatic temperament. Thus he became the persecutor of the first Christians. By the authority of the High Priest he fulminated against the sectarians, and they grew to fear him.

He was not content to limit his assault on the sect in Jerusalem; he wanted to attack the Christians outside the country as well. He set out on the road to Damascus, the ancient city where Jewish and Greek culture met and where sects and religious movements allowed to flourish.

On the way to Damascus, however, Saul was overtaken by "the spirit." He saw "Him" whose disciples he had tormented, and he heard "His" voice: "Saul, Saul, why are you persecuting me?" Anyone else would have experienced this as a dream and would have let the dream drift away. But not the weaver and the zealot Saul. For him this experience was a spiritual revolution, and his response would transform it into a historic one.

Saul became Paul. He went from Damascus to Arabia. He remained solitary for a while, working on his loom, weaving and binding the spidery threads of his imagination, and bringing a completed pattern to Jerusalem. He did not come to the Jews anymore, nor to the Pharisees, but to the disciples, to Simon, Hanania and the others. They refused to accept him, nor did they believe him. In their simplicity they could not understand how the recent enemy could suddenly have become a friend; and not merely a friend, but a fanatical supporter of the faith, one who exaggerated, one who bullied. He came to them and said: Do you believe in Yeshua? Do you consider yourselves His disciples, His messengers? Do you know at all what it is you believe in? Do you have any idea of what treasure you hold in your hands? Do you not see that the world is waiting for His arrival? Not the Jewish world; it is small and poor, and you are as well known here as He is. No one here will honor you or your piety. Go to the gentiles, to the Greeks and the Romans, they are more simple-minded, less critical. And when you come to them do not tell them your Jewish legends from Galilee. Do not talk about a rabbi and say that you merely want to give a different interpretation of the Torah. Address them with grand words; tell them about the Messiah, about the son of God, the redeemer of the world. They will believe you.

At first the disciples drew back in fear. This was too much for them. It was not what they meant or wanted. Having seen their teacher with their own eyes, having followed him from Galilee, knowing all about his life and his teachings, they could not follow Saul's fantastic exhortations. But they had to admit him into their midst, and he succeeded in confusing and overriding them. Yet they were not drawn to him, and he remained a stranger to them up to his very end.

Saul set out alone on his historic journey to the gentiles. It was a long way from Jerusalem to Rome, Athens, Cappadocia, Cilicia, Antioch and Corinth. The short, snub-nosed, bow-legged Jew made his way to all the bastions of Greek culture, and he talked, and he preached. He was laughed at, and he shrugged it off. He was beaten by Jews, for punishment, and by the gentiles just for the fun of it. He suffered the beatings and went on his way, preaching and weaving before the eyes of the world the wondrous legend of Jesus Christ, the son of God, the redeemer of the world.

"For two years he remained in the lodgings he had rented, taking in all who came to him, preaching about the kingdom of God and about all things relating to Jesus Christ. He did so in safety and in peace." Thus ends *The Story of the Apostles*, the only canonically acknowledged history of the disciples of Jesus and biography of Paul. And the man we leave in "rented rooms" at the end of his road is the same one he had been all his life. We do not learn any more about him. The life of Paul ends as suddenly as it began, and we are left in the dark as to how it had come about.

Later legends, however, such as the apocryphal *The Stories of Paul*, tell of a different end for the apostle. His imprisonment in Rome does not end as idyllically as the canonic text tells us. On the contrary, it ends in pain and in death. Emperor Nero orders his death by beheading and his soldiers carry out his order. They come to Paul as he is preaching to his Christian followers. When he sees the speculator, i.e. the soldier carrying the sword, he stands and, turning his face eastward, raises his hand and prays. After that he speaks in Hebrew to those close to him and then stretches out his neck towards the sword. As the sword strikes, a spurt of milk gushes out of the wound and spills on the robe of the soldier. That same night, around nine o'clock, the apostle Paul comes to Nero, who is surrounded by philosophers and generals, and says: "Emperor, here I am, Paul, a soldier of God. I did not die but I live on in my God. But you will soon be visited by great sorrow and affliction because you have spilled the blood of the righteous." And with these words he leaves the Emperor.

Once again we have a mixture of various elements, a fusion of two personalities. The Jew who prays facing eastward and speaks Hebrew before his death, and the miracle-worker, the sorcerer of the Greco-Roman fantasy, who can walk carrying his head in his hands. The same legend is also told of the last Greek miracle-worker, Apollonius of Tiana: milk in the place of blood, remaining alive after being beheaded, etc., etc. Small wonder, then, that Christian legends did not know how to deal with Paul, how to present him. In Jerusalem he had been "the Gentile." Simon (Peter) had fought with him and had been unable to forgive him for abandoning Jewish law, for eating with the gentiles and for following Greek customs. The Jerusalem *evyonim,* the first genuine Christians, had regarded him as a seducer, as Satan come among them. They claimed that he was not at all a Jew, but rather an agitator posturing as a Jew in order to marry the High Priest's daughter, and that he became an apostle of Christ when the Jews did not treat him with due respect.

The Greeks, the Romans and the gentiles, however, did not accept him as one of their own either. He was, it is true, a Roman citizen, but they always considered him a barbarian, a Jew from *Eretz Yisrael* who got exited and waved his arms around, who was prey to hysterical or epileptic seizures, and who preached crazy sermons about another Jew somewhere in Galilee who became a god. The philosophers of Athens and Rome were laughing in their courtyards. If God had to manifest Himself in the shape of a man, did it really have to be in some forsaken corner of the world? Should it not have been in Rome?

◆   ◆   ◆

In Paul's letters to the Christian communities of Rome, Corinth and Galatia, as well as to the Jews, that is to the community of Jerusalem, one finds a consistent motif: his astonishment at himself. Throughout all his words there resonates the question: How did I, the Pharisee Saul, the pupil of Gamaliel, a Hebrew among the Hebrews, a grandson of my forefather Abraham, how did I become a teacher of the new faith? Who am I that I shall dare to do this? How do I know that it is the right thing to do? And he takes heart and answers himself: I do not speak in my own name. I am a messenger. I work on behalf of the Messiah. I am obeying His orders, and on my shoulders lies the duty to tell the world what has happened in Jerusalem, on Mount Golgotha.

We are in the presence of a troubled conscience and of a compulsion. His conscience troubled him not because he was proclaiming a new faith, but because he had delayed doing so. Actually Paul carried out what all Jews before him considered to be their duty: to become missionaries to other nations. This had been the strongest Jewish urge, their historic task: to go out into the world and spread God's will, i.e. to let the world know their conception of God's will and of what He expects from man. Jews wanted to do it but had done nothing to carry it out. They talked among themselves about the redemption of the world, but the world did not learn about it. Isaiah and Amos, Hosea and Ezekiel all addressed the entire world, but they did so from their own land and were heard only by Jews. And when a Jew did manage to tear himself away from his home soil, speaking and writing in Greek, the predominant cultural language of the time, he lacked the courage to preach the Jewish dogma; he merely interpreted, conciliated, and built bridges, as did Philo of Alexandria. The only Jewish philosopher of ancient times, a Jew versed in Greek culture, a thinker, an adherent of Plato, and, at the same time, a Talmud scholar, Philo worked on proving that Moses and Plato, Judaism and Greek culture, were not as far from each other as was assumed. He tried to convert Plato to Judaism and to Hellenize Moses, but his efforts had come to naught. The Greeks had no use for the Scriptures, and the Jews had no use for a Platonic or any other philosophical system. Because between the "yea" and the "nay" there can be no compromise. One has to choose either one or the other. There is either a total rejection or a mere dogma confined to the paper it is written on; there can be no glowing words, no vital spiritual force.

Paul had been the first Jew to sense this. He did not go to the Jews; he had nothing to tell them. He could not impress them talking about "the kingdom of heaven," "the son of man" or the Messiah. They were familiar with all the nuances these words evoked. They were present when those concepts and images came into being. And when he went on weaving fantastic tales of the word becoming flesh, and the idea assuming corporeal reality, and the dream becoming history, they laughed at him. Then grew angry, and their anger turned into scorn. But the Jewish spirit was still striving to reach the wide world; it knew that history was awaiting it.

Paul went out into the world, to the nations who loved facts, who bowed down to reality, even when reality resided in a mere stone, plank, or human being. Paul brought the Jewish idea to the Greeks and the Romans, to the dominant nations and cultures, and he did not offer them a compromise, he did not seek conciliation. He came with a sharp "nay." He did not say to the Greeks: "Your philosophers are great, and your culture is beautiful, but it can be given a different interpretation." He did the opposite; he came to Athens and said: "You are walking in the dark, you do not know what the truth is, you are confused, your entire culture is worthless, you are barbarians. The truth, the light, the wisdom dwells in Jerusalem, among the Jews, with a rabbi in Galilee."

He came to the Romans and told them: "Your kingdom is built on sand. The only true kingdom is that of the Jews in Nazareth." It is true he called him the son of God, the Messiah, Christ (the anointed), the Master, but he presented to the Greeks and the Romans proofs of his new dogma by, once again, citing Scripture, and the Commentaries. A Jewish way to a non-Jewish goal.

Had Paul been born a few hundred years earlier, when the Jewish kingdom was still intact, when the people — his people — had not yet lost its strength and its courage, his mission to the nations would surely have assumed a different character. Then, too, he might have set out to weave colorful spider webs, to create a legend. All indoctrinators do so, especially those who promote religious doctrines. But his legend would have had a different, a more Jewish, a more intelligible, a more humanly possible tone. And he might, perhaps, have truly arrived at a conciliation between Judaism and the world, at a Jewish-universal culture. But Paul had been born too late; the bridge was drawn up, and Judaism had walled itself in, set itself apart. Nationalism prevailed over pure religiosity, and Judaism erected a partition between itself and other nations.

Paul had to leap over the partition, and the leap resulted in world-historical consequences. The tragedy of Jewish history, its greatest tragedy, was Paul. If only the tremendous task of planting the Jewish seed in foreign soil had been entrusted to someone more rational than Paul, to less of a braggadocio, as he called himself, to a healthier, a more balanced, a more intact personality. The weaver of Tarsus, the Pharisee, given to hysteria and sudden seizures, put the seal of his personality upon the young Christendom. He was a conflicted, guilt-ridden man and such was his dogma, the Pauline one, the Christianity that he had created. He talked too much but had not said the final word. He told parables and legends without a clear moral principle. And he always preached of guilt: a guilt that must be atoned for, from which one can be redeemed through one's own sufferings or that of another.

The erstwhile fanatic persecutor of Christians became the first pursuer and implacable persecutor of his own people, of his own roots. His life was spent in opposition to himself, in a struggle with himself. The struggle against his past became the soul of his faith and the *raison d'être* for his work; it was the achievement of his life. Simon had a sure, Jewish instinct: he felt that the Pharisee would never become a disciple of the young and kindly preacher of Galilee, and so he had been hostile to him. But Paul had the last word and was proclaimed the "rock" of the Christian church. He transformed Simon into Saint Peter, whose likeness became enshrined on a Vatican basilica in Rome. Countless masses come to kiss the feet of the old fisherman. It was Paul's only consolation or, perhaps, his only revenge.

Paul smiles. He has brought the Jews of Galilee to greatness; he has brought them there, but he does not intend to stop at this. The Pharisee has not finished his task. Sooner or later the way back will be found. The weaver of Tarsus is still seated at his loom, weaving. What pattern will emerge from it?

The New God

"God and the Messiah are dead. The Workman's Bund is alive!" This is the fool-ish, childish mantra through which young people once gave vent to their irreli-gious fervor. People laughed at it. They laughed not because they were so certain that God and the Messiah were not dead, but because of the "ersatz" they were being offered as their heirloom. God and the Messiah being replaced by the Workman's Bund of Russia, Poland and Lithuania — the exchange was too ridic-ulous. But one might consider its less humorous, more serious, even tragic aspect. And it is the Christians who have advanced this serio-tragic view, especially the American and German Protestants.

Contemporary fundamentalists have some justification for their bitter struggle with the Modernists. It is not — as in Catholicism or Judaism — a struggle between two dissenting groups, rather it is total war, an attack on God, a war against the "old" and for the "new."

Old, new — it actually sounds like a joke. Can you imagine talking about nature in terms of old and new, or about an old and a new logic? This is, indeed, an indication and a confirmation of the fact that when we stop paying heed to what is being said, concepts begin to lose their meaning, to split into old and new.

This above trend was set in motion by the Germans for national rather than religious reasons. They had arrived at the conviction that the culture of a people must be rounded out, enclosed, with its own center of gravity. A national language is not sufficient; one also needs a national psychology, a national philosophy and a national religion. This was the initial goal that Protestantism pursued. The Roman universal church is centered in Rome but spreads its message throughout the world, using the same rituals and the same language in Paraguay as it does in Comstock. The Protestants countered with the ideal of a national religion, a religion that should adapt itself to each land, each people, each language, and each era.

The Germans have pursued this concept a step further. If their religion is truly a national one, then what is their bond to Christianity? Why should they be tied to a literature that came into being somewhere in the land of Israel, brought forth by a people they dislike? Why should Abraham, Moses and David be their religious heroes? Why should Jesus of Bethlehem be their Messiah? And why should their God be the Jewish God?

The question is a logical one, and they have found a logical answer. Germans began to talk about a "German" God. But these German aspirations faltered in mid-flight. The German God failed to fulfill the hopes and aspirations of his people and the God of the supernatural state won out. And just like the pagan worshipers of the Fiji Islands, the Germans grew angry at their homespun, Prussian god. It is fortunate that they lack icons and holy statues because just like the Fiji Islanders they would surely have smashed them. And thus the Germans remained altogether without a god. Having long ago broken with the "Jewish," the "old" God, and being angry at the new, the "German" one, they were left with no one to praise.

The German idea of a national God immigrated to America as part of the German-Aryan-Prussian ideological baggage, and assumed the name of religious Modernism. Its leader, Father Charles Prentiss Potter of the Unitarian Church, has gradually worked his way through to the idea of an "American" God. He wants a new bible, new religious, holy symbols, a new God. He asks why the old Jews from Palestine should still serve as symbols for the great American democracy. Can one not do without them? Can one not find American religious symbols and leaders? Why not exchange the Jewish Bible with its prophets and its ancient glory for an American bible, a national one? And he proposes a new bible with tales of Washington and Hamilton, Lincoln and Woodrow Wilson. Is John Adams not our modern Deborah? And can Woodrow Wilson not take the place of Jesus Christ?

The nationalist American Modernists go still further, sharply rejecting the entire concept of God as the King of Kings. How un-democratic for an American to address God as king! At least let Him be called the President of Presidents! But even this would be un-American, would absolutely contradict the Monroe Doctrine, which states that no one may interfere in American affairs. The Modernist priest wants a new god, a democratic, American one, which means "God as helper, leader and friend." In summation: God and the Messiah are dead, long live John Adams!

We may let the Protestants fight this out among themselves. This is, after all, their own concern. What has captured my interest and that of all those interested in religio-philosophical questions is the remarkable change that the concept of God has undergone of late. The spiritual culture of our time has become shallow and clarity of thought has given way to sentimentality.

What is really at the heart of the long controversy between Judaism and Christianity? It is not mere Christian mythology, nor historic symbols and legends, for the difference goes deeper and is more radical. It is law against grace. Two world views are facing each other. On one side is a world view based on strict order, on cause and effect, on "because" and "therefore," on reality. On the other side is an idealized and romanticized view of the world, picturing a father surrounded by a beloved family. And when the children disobey and misbehave, the father indulgently forgives them.

Jews, too, of course, have been unable to withstand the lure of miracles. It is, after all, so difficult to renounce a childlike view of the world. Jews also speak of being forgiven. They also indulge in imagining that the judicial verdict can be averted, that the flow of events can be changed, that the order can be overthrown in response to a worshiper's pleas and suffering. But this is not an integral part of Jewish religious thought. This is merely Jewish history, not Jewish religion; it is the folk mind-set not Jewish metaphysics; it is not the foundation of Judaism.

It is, however, the essence of Christianity. Take away the idea of God as friend and helper and the whole structure collapses. This is also the cause of the profound crisis that gradually came into being within Christian religious culture. The first Christians had not yet thrown off the mantle of Judaism; the ancient Christian religion was Judaism with added Christian legends. But the nations never accepted Judaism; it was too stern, too "mercy-less" for them. They adapted only the story, not the idea. Gradually the idea vanished altogether, leaving only the story, only its sentimental interpretation.

Renan was the typical neo-Christian sentimentalist. He did not say anything novel, only what all Christians wanted to hear. His sentimentality flourished, and its fruit began to ripen. Renan's image of Christ as "shepherd," the sweet, sensitive man, the soft, good "son," gradually became associated with God himself. God ceased to be law, order, the beginning of all beginnings and its ultimate source. God himself became a friend, a helper and a leader. Europe is ashamed to put it so bluntly. There the old tradition of a strong, masculine, logical, and disciplined culture is still in force. Whatever may happen there, medieval philosophy, Spinoza and Kant did not lived in vain. They left their mark, shaping European thought.

America, however, is free. The masculine culture has acquired a feminine, sentimental touch. Thought has lost its power; and emotion predominates. And emotion is both seductive and inconstant. Today we feel one way, tomorrow another. Emotion is brutal, egotistical, lacking perspective, and the most sentimental, narrow, perspective-less emotional manifestation is nationalism. Everything is included, even the grandiose, unfathomable, abyss-deep, supra-human idea of God.

Nationalism? Well, what about my defense of the ancient Bible? Is this not also nationalism? Or my need to pay my respects to the prophets Deborah and Isaiah? Maybe. But therein lies the tragedy of the modern Jew: His Jewish essence is forever imbedded in the historic, emotional elements of Judaism. And yet — age, distance, unfamiliarity have raised history above this narrowness.

Philo of Alexandria achieved this, and the great interpreters of Judaism throughout the ages have carried it a step further. They lifted all the historic, time-conditioned elements out of Judaism. Thus, when I think of Job I am not concerned with the man endowed with sheep and servants; that Job has nothing to tell me. But the allegorical Job, the Job who is a pure idea, this Job serves as a symbol for me, just as he has been doing for the long chain of generations before me.

To lift man above his human limitations and place him within the eternal order, which means bringing him to the feet of the *shekhina*, the Divine Presence, this has been the path pursued by Judaism. And by Christianity as well, as long as it remained rooted in Judaism. Everything in the world is, of course, an allegory, the living as well as those who were once alive. Napoleon is an allegory and so is Lincoln, Julius Caesar and even Tsar Nicholas II. But because they are so historically and nationally conditioned, because they are such a part of reality, they are not symbols, they cannot become universal legends. The ancient Greeks tried to make Alexander of Macedonia into a legend, Victor Hugo tried to do so with Napoleon and the Bolsheviks tried with Lenin. But the essence of legends is that they don't grow where they were planted; they come into being on their own, and so do symbols.

Judaism has furnished the world with symbols and, for better or worse, they cannot be plucked out unless one tears out the entire root itself: the concept of

God. And what then? What remains? Nature? Humanity? This merely replaces one word with another.

What does Lord Dansom tell in one of his stories? The gods looked down on the proud city where men had erected lofty towers — and the gods laughed.

The Sixth Death of an Illusion

Not long ago Tchemerinsky, the noted actor and member of the Habimah Theater, told me of the curious events which followed their performance of *The Dybbuk* in Chicago (or perhaps in another American city). Tchemerinsky had acted
in the role of the *tzadik,* and his portrayal of deeply rooted Jewishness, of sincerity and profound faith, had made a strong impression on his audience. It was two
days later that a rich Jew, the president of a synagogue and of a large Jewish organization, approached him with the proposal that the Habimah should perform
every week in the synagogue (I am not sure whether it was to be on a Saturday or
on a Sunday). They should not, however, perform *The Dybbuk* or any other
drama, but rather a "religious play." The actors should enact…religion. Thus,
observant Jews would change their present ritual and infuse it with a new content, adapting it to modern life, or rather, create a new form of worship.
Tchemerinsky shared this conversation with me as one of those "it can happen
only in America" events.

The story is, indeed, both amusing and curious, but just as every jest contains
a kernel of truth, so does this curious event contain an element of reality and of
profound seriousness. In a remarkable fashion we have followed a path that led
through America, through spiritual impoverishment, through the destruction of
old worlds, back to the beginnings. From the cultural bankruptcy which carries
the imprint of American Jewry, the path leads to the original. The wheel has gone
through all its turns and has spun back to its point of departure. Starting with

205

magic, with the dance around the Holy Ark, with the Kohanim with their timbrels and the Levites with their songs, on to spiritual asceticism, through the mysticism of the Kabbalah and the dry intellectualism of the Rambam, through the emotional religiosity of the Hasidim back again to the timbrels and songs, to golden filigree pomegranates; back to illusion. The theater has grown out of religion; religion is making a comeback through the theater.

Back to illusion. What is its nature? One can understand, one can accept, all the concrete manifestations of life because they are the product of their times. But what about the content? There was a time when men were able to understand the illusion of religion, when they danced around the Holy Ark, when they sank to the ground in contrition. These were the outward manifestations of their spirituality, of their faith. But today? What underlies today's illusion? What is the efficacy of an illusion when it is known to be merely a play? And what is the power of a symbol which has lost its meaning?

Tchemerinsky's story came to mind as I was reading a booklet by the old wise man of Europe, Professor Sigmund Freud, the originator of psychoanalysis. The booklet of some ninety pages is titled *The Future of an Illusion*, the illusion being religion. I believe that Freud is one of the greatest minds that our century has produced and one of the wisest of all times. His wisdom consists not merely in being learned, not only in exploring and uncovering a new science. He is also wise in the deepest meaning of the word. He is a man who sees through the veil that shrouds life, that envelops all values. He is a man "who has eyes in the back of his head." This was the source of psychoanalysis.

Psychologists and psychiatrists had wrangled with the definition of "soul" and "spirituality." They had erected barriers between physical and psychic life, they had created "laws," and all of their formulae and systems were of little help. And this was because the psychologists were working with values and with concepts which were themselves problematic. Then came Freud who said: This way won't lead us anywhere. First of all, we must free ourselves from all existing values and concepts and follow the path of modern historians who ask: What is the sense of speculating about the "meaning of history," about its correlations and development, unless we know the historical data. To create a philosophical system is easy; you postulate a hypothesis, you bolster it with facts, and if the facts refuse to support the hypothesis, "well, so much the worse for the facts," as Hegel asserted. But in history, one must first uncover the facts, collect the material, dig, explore, research and only then is one able to construct a theory.

Freud adopted the method of "digging," of uncovering the stories of personal lives, following them to their very beginning. Man and his "spiritual life" begin already in the maternal womb. It is there that one's first motives, one's "humanity," begin. All the rest is development, either normal or abnormal. Throughout his long scientific career, Freud persisted in uncovering facts and in destroying illusions, and so have his disciples. Freud was wiser than most of his followers, who are more aggressive than he but also more superficial.

In his book *Totem and Taboo*, Freud already touched on the subject of religion and tried to understand it by approaching it psychoanalytically. But the subject of the book, the faith of primitive peoples, was treated too scientifically, too theoretically, to catch the interest of broader circles of society, and least of all of those who concern themselves with religious problems. Because such is human nature, we are perfectly satisfied when we see others being criticized but push away all suspicion that the criticism may be leveled at us as well. The generals and officials in St. Petersburg laughed whole-heartedly seeing Gogol's *Inspector General* performed on stage, completely unaware that they were laughing at themselves. Christian theologians are in total agreement with all the criticism of Islam and Buddhism, and Jewish theologians smile widely when they read one of Renan's sharp critiques, or Strauss' "Destruction of Christianity." And none of them deem it possible that the criticism could some day reach them. "Me? Why should someone criticize me, since I am in the right?" But when the ax of analysis, of merciless criticism does fall on them, then they cry out to the heavens, then they are beside themselves with rage.

Theologians of all denominations subjected Professor Freud's booklet to their fierce anger. Protestant ministers and Catholic priests were gnashing their teeth, religiously affiliated psychoanalysts expressed regrets at their mentor's "error," and even the rabbis girded their loins and joined in the "holy war" against the apostate from Vienna. It was a truly wonderful comedy, with all the "spiritual leaders" falling upon Freud, declaring that he does not understand theology, advising him to stick to what he knows, etc., etc. Just as if their concept of religion was as self-evident as a mathematical formula, just as if God could speak only to those who had graduated from a seminary, attained lucrative positions, and were delivering weekly sermons about "love to mankind," "God's grace," etc. Old Freud is sure to smile at this illusion as well as at the professional saints.

What was it, actually, that Freud said? Not more than Spinoza before him or many other thinkers of former times, the only difference being that he said it very simply, avoiding obfuscating terminology and remaining scrupulously objective in following all the paths no matter where they might lead. Spinoza stopped at a certain barrier. He denied Judaism but made some complimentary gestures toward Christianity, albeit without making any concessions to it. And even though he basically denied the religious concept of God, the word still remained a part of his vocabulary. Voltaire attacked both Judaism and Christianity, but he had prided himself on being a "Deist," i.e. having the "pure faith." One way or another, the matter of faith remained untouched. Freud, however, went closer to the question. He applied the ax to the very root and asked: What is faith? And he answered: an illusion.

"The scientific mind," Freud says, "pauses for a while when it faces religious problems. It hesitates. But in the end it steps over the barrier. In that process there is no standstill. The more men know, the more they liberate themselves from religious faith. First from the ancient, shocking dramatics and then from their mysterious appeal as well."

He analyzed, in broad terms, the ideas that produced the religious frame of mind. He pointed out their roots, how they came into being, and why they grew into an illusion. This illusion had, at one time, been needed to protect culture and human society, a need which gradually disappeared. And he asked the "learned ones": Why do you persist in holding on to an illusion? You do not believe in it. You know that this is only a form of cultural development which had once been needed but which is now invalid. But you are afraid that the downfall of the religious illusion would bring about the downfall of the entire culture, that streams of humanity would overrun the earth and that human society would be destroyed. "I," said Freud, "am free of that servitude." He did not share this fear, he had faith in culture, in the power of the intellect; he had faith in the creative power of truth. He did not preach Deism or any other "pure faith." Nor did he preach atheism. He only stated facts and demanded that modern man deal honestly with himself, whatever the outcome may be. This, he said, will lead us to no harm because a new power has in the meantime come into being: science.

The wise man has spoken the truth. As unpleasant as this may be for professional theologians, the fact is that today's faith is not faith, it is merely an illusion, which is more and more perceived as such, with people fooling themselves less and less. Men have ceased to believe, and priests and rabbis must, therefore, use extraneous measures in order to maintain their institutions: dance, plays, parades, ornate words and thoughts gathered from the four corners of the world. Yet all these are, basically, manifestations of self-deception. The yearning for the infinite, for the mystic feeling of "being one" with the universe, of the "I and Thou" and of "partnership," has nothing to do anymore with historic religions, notwithstanding the preaching of certain modern theologians, starting with Christian ones and followed by some American Jewish imitators. All this is akin to a rooster's inability to step out of his white, "magic" chalk-drawn circle. But this is a thing of the past, and once the rooster looses its fear the circle looses its magic power and only the chalk-line remains.

And yet! That mystical feeling of an eternal cohesion, of generations following generation, of the "I and Thou," how can it, how shall it, express itself? Only in science, only rationally? But the mind is so complex that what we call the "intellect" illuminates merely the surface. And what lies beneath the surface? To be sure, religion is a mere inheritance. To be sure, the intellect is the antennae, is the part of us that thinks, that explores, it is "the mover," as Aristotle would say. But sooner or later, and usually sooner, our explorations lead us to a stone wall. We cannot go any further, we cannot find a path to…to ourselves.

It seems to me that the final word about religious life has not yet been said. Chesterton, the sharp, witty critic of everything that is "obvious," made an intelligent observation in his last work, *The Eternal Man.* "Faith has died already five times and today it is still standing in our way, it is even growing." And he advises that we should not wait for the death of faith; we may look out for its shortcomings, its stumblings, but not expect its death. Meaning, accept it as a given, as the stars, the earth, as life. He may be right. We do not mind the stars, we accept them as we accept the world, as it is, even with its illusions.

But this very "acceptance," does it not contain the death of the illusion, its sixth death? And this illusion, it gives us no answer and no satisfaction. It does not offer us the bliss that men are so passionately seeking, without even knowing what this "bliss" is. What is the value of such an illusion?

The question is still awaiting an answer.

The Unknown Sanctuary

In Paris — in the city of all possibilities, all contradictions — one can also find the following curious, rare phenomenon: a man who is truly serious about his Jewishness, a man for whom Judaism is new and fresh, is an experience. There are, of course, in Paris as everywhere else in the world, enough Jews, both native and foreign-born. There are Jews from Southern France, from Alsace, Polish and Lithuanian Jews, rich and poor ones, those who are wholly, half or a quarter assimilated, and those who are half or one-eighth nationalist. You can find everything Jewish there except for one thing: freshness. Max Nordau divided Jews into two categories, dubbing one the "We are also Jews" group, and the other the "Jewish food Jews." But there is another category, the "Thus it must be, what can we do?" Jews. Thus we are born, thus we become, it is not our fault, it is our lot, our fate, let it be so, one must bear one's yoke, smile in the face of adversity, make a virtue out of necessity. And every other Jew, perhaps even every Jew, thinks, and sometimes says, "Why me? Why did I have to be born a Jew and bear this onerous heritage?" And even when he utters the prayers of thanks for having been chosen amongst all the nations he thinks: How much better it would have been if the "choice" had not taken place at all.

It is so natural, so human, to grow tired of oneself. Always the same; the same face, the same movements, and the same old reactions to the outer world. This is, perhaps, the only, and the most important, human argument against eternal life, even against the theories of eternal youth. Because man's greatest fortune lies in the fact that he undergoes change — today is different from yesterday, and each tomorrow is shrouded in uncertainty. How unbearable it would be if our reflection in the mirror were never to change. And this is what is happening to Judaism; it has grown old and matter-of-fact, it has become a habit. One has become so used to it that one scarcely notices its, one is not interested, no longer inquisitive. The only thing one does is draw up accounts, rush to conclusions, and come closer — one way or another — to a resolution, to an ending.

Yet suddenly you become aware of a strange phenomenon. There is in Paris a man who often attends the great synagogue on the Avenue Des Victoires, almost daily, for whom Judaism is still new. A Jew who does not look Jewish, who walks and talks in ways which proclaim him as belonging to a different people, an alien race. You would never have assumed that the old Frenchman is a Jew, and, furthermore, a pious, deeply devoted one. And little wonder, because he truly does not correspond to our definition of a Jew, nor to the image harbored by non-Jews. He is, in fact, a Frenchman from an old French family from Lyons. His name is Aime Palliere, and he is a convert.

Parisian Jews of my acquaintance had told me about him earlier, in the joking way Jews often use when talking about converts, and with the assertions that whatever a convert may have been before his conversion, immediately after, he becomes a beggar full of complaints against the Jewish people, and becomes a new burden to the community. So who needs them? And it is, indeed, a difficult question to answer. The Christians, for their part, do not pose such questions. They are happy when they succeed in "saving" a Jewish soul, and they derive much satisfaction from it. The news that a Jew became an apostate is spread throughout the land, is trumpeted about by the priest and by the apostate, and the church rejoices, especially the Catholic one.

Such a "saved soul" was Alphonse Ratisbonne, a French Jew, one of the minor, fourth-rate writers, a free thinker, a universalist. One day he chanced to enter a church, remained there alone for a minute, experienced a moment of grace and walked out an ardent, fanatic Christian. Here is another case: One day when the organist of a church fell ill just an hour before services were to start, and a substitute had to be found, the priest approached the nearest organ-player at hand, a certain Herman, to play just this one time. And this one time was sufficient for the Jewish organist. He left the church a Christian and soon became a priest — Father Herman.

The Christians know how to make use of the Jews who come over to them. They use them as a shield against their own non-believers. When the Catholic orthodoxy, for instance, needs a defender who will gladly shed his last drop of blood fighting modernism, it turns to a professor at the Catholic University in Vienna, a Jew from Galicia, who became Father Komer, and this "Father" lectures at the Viennese university about the inferno, describing it in great detail, and bringing forth a wealth of information, just as if he had spent years of his life there. Then there was the time when the University of Zurich decided to discontinue a course on philosophy because it was Catholic propaganda in disguise. The Catholic professor giving the course was a Jew from Odessa, Robert Zaichik.

But Jews cannot even do this for their own benefit. They cannot even make use of the rare times when destiny smiles upon them, when someone from the outside world becomes caught up in the Jewish stream. We think, we want to convince ourselves, that this is due to arrogance, to racial pride, yet deep inside we know that the real reason is contempt for ourselves, our feelings of inferiority. Those who told me about the convert from Lyons did so with a smile, and I shared that smile. But now this convert, Aime Palliere, has published a book, an autobiography. And I saw a vastly different picture, not a man who could evoke a smile or a pitying shrug of the shoulders, but a man who evoked profound respect and admiration. This Frenchman from Lyons, this heir to an old and beautiful culture, was able to perceive the "unknown sanctuary"; it attracted him, and he remained there. Indeed, the title of his autobiography is *The Unknown Sanctuary.*

He describes his journey for us. His point of departure — a very characteristic one for a non-Jew — was a picture book. He had, in his childhood, leafed through a Bible illustrated by Gustave Doré. It was a large, leather-bound folio with beautiful, fantastically naive pictures. Gustave Doré had painted the old Hebrews in such magnificent garb as we could never have imagined. To us, even Abraham, Isaac and Jacob appear as Jews from Yeshiva, with long beards, a long coat and yarmulke, slippers and perhaps even a red kerchief. But Doré perceived the Patriarchs in all their Oriental, sunny, shining splendor, radiating majestic superhuman greatness. The young Aime was enraptured by the pictures and fell in love with the Hebrews. It never occurred to him that the Brothers Kahn who were his classmates or the Jewish merchants or workers from Lyons had any relationship at all to the Hebrews depicted in Doré's Bible. The former were "Jews," petty merchants whom one did not like very much; the latter were "Hebrews," noblemen. But it appears, as a Christian writer put it, that there are not only souls who are "innately" Christian, but also those who are "innately" Jewish. And such a soul dwelt within Aime Palliere. He was drawn to religious thought. His mother had a dream of his entering the priesthood, but Aime was drawn to the synagogue. He learned Hebrew, he got to know Jews, he visited rabbis, he continued to read, to explore, to search, until he came upon a man whose words captured his interest, the well-known rabbi from Livorno, Eliahu ben Amozegh, one of the most remarkable personalities brought forth by Italian Jewry before it succumbed to almost total somnolence. He was an opponent of Samuel David Luzzatto, the famous rationalist and *maskil* who defended Jewish thought against Renan's contempt for Judaism. Ben Amozegh was not a profound thinker, but an original one. His passionate temperament found expression in a poetic style; he was the ultimate Spanish Jew, with all the highs and lows of the Sephardim.

Ben Amozegh developed a remarkable theory of Judaism and the Jewish people. He was the first one, even before Achad Ha'am, to have introduced priesthood as a function of Jewish life. What is Judaism? he had asked, and he answered: There are two levels of Judaism, two categories. The first is the universal one, which includes all of humanity. This is "Noah-ism." The commandments to the sons of Noah are the foundation of humanity's relationship to the universe and to mankind. Man needs no other principles than Noah-ism, which include all religious outlooks on the world. But in order to keep Noah-ism alive, there must be a second category of people who are willing to shoulder the heavy burden of being its zealous defenders. There must be priests. The priests are subject to all of the laws, all of the restrictions, all of the burdens. For them Judaism is as tradition has established it. Jews are the religious, spiritual guardians of the world; this was their role. Aime Palliere's thirsty soul drank a few drops from the ancient cup of Jewish mysticism, and these drops led him to becoming a Jew in the fullest sense of the word, in the sense of ben Amozegh, and, I would say, in the only possible sense. Because if we do not raise Judaism to a universal category, if we do not lead it back toward finding a new approach to culture, then our question is not satisfactorily answered.

Aime Palliere found an answer for his soul. He discovered what we do not see anymore, he perceived a fresh source, a holiness, where we see only an old synagogue and a drained pool. It was not the first such occurrence. About 15 to 20 years ago Martin Buber began translating into German Hasidic stories and legends by the Baal Shem Tov, Rabbi Nachman of Bratslav, and others. All of us, his friends and colleagues, smiled at this strange occupation on the part of a proponent of modern culture. Of what import are those mildewed names, those legends of bygone times? A fine German translation and a good introduction are of course very nice, but to what purpose? Who needs them? And yet, it turns out, they are needed; we see that the "strange work" has been fruitful. All at once Germans became aware that Jews also have their mysticism, that Judaism contains more than the shallowness of a Geiger and other German-Jewish apologists and explainers. They suddenly saw that Judaism has a countenance of its own, a life of its own, that it is a world which rests on its own foundations. They were surprised, and they were not the only ones.

We, too, began to ponder the meaning of *kavanah* and of *tzimtzum*, to ponder the beauty of the realm of Jewish spirituality. The alien mirror led us back to our own. We discovered ourselves. It is necessary, from time to time, to rediscover the "unknown sanctuary." We need to step back from it far enough so that it does become unknown, unfamiliar, loses its matter-of-factness, and then to re-approach it, experience it anew, repossess it if we can. It is possible that some will not be able to find it; they do not have to, they are not meant for it. But for the ones who will find it, who will discover it, it will be an experience and an opening. It will be a fresh source.

The renewal and rejuvenation of Judaism can come only from the converts. But not just from converts like Palliere who came to us from the Christian environment, but from Jewish converts, from those who distanced themselves from Judaism, put it aside, and who, in order to see it more clearly, had submitted themselves to the penance of straying, of going out, far, far, away, in order to find their way back. Whether they will do so remains to be seen. For now, the search is sufficient.

The Hidden Away Ezra

Scanning the shelves of Christian theological libraries, you will find a thick volume, the *Apocrypha*, the hidden books, which speak in Greek and Latin, but whose source, spirit and content are Jewish. They are part of the ancient, rich Jewish literature that the sages of the time had consigned to be hidden in a secret place, called the *genizah*. Who made the decision as to which books were to be hidden and to what end, is one of the mysteries of Jewish history, and one of Judaism's paradoxes. A people that has always prided itself on its spirit, and on its Book, a people that had renounced everything, all beauty, all ease of living, for the sake of spirituality, this people had the strange idea of doing away with a crucial piece of its literature. Old and accomplished at a time when other nations had been still in their cradle, this people, filled with experience and deep wisdom, had denounced its own creations.

Babylon and Assyria had their songs, tales, plays, scientific explorations and travel descriptions, while Egypt had amassed its treasures and Greece had produced a mirror image of itself. Only the Jews had banned, erasing from its folk memory, all things that did not carry the stamp of holiness; everything that, for one reason or another, had been deemed unsuitable for inclusion in the Holy Writ. But for what reason? It is truly difficult to understand why Proverbs or the Song of Songs or Job were included in the Bible, while various other books were not. Actually, their inclusion might have proved a more effective hiding place.

Rabbi Akiba wanted to put Kohelet into the *genizah*, and only the stature of its legendary author stayed his hand.

Thus it was that ninety-nine-percent of its creative output was lost to the Jewish people. Only twenty-four books remained, along with some fragments rescued by Christian theologians in Syria, among them the most remarkable ancient Jewish document, the Fourth Book of Ezra. There exist various translations, in Greek, Latin, Ethiopian and Armenian, but no one has seen the original text. One hypothesis gave birth to another, the most generally accepted one being that a Hellenistic Jew, steeped in Greek culture, had written the book in Roman times, following the destruction of the Second Temple, and had, according to an old tradition of attributing current writings to ancient personages, signed it with the pseudonym Ezra.

The Book of Ben Sirah was also discovered in the *genizah* and was, as it were, put back into the "womb of Israel" — or, rather, restored to a new life, to an organic cohesion with the Jewish spirit. It was, indeed, miraculous the way Solomon Schechter discovered the Hebrew original in the Cairo Genizah, located in the attic of the old Cairo synagogue, in between crumbling pages of old prayer books. The fate of The Fourth Book of Ezra was less dramatic. A Jewish scholar took pity on it and freed it from its apocryphal, Christian-theological prison. Dr. Aaron Kaminka liberated not only the text but also its author. Actually, it had always been clear that Ezra — our Ezra, the scribe, the builder of our religious system, the actual shaper of the historical Jewish configuration of Biblical books, the politician and lawgiver — that this realist and rationalist could not have been the author of the mystical poem that bears his name. The book itself contains a hint and an indication. The Syrian text, for instance, introduces the work as the "writings of Ezra the Scribe, who is called Shaltiel: 'I, Shaltiel, who am also Ezra....'" But why should Ezra be called Shaltiel? The Midrashic interpreters began to explore this question, and a legend began to grow up around Ezra, whose real name was said to have been Shaltiel and who had been a member of an aristocratic family in exile in Babylonia.

Upon his return to Jerusalem, Shaltiel took the name of Ezra and set out to discharge his mission. But the legend does not correspond with historical reality, or with the personality of Ezra the Scribe. Dr. Kaminka, in his turn, endeavored to solve the problem in a very original way. He posited the hypothesis of an error, the name "Ezra" being merely a misreading of the actual name "Assyr Shaltiel," with the name Assyr, which appears in the Syrian and Arabic texts, having been translated into Asra, which in subsequent translations became Ezra. But who, then, was this Assyr Shaltiel? Dr. Kaminka has "discovered" him, too: He was no other than Prince Assyr Shaltiel, the son of last king of Judea, a prince born in exile, a prince in captivity. Thirty years after the destruction of the Temple, years full of the pain of exile, the poetic prince was moved to write a poem of deep pessimism and despair, a poem of great pathos and profound humanity.

This is the hypothesis of Dr. Kaminka, and I do hope that it is correct. It has the excitement of a historical discovery and the magic of awakening, the awakening of a sleeping prince, the legendary Prince of Judea. The ancient theological mist dissipates, and the ancient forgotten picture acquires color and comes to life. At the rivers of Babylon sits a young prince, pouring out his sorrow and his dreams, pouring it out in a song of Zion. And as he sings, his vision transcends his historical reality, the fate of his people and his land, which become part of a universal drama, part of a tragedy enacted by God. All the questions raised by life, all the manifestations of cultural growth, are here represented as part of the historical phenomenon which is called Judaism, which contains within itself all the challenges that life poses, all the manifestations of human cultural development. He sees, then, not a small people from the hills of Judea that has lost its independence, with himself merely a captive prince (such events were rather commonplace in those times, and Babylon was full of exiles). He sings of mankind searching for the meaning of life which it had lost, searching with passion and with yearning and demanding an elucidation of the mystery of the world. He sings of man who had lost the thing he had loved so much, and who cannot reconcile himself to his fate.

I read chapter after chapter of the magnificent Hebrew translation. Dr. Kaminka has achieved an exquisite artistic feat in drawing the exiled prince in his native, linguistic garment, and I begin to understand why the sages of the time had consigned this book into the *genizah*. Assyr Shaltiel, the Prince of Judea, asks too many questions and leaves them unanswered. His forehead is deeply creased and will not relinquish its frown. He is not to be soothed by the hackneyed answers of Jewish theology and metaphysics. This is a Job who refuses all consolation and remains unimpressed even by the cosmogonic argument, which challenges the doubter with its "Where were you when the world was created?" And he keeps on asking, "Why, oh God, do you dislike the Jewish people? Why have you delivered us into the hands of so many enemies?" And when an angel asks, "Do you care more for the people than for their Creator?" the prince whispers, "No, but my pain cries out from within me." He cannot disguise his despair. "To what purpose was I born? Why did my mother's womb not become my grave, to save me from witnessing the suffering of Jacob and the sorrow of Israel?" And he probes still further. "What will bring the end of Jewish sorrow, and when will it come?" He receives the mystical, magnificent, dramatic answer. "One world ends with Esau, the second begins with Jacob. Do not ask about the interval between the heel and the hand."

The visionary, the questioner, is dissatisfied with the obscure answer. He probes further, deeper, and the problem of one nation grows into a universal ethical problem. Worlds come into being and die out, and sins are being punished. But why? Wherein does man's guilt lie? All men feel sorrow, but the cattle in the field are enjoying their life. Children of men sigh and weep, but the cows and sheep are content, and thus they are better off than we are. They do not await judgment, and they know no suffering. And what does it avail us knowing that things will be better in some distant future, when our present life is so full of affliction? To these steely questions the angel offers various answers, hesitatingly, as if aware that they are mere subterfuges and that all that he says can be encapsulated in two basic ideas. The first one is: "When the Supreme One created the world and man, He had already pronounced the judgment and formulated His law." This is the mathematical, the hidden argument which deals with eternal matters. The second idea deals with man, with time, with his limited lifespan and with morality. "I will come to those who will come to me." This is an ancient Jewish concept that had found its best and briefest formulation in the old saying: "If you enter my house, I shall enter yours." This is the theme of the covenant, the tie between man and God. "I give, you give — we are partners."

This feeling of partnership gives rise to the elitist, I am almost tempted to say Nietzschean, concept of the superman. The angel discloses the secret to the visionary that "This world was given to the many; the world to come will be given to the elite." In other words, the historical process is one of selectivity, of choice. Not everything that exists is worthy of existence. Life must be earned. Thirty years after the destruction of the First Temple these thoughts were written down by Assyr, the Prince of Judea, the eternal prisoner of the world, as he sat on the shores of the rivers of Babylon. He meditated and experienced metaphysical visions. He posed questions, and the answers did not satisfy him. This is why the scholars, the sages of succeeding times, had hidden him away. They were frightened by the breath of his reach; they grew dizzy looking into the depth of the Jewish spirit. They knew that no man and no people can survive atop a mountain or in the depths of an abyss, that one can live neither in elation nor in despair. They had wanted to save Jews for life that, its imperfections notwithstanding, was still life.

But now the Prince of Judea has arisen from its Biblical tomb and asked: "To what end?" And his voice resounds from the depths: "Has Esau's world come to an end already? Has Jacob's world finally begun?" And today, just as three thousand years ago, comes the answer: Between the heel and the hand, do not raise any more questions, Assyr, do not ask, you imprisoned one, because the answer has not yet been given." And the Prince sleeps on, dreaming his transcendent dream of the world to come, a world hidden in the folds of time.

E Finita La Commedia?

Does this mean that the comedy is finished, the curtain is lowered, and the spectators may applaud? Does this mean that still another chapter has ended, the chapter of Messianism? It had begun with the golem, with the lump of clay that, on a dark night in Prague, the Maharal kneaded and shaped, forcing it to become man. And going through stages of ecstasy, faith, doubt and despair, the Maharal arrived at the final conclusion that the golem is the Messiah, that the Messiah and the golem are one and the same. Not the powerful Messiah ben Joseph, or the kind, compassionate Messiah ben David — neither reason nor the heart should rule the world — but the golem. And so the dream of countless generations ends in a heap of dust.

Ah, listen:

> Ah, listen, listen some more
> To the wonders of the small Messiah.
> Once there was a clump of clay,
> Once there was lifeless matter
> Hidden in the clump of clay,
> In the darkness of lifeless matter.
> And the clay was dreaming
> Of a smiling face,

> Of a caressing hand,
> Of a kiss from warm lips.
> Thus had also dreamt
> Moses in the desert,
> Hanania in the desert;
> The same dream
> Had the son of David in the desert.

Thus sings Jossele, the golem of Prague, to the many people who had come from the four corners of the world — he sings the song of redemption, at the Messiah's festive meal. This is how H. Leivick ends his struggle with Messianism and the golem dream. He has begun it as an epic, a lyrical tragedy, and has ended it as a comedy. He knows this is true, and so he gives his new Messiah drama, his Messianic fantasy, a very symbolic title, "The Redemption Comedy," subtitled "The Golem Dreams."

Composed as a dramatic poem, it is a drama in its style and structure, in its scenes, pictorial descriptions, dialogues, and even its dialectic. It is also very confusing, and part of the essence of a drama is the need to arrive at a conclusion. And when the way is a contorted zigzag, then the human characters remain nebulous, mere silhouettes and marionettes, and do not attain the status of living human beings.

And thus it is in Leivick's comedy-drama. The grace, the lyricism of the beautiful golem legend has melted away, and it has become an acceptable folk tale. Yet I am overstepping my bound. I am not interested in making any critical literary analysis of the drama, for this is not the way I want to approach the problem Leivick has posed, the most important problem of our time and, therefore, of concern to me and demanding attention from all of us. Leivick is, perhaps the only Jewish poet whose ear is attuned to what our time is telling us, and is one of the very few, in the Jewish world, who is struggling with it. And, therefore, it is not the fit of the costume that matters, but the body beneath the costume, that of our tortured, banal, miserable "redemption generation."

It is no accident that it is during the last fifteen years that the Messiah idea has spread so widely among Jews, as well as throughout the entire world, in every country and in all nations. Everywhere there are eyes that search, hands that are stretched out, lips thirsting to kiss the hem of the Messiah's robe. The air is filled with Hosannas.

Up until 1918 men had believed in the law; after 1918 they began to believe in the will — the will that moves mountains, that leads us from all the valleys filled with misery to the lighted mountaintop where miracles are performed. Leonid Andreyev, the deeply intuitive and mystical Russian poet, had cried out "Come Master, come Redeemer," at the time when all his horizons were covered with fog. And, emerging from the fog, he had seen the apocalyptic figure of Lenin. His outcry had come not out of faith, not out of a joyous expectation, but out of profound despair and infinite bitterness. A world was being destroyed. Where once there had been some kind of order, a system, a structure, there now was chaos. And here comes someone and says: "I will rebuild, I know how to save you." And so one responds: "Good, come lead, and let there be an end to it!" And a wave of a new faith in man swept the world, a belief in magic. Magic is not like mysticism, which, undefined and impossible to grasp, hides from life, as if behind a veil. Magic is based on the belief of primitive human beings that man can over-rule the Law. It is summarized, if you like, in an old Jewish saying: "God orders, and the wise man ignores it."

It is, actually, a remarkable cultural-psychological phenomena that just as all faith systems are wavering, it is the most primitive religious concept that has assumed a central position — that of Messianism. It is one of the most extrane-ous concepts of all religions, because it is so old, so archaic, so primitive. A Chris-tological concept that was already at the birth of Christianity a recidivism, a return to a forgotten, surpassed beginning. Jews and the cultured peoples of the Greek-Roman Western lands had already come up with a concept of a universal system, of an order and a law that no one could change — no one could be a sub-stitute for anyone else; no one could redeem anyone else. It is a system of respon-sibility and of human maturity. Then there came primitive people who rebelled against taking on responsibility. They wanted someone else to make decisions; they wanted to be led; they wanted to follow. They were afraid of loneliness, afraid of facing the secret of the universe. Let there be a partition between us and the world, they cried, and they unrolled a curtain, painting on it the head of the Messiah.

Little by little, the curtain was lifted, and the horizon became visible. And thus it remained as long as things were proceeding normally and life was bearable. But when a catastrophe occurs, then the curtain with the Messiah head is once again lowered to face the world. And all over the world there arises the call for the Mes-siah, in all languages and all variations. All the believers and all the unbelievers, all those who are discouraged, lost and despairing come under the spell of a new illu-sion: redemption. And even among the Jews there have been many who responded to the magic of the word. And yet the Jews are the only ones who have constantly distanced themselves from Messianism. The Messiah does, of course, live in legends and in poetry, but for the living, thinking mind he is a mere dream, without any definite shape, hovering somewhere until the advent of the end of days. And even then we cannot be sure who will be redeemed and how. Will might prevail or will kindness? Innocence or guilt? Will the redeemer be the Messiah ben Joseph, or the Messiah ben David?

Jewish thought, however, decided to make peace with the redemption motif, to take it seriously and fill its own vacuum with it. For not only had we lost the will to change the world, we had also come to scorn the world. Hastily, enthusiastically we latched onto the national redemptive motif. But we soon came to feel that God is not contained in the land or in the language, and that this is not the beginning of redemption. Then hopes were rekindled in the fire and the social melting pot of the revolution, and again a voice was heard: God is not in the fiery storm; this is not redemption.

Where, then, is it to be found? In the ancient revelation of Elijah, in the "still, small voice," in the purified and profound, humanely responsible solitude? The dialogue of our generation revolves around this question. It is a dialogue that does not lead to an answer and has not yet achieved a polished artistic formulation. And thus it is with the comedy of redemption by the highly sensitive poet Leivick. Here each of the Messiahs has his own aims. The son of Joseph wants power, justice and order. Hanania, the son of David, the desert Messiah, wants purity and innocence. The son of Joseph kills a world, and Hanania rescues the world by chopping off the head of Joseph's son with his own pure hands. And having covered his hands with blood, he, too, is unable to do what he wants to do, to liberate the world from blood and death. He must atone for the blood he has shed, even if it was shed with justification. Because the law prevails, the law must still be obeyed. And yet, ancient Jewish mysticism says: When the Messiah comes, the world will be freed from the law by compassion. But is this possible? And when Hanania the son of David falls, who will replace him? So we are returning to the old source, not to any idea, or to any one man, or to any passing event, but to the eternal, the constant, the golem — the clump of clay that becomes a body, the blood that turns into wine.

"Humanity is groaning underneath the yoke. It does not know that its future depends on itself. It alone can determine whether it wants to go on living. And it must, furthermore, ask itself whether it wants to go on living in a way that shall be felt on our rebellious planet, as it fulfills the world's essential function, to create gods." This is the way the great mystical realist, Henri Bergson, ends his last important work, *The Two Sources of Morality and Religion.* And it focuses our attention on the need to make decision: whether to choose subjection to the tyranny of magic and of Messianism, or the freedom and responsibility of mysticism.

H. Leivick had struck a bargain with Messianism — the golem must first become a human being. Redemption will come only when the golem achieves the transformation. The comedy of redemption before and up to his time was enacted by various Messiahs wanting to redeem man, not knowing that man did not yet exist on earth. The golem may, perhaps, not become man until the end of days, but what choice do we have? We must wait.

The Tragedy of Hasidism

✦

"One must not age" — Rabbi Nachman of Bratislav

Ever since Jews had begun to "modernize" Hasidism, to make it fashionable, to fill the press with boring and, at times, rather ludicrous stories, I have found myself reacting to it very negatively. It really annoys me to read, again and again, about the holy legends, the eulogies of the Baal Shem Tov and of all the other "pious Jews," of their miracles and their wise sayings. It seems to me that this is diminishing their stature, akin to taking a precious stone and cutting it into small pieces, or to opening an expensive bottle of perfume and pouring it into cheap samplers until the perfume loses its aroma and itself becomes dirt cheap.

The question arises: If this is Hasidism, if all that the journalists are telling us is true, then what is the value of Hasidism? Why should one disinter it? Why should one impose its spirit on the Jewish soul? Are we children waiting to be told stories? Or are we, perhaps, so old that we are living mostly in the past, even if that past should have been a foolish and a meaningless one? This is the tragedy of the Jewish mind. It does not move from the spot, it is spinning in a circle and always comes back, always returns. Where to? We do not know it ourselves any-more; we only feel that something is out of order; we only see that the wheels have gone rusty. And yet, if one looks closer into Hasidism, if one goes directly to the source, there opens up before us another, unexpected perspective. Hasidism appears to us in quite a different guise.

In front of me lies a Hebrew book, *Sefer Ha-Hasidut*, (*The Book of Hasidism*), by the noted Bible scholar Abraham Cohane. It is, truly, a book of and not about Hasidim; nor is it a semi-fictional, trivialized interpretation and adaptation of the idiosyncratic phenomenon that is Hasidism. It brings us just the unadorned text, the original itself. It is an anthology of Hasidic literature from the Baal Shem Tov to Rabbi Nachman of Bratislav. There are excerpts from books, letters, legends, aphorisms, everything without commentaries, in their old, pure form. And this is as it should be. Hasidism is not folklore, nor is it a precocious form of literary art. The Baal Shem Tov and his disciples did not live and struggle to have mediocre people retell their lives and turn them into foolish tales to entertain small children and childish adults. They had intensely pursued a goal; but what goal was it? What had constituted the core and the root of their soul?

I must confess that this book has given me a different slant on quite a few things. I have always been rather partial to Rabbi Levi Itzhak of Berditchev, as he used to refer to himself. He is, of course, the most popular figure in the gallery of saints to whom Jews have been genuflecting in the past few years. His songs are being sung, and his cited prayers contain so much compassion, sweetness and freshness that I wish I could visualize what he had looked like, this remarkable man who had started out as revolutionary and had ended up as a worshipper in the synagogue of his small city.

He starts out with "Good morning to You, Lord of the universe. I, Levi Itzhak from Berditchev, have come to you with a question: What do You want from us? Why are You looking with disfavor on the Jews?" Strong, forceful, heart-rending words, right? And how does he end it? "*Iskadal v' iskadash....*" "May Your name be exalted forever." The beginning does not fit in with the ending, has no connection with it. The harsh question remains unanswered. And if one does not get an answer, why persist in posing the question? If one lacks the courage to pursue a matter to its final conclusion, of what use is the bold beginning? Is this not like gathering all one's strength, flexing all one's muscles, to pick up a straw?

He proceeds to manifest his religious ecstasy in appealing to God, extolling God, vowing to serve God. These words are constantly on his lips. But who is the God whom he serves, whom he seeks, for whom he yearns? The more one reads, the more unintelligible, pathological, hysterical he becomes. The rabbi of Berditchev was unable to call on God without being caught up in enthusiasm and manifesting it by leaping, whirling around, dropping to the floor. It was a kind of dervishism in its most exalted form. Even rabbis could not accept it, were unable to understand it. They could not accept the exaggeration, the lack of boundaries, the personal appeal to God. Judaism maintains a distance from God. There is only the all encompassing Torah, and therein lies also its strength. The rabbi of Berditchev had eliminated the distance.

Can you imagine anything more un-Jewish than the story of the merchant, told about the saintly Rabbi Levi Itzhacon? It was the eve of Yom Kippur, and the rabbi does not let his congregation go home. He sits down on a bench and summons Leibushon, the most important merchant of the city. "You are an important merchant?" he asks.

"Yes."

"Can you undertake a business deal for me?"

"Of course."

"All right, this is my business. I want to make a deal with the Master of the Universe. I am offering Him my sins in exchange for a pardon from Him. What will be my profit?" Leibushon gets confused, does not know what to answer. The rabbi answers himself: "My profits are children, life, wealth — and all this I give away to the people of Israel."

Beautiful? Perhaps. But is this religion? Is this Judaism? Or is this theater, perhaps even simply hysteria? Who had given him the authority to pull the Jewish soul down to the market place, to the level of striking bargains? For the one who lifts the market place to the level of heaven pulls heaven down to the level of the market place. And this is what Hasidism has done. In clothing their words and parables in mystical splendor, they have abased and trivialized the Jewish spirit. They have diminished not expanded it.

This was the work of the rabbi of Berditchev, of the "smooth as silk" Leib Sharham, and of many other "saints" who had stepped out of Ukrainian Judaism onto a Jewish side road, an overgrown, thorny road. They did not enrich Jewish thought; they have hindered its development by trivializing it. Dancing upon tables in their stockings, repeating wild, inane newspaper reports, making up stories…This is what they had brought into Jewish culture. And what has remained? A few songs, a few stories, an unintelligible legend, and a few ashes from an extinct straw fire.

It would be most interesting, most instructive, to analyze, critically and psychologically, step by step, character trait by character trait, every one of the great Hasidim, all the various figures in the Hasidic movement. There is a difference between the Ukrainian, the Polish and the Lithuanian rabbis. The Ukrainian one is pure emotion, is more given to folklore, more a child of nature. The Polish one is better dressed, better mannered, more learned. But the most interesting type of them all is the one from Lithuania, represented by Rabbi Shneur Zalman from Lodi, the compiler of the *Tania*. He had connected mysticism with its thought process; he had molded feeling into a system.

"I have no need of a Garden of Eden, I have no need of a world-to-come, I want You, just You!" says one of the prayers in the *Tania*. And this is, perhaps, the highest, the most mature expression of Hasidic thought, the only possible vision of the path it had wanted, but had been unable, to carve out. The Garden of Eden, the world to come, the entire Jewish mythology, had suddenly lost its grandeur, and was discarded. "I only want You!" This thought, this search, this striving to uncover the secret, this had become its central point, its focus. But it is only a beginning. If the mythology has become worthless, why not go beyond it? If the only thing that is essential is God, then why carry on with the entire traditional ballast, the whole load that Judaism had put on the shoulders of Jews? You cannot find Him by reciting prayers or learning *Gemarah*. And why tie up the history of the world and the mystery of the universe with the Jews?

The *Tania* posed this question, not knowing where it must lead. It, too, had contented itself with incomplete, ready-made answers, had stopped in midstream. Only one among them could not stop, had suffered from the self-imposed boundaries, had felt the great spiritual tragedy of Jewish mysticism, of its imprisonment, and that was Rabbi Nachman of Bratislav. Traditional Judaism had condemned him, and, perhaps, justly so. A story is told about a Hasid coming to Rabbi Talnet to ask whether it was all right to marry a girl from Bratislav. Rabbi Talnet had answered: "This would be a misfortune. When I was living in Vasilkov, I used to see scorners go to Kiev, and now I see them go to Ouman," i.e. to Bratislav. The scorners and the people of Bratislav were occupying the same rung of the ladder. Sharp words, but they had contained a bit of the truth.

Since the time when Judaism had halted in its development, there had not been such a spiritual revolutionary in the field of religion as the rabbi from Bratislav. "One must not age — one must not be an old, wise man, an old Hasid. It is not good to age, one must always begin anew." This teaching was directed at a Judaism that is founded on the concept of age, that prides itself on being hoary — "Israel the gray-haired," "God the ancient." In his protest against age, in his demand to do away with all that is old and to be constantly erecting new foundations, Rabbi Nachman of Bratislav was the most daring, the most destructive, the greatest revolutionary in Jewish history. He was more revolutionary than Shabbati Tzvi, more so than all the others who had wanted to renew Judaism. Because they had proceeded from within old concepts, they had not reached the essential core. The rabbi from Bratislav had started with a novel concept; he knew it, and had said so. He only had not known how to join the new Judaism to the old one. "How does one become worthy of being a Jew?" he once wailed. "How does one do it?" And underlying the wailing was a feeling of futility, a feeling that being a Jew was unachievable. He had hoped that *Eretz Yisrael* would help, that he would find there the key to the understanding of the essence of Judaism, and of its connection to the world and to God. He had returned full of doubts and anguish.

He had gone to *Eretz Yisrael* to make peace with old age and had returned to tell the wonderful story of the seven beggars, which makes the point that the oldest is the youngest one, and asserts that the child, the beginning, is the one closest to the mystery. The rabbi of Bratislav, however, had come too late and had lived in a community where he was not able to exercise a fruitful, progressive influence. Had he lived a few hundred years earlier, when Jewish thought had been younger, fresher and more courageous, and had he lived in a community of cultured people, like those in Spain or in France, the rabbi of Bratislav could have led Judaism onto a new path. He could have freed it from its inherited judgments; he could have loosened its wings. But he lived in the Ukraine, in an environment of fear and of sorrow, and his words had fallen like seeds on a stony ground. From the magnificent spirit of the Bratislav rabbi remained just a few fragments, a few words, some lovely stories — deeply philosophical ones, and therefore little understood — and a grave in the cemetery of Ouman.

A storm had passed through and had left behind a sigh. And this is the tragedy of Hasidism. Old age remained victorious.

About a World that is No More

It has only been a short while since death overtook it, yet it has already become a grass-covered tombstone. What was a lively world with its own coloration and its own music is now a neglected relic of times gone by. And yet, from time to time, a voice reaches us, a voice coming from somewhere, a voice out of the past, telling us about life as it once was lived.

Does anyone today view the Hasidic world as part of real life? I may be mistaken, but it seems to me that it has become merely an object of archeological, historical studies, a part of antiquity. And I am always overcome by a sense of wonder as well as of puzzlement when I come across a person who still has a purely personal relationship to Hasidism. And this is what I felt when I came across H. Itzhak Aven. There is among us a Jew, a man like all men, walking the streets of New York, riding the elevators, speaking an Americanized Yiddish, writing for the newspapers, interested in politics, in matters concerning Europe as well as Palestine. Yet this man's heart is filled with love for something that is very old and incomprehensible, and he lives spiritually in a world which is further removed from us than the tomb of Tutankhamen.

I have read a great deal of Hasidic literature. It has, of late, become quite a fashionable pursuit among Jews. The very fact that we have already moved so far away from Hasidism may be endowing it with the interest of a historical phenomenon. Or, perhaps, does a longing for a little bit of beauty, inspiration and a spiritual awakening move us?

230

But all the writing that has come my way has been literature and history, texts and commentaries. Itzhak Aven is not a historian, and his writing is not literature as we define the word, i.e. a content poured into a pre-made mold. His writing is autobiography; it is the baring of a soul. His book *From the Rebbe's Court* is more than a historical account, it is a human document: a book not about Hasidism, but a Hasidic book itself; not a study of religion, but a statement of faith. It is a religious book in the purest sense of the word.

The author may have intended to create a "literary" work, since he is, after all, living in New York and writing for Jewish newspapers. Fortunately, he did not succeed, in spite of an ample use of irony and humor, a rather slangy Yiddish and sudden interjections of English words in the midst of Hasidic orations. But it is the very artlessness of language and form that makes this such a warm-hearted and interesting book. The man of faith, the Hasid, struggled with the writer and prevailed. This is especially gripping because it is the first time that a Hasid has retold, in his own way, the stories which have been languishing like dried leaves among the pages of historical and literary writings. For the first time, to my knowledge at least, a rebbe's "court," the entire idiosyncratic, legendary world, has been described from inside out, as it were, by someone who has not forgotten, by someone who, spiritually, still inhabits it.

In Christian literature one finds many books by mystics, not only about but also written out of mysticism, providing psychologists with great treasures. In his famous work on religious psychology, William James explored these outpourings of the soul, from the Confessions of St. Augustine and of Santa Theresa, to the poems of St. Francis of Assisi. It is a rich and colorful literature, opening up for us depths and horizons.

Jewish religious writing is poor in this respect. We have religious writings, we have books on mysticism, but we have only treatises, no "confessions," no breast-beatings, no analyses of personal experiences. We do have legends, but the source from which they arose, the psychological process that created them, is hidden and covered up. Itzhak Aven uncovers a source for us; he shows us how the Hasidim created their world, how their legend came into being. What he unfolds before us are not mere facts, but a drama, a play in which he, himself, is one of the players. He had, personally, been a part of a rebbe's court. He stood on the sidelines as his *rebbe* stepped out of his abode. He witnessed how an old Hasid swept the dust off the stones, which were to be honored by the touch of the *tzadik's* feet. He himself sat in the tavern where Hasidim were telling stories of the Bal Shem Tov and the Magid of Mezerich.

Aven, having been a player in the drama, endows his story with a tremendous vitality and holds one's interest with the grip of a suspense novel and the charm of an ancient Eastern legend like the tales from *A Thousand and One Nights*. And you forget that all this took place quite recently, almost before your very eyes. You cannot fathom how this could have possibly happened, and your wonderment extends to Jewry as a whole. It is, indeed, a remarkable people who can bring forth such tremendous contrasts. On the one hand Judaism is part of modernity, part of European culture, of *le dernier cri*; on the other hand, it is evocative of a lifestyle that might be found only in Tibet or in some remote corner of India. It is, indeed, a complex people, who can simultaneously bring forth a Marx, a Lord Beaconsfield, and a Magid of Mezerich. A few miles away from Sadagora lies Tchernowitz, a town inhabited by nearly assimilated Jews who read the *Neue Freie Presse*, are fighting for political autonomy, and attend high schools and universities. While in Sadagora there is a "court," a "Jewish kingdom" apart from the world, a kingdom with its own laws, rituals, customs and ambitions.

I can imagine what an Englishman like, say, Sir Oliphant, the enthusiastic Zionist, would have thought had he seen the rebbe's court. If he were far-traveled, he would have thought of Tibet and the court of the Dalai Lama. There is no other possible counterpart. He might also have experienced a twinge of envy, just as we modern Jews are, at times, beset by envy of the Jews of times gone by. We live in a world ruled by "you must"; they lived in a world of joyous assent. We live in a world that thirsts for answers; they lived in a world that had the answer. They knew a secret that is hidden from us. How can we understand what it means to be ecstatic, to be entranced by a leader, a teacher, a rebbe? How can we enter into a psychology of people who never questioned but always accepted, who transformed each word, the smallest act of their spiritual leader, into a symbol?

Yet, as I view the spiritual life of our time, I begin to understand whence comes Judaism's great strength. I say "of our time" because this is the first time that we Jews have stepped out of our sphere and have joined the spiritual life of the world around us. It is the first time that we have truly abandoned Judaism and have espoused the guiding principle of the world around us: individualism. The Jewish world has had leaders that the non-Jewish world never did. Leaders who did not lead by imposition and power, but were freely chosen spiritual leaders.

For thousands of years the world was waiting for a spiritual leader, for one who would unite nations and countries, the past and the future. The world was waiting for such a "human bridge," and he failed to arrive. Kingdoms were vanquished, and nations perished, but a leader did not come who would state: You and they are brothers, you and they are children of one Father. You and those who have come before you are links in a chain. And then Judaism arrived and gave the world the Messiah concept, gave it Jesus.

Much as the world misunderstood Jesus, it nevertheless gained something from him: it used him to stop its disintegration. The bridge Christians built was made of paper, but it was still a bridge. Judaism has not needed such a bridge because Jews have absorbed the vision of the Messiah into their life, a Messiah who will unite the world when it is ready for Him, because Jews have viewed life as a preparation and as a path. In other words, for Christians the Messiah is a bridge, while for Jews he is merely a bridgehead.

It is, therefore, a pure misunderstanding to say that Judaism is essentially rationalistic, because a rationalistic view of the world, a cerebral religion, is an impossibility. As rational as they may be, it is not the laws, rituals and intellectual discourse that have upheld Judaism, but rather its mystical core, as shown by the Kabbalah, Shabbati Tzvi and Hasidism. Overlain as it is with rules, order, hierarchy and a quasi-governmental organization, at its core Hasidism is still mysticism, the conviction that man is merely a symbol and that each generation is represented by a "perfect man," a *tzadik*. This is the substance and the essence; all else is mere formality. One *tzadik* may adopt the way of kingly splendor, another may choose a modest life, but these are merely temporal distinctions that change and pass. What remains is the essence, which abides within the Jewish soul.

A world that is no more has, for a while, stepped out of its grave and asked: Am I altogether dead? And asked further: What have you, my heirs, done with the inheritance I have bequeathed to you? And the world awaits our answer.

Our Golden Legend

A few hundred years ago, the Archbishop of Genoa, Jacobus de Voragine, set out to collect all the folk tales and legends about the Christian saints, martyrs and church luminaries which had come into being in the preceding thousand years. He called his collection *The Golden Legend*, not thinking — and, surely, not intending — that these tales of pious men and their deeds should become not only a summation, but also the end, the conclusion, of an entire religious cultural epoch.

Of all human emotions, the one which is most akin to faith is love. I do not know how much truth there is in the words of the Russian poet who wrote, "...a thought put into words becomes a lie..." Still, when a lover is able to express his love, his passion, in precise, measured words, when he can impose the yoke of analytical thought upon the complexity of his feelings, we may well suspect that his feelings themselves are becoming less stormy, more settled and more abstract, and with that, less magnificently intoxicating than they had been before the process of crystallization had set in.

Faith, like love, is a collective emotion, with all of the qualities and character-istics of eroticism, albeit generalized and objectless. An emotion that is at its stormiest, most intense and most ecstatic when it is closest to its source, when it cannot achieve adequate expression, when it cannot be confined to a formula. The Buddhist seated beneath a tree constantly repeating some random Sanskrit words is not concerned with their meaning; he uses them to wall himself off into solitude, and they become a thread on which to string his inchoate feelings. The most impassioned prayers, the prayers that warm our hearts and inspire us, are conducted in partially unintelligible language, replete with complex, esoteric symbolism. Anyone who has heard Hasidim sing, who has listened to the sweet pianissimo of the mystical *niggun* rising to its fortissimo and the choral ending, knows the power that the irrational exerts over man. None of the singers, perhaps, understood the words or perceived their profound meaning, but this was not necessary. It was, indeed, the very opaqueness of the words that allowed feelings to find an ecstatic release. A "clarified" faith, one which is intelligible in all its details, one which lacks deep, dark underground passages and high, cloud-piercing towers, such a one is a mere abstraction, a thought-constructed, sterile faith.

As faith loses its power, literature comes into being. The Middle Ages, pious and steeped in mysticism, had produced merely folk legends about the lives and deeds of their saints. As religion settled into a petrified dogma, faith sought refuge in literature. And it is interesting to note that it was, precisely, the great skeptics who found themselves captivated by the holy legends and mystical literature. Voltaire fought this with derision because he still considered religion as a powerful force that had to be combated. But Anatole France could already allow himself the luxury of smiling indulgently at the yellow pages and of retelling anew in his own, ironic way, those alien, golden legends of the Middle Ages.

Thinking about Hasidism, I often feel that the entire movement came truly to an end at the moment I. L. Peretz wrote his Hasidic tales. The enlightened spirits of the preceding generation derided and fought Hasidism because it was, for them, still a living reality. But Peretz saw merely a corpse, and he proceeded to embalm it and to wrap it in rare linens, to preserve it as the Egyptians had preserved their mummies. It is not at all accidental that the so called Hasidic literature grows stronger from year to year and that Hassidic motifs become more central in contemporary dramas, novels, essays and songs. But stranger yet is to observe how great an impact these fantastic tales of another time have on the non-Jewish world. The first appearance of Martin Buber's German translation of the Tales of Rabbi Nachman of Bratslav created a sensation not only among German Jews but also among wide circles of the German intelligentsia. And, even today, we see that the only Jewish dramas that have been able to attract the attention of the cultured world, are *The Dybbuk* and *Yoshe Kalb*. Non-Jews perceive in it something that we, perhaps, are not able to feel at all; they see it as the Jewish Golden Legend. We, ourselves, are still too close to the source, and do not yet have the required distance.

For us, the old Hasidim and *tzadikim* are simply bearded Jews wearing caftans and speaking in an outmoded way — they are a phase of life that we have just left behind us, and we tend to be rather irritated by them. But those who view them from a greater distance, the non-Jewish world or modern Jews who have grown up in the New World and have not experienced Hasidism as a way of life, they see it merely as literature, legends, dramatic plots. For us the theme itself maintains its power, but the others are intrigued merely by the form, or, even more, by the essentially human, heroic attributes hiding underneath the beards, the sideburns and the long satin gabardine coats. This is not surprising, since life cannot be sustained in the thin atmosphere of abstract thought. Today's Jewish generation is seeking a way to reach the sources, the basic foundations of Jewish consciousness and Jewish religiosity. Synagogue services and sermons on Jewish ethics and Jewish nationalism do not nurture their imagination, which craves colorful imagery. And it is not so much Judaism that they are looking for, as Jewishness, the quintessential Jewish human being, the Jewish legend. And they find it in Hasidism.

A few years ago, a German-Jewish rabbi came to see me and invited me to join the enthusiastic members of his "neo-Hasidic cult." To all my questions about the meaning and purpose of his group his answer was: "I cannot explain it, I cannot formulate it, I can only feel it." Which indicated to me that this was more than a daydream by a rabbi wanting to weave together loose threads of religious aspirations, that it was, rather, indicative of something hovering in the air, in the Jewish air of today.

Just because Jewish life has become such a difficult and tragic problem which no one can evade anymore, just because it holds us in its grip like a nightmare, a yearning to find a place for oneself in Judaism is becoming ever stronger, and the urge towards Jewish mysticism is growing. Rabbi Louis Newman's *Anthology of Hassidic Literature* had already been symptomatic of the mood of the time, but Newman's work is a mere collection of bits and pieces and, at best, a primer of Hasidism. Today's youth, however, wants to go to the roots; it wants to immerse itself in the romanticism of Hasidism. And this desire has called forth a work that can have great meaning for today's Jewish youth, *The Romance of Hasidism* by Jacob S. Minkin — a book for youth. The well-versed scholarly reader may, perhaps, not find in it what he is looking for, namely the Hasidic philosophy and its view of the mission of Judaism. No Jewish scholar has, as yet, undertaken such a study. More is the pity, since it would be truly worthwhile to apply all the keenness of philosophical analysis not only to the metaphysical ideas of the Kabbalah, of the Zohar, but also to the strictly developed system of Rabbi Moses Cordovero, and that of the Ari or, or in later times, to the *Tanya*. This is so because these idiosyncratic, archaic works rest on an entire, highly original philosophic structure. There we find the deepest source of the Jewish view of the world, deeper than the officially accepted Jewish thinkers have fathomed.

Jacob S. Minkin did not dig that deeply, nor was it necessary for him to do so in order to achieve his purpose. What he set out to do, consciously or not, was to give American Jewish youth an access, in English, to a glimpse of a Jewish humanity which has already vanished into eternity, to create a golden legend which would, once again, become a source of inspiration; and this he has achieved splendidly. His book is alight with his own enthusiasm, which precludes all critical probing, it glows with his own faith in the legend. And this is good. Had Jacobus de Voragine been already an Anatole France, his *Golden Legend* would not have become a historical phenomenon, since it is naiveté which first has to break the ground for depth-penetrating art, an art that creates not only verbal imagery but which also undergirds our thinking and our lives, which becomes the very essence of life.

The Middle Way

I recently experienced a rare pleasure — a reader responded to an essay not with approval but with something that is a thousand times more valuable, with understanding. His interest had been caught by an expression I had used in passing in an article without any philosophical pursuit, the Middle Way, which is the teaching of *binui*, of moderation — the teaching of the Habad. The reader's keen response, in turn, resounded in my mind, and thoughts spun about, anxious to take shape. But I know that the time for this has not yet come, and when it comes it will be a difficult task to get at the roots of concepts whose origins are concealed. As Nietzsche once asked: "You want to know where I stand — do you know the depth beneath my feet?" Depths underlying not only one's personal life and thought but collective life as well — the life and thought of Judaism.

In our present time this is, indeed, a cardinal question. Whether we will it or not, we cannot escape it, we cannot hide from it, we must seek the "Jewish Way." It has always been thus. In times of crisis, of danger, of peril and hopelessness, came the *tzimtzum*, the concentration, the setting of limits, the penetration into our own depths, the seeking of the way to ourselves. This is especially true today, when we are faced with questions not only about Jews but also about Judaism, when the Jewish question is a difficult one for Jews themselves. Officially and publicly we present a proud front, but privately, among ourselves, we are attacked by doubts: Is this, perhaps, the last time we will lower the pitcher into the well before it runs dry?

We are talking about Jewish values, the Jewish word, the spirit of Judaism, which we still expect to accomplish wonders; but what lies behind the words? We know where we stand with religion because, while we have not as yet arrived at what Freud termed "the end of an illusion," we certainly find ourselves at the beginning of the end. Religion, at least for the younger generation, has lost the clarity and the burning intensity it once had, and its view of the world is taking on an entirely new form, still undetermined, still shapeless, but essentially a non-dogmatic one — a religion without faith.

Those German apologists and interpreters of Judaism who focused on ethics were not altogether wrong, except that their shallow approach served to trivialize all of Jewish ethics. They have blended two concepts: the content of ethics and its form. Content means generalized, formulated ideas; words. Whereas form implies action and is like a churn which takes in a great variety of material but then forces it into a specific configuration. And what we are seeking today, what we are seeking with the greatest intensity of our thought and our will, is the form of Jewish life, the Jewish way. I often find myself puzzled by the question: Why are we not bringing forth any Jewish philosophical systems? It may be that they do exist, such as Hermann Cohen's philosophy. And, perhaps, if we were to penetrate deeply into the thought processes of Bergson and Husserl, the most prominent thinkers of our time, we might find there what we are seeking. These, however, are only hints, allusions; the concealed Torah. What Judaism needs, though, is a clear, unreserved reflection and discourse, first among ourselves and then with the rest of the world.

My own search for the interwoven strands of Jewish thought has led me to look for them in fabrics of such intricate design that it is almost impossible to get at the basic stitches — to present Jewish concepts in a universally intelligible form. Often I find treasures. Take the very idea of *binui*, the Middle Way, a deep thought buried in a book that is not easily accessible, that lacks any orderly arrangement, that is written in a moralistic, religious tone and that addresses itself to readers who are singularly unsuited to pursue the thought and to continue building on its foundation. It is difficult for modern man, accustomed to following the mandates of logical thought and conclusive argumentation, to get into the spirit of a book such as the *Tanya,* a collection of aphorisms, presented in an unstructured, unorganized form, by the founder of Habad.

Years back I tried to find my way to the essence of the book but became discouraged by its format. I was looking for philosophy but found only scriptural verses. It was H. I. Bunin's clear summary presented in his *The Teaching of Habad* that gave me insight into the *Tanya*. I went back into the old, yellow-paged original, and this time the words came to life. I saw the Jewish spirit wrestling with the world, seeking to approach it, on its own terms, and in its original and therefore fresh way. I say fresh and original because the distinctive quality of this Jewish theological thought is that it is almost free of mentors. Each thought must break new ground, or nearly so. These thinkers are not building on prior concepts, they do not transform the history of philosophy into philosophy itself, they feel no obligation to dispute all the thinkers who preceded them, nor could they have done so, having never read any of them, not even the Jewish philosophers of the classical period.

There stands before us a remarkable figure, Rabbi Zalman of Liadi (1747–1812), the author of the *Tanya*, the rabbi of a small town who spends his life studying Torah and Hasidism and who has never come across the *Guide for the Perplexed* or the *Kuzari*, to say nothing of the writings of Chasdai Crescas. A Jew who has, surely, never heard the name of Spinoza and who creates an ethical, philosophical system, without being in the least aware of it. He grasps the threads of the Kabbalah, weaves them into new patterns, drawing them into their logical conclusion, yet doing this in an almost unselfconscious way.

I will not unfold here the system of the *Tanya*, if for no other reason than that this would mean going deeply into the philosophy of the Kabbalah, into the mysticism of the Ari, and of Cordovero, one of the greatest thinkers Judaism has brought forth. It is a system based on a dualism that is inherent in nature, and on the split that exists in the world. Rabbi Zalman of Liadi could be brought into the mainstream of philosophy very simply by a mere change of terminology — it is the language which stifles insight, those weighty words which almost defy translation, those multi-colored Hebrew and Aramaic expressions, so filled with meaning that cannot be transmitted in clear, definitive words. This alone makes this writing so difficult to understand and to explain. But yet, if you labor long enough, you can reach solid ground, you can arrive at the theory of good and evil, the good inclination and the evil one, the two basic principles, which both have their legitimate place in the world. The world contains nothing that is superfluous, says Moses Cordovero in his *Elima Rabati*, and he points out that the purpose of evil is to grant mankind moral and spiritual autonomy. Without basic evil there can be no free will, no opportunity for man to struggle toward higher values.

It is this concept of spiritual and moral freedom and of man's constant struggle to achieve it that the rabbi has developed into the main theme of the Middle Way, into that of the man in the middle, of the average man, of mankind altogether. Because every man stands between the two poles, every man contains both good and evil qualities, carries within himself all the colors of the rainbow, from the faintest to the strongest; every man symbolizes the human striving to overcome his lower nature. And he goes even further: The purpose of all creation (creation being *tzimtzum*, divine self-limitation, the compression of eternity, of the infinite) is to give birth to man, to suppress the negative principle, and to do battle with the dark side of the world.

Modern science takes, actually, the same approach — man represents the final stage of development of life on earth, because he is the only organism that is autonomous, free, that can govern matter, control its own environment, and, most importantly, rule itself. The aim of culture is to subdue instinct, which means to free oneself from blind necessity. Man equals freedom, and freedom equals thinking; this is the dictum of the *Tanya* and, I would say, of Jewish philosophy altogether. "Sovereignty of the spirit" is the rabbi's idiosyncratic term, which has its parallel in Spinoza's intellectual love for God. Intellect is love, to understand is to love, because understanding means becoming one with the understood. Thus, quite unexpectedly, there emerge two Jewish thinkers: Spinoza in Amsterdam and Zalman in Liadi, the one who went outside the Jewish fold and the one who founded a Hasidic sect. And does not Bergson's idea, put forth in his *Creative Evolution*, have its roots in this Jewish thought? Does not his philosophy rest on the theory of a downward development, a descent from a universal energy followed by an ascent through the will and through intellect? Bergson's teaching has been called the "philosophy of freedom," and the thirst for freedom, the responsibility borne by each human being, the proud principle of accountability, finds its resonance in the words of the rabbi: "If I am not responsible for myself in this world, then what do I amount to?" Every man is a world in himself; no one can take his place, and no one can redeem another person or change him. No one, not society, nor the state, nor any collective identity. There is no collective organism, there is only a collection of individuals, each one free to be himself, with his own internal struggles, each master of himself and subject only to the powers of infinity, of that which has neither shape nor name.

With its roots so deeply anchored, Jewish thought bravely faces the world, not apologetically, not latching on to the newest contemporary thinker, nor to Buddhism or Taoism, but rooted in its own soil. Jewish faith? Yes, faith is a private matter; whoever has it, has it. But the sovereignty of the spirit, the struggle against the instinct that resides in the subhuman, is growing stronger and sharper in the world. The free acknowledgement of the other, of the negative in the world and the struggle with it — this is an unsentimental and unromantic philosophy, but one with the clarity and the impact of a mountain spring; a philosophy from on high. Yet the very exaltation of theoretical thought is balanced by the injunction to moderation and realism in the conduct of life. The highest idealism notwithstanding, the world can neither be denied nor overcome. Darkness remains even in the face of the existence of light. We are able to understand this, but we cannot overcome it, except within ourselves, because the final aim of the world is the human personality, and this means the freedom of moral decision.

And this, dear inquiring reader, is an outline of the philosophy of the Middle Way, the Jewish philosophy of life that awaits its day in the sun. It waits, and the world waits, because the world always pays heed when Jews enunciate their true thoughts. It knows that these thoughts have deep roots.

The Wreath of the Holy Ark

Everything depends on luck; this holds true even for a wreath. Rabbi Johanan once gave us the lovely vision of the three wreaths: one is a wreath of the sanctuary, the second is the wreath of the kingdoms, and the third is the wreath of the Holy Ark. Aaron had been worthy to receive the first, David had claimed the second, but the third still rests in its place, and anyone who so wishes can claim the wreath of the Holy Ark, the wreath of the Torah.

The priestly service is a thing of the past, for the kingdoms are no more. No one can modify them as they are in the past, inaccessible to us. Yet, preserved in the depth of human memory, they are, in their extinction, more momentous than they had been at the time of their existence. What was the priesthood when it was still an institution? Comprised partly of dervishes and partly of Brahmins, the priests were a thorn in the flesh of the people, deriving profits from the piety of the masses. And the kingdoms? Ineffective kings ruling over a politically weak people, always dependent on the whims of their neighbors, be it Assyria, Babylon, Egypt or Rome, they were rarely free and autonomous. Reality had dried out the priestly and the royal wreaths, but legend brought them back to life, granting us the gifts of blooming, purple-flowered wreaths.

Only one wreath has not been submerged in the folds of history — the wreath of the Holy Ark, the wreath of the Torah. And everyone feels free to pick it up, to adorn himself with it, keeping it for a while and then putting it back. And each time the wreath loses one more leaf. Who knows whether this is still the same

243

wreath? Perhaps parts of it have remained somewhere else, in Babylon or in Cordoba or in some small Polish or Lithuanian town which may not even be listed on the map? And who knows whether the Torah wreath that in our days is going from hand to hand, and from head to head, is not a wreath of artificial flowers, with neither scent nor luster?

I often wonder why I am so disconcerted by the new Torah impetus that is emerging in American Jewish life? Have we not, for years and years, called for a revival of spirituality? Have we not fought with bitterness and sarcasm against the ignorance that is gaining so much ground in America? Have we not steadily preached: make room for Jewish thought, for Judaism? And it has happened: Lawyers, bankers, businessmen and insurance agents attend kosher banquets, listen to heated rhetoric and sermons about Torah and Judaism, give or pledge money, applaud, take pictures and agree that New York needs a Yeshivah. If the speeches deal with Jewish education they, again, are ready to agree: You want *cheders*? Good. A *Talmud Torah*? Fine. An orthodox theological seminary? Agreed. A seminary of modern orientation is fine too. Everything is satisfactory, as long as it concerns Torah, as long as it concerns Jewishness.

This is the reason that I always leave these banquets and Torah-feasts with such a feeling of disquiet and chagrin, the constant preaching about Torah and Judaism ringing in my ears. It is precisely when I watch the assembled audiences being inculcated with "the pride of the Jewish people" that the sad and prophetic words come to mind: "Sooner or later, the Jewish people will forget the Torah." And, who knows if the "later" is not already very, very near?

This holds true not only in America but everywhere, even in Russia. When I hear news from Russia about the Bolsheviks closing the schools, persecuting the rabbis, forbidding the teaching of Hebrew, etc., etc., I am not very scared. It is, perhaps, Judaism's best protection against assimilation, because no spiritual force can exist without a struggle, without opposition and affliction. And the harder the struggle, the stronger it remains. And if the Bolsheviks, the Jewish Bolsheviks, come forth with a different view of Judaism, this is not a struggle until death. It is a struggle for survival, a process of purification. Whatever has grown moribund falls by the wayside, and whatever has retained its vital force remains. And when the storm in Russia passes, when life returns to its normal grooves, we will see a new, purified Judaism, a Judaism which has found its meaning.

What bothers me, however, is the old Jewish intelligentsia that finds itself partly in "exile," and partly in Russia. It has suddenly divested itself of the Russian Jewish charm, it has surrendered. Not long ago I met in New York one of the former leaders of Russian Jewry, one of its principal intellectuals. At home in St.

Petersburg, in his own environment, he had been a Russian Jew, and that means an idiosyncratic type of Jew; the only Jewish variant that has found a bridge between being Jewish and being universally human, the Jew who had easily and elegantly walked along a path leading from the synagogue and the study house to general culture. It is true that in St. Petersburg and in Moscow, in Kiev and in Odessa, one did, at that time, also talk about the uniqueness of Judaism and of its future. But there was a different meaning and a different certainty underlying their assertions and their questing. It had been a sincere desire to deepen and further develop Jewish thought, to extend its trajectory.

And here I meet him in New York. He is suffering in exile, feeling sorrow for old Russia. He bemoans the Jewish Diaspora and is angry with the Jewish people that has spawned so many destroyers and demolishers. He longs for the fleshpots of the past, completely forgetting that each historical phenomenon contains its own cause and that the Bolshevik catastrophe is a result of underlying reasons, is rooted in Russian history. The old intellectual had completely changed his tune. And I suddenly heard the old, familiar German-Jewish West European formula: Religion is for the people. Judaism is an institution whose purpose it is to uphold the existing social system. Torah becomes a wall supporting the interests of one group versus another. The Jewish spirit is treated as a political platform. I almost did not recognize him, or, rather, I have only now recognized what "Judaism" meant to the old, well-established Jews, the fanatical supporters of the existing order, who had felt so much at home in old Russia.

What a distance between this Judaism and that of the prayerhouse, the Judaism of asceticism, of self-denial and of transcendence; the Judaism that sees itself as a sacrifice on the altar of universal redemption, and, as such, being chosen and unique. What an abyss between the Judaism of the comfortable pillars of society and the stormy, seeking, restless Judaism of those involved in the mystical Judaism of Gershenzon, the Judaism of the eternally burning thornbush.

Having listened to the perorations of the old Russian leader, I began to ponder the fate of Russian Judaism. If a few years of suffering have already robbed Russian Jewish life of so much of its vitality, courage and luster, what will happen in the future? Will Judaism all over the world go the way of Western Europe, of the Judaism by emissaries? The very clever observer and politically astute former king Ferdinand of Bulgaria once made a very stinging comment about Zionism. Someone had asked: What is Zionism? And he answered: "A Zionist is a Jew who pays others to go to Israel." Ferdinand had in mind the Zionists he knew, the Western European ones, but he could have said it not only about European Zionists, but also about American ones, and about Jews in general. Today a Jew in Europe or in America hires someone else to do his praying and his Torah study, to assume the yoke of following the precepts, to free him from spiritual unrest.

This is, actually, the entire significance of the new "Torah enthusiasm" that has now sprung up in America. Torah, yes…but for others. Jewish education, fine…but for others. Let some idlers spend their time in Yeshivahs; let a few hundred, or a few thousand, children wear yarmulkes, learn Hebrew and become religious. This serves us fine in the eyes of other people. The Christians have their own struggles between fundamentalism and modernism. They talk, day in and day out, about church and about religion, meaning mainly politics and conservatism, and we would do well to keep pace with them. We must show them that we are like other people, that we, too, care about God and not only about business.

There is no secrecy about it. Our American Jews are too naive to dress up true faith in the robes of philosophical or theological oratory as the German Jews used to do. Germany had demanded profundity from its Jews; America demands simplicity and naiveté. One does not even need to make the effort of lifting the rough-hewn prophetic mantle off the Torah; one merely needs to overlay it with a mantle of gold. Anyone who so desires can take the wreath off the Ark and put it on his own head; anyone with enough money can adorn it with beautifully bejeweled, shimmering flowers. It becomes a lovely, rich wreath, but artificial flowers do not bloom. And a Judaism that does not grow and bloom is a Judaism that must die.

How lovely, how entrancingly did this wreath once bloom when Judaism was still so poor and so naive, serving no one but itself, when it had no other purpose but to hear. This, too, has passed. This too, is already history.

And so it is. Everything depends on luck, even the wreath of the Holy Ark.

Texts and Histories

Round and Round the Book of Books

They dig in Ur; they excavate in Kish. Each day brings new developments and new discoveries embedded in sand, clay and stone. Treasures are found in ancient coffins, and treasures are still lying in wait in attics and cellars of erstwhile houses. Treasures from times long gone whose impact yet extends up to this very day, a past that is stronger than the present. And who can tell what the excavating spade may still bring to light? Who would have predicted, some twenty-five years ago, that in Susa, the old Persian capital, a stone monument would be found bearing the etched inscriptions of the Laws of Hammurabi, the law-giving king of Babylon, a document that sheds an entirely new light on all of ancient history and spreads a shadow over the history of Jewish religion?

One stone added to another and the enigma of Jewish culture is coming closer to its solution. Of course, there are those who look at this with jaundiced eyes, the members of both the Christian and the Jewish fundamentalist camps. They do not want to know the truth; they fear it. In Jerusalem I was told that when archaeologists had begun to dig around the third city wall, there had been an immediate protest on the part of the priesthood; and petitions were sent to the British government to stop the excavations. The excavation of the third wall did not fit into their scheme of things because the uncovering of the third wall would have given the lie to the evangelical crucifixion account: Golgotha would not have been Golgotha, and the Via Dolorosa, the route which Jesus, according to the dogma, walked to his crucifixion, would have been a mere legend. And if this account is only a product of human imagination, then why not all the rest?

It is, however, childish to close one's eyes in order not to see the truth, as if truth could be affected by our willingness or unwillingness to acknowledge it. Jewish fundamentalists, as well, do not approve of any Bible criticism whatsoever. For them all things are as they should be, and they are willing to reconcile all contradictions and accept as truth all the historical impossibilities and legends in order to stave off doubt, in order not to have to reflect on it. And so they counter all questions with one answer: "Chutzpah!" "What chutzpah!" laments S. D. Luzzatto. "What impertinence to assert that Isaiah's prophecy of Koresh had been written later, in Babylon." For Luzzatto everything was chutzpah, even Spinoza's wonderfully clear analysis of the Bible. And if this is the attitude of such a luminary, a scholar reared in the European cultural tradition, what wonder then that ordinary Jews, Jews without the benefit of having had a taste of world culture, should wring their hands and rend their garments when anyone applies the method of historical criticism to the Bible. This attitude, alas, has spread until it has become generally accepted that there are certain boundaries that must not be transcended; so far and no further! The entire realm of Jewish thought has become subject to one single method of exploration. One may investigate certain designated areas, one may link one wall to another, and one may interpret the configuration, but one may not search for the truth in the spirit of free inquiry. One may not remove a section of the wall to discover what lies behind it.

Jewish scholars and critics pride themselves on their readiness to measure and analyze all phenomena and to throw all their findings onto the scale, all except those that pertain to Judaism and its historical roots. Then the spirit of free inquiry deserts them; then they take fright. Even the freethinkers among them are often heard to ask: All right, assuming the Bible is, indeed, as the Bible scholars assert, a mere encyclopedia of ancient wisdom, traditions, and legends, where does this leave us? If you take away from us The Book, the Book of Books, what is to become of the meaning of our existence? If you demolish the uniqueness of the Bible, you likewise demolish the uniqueness of the Jewish people. And then we shall stand all alone in the world, without even the support of our forefathers.

This may be a valid argument, but only as long as the peoples among whom we live believe that the Bible is a divine document handed down specifically to the Jews — only so long as we are accepted as the rightful heirs of the Bible. But what would happen should their faith weaken? For this is what is happening more and more each day. One hundred and fifty years ago it was widely believed that the Book in its present form had come down from the heavens, that it had been dictated to Moses from above. How many educated non-Jews truly believe this today?

Historically speaking, the Bible is no longer at the center of the spiritual world. It has been absorbed into the flow of history. It is, of course, rated as an achievement, and it is legitimate to view it as the end of one period and as a point of departure of a new, universal culture; but it has ceased being a mystery. And the time has come for us to admit to ourselves that critical assessment of the Bible must be continued. We Jews began this work long before the Christian world had the courage to tackle it. In the Talmud already we find probing allusions and conjectures, pursued at greater depth by Ibn Ezra and by Spinoza. Today, two Jewish scholars, Dr. M. Soloveitchik and Z. Rubashov, truly deserve great credit for having had the courage to introduce Bible criticism into Jewish literature with all its findings and conclusions.

Perhaps for the first time in literature, not only in the Jewish or Hebrew but also in the general literature, we see unrolling before our eyes the struggle that has been raging around the Book of Books. It began in the faraway past when the struggle concerned the codification of Jewish tradition, and has continued up to the most recent explorations, whose sole purpose is to gain knowledge and understanding of the historical development of the Jewish people. A remarkable canvas: We see a world resting on a book, we see a people for whom this Book is its sole *raison d'être*, consolation and hope, an inexhaustible source of inspiration and a key to all mysteries. This Book is an axiom. Does one doubt a mathematical axiom? And if one should do so, what would be the result? Any attempt to deny basic mathematical axioms would destroy our ability to comprehend the world and to deal not only with its scientific attributes, but with the practical aspects of daily life as well.

Mankind has changed little throughout the ages. Thus, a thousand years ago there were also dissatisfied critics and searchers who felt that there were some incongruities among certain Biblical accounts and who realized that not all Biblical writing maintained the same literary *niveau*, or the same character of narrative. History and legend, ethics and hygiene — how to weld them together into an organic unity? And already at that time there were those who concluded that the Torah speaks allegorically, but that ordinary man interprets it according to his limited intelligence. The sharpest, perhaps most radical criticism, however, came from the mystics, from the Masters of the Kabbalah, who interpreted all Torah as a single allegory, as a philosophical statement expressed in images and parables.

We, today, are no more in need of *pilpul*, nor do we have to interpret the Flood, since the epic of Gilgamesh, the old legend of Babylon, makes things clear to us. We know of the existence of the ancient Eastern legend, and whether its hero is called Noah or Utanapishtim of Babylon, the text is almost identical. And when one Bible scholar after another points to the differences between the parts of the Bible where Elohim predominates and those where Adonai has taken His place, when they look at the text in varying contexts and reverse the order of events, we no longer get frightened.

There was a time when scholarship had gone to the extreme of altogether denying the historical reality of the Bible. Their denial was directed not only at the account of the Creation of the world, but also at the actual existence of Abraham, Isaac, Jacob, Moses, Isaiah, etc., considering them symbolic representations. Thus, Abraham represented the sun, Sarah the moon, and even today we have Professor Edward Maier claiming that Abraham and Sarah had been two local ancient Semitic divinities who, in the course of time, had been endowed with pseudo-historical personalities. But that is, perhaps, an extreme case. The scientific explorers of the Ancient East, on the other hand, the archaeologists and philologists, have been uncovering more and more proofs that what the Bible tells us is not mere fantasy, but is based on actual events, which, in the course of time, came to be told and retold in differing ways. The bricks of Assur and the stones of Egypt and Persia yield up the sayings of "Israel," the stories of "Jacob-El," the mention of the "Haviri," the Hebrews. Thus, no one will be surprised if somewhere from beneath the soil there should emerge the figure of the least understood, the most important leader of the Jewish people: Moses.

The work has only begun. The history of the Jews has yet to be written, but a perspective is emerging of a Judaism that has existed without and before the Book. We come to see a people that had existed hundreds, if not thousands, of years prior to it. A people that had created a culture, sung songs, created a society and laid the foundation stone of a new religion. There are hints of that in the Torah itself. The ancients themselves were aware of the existence of a hidden treasure of stories, documents, and recorded traditions. The Torah, the Bible, was for them not a foundation, not a point of departure, but a roof, a point of arrival. It mirrored only one part of Jewish history, be it its spiritual or political aspects. The Kohanim had prevailed; Ezra had put his stamp on Judaism, choosing and eliminating the data to be included. Jewish thought had become hemmed in; it was forced to fit itself into a smaller framework, or else to hide somewhere in caves.

It is out of the caves that, later on, Jewish mysticism emerged, bringing in its train consequences of world-historic import. And Adolph Frank is surely right when, in his famous book *The Kabbalah*, he moves the origins of the Kabbalah back to ancient times, to the times when all of the Jewish tradition was in the process of being established. Then there had to be two streams of thought in Judaism, two ways to choose from: the way of the priestly Torah, or the way of mysticism and philosophy. The priests had prevailed, which meant that the other stream had to forge its own bed and, in the end, had to break out of the Jewish camp, flooding the world.

The task of the present generation is to gain a clear perception of the essence of Judaism. It must reexamine its past in order to build its future. And, perhaps, in the process, we will find a new access to the *genizah*, to the ancient, closed, shadowy past, which leads to the path of religious creativity. From criticism to mysticism, thus the way leads.

Reading the Book of Ruth

I have been browsing in the Book of Ruth. Preceded by the colorful Song of Songs, and followed by the bleak and sorrowful Lamentations, the Book of Ruth comes to us as a breath of spring. We see fields and tents, laborers and women gathering corn, and we see Ruth, the quiet daughter of Moab, faithfully working in the path of the people she has chosen as her own. It is a book about the only human being in the Bible who chose to become a part of the Jewish people. The only one motivated not by love, faith or a search for happiness, but by pure, deep humanity. A lonely person who sought to join those who were alone.

And from the Book of Ruth, from the old, naive tale, my mind wandered to the Midrash. From time to time I get the urge to return to the Midrashim, a collection of books unique to the Jewish people. No one can understand the hidden treasures of the Jewish spirit, the implicit messages nestled between the lines that get handed down from one generation to the next, the range of Jewish lore in all its variety, unless he knows the Midrash. It is a prism that breaks a ray of light into a multitude of beams, beams of many colors, illuminating diverse times. It is Jews talking to each other across the barriers of time and space. Thus, a note struck amidst the sun-filled fields of Moab finds a faraway echo in Babylon, in Persia, in Alexandria, in Rome. The tread of thought rolls capriciously along intertwining, intersecting roads — a challenging word or an unexpected name will elicit a new idea, but always in pursuit of the same theme. The old sages are masters of roaming afield, but always with a purpose in mind. They lead us up and down a road, branching off to the right and to the left, then suddenly we find ourselves on the path leading back to the beginning.

And so the stream of Jewish thought flows its way around Ruth, the corn-gleaning Moabite, and leads us on mysterious byways towards a wondrous personality, the most puzzling, the most profound thinker to be found in the realm of the Jewish spirit — Elisha ben Abouya. Transported to the market place of old Tiberius where Rabbi Meir sits and preaches the Torah, we see his teacher, Elisha ben Abouya, approaching on horseback. The loyal, saddened pupil wants to know how and why his teacher has become an apostate. And the teacher answers that he has come to see that those who observe all that is written and commanded and who do good are rewarded with pain and with death, that the pious and the righteous perish and the sinners remain victorious. Seeing this, he had changed, becoming the "Other."

Now facing him, in my mind's eye, is his friend Akiba ben Joseph, smooth and clever, ready to make all manner of sacrifices for his people, for his faith, ready to die for it, and yet not ready for the ultimate sacrifice — for loneliness. Akiba represents one side of the historical coin, one face of Judaism, and Elisha the other. Elisha had struggled with God, to understand His truth, while all around him he perceived existing contradictions between precept and reality, contradictions he could not accept. He demanded all or nothing.

On the other side stood Akiba the orator, Akiba the preacher, Akiba the conciliator. "Yes, there is constant contradiction, but the contradiction is only an apparent one. It stems from the fact that we view things from only one angle, that we look at only one dimension, that of earth, life, human events. But if we extend our line of vision into a new dimension, towards heaven, the future, the world to come, then all contradiction is solved and the Word is true." And Akiba ben Joseph had preached and had conciliated the Jewish people into history. He had sacrificed his own life in order to enable future generations to live, and not to despair. Akiba's accomplishment overshadowed and cast into oblivion the heroic gesture of Elisha ben Abouya. Akiba ben Joseph has entered history as The Jew, Judaism's spiritual and historical hero, while Elisha ben Abouya has become a sideline figure, the ousted one, the Other.

The time of Akiba, however, is coming to an end. Compromise and conciliation have run their course; one can no longer bridge contradictions with words, or mask them with parables. Our times demand and our souls cry out for intrinsic harmony between precept and fulfillment. And Elisha is being resurrected for the sake of his teaching. And what was his doctrine if not the one we are yearning for today, an uncompromising, one-dimensional doctrine? We have gown weary of the moral, religious and spiritual compromises advocated by Akiba, of the unending task of reconciling what is with what might be. We have had enough of compartmentalization and of itemized bookkeeping. We see people preaching one thing before ascending to power, and doing the opposite once they have achieved it. We see people who seize the first opportunity to betray the best that is in them — conflicted people, at war with themselves, torn between two worlds. We see realists who understand Judaism, but, "you know, one has to consider circumstances…see things in perspective…" How small have people become?

So many sermons are being preached, so many clichéd speeches delivered, and no one knows anymore what is good and what is bad, what one may or may not do, what one must or must not do. I sometimes wonder if it is possible that the people in Moscow or in India, the fanatics and the ecstatics, who reject all compromise and all conciliation, are closer to the truth? I consider the idea for a while, and then I try to visualize these people. Having no first-hand knowledge of the people of India, their images remain shadowy, but I do know the people in Moscow; I can see their hard faces in front of me, and I can feel their cold disregard of human needs. I know the censorship that they exercise over their thoughts, their fear of facing the truth, and I know that the truth does not dwell among them. It is not there that the new man is to be found — the new Elisha, a man who treats himself sternly but is gentle towards others; a man who lets his thoughts lead him where they may, but who retains a firm grip on his actions; a man who has the courage to be different and to be lonely.

Thus matters stand, I am afraid, not only in India and in Moscow, but everywhere else where doctrines are being preached, where men sacrifice themselves and others for holy causes, whether old ones or new ones. Akiba ben Joseph, a universal figure, is still going around the world, spreading his nets of conciliatory compromises over people, and Elisha is still, the Other.

It was a long leap from Ruth, the quiet daughter-in-law of Naomi, to the passionate figures of Akiba and Elisha, and I do not know myself just what propelled me. I do not know what has pulled me away from the sunny fields of Moab onto the thorny, overgrown paths of history. The ancients have led me astray, and the old, restless Jewish spirit that does not allow for any surcease, nor countenances any idyllic endings, pulls me ever onwards, towards the unknown, towards the strange, towards the other. Then it turns back, longingly, to the quiet, secure, magnificent wholeness and loyalty of Ruth. "Do not tell me to abandon you, to leave you. Where you go, I will go; where you sleep, I will sleep. Your people are my people, and your God is my God." The only loyalty that transcends all others:

"Your God is my God." Perhaps this is the only way to a new Elisha. Or so it was for Ruth in Moab, when the world was young, so very young.

Kohelet

Wedged between a mournful poem and a hope-filled tale of action is a book of calm humanity, the only universally human, ageless work of eternal truth to be found in all of literature. Easily understandable, accessible to everyone, it is a work of utter simplicity and is, thus, also a web of the most intricate design. On one side we have the book of Lamentations, on the other side the book of Esther, and between them Kohelet. As Goethe said of himself: "A prophet to the left, a prophet to the right, and the world-child in the middle." Lamentations pleads: "Remember the past! Turn us unto Thee! Remember our days as of old!" It is a plaintive plea from generation to generation across the stretch of history, the tragic history of a people. And the Book of Esther commands: "…these days shall be remembered and kept throughout all generations…nor shall the memorial of them perish from their seed." This, too, is a tragic commandment, coming from a people who had already withdrawn from the outside world and drawn up the bridges, a people happy just to be treated in a human manner. But the wailing proved too strident and the rejoicing too insignificant; both led into valleys of decline. And between these two valleys arose a mountain, calm, clear and cold; a book of wisdom which was not afraid of its own courage; a monument to thought, playing with all the possibilities and squarely facing all the consequences, a book in which affirmation and negation meet and acknowledge one another as mirror images of the same being, a being created by our fantasy.

No one knows the author's identity. All those who have tried to put Kohelet into a historic framework have merely expressed unfounded opinions, given way to more or less poetical conjectures. And truly, we would gain very little from knowing Kohelet's name or even what century he lived in, since the timelessness of Kohelet's thoughts renders worthless all historical references, all efforts to assign them to a specific time and a specific space. The truth he enunciates is the truth of the ages, of today, of yesterday, of the faraway future up to the End of Days; this will be the only truth about man.

I know that my own conjecture is not based on any historical data, yet I find its lure hard to resist. All of Kohelet often seems to me a parody conceived by a genius, a parody of all of philosophy and of the entire religious view of the world; the reaction of a person who suddenly realizes that "the king is not wearing any clothes." The product of a culture as it ripens, becomes overripe, and approaches autumn. I do not know whether it happens by incident or by design, but I find it truly remarkable that Jews read the sayings of Kohelet during the fall holidays. It is the time of ingathering, when everything is ready: the product of hard, sweating labor, of sowing in tears, and of reaping in song, is already gathered and stored in the barns. People rejoice in the fruits of the Jewish soil and the Jewish spirit; people rejoice in the Torah. And then, in the midst of the ecstatic celebrations, there arises a biting, daring, deeply human, life-transcending doubt which asks: What is it we are celebrating? All is vanity, vanity of vanities, nothing more.

Jews and non-Jews have given ecstatic accounts of what constitutes the essence of the world. The Greeks gave us the formula: everything is being, being in all its varied forms — water, fire, matter, spirit; being in its abstract form. The Jewish formula is: Everything is the manifestation of God's will. And the anonymous rebel counters: All is smoke, steam, vanity of vanities. Please note that he does not say everything is nothing, because "nothing" can also be a mathematical function, a beginning; it can be, and it was, so used by the Gnostics, by the Mystics, by Hegel. Smoke, steam: they are a "something," but they are only insignificant by-products of former existences. The core of Kohelet's thought is contained not in the pessimistic concept that all is vanity, but in his critical relationship to existence. He expresses not pessimism, but negation; not bitterness, but moderation. It is the recognition of limits: "That which has been is that what shall be. And that which has been done is that which shall be done." There is weariness everywhere, and words have lost their import and their meaning, because all existence is mere smoke, a remnant of an extinguished fire, or mere steam, a remnant of water that is no more; and all creatures are configurations emerging out of smoke, nothing more.

It is a book written by the greatest ironist, the most courageous and the most dispassionate book that has come down to us from the ages. It is a book of irony, not of satire or derision. Irony is a concept and a word coined by the Greeks. But neither Socrates, nor the thinkers who came after him, nor the poets who used laughter to combat the world had been true ironists. Irony starts with man himself, within his own being. The moment Socrates announced that his task in life was "to know myself," he stopped being ironic; he had come to take himself and others seriously. The ironist says: Let us say I do get to know myself, what will happen? And if I do get to know the whats and whens and wherefores of events, what will this avail me? I shall know that I am a drop in an endless ocean, a breeze in the wind, a link in the chain which encircles the world and from which there is no escape. "That which is crooked cannot be made straight. And that which is wanting cannot be numbered." Strength, weakness, all will be forgotten, and the wise man dies as surely as the fool. And furthermore, if we go beneath the surface, we find that "what befalleth the son of man, befalleth the beasts." And that in the eyes of eternity they are equally non-existent.

Kohelet — it may be a name, it may be nothing more than a word to describe a "collector," as the Greek translator of the Bible interpreted it, naming this book *Ecclesiastes*. Whether it be a collection of sayings or an original creation, someone had to put it together, someone had to put his stamp on the work. And that one had been a great ironist, a great minimizer of human importance. We can see it in the book's very beginning: "The words of Kohelet, the son of David, a King in Jerusalem." No more do we read "David King of Israel," as in the Proverbs, or just "David," simply, matter-of-factly and, therefore, majestically, as in "Psalms of David," and "Prayer of David." All we have is "David, a King in Jerusalem."

This offhand, superficial link to the whole history of Israel and Jerusalem is itself already a negation, a minimization, an ironic silence. There was a king over Israel and Jerusalem, and if so, nothing came of it. He tried to accomplish something, but his efforts came to naught. He wanted to attain truth, an essentially futile striving since it is an impossible achievement, an achievement beyond our ability, outside of our realm. This is Kohelet's basic concept, which those who came after him reshaped to fit their needs. Men of ardent faith filled it out with piety and ethics and philosophy, trying to soften and sweeten the bitter fare. The wisdom of the Proverbs, the pathos of the Prophets, a religious outlook on the world, all this was added on. But the force of the original thought pierced its way through the added layers.

Aha, we think, now he assumes the tone of a veritable moralist: "…say little…discharge your vows to God…fear God…." etc. But then his tone changes:

There is nothing better for a man than that he should eat, drink and make his soul enjoy pleasure for his labor. And men are commanded to don white garments, anoint their hair with oil and "...whatever thy hand attaineth to do by thy strength, it shall do." Epicurus could not have said it better: It is the philosophy of eat, drink and be merry, for we live but once. But then we hear the original voice of the real Kohelet: "It is better to go into the house of mourning, than to go to the house of feasting. For that is the end of all men, and the living shall take this to heart." And, finally, "What import does it have for man whether he does one thing or another? And who can tell what will befall him in his lifetime?"

Kohelet negates basic human assumptions; he is almost an outsider, standing apart from history, the only one in the entire Jewish world without any historic ties. The prophets were part of their historical times, and Philo was shaped by Jewish history. But Kohelet, except for the pseudonym and the remarks about the kings of Jerusalem, stands outside the narrow enclave that is called history. The sages almost succeeded in suppressing Kohelet; his fate hung on a hair, because the ironic, deeply metaphysical, anti-historical Kohelet did not fit into the national vision of those who wanted to reconstruct Jewish life on an entirely new foundation, and wanted to create a people who dwell in memory. Whether by happenstance or because the collectors wanted to preserve, in one single volume, this variant of the Jewish spirit as well, Kohelet was allowed to remain in existence. It is the final and only expression of a rich, many-colored, mature spiritual life, a life that includes all the peaks and valleys of human experience, a life that already reached the top of the mountain.

It may be that the sages were right. A people steeped in a Kohelet-mood was not equipped to stand fast, to fight, to endure. Kohelet was not able to become a sectarian and a martyr. With his view of the world one does not lose a Jerusalem of stone and of gold in order to win a Jerusalem of pure spirit. Such a mood is not conducive to history making. And thus, Kohelet, while not suppressed, was simply overlaid with Midrashim, with interpretations, with a prayer shawl of purest wool.

But the old ironist of Jerusalem smiles on the book that stands between Lamentations and Esther, and he is not surprised. All that is happening has happened before, and there is a time for all things, time also for his soaring truth. It seems to me that his time has come, must come, because it is fall, and the harvest time has gone; because we reap in tears what we have sown with songs. And in time of pure history, it is Kohelet, standing above all history, who is the guardian of the key.

The Sealed Book

It was 1,420 years ago that The Book was closed and sealed. It was the first such completion. Up to that time nothing in Jewish tradition, in Jewish thought, had been firmly fixed; all had still been in the process of evolving. Jewish thought had changed from generation to generation, developing new systems, different angles of approach, and a variety of viewpoints. The different systems coexisted and came together in a fluid totality in the interlocking teachings of the Talmud. The Talmud, until then, had been a teacher, not a finished codex, nor a Torah that must not and cannot be altered. It was a vigorous living spring, always ready to seek out new paths.

Today we ask ourselves: How was it possible to convey such a tremendous amount of material as is contained in the Talmud by way of mouth, from person to person, by memory? We are so used to books, to the written, printed word, that we are unable even to imagine a culture based on pure memory. A memory containing not only the written Torah but also all the commentaries, every word that was spoken, and when, by whom and to whom it was addressed.

It is, perhaps, the only such instance in all of world literature. The Greeks did not follow this path. Their art of writing was closely linked to their thought process; they did not rely on memory. The Talmud was not only the sole such phenomenon but also the most remarkable. It was the product of a culture that developed in an impersonal, collective fashion. It was the manifestation of a culture that never knew the meaning of form, of style and of conclusion. There is

262

something in the Jewish spirit which stands in absolute opposition to the individual; man counts for nothing, and what matters is the public good he serves. The individual vanishes; the collective remains. The Greeks and the Jews were living in close geographic proximity yet separated by abyss-deep spiritual differences. They lived in the same universe and faced the same problems of man's interaction with external forces and with his inner world.

The Greeks pursued science, i.e. the mastery of natural forces, and philosophy, the discovery of the self. Greek thinkers followed their own path, creating their own view of the world, paying no heed to each other. Heraclitus took no notice of the conclusions of Pythagoras, and Plato did not trouble to acknowledge Heraclitus. It was inevitable that schools and academies would be formed, with stronger thinkers leading the more average ones. But neither the written history nor their orally enunciated contemporary interpretations carried the stamp of authority. The artistic, creative instinct of the Greeks drove them to build up systems, each one in its individual, idiosyncratic style.

Jews were living in the same world, facing the same questions, the same concerns, the same fear of death. How did the Jewish spirit respond to these challenges? The Jews lacked the artistic impulse. They had great, profound, sharp thinkers, but they were not artists. Not one of them, therefore, made an effort to collect his thoughts into a system of his own, to put his personal stamp on the work of his lifetime. Imagine what Jewish culture would have looked like if Rabbis Akiba, Ishmael, and Gamaliel, if Elisha ben Abuyah or Rabbis Meir, Tarfon and Hillel had each wanted to systematize and complete his work? We would have today one of the most remarkable libraries. We would have a cultural treasury of tremendous potential, since each one of them had been a great personality.

Rabbi Akiba alone is already a treasure, a spiritual force of first rank, a thinker who could have occupied a place in universal culture next to Plato and Aristotle. He was not only a strong personality, a national figure, a leader and a fighter, but also a thinker. He uncovered a new method and led Jewish thought away from a slavish dependence on the written word. The Torah for him was merely a casket waiting to be filled with content. What he called the method of discourse was, actually, Greek logic at its most profound. It was the Socratic "guiding skill" which helped the child to proceed from one developmental stage to the next. There was opposition against this method of inquiry. "Akiba, how far are you going to go?" asked Rabbi Tarfon. "How long will you continue heaping your thoughts upon the Torah?" But Rabbi Akiba did not stop. He discovered, amassed and added new content to the traditional lore. Rabbi Akiba, however, was also a child of his time and of his people. He lacked the strength, the will and the need to dedicate himself fully to this work. He remained a teacher and a leader. He was not a writer.

This held true for all the other thinkers and developers of Jewish thought. That is, until the time came when the creative source ran dry, and the living word was caught and cast into a book: the Talmud. A book? A book has a beginning and an end; it follows an orderly process. The Talmud has neither a beginning nor an end. This most remarkable phenomenon in the world is as wide and as deep as an ocean, with neither shape nor point of entry. Everything in the Talmud is idiosyncratic, its form, its language, its content and its method. It is the spirit of the Jewish people, mirrored in its alphabet, crystallized in its words. It is a book that exudes tremendous charm when read in the original, and becomes alien, unintelligible when read in translation. The great German Jewish scholar Zachariah Frankel once said, "One cannot study the Talmud with a dictionary; one can never teach anyone to understand the Talmud in translation. It really cannot be translated."

One can, of course, translate everything. But the original charm, the magic of words, the acuity of logical nuance, all that makes the Talmud what it is, all that disappears. This holds true not only for translations into German, French and Russian, but also for a translation into Yiddish, into the language which for hundreds of years has been the mediator between the Talmud and the Jewish people. The mediator? No, that would have been too much. The art of studying was not about translating the Talmud and interpreting the words, but rather avoiding all interpretation and the search for meaning. The words attracted no attention, nor did one even take the trouble of reading the Talmudic text in a grammatically correct way. One intoned the thoughts in a traditional singsong. One studied the book not as a written text but as a living source, as if one were hearing the discussions between Rabbis Hillel and Shamai, as if being among their pupils and listeners. No one instituted such a method of learning; it emerged by itself, evolving out of the way the Jewish people viewed the Talmud as a living organism.

Fourteen hundred years ago Rabbis Ashi and Rabina closed the Talmud. But the Talmud resisted; it did not accept the closure. It continued to struggle for freedom of movement until the passage of time defeated it once more. And this time it had remained closed, locked and sealed. Our generation has added its seal to the closure.

From time to time there emerges a romanticist who wants to lift the seal, to unlock the book. One such romanticist is Dr. I. M. Zalkind, who shouldered the task of translating the Babylonian Talmud into Yiddish. The first volume, the

Tractate *Berakhot*, has already been published in London. I do not want to enter here into a critical review of the translation or the commentaries. One can, of course, find many linguistic mistakes, and one may not always agree with the interpretations, but this is of small concern to me. What I am most interested in is the undertaking, not the execution; not the literal translation, but its sound and its tone.

When I open a tractate in the original, an idiosyncratic world opens up before my eyes. A world peopled with figures from ancient times, a world filled with shadows out of the past. These shadows come to life for me, they move, they wrinkle their brows in dispute with one another and then relax into telling wondrous legends. I open the translation wondering if it might bring forth the shadowy past in a clearer, simpler, more intelligible way. But no, the entire ancient world has vanished; all that remains is a dead text, often uninteresting, always alien. I do not recognize the Talmud. And the reason for this is clear: One can read Plato or Aristotle in any translation because you can transpose something that is fully formed into another form. But you cannot translate, transpose, capture the movement of the atoms. And the *Gemarah* is, or was, the movement of the atoms of Jewish thought.

It may be that such a translation is needed; it may be that it is necessary to bring present-day Judaism closer to its cultural past. It is surely a praiseworthy achievement, and I admire the diligence and the enthusiasm of the translator. But I doubt very much that this is the right way to achieve it. The Talmud is the Talmud. It is not a book. One has to accept it as it is, or not all. One learns Talmud; one does not read it. And if one studies it, one has to do it in its own language. One must not make Jewish culture too accessible; one must not minimize the effort needed to reach it. It is difficult to find one's way to Jewish culture, and therein lies its originality and its beauty. If someone wants to reopen the Talmud once again and lift the seal of the lock, he must work as hard at it and as persistently as did our fathers and our grandfathers. It is hard work, but it is worth the effort.

The Jewish Form

A Talmudic legend tells us of the time Rabbi Abahu and Rabbi Meir arrived in a city at the same time to teach at two congregations. Rabbi Abahu was speaking about the Agadah and Rabbi Meir was teaching the Halacha. After a while people started leaving Rabbi Meir's lecture to listen to Rabbi Abahu. Rabbi Meir was unhappy about this repudiation, but Rabbi Abahu consoled him with a parable: "Two vendors met on the same street. The first one was offering diamonds, while the second one was selling housewares, such as spinning wheels and needles. Where do you think the people were flocking to, if not to the second stand?"

Rabbi Abahu was modest. But in his modesty, in his downplaying of his own achievement, he uttered a great truth. It is the truth underlying the way in which the Jew relates to the Agadah, to the legend, to poetry, to form. He "merely," naively transformed the housewares into diamonds.

The Jews are a remarkable people. They are engaged in a constant struggle with human nature, struggling against all that speaks simply to the heart and to the imagination, against all that is light and beautiful. Jewish history is in constant warfare against the primitive human elements within us. The more we distance ourselves from life, the better. The greater the difficulties, the more eagerly we pursue them. Is there anything more difficult to follow than the Jewish Halacha? It looms as a craggy mountain, and each time we traverse it we have to clear a new path and shift the rocks. One has to sharpen one's wits and raise one's cognitive capacity to the nth degree in order to perceive its coherence and logical sequence. One cannot achieve this with the usual methods, such as our European-Aristotelian logic that forms the basis for Western European philosophy and science. This kind of logic does not suffice for the study of the Talmud, which requires a different approach, requires broader basic assumptions. And present-day scholars have used great acuity in extracting from the Talmudic formlessness a logical coherence, and in demonstrating its validity and its technique.

It is possible that future thinkers will have to penetrate still deeper into the methodology of the Halacha. Science feels hemmed in and hampered by the processes of Greek logic; it is looking for new approaches. There is a long line of searchers, extending from Francis Bacon to Bertrand Russell to the Jewish-German logician Edmund Husserl. We sense that the world is not resting on the simple, clear Aristotelian laws; it will not submit to them; it is straining to escape them. And Talmudic logic, as difficult and as diffuse as it may be, is, perhaps, more fruitful than the established, completed, petrified logic of the Greeks. And it is this very difficulty which endeared the Talmud so much to the Jews. Jews do not want smoothness. They dislike completeness, the flat, straight, measured way, with a given beginning and end. The Jews pursue a zigzag path, a path that leads up, comes down and ascends anew. At times the path disappears altogether, and one stumbles along until it suddenly reappears, opening up a new, unexpected vista.

This frame of mind may, actually, account for the fact that Jews did not engage in creative arts, and that, even today, Jewish artists tend to be restless, discontented, unable to adapt themselves to established forms, always searching, conflicted, always negating rather than affirming. The Jew drives ahead too fast, feels too intensely, creates no transition between one state of being and another. But art stands and falls on transitions, on the in-between.

One cannot even imagine a Jewish *Iliad* or a Jewish *Aeneid*. If the Jews had been embroiled in a Trojan War or had come up with an Oedipus legend, they would have told it in a few words, just as they related the Creation of the World and the Flood in a few chapters of *Genesis*. The Jew focuses on the heart of the matter not on the accompanying details. He is not interested in knowing how Noah looked or how he was dressed; he was satisfied with learning that "Noah was a righteous man, he was blameless in his age." How the Greeks would have embellished the story of Abraham and Sarah, or such a dramatic tale as the *akedah*. The Jew contents himself with the general outline; the details do not matter to him. And even when overtaken by a yearning for art, for details, for characterizing traits, for the "in-between," he is unable to accomplish it. He cannot hew out any marble statues; he has to content himself with drafts and with sketches.

Many have tried to develop and flesh out Jewish legends. The Midrashim were the greatest artistic endeavor of the Jewish people. But they, too, did not go beyond the initial elements of art, beyond the idea, the content. They gave us diamonds but failed to polish them; they gave us blocks of marble but no statutes. The only attempt, in our time, to come closer to solving the problem of form was made by Bialik. His collection of *agadot* in Hebrew is, perhaps, the first attempt to polish the diamonds, to shape them into a form of art. His artistic instinct showed him the way, the way of art, i.e. height and depth, contrasts, fulfillment and despair.

What about the same legends without an artistic recasting? What about Rabbi Abahu assigning to them the value of housewares? They turn out a bit more folksy, but too Jewishly folksy, too amorphous and without style. Here I have before me such a collection of Talmudic legends in three volumes, translated and arranged by Tcharik. Tcharik made the greatest effort to assemble the pearls of the Talmud, be it the Babylonian or the Jerusalem one, to let the people hear Jacob's voice anew, as it were. It is, undoubtedly, a needed and a useful work. While there may be a doubt as to the need for a Yiddish translation of the Talmud, i.e. of the literature of the Halacha, there can be no doubt at all of the urgent need to bring the Midrashim into Jewish life. The impoverished and parched Jewish soul is, indeed, thirsting for a chance to experience a new flowering. The people's hidden, instinctive aching for beauty yearns to show what we are capable of achieving.

Alas, there is a "but." Tcharik showed more love and devotion for his work than his ability to execute it. He was unable to pour the old legends into new vessels, or, at least, to preserve the old, original charm of the East. It would lead me too far afield to subject every legend to a comparison with the original text. But let us take the legend of David's field. Tcharik transmits the legend, but what is lost in the translation is the remarkable vitality of the story. "David sits down to learn Torah," is Tcharik's translation of the original, which reads "David devotes himself to the Torah." The words describe the same action but in ways which resonate in a completely different way. To "learn Torah" makes one think of a schoolboy at his desk; to devote oneself to the Torah evokes the aura of the East. The Midrash tells about the sages of Israel who come to see David. Tcharik calls them instead "the leaders of the people," and this phrase brings in a dissonant tone. The *Gemarah* says: "They have sought guidance from the *Urim* and *Thumim*." Tcharik then explains: "They were considering the chances of winning the war." Why did he need such an addition? It is not contained in the text; it changes the mood and brings in another atmosphere.

And another example. There is a small Talmudic legend from *Yebamot* about a Greek who wants to become a Jew. The Talmud says that he is asked why he wants it, and does he not know how hard it is to be a Jew? He is accepted when he replies: "I know it, and I feel that I am unworthy." The implied meaning is: I am unworthy of becoming a vessel for so much suffering and greatness. It is a proud, beautiful and uplifting answer. Tcharik translates it thus: "I know it, but because of it I consider it an honor to become a Jew." And the answer loses its beauty.

I could cite other examples but I do not want to enter into a philological and critical discussion. It only pains me that such a work as the translation of the Agadah has not been done in a more artistic way, in a more modern, and, I would say, a more literate language. I regret that we do not have a Yiddish translation of the Agadah that could measure up to Bialik's Hebrew rendition. We need it. The unpolished diamonds left to us by the ancient Jewish imagination are awaiting their refinement, are awaiting the new, artistically awakened Jew.

A Treasury of Allusions

Every time I pass a Jewish bookstore, its shelves overflowing with books of rabbinic exegesis and sermons, I remember the rabbi of my schooldays, Rabbi Aaron Meir Dragitschen, who had found his way from Lithuania to Ouman. Throughout the week he taught us *Gemarah,* but on Shabbat he assumed another role. On the Sabbath he became a preacher, a sermonizer, an orator. And we, his students, were aware of how much mental strain and effort went into the preparation of his sermons. I do not know why it was so, but we suspected that he was not a great scholar. Perhaps it was due to the fact that he was not very astute, that he could not find his way out of the maze of Talmudic debates, and that he was unable to evoke in us the desire to pose questions, to hone our brains by "lifting mountains and demolishing them," as the Talmud enjoins us. We perceived, however, how he truly revived, expanded, caught fire, when he approached the Agadah and the Midrash. And he used to quote with enthusiasm the famous saying from the *Sifrei*: "If you want to know God, study the Agadah."

We students felt, however, that this was merely an excuse. Our *Gemarah* teacher just did not have the gift to deal with the *pilpul* and with the harsh logic of the stern Halacha. He was drawn to poetry, to the legends, to the literature; this was what he knew, what was accessible to him. And a few years later an eminent scholar came to teach the *Gemarah* to those few persevering and began with a warning statement: "Those who have composed the Agadah, and those who are studying it, are wasting their time." Yet he, Rabbi Joseph Ben Levi, had never even looked at the Agadah.

Thus we found ourselves between two poles: the strict injunctions of the Halacha, and the liberal interpretations of the Midrashim, until life cut our ties to both. We began to see the teachings as dealing merely with the past, with long dead generations and without any relevance to our present-day life. All this lore was the province of historians, of students of literature, of all those who devote themselves to exploring the past. Yet the very fact that our current approach to knowledge, in all its aspects, has become historical and coolly objective, may lead us to explore both Halacha and the Midrashim more seriously and more incisively. The further we move from the historical reality of daily life, the sharper grows our perception. We are only now achieving the right perspective on the ancient spiritual life of the Jewish people. The Halacha becomes the key to the sociology of Judaism, while the Agadah opens up ways for our understanding of Jewish thought, an intellectual complexity that has never achieved a clear formulation and which has always struggled against codification.

The beauty and the vigor of Jewish thought has always been the "not-saying-it-all," not following a thought to its final conclusion. It was a thought afraid of where it might lead and which, therefore, broke the thread at a critical point. It is a thought suspended in eternal tension between sharp concentration and veiled hints and allusions. And the more we learn of it, the darker it becomes, the deeper and more concealing.

Christian and Jewish scholars have more than once pointed to the fact that there is no creative Jewish philosophy. Even medieval Jewish philosophy is not original, being a mere interpretation of existing systems, a harmonizing of religion with Greek and Arabic philosophy. Militant proponents of Judaism are endeavoring to prove the opposite and are basing their assertions that there is a purely Jewish philosophy on a Talmudic scrutiny of the Rambam or of Saadia Gaon. They think that pouring over ancient texts can rehabilitate the Jewish philosophical reputation. They are laboring in vain. Jewish thought does not manifest itself in systems or in methods; it is never crystallized, never complete, never putting an end to further pursuit. It is spread out and scattered; it is fragmented; it is mere allusions, always a beginning, or a continuation, never an ending. It is almost impossible to combine all the separate fragments into one complete picture, to make even a mosaic. The *Zohar* attempted it. It wanted to place under one roof, to combine in one system, the thoughts of past generations, all the Judaic philosophic searchings and arguments; but it did not succeed. It wanted to fuse the scattered, glowing, shining sparks into one great flame, a holy light; but the sparks lost their glow and became extinct. If we want to fathom Jewish thought, we have to go the source. We must do so without hoping for a universal vision, for a *Weltanschauung*. A different approach is needed. Jewish thought is multi-colored, and therein lies its worth.

There lies before me a book which, to my mind, is of much greater worth than all the attempts to compress the wide spectrum of Jewish thought into systems and subject it to scientific validation. It is an artlessly conceived book, without recourse to any philosophic or, even, scientific-critical methods. The material has been collected and assembled with utter simplicity by an old-fashioned Sephardic rabbi. The book is titled *Torah Shelema* (The Whole Torah), and the author is a Jerusalem rabbi, Menahem M. Kasher. In his introduction, however, Rabbi Kasher states that he is laying no claim to authorship, citing the words of the *Gemarah*: "Pray do not draw any conclusions, and pray do not interpret. Please tell it simply, in an orderly fashion." He is not an instructor, nor an interpreter; he is simply assembling data in an orderly fashion. He has undertaken a difficult task of gigantic proportions: to extract from the extensive Midrashic literature all the commentaries on the Torah. This actually means providing historic annotations to the Torah. It means fusing for the first time in an orderly fashion the two Torahs, the written and the oral, into one organic unit in order to make it the whole Torah.

It is a gigantic task. Two volumes have appeared already, and they have reached only the second chapter of Genesis, which means that when the book is finished it will occupy an entire bookcase. It will become a library unto itself. As was said, the method of the compiler is not a modern, scientific one. He only selects and compiles commentaries, he does not expound their historic backgrounds nor, even, their linguistic idiosyncrasies. But this does not matter. We are well supplied with historians and philologists, including William Bacher and his well known work on the Midrashim, and Louis Ginzberg, with his monumental work in English, *The Legends of the Jews*, especially volumes five and six which contain annotations and explanations. What matters is the material itself; what is important is the collection. And what a fabulous collection of Midrashim is being offered us! Old, forgotten, hidden treasures have been brought to light. Midrashim from Yemen, Midrashim still in manuscript, Midrashim from all corners of the world are assembled here. Take the first passage from Genesis: "In the beginning…" It is a stone-hewn sentence, a pillar, surrounded by a forest of pillars: the Chaldaic Targums — Onkelos, Jonathan ben Uziel and Yerushalmi — as well as Rashi, *Gemarah*, Midrash, the *Zohar*…290 items about the first passage alone.

I am reading (if you can call it reading, if it is at all possible to read such a book the way one reads any other book), and thought after thought flashes through my mind, following spark after spark, allusion after allusion. Generations are calling to each other across the stretches of time, talking things over. Here you find a profound observation, there a poetic figure of speech, and further on the sigh of a fettered thought and then a smile, the smile of a skeptic. And you see the Jewish spirit at work, weaving its pattern, breaking off the thread and resuming its weaving with so much passion and such profound despair, the despair of ever reaching the goal.

You turn a page and you read: "In the teaching of Rabbi Meir was found a remark: 'and behold this is very good — and behold, death is good.'" Rabbi Meir, an apologist for death! Rabbi Meir expressing a Buddhist thought! One remark, one word, and Rabbi Meir expands in front of our eyes to an even greater stature, becoming Rabbi Meir the philosopher.

Turn another page and you come to a passage from a Midrash on exultation: "In this hour David was so filled with joy that he erupted in folly and out of his folly he fashioned his song. And God said to him: 'This folly is good!'" And you see before you a strong, rebellious Jew who did not want to separate the world from folly; you see a realistic moralist. And then comes one who thinks in economic terms, a historic materialist: "Said the rabbi: 'When there is sufficient bread in the world, then there will be peace in the world.'" Peace and bread, peace and money, politics and economics go hand in hand.

I could fill entire pages with quotations, with wonderful sayings, but it is not necessary. The beauty of these ancient words and thoughts is that they stand alone, isolated, and one must go to them, seek them out, dig a path to their depth. What a pity that my old Rabbi Aaron Meir had not lived to see such a book, to have such a treasure. How happy he would have been. He was not destined to have it. And this is the way it usually happens in life: Those who were really in need of the book, the preachers, the sermonizers, the bookworms, they are gone, and those who now have it do not want it anymore. Except for the historians, except for those who want to rethink Judaism's historic configuration and to gain a deeper understanding of it. They form the exception, as well as those who are still able today to understand the allusions of Jewish thought and who want to develop the allusions into concepts — if this is possible.

Telling Throughout the Night

They had been sitting up the entire night, a spring night, telling the story of the Exodus from Egypt. "What did they tell?" I was asked by a child who, unlike her elders who were content to accept given facts and clichés, was young enough to be curious and to ask questions, yet old enough to understand an answer, even if it did not conform to the accepted text.

"What was it that kept them talking the whole night long? Surely they did not retell, word by word, all that is told in the Bible, all that we read in the Book of Numbers and the Book of Exodus. And even if they had, would that have taken the entire night?"

"They have told a story which views things from a different perspective, my child, a story which was never written down, a story which the priests and the scribes suppressed and erased from memory. They told the secret of how history is being made."

"Tell me, tell me!"

"Even if it takes the whole night?"

"I am ready for it," said the child, with glowing eyes.

And I began to tell, although sure that but few of my words would reach the ears of the child. I knew that very shortly the child's eyes would close, lulled by the almost melodious tone of the tale, because any tale built on orderly progression possesses an inherent rhythm, and rhythm, in the end, turns into melody.

And because I knew it, I was able to loosen the bridle which constrains imagination, the myth-creating, history-weaving imagination and tell....

In the city of the white walls, the city of Memphis, and in all the smaller and larger cities of upper and lower Egypt, life was in turmoil. The calm and order of the past evaporated into thin air, as it were. Revolution, the dissolution of the small, feudal princely states, the downfall of the old feudalism, strengthened the power and majesty of the king, the pharaoh. The old, naive, African way of life, thought and belief vanished. New designs were being woven on the ancient loom, designs originating in Asia, and forgotten cultures were coming to bloom again on the hot Egyptian soil. Half buried in the sand of Sahara, the sphinxes, half man and half beast, were keeping vigil over the fate of men and were smiling their mysterious, not-yet-human smile.

In the academies of Memphis scribes were etching images on stones, painting signs on papyrus, preserving the treasures of knowledge amassed by generations, knowledge of ways of measuring and of calculating, of damming the rising water of the Nile and of regulating its fall. They wrote down everything that had happened and that had to happen. Deep and searching thoughts, along with daring words, were being etched in stone, were being painted on the thin papyrus sheets. Some were telling of the customs of alien people in unknown lands, others were talking about the Asians and, especially, about a remarkable tribe called the Hebrews, a nomadic tribe with just one aim in life — to wander and to fight, to fight anyone willing to engage in a fight, their hands always raised in a striking position and in each hand a knife. The scribes told not only about foreign lands and strange peoples, but also about mysterious gods: gods of a thousand shapes, gods with the head of a bird or the body of a serpent, gods who wore masks of the ever-changing ways of the world. One of the scribes, however, was etching and humming to himself the *Song of Aton*, a psalm of praise to the only god of the universe: "You arise in your splendor on the horizon, Aton, you source of life. When you appear on the sky, you fill the earth with your beauty, you are great, you are beautiful, you illuminate the earth." And the wondrous hymn closes with the lines: "You extend yourself into tens, hundreds, thousands of forms, into countries and cities, fields and roads. You are in my heart, no one understands, no one except myself, your son, flesh of your flesh, Ichnaton."

Pharaoh and his priests were not asleep; they understood the peril that lurked in the Aton songs and meditations. They remembered the times of Ichnaton, the apostate, who turned away from Amon-Ra and pitted himself against the entire established order of the world, wherein the kings are ordained as absolute rulers on earth, and Amon-Ra rules the heavens. They did not forget the revolutions which had shaken up Egypt, the land of the white and red crown, nor the keepers of order who had persecuted those who preached and continued to adhere to the apostasy of "Ichnaton the damned." Pharaoh's chains came to weigh heavily on those who embraced freedom of thought and their prison cells were dark and dank.

The revolutionary thinkers left the metropolis, fled far away from the center to the city at the border of the land where Asian tribes were living, tribes who had once flocked in from Canaan and from other lands, nearby lands and those far away. They lived in a world of their own, with their own peculiar customs, their own, different way of life. You could not find here the refinement of Egyptian life, nor the ironic wit of the seers and magicians, only the desert-hot passions of peoples who have not yet lived out their allotted time, who have not yet completed the circle of their existence. An active volcano not yet cooled down. It was to this human encampment that they came to seek refuge, these spiritual revolutionaries, these seekers of a new truth, Egypt's passionate intellectuals. But they expressed their thoughts in ways which were too literary, too spiritual, too mysterious to be understood by the masses, who heard only one theme: the call to freedom, the song of wandering.

Among all the peoples and tribes in the encampment, the most restless and most inquisitive group was a small band of people called the Hebrews. They listened avidly to all that Prince Moses the Egyptian was telling them, all the songs he was singing to them, all the secrets he was uncovering for them. And as they listened they were reminded of their own ancient traditions and legends which had been passed on from one generation to the next and which had grown more beautiful and more heroic with each retelling. Legends of the Fathers who rebelled against the old worldview, who bore testimony to the existence of God and refused to serve any man, any king, even one who wore two crowns, a white one and a red one, the two-fold crown of Egypt.

The time came when the guardians of law and order, Pharaoh's officials and soldiers, became aware of the disquiet which had begun to spread along the border, and they began to mete out punishment. "Let them do hard labor, let them sweat in the sun carrying bricks, let them build and produce; this will stop their thinking and their dreaming," decreed those in power. Those who expressed discontent were imprisoned, their leaders hunted down, one revolt after another suppressed in blood. The seeming impossibility of any successful, prolonged struggle caused a split in the ranks of those persecuted. The older, wealthier ones sighed plaintively: "What do they want from us, those who are trying to seduce us into rebellion? All of Egypt is calm; everyone is satisfied. It is true, of course, that Pharaoh makes demands and that Pharaoh is an oppressor, but this is the way of the world, this is the law of life on earth, and one must obey it. Life is really very good in Egypt; why should we provoke the lion of the desert?" Thus did the old and rich ones talk among themselves, and they came to the decision to turn over to Pharaoh's men Moses and the group of Egyptian intellectuals who joined the Hebrews. "We will not tolerate being used to protect strangers," ran their argument. "We don't want to transform the entire world. We simply want to live like everyone around us."

Moses got news of the plot, and he and a number of his followers left the settlement at night, escaping into the desert. "Those who want to go in search of the unknown God, the nameless God, who is greater and higher than Aton, more severe than he, more demanding and more proud than Egypt is at its most magnificent, follow us!" The call was transmitted from ear to ear, and one after another, they stole away from their dwellings, young warriors filled with a thirst that cannot be expressed in a word or contained in a concept; a thirst for wandering.

Thus began the greatest, most fantastic epic of world history. An epic which has its beginning in the most distant past and its ending...its ending at the end of time. Verse after verse, song after song, and always back to the beginning, to the hot spring of Aton, in the sand of the desert.

"You know now, my child, what it is that they have been telling throughout the night about the Exodus from Egypt. What we are telling now is the completion of the story, the national-historical event. But the story which is told on the night of the "order," on the Seder night, is truly the story of the source, of ancient stirrings, of that which transcends nationality and language and country, which is greater than man and higher than an "Aton." But only those whose ears are attuned to the deepest tones can catch it, that old, concealed and suppressed tune, the song of eternal disquiet, of the ever-readiness to be on the way. Do you hear my child?"

But the child did not hear; she had fallen asleep with her head on my shoulder. I knew it would be so. Children may ask questions but lack the patience to wait for the answer. Adults, on the other hand, may perhaps muster the patience to wait for the answer, should they ever gather the will to ask questions.

The Two Walls

Some years ago I was asked by a London paper to write an article about Hanukkah. I was younger then, more hot-headed, more apt to give voice to all my thoughts, to matters which seemed vitally important, and so I wrote an anti-Maccabeean article. I did not do it because I delight in paradoxes, in the "maybe it's the other way around," but because I sincerely believed that the Maccabees had committed a historic injustice. They had barred the path of Hellenism, and their struggle had eternalized the conflict; they had created a prologue to the great historical passion-drama called Judaism. My question then was: What drove them to do it? And I ended with the hope that I would never again be asked to write about Hanukkah.

Years have passed and here I am writing about Hanukkah, not on anyone's request but on my own volition, driven to it again and anew by the old, eternal question: What is the meaning of Jewish history? I am often told that this is an individualistic, "elitist" question, merely an idle cogitation, or as H. Rosenfeld recently characterized my entire way of problem-posing, a question for a Rambam. I do not wish to argue the point except to say that the individual has the same rights as the collective — what is, after all, a collective if not an assemblage of individuals?

On every possible occasion I ask the question of the meaning of Jewish history — the meaning not in the mystical sense of having been determined by a Supreme Providence, nor in the sense of purpose, but a meaning in the sense of content, of substance. When we talk today about the meaning of Roman history or of the French Revolution, of events long passed, without any direct bearing on our present, we aim only to understand the basic motives underlying the facts, to make sense of what has taken place. We scrutinize the multitude of events in the light of the results achieved — success or failure — and lay bare their substance, their inner core. And since history may, indeed, not be a teacher capable of transmitting a useful pattern from one generation to the next (because humanity is governed not by reason but by the will, passions and the interest of the moment) it is especially important to understand the nature of our present moment, our today. And this may also account for my striking out in various directions, pursuing paths which turn out to be dead ends, or which meander aimlessly, or which lead me back to the same old wall, the wall which is also a gate. I knock, and I plead, "Open the gate!" But there is no answer, not yet.

It seems to me that we can approach history only through images, that this is the only way we can relate to historical events. And so I see before me two walls facing each other throughout the ages, at once enemies and partners. By itself, each wall is merely a ruin or a gravestone. Together, covered by a roof, they form a dwelling. The essence of a dwelling is that the opposing walls shall never come together, shall always oppose each other. Should they lean towards each other, becoming one, the structure would collapse.

Two walls — on one we find the pronounced Tetragrammaton, on the other we find the beautifully painted, elegantly clothed figure of the eternal Aphrodite, with her wise, charming, enchanting smile and Venus emerging radiant and laughing out of the ocean waves. The wall with the sacred name on it bears rows of prohibitions, of "you shalt not." Each "no" is a barrier, and every "shall not" a guideline, a directive. You shall not do this means you must do that, in such and such a manner must you conduct your life, this is the way you must follow, this is your way, the Jewish way.

On the other wall we find a world of possibilities — sometimes things are done one way and sometimes another. One may do anything; everything is allowed. And should there be anything one may not do, then this is stated with regret. Venus-Aphrodite. Venus emerging from the foam is so tolerant of sin that she does not even concede the concept of sin. Not that the Greeks did not struggle with a feeling that there was in the world such a thing as sin, or, as they called it, hubris. Hubris was a theme of the Greek tragedies, but it did not become a part of Greek thought or of Greek life. On the doorsteps of the Greek house, by the Greek wall, played Aphrodite's only son, Eros, blindfolded, aiming his arrows at those who passed by. On the doorsteps of the Jewish house, by the Jewish wall, sin was crouching, Sphinx-like, consumed by burning wrath, and lying in wait like a feral beast, like a faithful watchdog ready to jump on the unwary passer-by, on the stranger. Eros was provoking sin, and sin was baring its teeth. And thus the two walls were facing each other in an oddly companionable way: two walls, under one roof, never blending into each other, never separating from each other.

If we compare the Maccabeean struggle with the grandiose struggle against Rome we find the same national heroism, the same stubborn nationalism, even the same religious politicking, but the tone is different. The Maccabees struggled not only with the Greeks, but also with themselves. They, too, had loved the sweetness, beauty, lightness and luminous depth of Hellenism, and they had fought for their spiritual survival, not their physical one. Their struggle had not been one of narrow nationalism. They had, after all, traded one dependency for another as they sought Rome's protection against the Seleucids and the spirit of Hellenism. But they had not minded it because they felt a part of the political stream of life, part of the world. They felt they were the only people truly to enact world history.

Can one really imagine what would have happened if the Maccabees, following the example of the Jerusalem Hellenists, had dressed like the Greeks, put grape leaf wreaths on their heads, and sung lovely Greek songs accompanied by harps? The world would have become Greek in language, in sound, in character and in thought, and Venus and her son would have ruled it. A wall — colorful, marvelously beautiful, but still only a wall. An ornate, a golden gravestone, but only a gravestone. The Maccabees did not allow this to happen. They neither wanted to reform the Greek world, nor to destroy the second wall. As a people with a sense of history, the Jews have always understood that there is a need for a dual outlook on the world, that man must have choices. Truth is a choice between this path here or that one there, and the very "or" presupposes the existence of both the "here" and the "there."

The Maccabees fought and won because spiritual struggle knows neither defeat nor conquest, and this was a struggle in which Jews have always manifested their strength. Even though they did not conquer, they had attained their goal — they had preserved the two-walled structure. Rome, later on, put its own roof over both walls and then added two more, transforming the Greek and the Jewish worlds into a new one, the Roman world, a political empire ruled by might. Yet the basic pattern could not be changed. Eros is still confronting sin, both needing each other, both actors in the great, eternal play — the mystery of man and God.

Once I had been inclined to argue with the Maccabees: Might it have been better to let the Jewish world go under gracefully, to let Judaism and Hellenism fuse? But the years have taught me: What is, is, and cannot be otherwise. Waters cannot flow one into the other nor can souls merge with each other; rooted in their own soil, they face each other, wall facing wall. Some contests are won, others are lost. At times, a certain atmosphere, light, and touch of an artist's brush will soften duality into harmony; at other times, the contrasts are revealed in all their sharpness — bitter foes, snarling at each other with bared teeth. And together the two walls make up the world of today, as they have from times immemorial and, undoubtedly, as they will tomorrow. No one has lived in vain. Everything has a meaning.

When Abraham was Still Young

He was very young and was still called Abram, simply Abram, the son of Terah. Legends tell us that Terah was a storekeeper, a merchant, who did a brisk business trade in all kind of religious articles. His store, stocked with fine, rich wares, was one of the best in the old city of Ur-Kadesh. Was there anything one could not find in Terah's store? Were you looking for big gods? There they were: Ea, the biggest God of the heavens, and his son Marduli; Gibul, the fire god; Nindar, the grim, evil god; and many others. There were the Ammakinm, the earth-spirits, and gods in various shapes: a human head joined to the body of a lion, a giant man with wings, or a man with the body of a fish. Everything could be found in Terah's store.

The pious men of Ur-Kadesh used to flock to the store, bowing deeply to the statues that lined the walls and prostrating themselves before the gods they were about to purchase. They pleaded for their favor in long or short prayers. Then came the haggling between the store owner and the customers, until, having obtained the best possible price, the men and women of Ur picked up their gods off the shelf and carried them to their homes or to the great ziggurat, the tower which served also as the town's main temple. Jewish legend relates, with its idiosyncratic humor, of the time young Abram found himself alone in his father's store, Terah having gone into town to take care of an especially large order, and began a theological disputation about god and the gods, and ended up almost ruining his father's business. It would appear that the citizens of Ur did not think much of freethinkers and philosophers and did not take kindly to a young merchant's audacity in expressing his heretical views. Terah's business rapidly began to decline, in the end forcing him to leave Ur together with his sons Abram and Nahor.

The rest is well known. Terah died in a foreign land, unable to forget his homeland, and Nahor did not accomplish much; only Abram managed to work his way up. He changed his name — an old Jewish custom — and Abram turned into Abraham and became…well, we all know what he became and feel it in our very bones.

It was not so very long ago that it was the rage among historians, and even the well educated, to smile at the mention of Abraham. The entire Biblical story, told in just a few lines, was seen as so fantastic, so unhistorical, that it must have been a legend. Imaginative historians sought proof in various nooks and crannies that Abraham was merely the name of an ancient god, though it was not altogether clear what kind of god, a sun-good or a moon-god. Even a scholar of the caliber of Edward Maier, a truly eminent researcher, made an effort to prove that Abraham and Sarah were the names of two local Canaanite gods and that it was a latter-day legend which transformed them into the parents of the Jewish people.

The doubt about Abraham's reality stemmed mostly from the inability to conceive of the actual existence of Ur-Kadesh and to accept the reality of the flood, the tower of Babel, etc. One interpreted the Bible, as the Bible intended it, from a universal perspective, which led to the fantastic tales woven by historians around the Biblical legends. The flood? A universal flood? When did it happen? Where are the geological proofs? There was a time when one assumed that the legend of the flood, which spread over the whole world and can be found in the mythology of various, far-spread peoples, is an allusion to a great geological catastrophe which once, in by-gone times, split the earth asunder, separating Europe from Africa and Asia from America, destroying an entire, highly cultivated continent, which Greek legend calls Atlantis. Viewed from this broad perspective, the entire Biblical legend, and, obviously, especially the one of Abraham and Ur-Kadesh, lacks all historical value.

Most recent scholarship, however, has reined in imagination. Instead of universal history, the Biblical chronicle has become the story of a certain land, of quite a narrowly determined one, just as it says in the Bible, the history of Mesopotamia. It is the land between the rivers Tigris and Euphrates, the land that extends, in the East, from the Persian Gulf to the Syrian desert, to the kingdom of the Medes, which extends into Central Asia up to the Caspian Sea, in the north of Armenia, to the land that was once called Urartu (Mount Ararat), and in the west to the cradle of the Semitic peoples: Arabia. Up to the 19th century no one harbored the slightest doubt that the land between the two rivers had been a purely Semitic land and that its history was exclusively that of Assur and Babel. And truly, we find in the Bible names like Shanor; we know of commerce and industry, of cities, or capitals, such as Alsor. Genesis tells us of the war conducted by four kings against five others: Chedorlaomer, king of Elam; Tidal, king of Goyim; Amraphael, king of Shinor; and Arioch, king of Ellasar. But all these were such incomprehensible, fantastic names, names without even a Semitic ring to them, that they were, so to say, politely ushered out of history. That is, until 1842, when a French consul began excavations on the sites where Nineveh and Calah once stood, reactivating Oriental research and starting a new chapter in the history of the ancient East, changing ancient legends into realities. The Englishmen Layard and Rawlinson came to Mosul, and there were excavations after excavations in the palaces of Sennacherib and Shalmaneser; and the relics of Babel and Assur bore testimony to their past.

The research went still deeper when George Smith took on the task of studying the libraries found in the palace of Sennacherib, filled with small, baked tiles, and covered with mysterious, cuneiform characters. Tremendous patience, industry and acumen prevailed over the ravages of time, and the world beheld, emerging out of the sea of the past, an ancient culture with a language which had been old already when Abraham was still young. There emerged from its grave a culture of iron and bronze, the culture and the language of Ur-Kadesh, of Akkad, Erech, Kish, etc.

The German philologist Paul Haupt and others did their best to fit the surviving inscribed shards together, to systematize them, and then, with the help of old tile grammars and dictionaries found in the ancient libraries of Assur and Babylon, they brought forth a grammar of the Sumerian language. It is a language completely unrelated to any either Semitic or Aryan languages, closest in sound and structure to the Turco-Tataric dialects, and scholars have classified it as one of the so-called *Turanic* languages. Their characteristic trait is the absence of grammar as we understand it. Words are simply strung together, they are not declined, modified or defined in any way. The grammars of the Sumerian language which have appeared so far contain, perhaps, more imagination than true science, and the philologists have yet to agree on the question of the roots and origin of the ancient Sumerian language. It is still impossible to say whence the Sumerians came and when. Were they the first inhabitants of Mesopotamia with the Semites coming later, taking over the land? Or was it the other way around: were the Sumerians the ones who had come from far away and, for a span of time, had become the rulers in the "land of the two rivers"? It is a question which science still cannot answer. This applies not only to the older scholars such as Rawlinson, the author of the well-known work *The Five Great Monarchies of the East*, or Lenorman, the scholar of the culture of the Kushdim, or Hamel and Delitsch, but also to the most recent scholar in the field, Professor C. Leonard Woolley, the excavator of the Sin-temple (the temple of the moon-goddess) in Ur-Kadesh; even he cannot give a clear answer.

Perhaps one must dig even deeper and explore even further afield before one can arrive at a more or less satisfying result. But even current archaeological and historical explorations open up a remarkable panorama to view. An ancient, closed book has opened up to us, and we can read in it the history of generations which vanished even before History began. A mere two thousand years ago the ancient Syrio-Greek writer Berosus wrote the history of Assur and Babylon and told the following: Long ago there came out of the sea someone by the name of Aanes. He was, at once, a man and a fish — half-man and half-fish — and Aanes brought with him science and the arts. He taught people the art of writing and all the other knowledge, and since that time no one had added to that knowledge.

A ridiculous legend, but one which has received a certain amount of historic confirmation. Aanes, half-man and half-fish, is none other than *Ea-An*, the God of Water of Sumerian mythology. And the entire legend means only that the Sumerians brought with them to Mesopotamia a rich culture and that they laid the foundation for the further development of Sumerian and, consequently, of European civilization. And their history begins at the point where the Bible offers its first thread, with the flood.

First come legendary and fantastic numbers. The list of kings is divided into two parts: the kings who ruled before the flood and those who ruled after. The name of the first king on the list is Alulis from the city of Nunk, and he ruled for eight *sars,* which is 82,000 years; after him came Alalgar, who ruled 36,000, etc., etc. There were altogether eight kings in five cities and the span of their rule was 250,000 years. "…and after that came the flood. And after the flood the kingdom was sent to earth from above." Thus begins the chronicle of Sumerian history. And when you join this with the famous Babylonian flood-tale, the so-called Gilgamesh epic, where the flood is described almost as in Genesis, when one weaves together all the threads of tradition and history, one can form a clear picture of the flood. From a legend it becomes a historic fact.

Thousands of years ago, six or eight or ten thousand, a great natural catastrophe took place in southern Mesopotamia. The rivers overran their banks, the water flooded the surrounding land, and the entire population perished. Only the

Sumerians, who had brought with them from their own homeland the custom of building their homes on platforms (as was done in ancient Switzerland), survived the flood and pursued their culture. Thousands of years passed and the Sumerians had settled and become the rulers of Mesopotamia and spread their dominion far afield. Ur became their first capital, the first big city they built. And their first ruler, or *petish* (the word has remained in the Hebrew language), was called Meshannifada. His dynasty lasted, according to the Sumerian chronicle, 127 years. A brief span of time for such an old history, but because it is so short, it is already historic, already in the right period.

Cities also grew, and a society came into being. The ancient religion took on a more refined shape. The *petish* was a ruler and a high priest at the same time. The city lived under the protection of a special god, and in honor of the god ziggurats were built: tall, many-floored temples, similar to the Indian pagodas. The ziggurats were built on high hills, and the height of the buildings left such an imprint on the imagination of their neighbors, the Semites, that, in years to come, it gave birth to the wondrous legend of the Tower of Babel. Once again, reality became enlarged and broadened until it took on super-human dimensions. This is, actually, the entire task of human consciousness: to raise reality to a symbol of eternal values.

Two thousand years passed, or perhaps more, and Ur-Kadesh went through its third dynasty. Its northern part was already entirely Semitic, and only the south remained Sumerian. Nineveh did not yet exist, but the same townlet that the Sumerians built and called Ka-Dimiri came under Semitic influence and changed its name to Bab-Ylon. Babylon grew. Not yet a rival in power and culture to Ur or Alsar or Eridi, it was already a cloud on the Sumerian horizon. Ur-Nauum and his son Bir-Sin, the last great *petishim* from Ur, struggled for power over Mesopotamia. They built tall temples, and surrounded the city with tall brick walls. The Sumerian scribes wrote down the old traditions, laws and prayers in order to preserve a culture from dying. But the end came. The last of the Sumerian kings, Bir-Sin, struggled in vain against the Semitic onslaught. Amiru and Elim rose against Ur and destroyed the ancient people. And the last document of Sumerian history, the pillar of Ur-Namu, which was found in the ruins of the city of Nipur, bewails the misfortune of the destruction of Sumeria thus:

> And when they have overthrown, when they have destroyed
> the order,
> And when Elim had devoured all things like a Mahal, how
> they have changed you, Sennir!

They have rooted out the holy dynasties from the temple,

They have destroyed the city and razed the temple,

They have taken over the reign of the land....

With this lamentation Sennir and Echad were buried, wiped off the earth. And this took place when Abraham was young, in the time of Ampral King Shinar, i.e. Hammurabi, the lawgiver of Babylon.

The kingdom had fallen, the language forgotten and the people itself become a legend; but their legacy remained. Absorbed by the Semites, covered up by layers of another culture, re-interpreted and transformed, the work of the Sumerians yet became the point of departure for further development. The laws of Hammurabi, the first judgments proffered from the altar, constituting, if not the basis, still a model for Jewish lawgiving, were nothing more than the ancient laws of Sennir and Akkad. The East owes its architecture, the foundation of its way of life and also the rhythm of its poetry, to an alien people that disappeared five thousand years ago.

At the Foot of the Old Mountain

The other day one of my colleagues, a *maskil* who considers himself "enlightened," asked me half in jest and half in earnest: "Will you now perhaps write, in keeping with the holiday spirit, on a subject of great importance and in the style you favor: mist shrouded mountains, thunder and lightening, a trembling multitude that accepts everything while scared to death, a most beautiful tale of power, the power that the spirit, the word, exercises over man?" I smiled but said nothing, and we went our separate ways.

At first I dealt with his comment as a rather unfriendly witticism, almost a mockery, at any rate an insinuation, since my rationalistic colleague often remarks ironically on my interest in so-called mysticism. But soon the subject of a theme took hold of me. Indeed, why not? Why not submerge myself into the thoughts and the feelings that permeate the most remarkable celebration that exists in the world, the celebration of an idea? It does not matter that thousands of years have covered it with a web of customs that contain little of its greatness and majesty. Nor does it matter that the majority of the holiday-observing, pious or simply custom-following Jews have only the slightest idea of the basic holiday motif. Shavuot is being celebrated with traditional greenery, with dairy dumplings, with Shavuot hymns and with the lyricism of the romantic story of Ruth. But at the back of all the historic events and customs, at the back of all this cozy Jewishness, there stands a bleak mountain, deep, deep in the desert. There stands a powerful, mountainous, rocky concept, the concept of law; and above it, an even loftier concept; the acceptance of the law.

They were wonderful, superb dramatists, those ancient scribes who fused ancient legends with chronicles and memories of various groups and tribes, and extracted from this molten mixture the grandiose images that have transformed the old Jewish stories into a universal book, the Book of Books.

The dramatist creates his work of art by uncovering the essence of the central characters and the main motifs concealed within the endless confusion we call reality. The fewer the characters, and the more consistent the motif, the greater the dramatic impact. Can we find, in all of world literature, a single scene culminating in as powerful an artistic climax as the scene around Mount Sinai, the forbidden desert mountain? Clouds surround it, thunder and lightening rend the air, the mountain spews fire out of its caves. At the foot of the mountain stand a people, man pressing against man, transfixed in awe and in elation. And words, fiery, lava-hot words pour from the mountain into the valley. The people collect them and etch them into their hearts — for all times, for all generations.

At the foot of the mountain lies an encampment of shepherds who escaped from lowly servitude and were wandering in the desert, without a past, without a present and with a very uncertain future. This encampment imposed upon the poor shepherds the burden of the entire world; a burden which no one can sustain and which no one can throw off. A few days earlier, just before they had assembled at the foot of the mountain, they had been free men, as free as all the preceding generations had been, as free as the sand of the desert. And in the course of one day they had become fettered, laden with chains forged out of — what? This is, perhaps, Judaism's most interesting problem, the altogether crucial one: the turning away from absolute freedom toward containment and necessity. What is freedom but a word and a yearning? It has never existed; it will never exist. Not one of the world's creatures is free. Everywhere are iron gates, boundaries, barriers, even for the blades of grass in the fields, the waves in the ocean and the wind in the desert. Let two people come together and there will be power, oppression and dominance. One will command, the other will comply; there will be no equality. Freedom can be obtained only in solitude, but man has never led a solitary life, nor can he do so. Even when he is alone, a Robinson Crusoe, is he really free, can he do what he wants? Is he not imprisoned on his island, and must he not, in the end, depend on his man Friday?

Driven by his need to find meaning in life and in his own existence, driven by his need to find himself, man rebels. He wants to persuade himself that, indeed, as a magnificent ancient poem goes, "man wields the greatest power in the world," that he is, at any rate, its most important element, its core, its point of departure, and its goal. Each person sees himself as the center of the universe; his own being is of greater importance to him than the sun and the stars. All of the cosmos revolves around him. The world begins with him, and without him it loses all its meaning.

When the downfall of man began, who could stop it? Who had the power to do it? There was, of course, the power of iron and of fire, of whips and of swords. This power does lie in human hands. But it is not enough. Neither prison nor death can eradicate the rebellion of the soul, can still its yearning. None of the laws that ruled the nations could prevail over man because they had been forged without his agreement. He had not helped erect the barriers, he had not sanctioned them. Judaism's greatest achievement, its very essence, lies in postulating, for the first and only time, that limitation must be freely arrived at. At the foot of the old mountain, man, for the first time, decided to abdicate his rights. This is the primary, magnificent presentation of the original ancient drama. It was those who followed, the weakened and conflicted ones, who brought in elements of power and of constraint. And none of those preachers and commentators on the Bible felt that they were weakening the importance of Judaism, of its universal-historic character, by introducing the concept of constraint. To have the mountain tower over an encampment of helpless human beings and announce: "Either you will do my bidding, or this shall be your burial place," as the Midrash depicts the Sinai-drama, is a weakening, nothing more than a reduction of a significant psychic process to a mere physical occurrence. Faced with the choice between obedience and death, the poor desert wanderers bowed their heads and obeyed, thus placing all of Judaism into the realm of general human history, a history of power and of fear. In their own fashion the Midrash writers were, of course, historically correct. Jewish history has been one of need and pain, of generations living under force and oppression. The history of the entire development of Jewish thought has been one of a long, difficult struggle of man against the established order, has been forged out of heartache and suffering.

Each year we learn more about Jewish history, how tribes united, how variegated splinter groups had joined them, how various old races had come together in order to create a people, the Jewish people. There are names in the Bible of peoples who had vanished even before Abraham left Ur, names which until now have been thought to be fictitious, but which have now acquired validity and content. Philology, excavations in Asia Minor, and historical research have delved deeper than ever before and have truly revived the dead and the buried. The different concepts of Judaism have also emerged from within the fusion of various elements: The laws of Hammurabi, old Aryan ordinances, the knowledge of the Sumerians, ancient mysteries and legends, all this has found its way into the only book the ancient world has left us. But the artists who created the Book were spurred by a basic concept, a central idea: the concept of will. They brought it to life in a giant scene that is at the center of all other developments, the dramatic events that took place on Mount Sinai.

The idea was that men subjugated themselves freely and in ecstasy, that man sanctioned his renunciation of personal freedom. And this was the first introduction into human culture of the concept of moral law, of the words "thou shalt not," not merely because you are forbidden to do it, not just because you may be watched by a guard with a sword or a whip, but because a voice within you does not allow it; one pledged one's word, and one must keep it. Thus, at the foot of the cloud-covered mountain, conscience was born. This is, actually, the central concept of Jewish history, a concept that most Jewish thinkers, be they ancient or modern, have altogether forgotten. Judaism is usually viewed either religiously or historically, and this is not enough. Religion is philosophy wrapped up in rituals and, as philosophical thought changes, rituals become a burden. Because an event took place once does not mean that we have to go on reenacting it; the past, by itself, does not sanctify life.

The ineptitude of all modernizers and renewers of Judaism stems from the fact that they want to adapt it, in one way or another, to a fluid, passing moment. They want to rescue theology by way of social reform, thus befogging and trivializing both. Had Judaism been nothing more than a theology out of the ancient East, burdened with rituals out of the hoary past, it would have lacked the strength to survive for so long; it would have long ago died a natural death. But the mystery of Judaism is a deeper one; it is a psychic liberation, which means gaining freedom through submission. Only one man understood the fathomless depth of this idea, understood the ways of freedom and of necessity, and this man, Baruch Spinoza, was rejected by Judaism.

The confrontation between Spinoza and Judaism is also a continuation of the Sinai-drama, in that it is, again, the rebellion of man against an idea, the rebellion of Jewish man against the Sinai-idea. And the struggle continues; the Sinai-drama is not yet finished; the last act has not been written. Once again there is need and there is pain; man wades through oceans of blood toward his ultimate rebellion and toward ultimate peace, peace with himself and with the Sinai-established necessity. A superhuman struggle is taking place between conscience and the world. And, as in the first act of this grandiose drama, so in the last one: A frightened nomadic people, encamped at the foot of Mount Sinai, became the world's chief actor, a people who feels that the responsibility for the world rests on its shoulders. A heavy responsibility, but we must bear it. It is our fate.

The Transmigration of a Shekel

The well-known coin collection at the Cluny Museum in Paris was the scene of great excitement. People came and went all day long — gray-bearded and bald-headed professors, artists and simply the curious. And among the curious visitors were mostly Jews, Russian, French and even American Jews. They were all crowding around a table on which stood a small box made of glass, containing a few new coins. They were gleaming, young and pure as a newborn child, spotless and stainless. The coins were of varying sizes and coloration, with Hebrew inscriptions on one side and Arabic ones on the other side. But the Arabic inscriptions could not be seen because it was the Hebrew side that was facing the public. "Out of respect for old age," the director of the museum explained, an old man with deep-seated, burning eyes, the eyes of a dreamer.

The public stood and stared. The director translated the words engraved on the coins, explained the historic context of their origin. He told the remarkable story, thousands of years old, of the shekel, of the Persian drachma, of the Syrian prutah and of the Roman dinar which had all been resurrected at the same time. Their path had been a long one, and in broad strokes and in almost poetic language he portrayed the remarkable transmigration of the coins and the transmigration of a people. After the professor's lecture the visitors left, the gates of the museum closed, and it grew quiet. The professor remained alone in the still, isolated hall, as alone as only art, as only the spirit, can be. He went over, once more, to the glass box containing the new coins. He looked at them with love and with wonder, then slowly lifted the box with the awe of a mother viewing her newborn child and carried it to a table in another corner of the room where other coins were reposing beneath a thick glass top — old, mildewed, misshapen coins, without any intelligible inscriptions or symbols. He opened the lid and added the few new coins, now resting on velvet pads. He closed the lid and stood there, looking at the sudden encounter of generations, the gray-haired with the young and green.

Whether it was due to the stillness or to his nervous tension, the professor soon began to hear a strange noise, a sound like a gentle tap on metal, that usually goes unheard, more a rhythmic vibration than a full sound. The sound grew stronger, more vibrant. "New guests?" asked an old, almost shapeless coin. "Who are they, were they buried under a mountain, a hill? Where do you come from, and who are you?"

"From Jerusalem," came a childish, bell-like voice.

"From Jerusalem? Are you kinfolk, resurrected in the City of David? Where did they find you?"

"Find us?" The young voice began to laugh and was joined by the others. "Find us? No one found us. We have just been created. We have just now emerged from the fiery oven where we have been melted, and from under the hammer which has hammered us into shape."

"Just now?" retorted the old rusty voice almost angrily. "What do you mean just now? How can anything take place just now in Jerusalem? I don't know who you are, but you seem still to be children, and as far as I can remember, only the old ones remained in Jerusalem. Who are you, then?"

The young voices announced cheerfully: "I am a shekel," and "I am drachma," and "I am a dinar," and "I a prutah." For a moment quiet reigned in the box, the quiet that is full of suppressed sighs, the stillness of remembrance.

"Well, well," rasped the hoary voice again, "so you are a shekel and a drachma, a prutah and a dinar, and you are so young, just born. Good, children, now I will tell you who I am, who we are. I, too, am a shekel, and those lying next to me are also a drachma, prutah and dinar. I am the grandfather; they are the children and grandchildren, which means that you are my great-great-grandchildren. I cannot see you very well, since my eyes have grown weak lying in the dark for too long, and the many years of silence have made my voice rough. Can you see me, my children, can you hear me?"

"Yes, yes, grandfather, we can see and hear you. Tell us why you are so old and so broken up. Tell us what has happened to you and why the others remain so strangely silent."

"Old and broken up. Yes, for years and years! You don't know what I have experienced, what hard times I have lived through. I remember…I recall…who knows how long ago it was? I remember the first time the hammer descended on me. You see, my children, I am immeasurably old and do not really remember all my years. I see them passing by like shadows.

"Somewhere there is a sunny land, with weeping willows providing welcome shade on the shores of its river. The people who lived there had long, braided beards and their heads were covered by tall hats. There was also a multitude of other people: people with blunt noses and high cheekbones, like the Tartars; yellow complexioned ones, wearing round hats; and others, tall and stout, with black hair and plaited beards. All languages were spoken there and trade flourished in ripened saffron, pearls, silk, spices and ivory. Outlanders were bringing in their merchandise, and the men and women of Babylon were trading with them. Pieces of silver were held up, measured and weighed, then put under the hammer and broken up. Upon the broken pieces a lighted needle inscribed three letters: *shin, kuf, lamed*. How this had hurt! How painful were the first years of my life!

"I wandered from one land to another, from Babylon to Assyria to Canaan, participating in all the celebrations, serving all the gods, the sun, the moon, and the stars. The gods Baal and Dagan, Moloch and Astruth — their names were etched and burned into me. Until one day I fell into the hands of Abraham, the Abraham of old, the son of Terah from Ur-Kush. I was almost among the 400 shekels Abraham paid to Efron for the cave of Machpelah. Only the fact that I was then already old and battered saved me from falling into the hands of this dreadful man. Efron the Hittite, a wily, experienced merchant, said to Abraham: "Give me a shekel I can do business with, for the merchants of Canaan won't accept such a shekel." So I remained with Abraham, and he beautified me, etching an old couple on one side and a young one on the other. I became an heirloom, handed down from generation to generation, from son to son. I became an integral part of their life. And when David the singer, David the king, came along he took me out of my casket, ordered that I be melted down and that one side should bear the inscription 'Jerusalem the Holy,' and the opposite one 'King David,' and that a tower and a palm branch be added as an ornament.

"This was a happy time for me. I felt young again and new; I forgot all my previous troubles with Moloch and Dagan in Babylon and in Assyria. But time passed, and I was back again in Babylon and barely escaped becoming a Babylonian coin with a new name and Nebuchadnezzar's image etched on my back. Fortunately, my masters had grown wise; they closely watched and protected me, refusing to surrender me. Thus I returned home with them, old and worn out, just as my people itself.

"New coins were being minted. The Persian drachma began to circulate widely, and the Greeks began to replace us with their drachma and talents, so that we were almost forgotten. Worse yet, the time came when the Greeks tried to destroy me altogether, to erase my name and deny me all respect. But then a savior appeared. I was again released from my imprisonment, and re-minted with a new image etched on my back, that of a portion of manna, and my face was adorned with the inscription 'Jonathan the King.'

"Time passed, and more time — it is so difficult to remember all the pain and suffering — until one fine day a Roman appeared with a sharp sword, broke open the casket in which I was resting, threw me into an oven, melted me down and then etched into me the stamp of dishonor: *Judea devicta*, — Israel is conquered — beneath the hard, cruel face of Emperor Vespasian. I was taken to Rome together with my comrades the drachmas and the prutahs, and we were then sent out over the seven seas to show off their pride of conquest and their contempt for us. I was passed on from hand to hand. From Europe to Africa and back to Asia, but never, never once, back to Jerusalem.

"And I have been here now for many years, not knowing what befell those who had been so near and dear to me. I was lying somewhere in a big coffin, in a cold land, beneath ice and snow, yearning for a bit of sunshine and for the sound of my native language, for the colors of my homeland. Years passed; the rain, the dampness, the cold had almost totally destroyed me. My only dream, my only hope, was that someday the moisture of the earth would rust off the old spot of dishonor, the Roman inscription and face, and that I would be returned to my ancient land naked, as the dead must be buried.

"But then I was found, cleaned and polished, and the shameful words *Judea devicta* were brought to light; I lay hopeless and in sorrow. Do you, my children, also bear those words upon you? Is Rome still living? Is Judea still defeated?"

The young coins laughed merrily and answered: "No, grandfather. Rome died long ago and Judea is no longer defeated."

The old coin sighed again: "How often have I heard this, and how often did a master return, a new conqueror bringing his own melting pot!"

"We will not allow it, grandfather, we will not let ourselves be melted again. We either remain as we are or we will be nothing."

"May it be so!" said the old coin. "May it be so!"

Stillness descended again upon the coin casket. The professor came to and rubbed his eyes. It had grown dark. The only glimmer came from the new Jerusalem coins in the glass casket. And the old professor smiled.

In a Small Room

It is an old truism: One can see more in a drop of water, when viewed under a microscope, than in the great ocean. We do not merely get a view of the world reduced to microscopic proportions, we get a view of a much more varied world. Because the most manifold, the greatest, the most wonderful and wondrous phenomenon in the world is the cell. But you can see it only through a microscope, be it a technical or a mental one. This means that one must concentrate one's full attention on one point, and make it one's point of departure.

Observing the storms in a teacup that pervade Jewish life, listening to speeches and finding myself drawn into the thick of the melee, I often wonder: What underlies this struggle. Where is its core? Is it like a tulip, a beautiful goblet of colorful petals which, when separated, reveals only a vacuum? Or, less poetically, is it an onion? You peel off layer after layer, shedding tears as you do it, and when you reach the last layer you find that your tears were shed in vain, for there was nothing at the center.

If I change my focus from the Jewish drop to the Jewish ocean, another metaphor comes to me: the labyrinth that is human life, and thread that might lead Jews out of its maze. The thread breaks or is lost in various places and times in the course of human history. But other nations do not search for it so intensively. To go astray causes them no anguish. Life for them is an end in itself. Jews, however, are always searching for the thread.

New York City is now celebrating its 300th jubilee, and the grand New York City Public Library on Fifth Avenue is observing the occasion with an exhibit of rare books, documents and manuscripts. The large rooms are given over to the history of the city, to unique books, maps and documents of a time when there was, as yet, no New York, no Manhattan, but simply Hudson Bay.

It is interesting but nothing more. What was a small island grew into a metropolis. This is, certainly, a momentous and impressive event but, overall, a natural one. Out of chaos emerges order; what is small becomes big. This is not the first time this has happened, and it will happen again. History is monotonous; it keeps on repeating itself. Visitors who come to admire the exhibit do not know that tucked away in a small room lies a treasure whose importance transcends even the splendor of New York City.

At first glance this is, merely, an exhibit of bibliographical rarities. There is the oldest manuscript of the Bible, older than the famous St. Petersburg Bible, which, up until recently, had claimed this distinction. There is the first printed book in Africa, there are Aboudarham's Hebrew commentaries, and other such antiquities. Dr. Joshua Bloch, the head of the Library's Jewish Division, proudly showed me all the bibliographical treasures he had been able to collect, and my bibliophile heart was, for a moment, aflutter with pride and awe. But soon my attention was captured by something else. I saw before me living Judaism in all its wondrous adventurousness. Day after day I returned to that small room, standing for hours before the glass cases, looking at old documents, inhaling the emanations of the spirit of the past, a spirit as old and as strong as death.

There is an exhibition case devoted to the Samaritans. We see a Samaritan Pentateuch from the third century BCE, written in Phoenician characters, wondrously formed letters that bring us closer to ancient times. They become a connecting link between the Jews and the rest of Asia Minor, plunging us into the old, mysterious life on the shores of the Mediterranean — the cradle of all of modern culture. One document carries a notation: "Written by me, Abraham Ben Israel, Ben Abraham Ben Joseph, the King of Israel." Who is this Joseph, the King of Israel? And what did the Samaritans mean when they said "Israel?" Would they have accepted me, as I gaze at this square lettered manuscript, as a son of Israel? And do we, the Jews of today, truly share the same roots with those preservers of history? Did they die so that we should live? Are we their goal and their fulfillment?

For thousands of years the Samaritans, with their books, calendars and prayers, had clung to the same piece of land, the city of Schechem. But they would soon completely disappear, even as they had been safeguarding the patrimony of their historical rivals, their hostile brethren. They had been safeguarding them for the wanderers who were returning to the land, the wanderers who remained faithful to the pull of their soil.

Then we come to an exhibit case for the Karaites, those who took their Judaism too literally, those who could not adapt. We see the Pentateuch, the prayers and the Laws of Anan, the founder of the Karaite sect. I read a few words of an old Karaite penitential prayer: "Hear ye strayers and sinners, and tremble because the affliction is great." And I am overcome with a feeling of compassion for these Jews who walled themselves in, keeping apart from their fellow Jews, a dried-out branch of a blooming tree.

History has not treated them kindly. It placed them among the Tatars, and almost turned them into Tatars. There is a Bible written in the Tataric language, using Hebrew letters. And I remember seeing a Tatar, with his yellow features and red beard, a round hat stuck on his head and wearing a long robe, walking along the streets of a Russian town, proclaiming: "*Shurus, burus*, old clothes for sale." Is it possible that those Tatars were also Jews, were Karaites? Were those Ahmeds and Abdullahs perhaps also brethren, only we did not recognize them?

Then we come to Persia. Another country, a different spirit. You feel the breadth of the old mountainous country. There are books on a variety of topics, pious and less pious ones, poems and romances. The romances of Azashir and Ezra, i.e. of Ezra and Ahaseurus, the king of Persia, have beautifully executed colorful illustrations. One shows Ahaseurus sitting on his throne, a Persian with Tatar features and long whiskers, and kneeling before him are two Jews, one of whom is Ezra. Ahaseurus' eyes are void of impression, while the bowed figure of Ezra projects self-assurance and pride. More romances, mundane ones, like the romance of Shahin Nizama, and others written in Judeo-Persian, the beginning of a Jewish literature of its own. A beginning which did not lead anywhere. Yet, who knows what impact it may have had on the masses of Persian Jews?

In fact, what do we actually know about this faraway, deserted twig of the old Jewish tree? A strange phenomenon has occurred: The elders have become the younger ones, and the younger ones have become the elders. At the time when Persian Jews were leading lives of splendor, the Jews of Europe were living as barbarians in barbaric lands. They led the lives of Slavs and of Germans, hiding out on the steppes or in the forests, losing almost all the vestiges of Judaism. Persia, at that time, had great Talmudic academies, *geonim*, scholars, thinkers and writers. Jewish pride was then abloom in the mountains of Iran. Yet today, Iranian Jews look with envy and with pleading at their younger, faraway, successful brethren, and seek their assistance in everything, even their Jewishness.

I go on to another exhibit case, and find another country: China, the greatest mystery in Jewish history. Who were the Chinese Jews? Who knows what wind brought there a few Jews from Jerusalem and opened a path for Judaism in the most isolated of all lands? Ages ago there was a Jewish temple in the city of Mai-Fung-Kai. Its building plans have been preserved in ancient manuscripts. It was a Chinese pagoda, following Chinese style and taste, and yet, it was Jewish. One sees a "seat of Moses," a table of incense, even a table for sacrifices, and, further on, a reception hall to receive the *tchaa*, the governor of the city. An intriguing mixture, indeed, of Chinese and ancient Jewish cultures. But above all these curiosities rises one portal, and on it is etched the ancient watchword of the Jews: *Shema Yisrael!*

The Chinese Jew has disappeared, leaving almost no trace behind. But then, in 1875, a Russian Jew, a former student of the Volozhiner Yeshivah, came to China. His name was Samuel Schereschevsky, and he bore the title Reverend. He was a bishop, a missionary. The Russian Jew came to China as a Christian missionary. He translated the Scriptures into Mandarin. And there is his picture: an old Jew sitting at a table, and next to him are two Chinese. They are studying the Torah, in Chinese. Thus, one way or another, following the Jewish or the Christian path, the Jew came with his own book, and had spread its teachings among the Chinese. Reverend Schereschevsky told his Chinese listeners about Abraham and Sarah, about Moses and Aaron, all these stories told in an ancient land, with its still older, still more incomprehensible, culture.

They are touching, these fragments which have remained of Chinese Jewry, even in its comical aspects, even when they transfer Hebrew letters into Chinese ones, changing the r's into l's. The twig was too far removed from the trunk and dried up.

Yellow Jews are soon followed by black one, by those from Indochina, and then those from India, thin and brown, looking just like Indians, as seen in the illustrated *Haggadah* from Calcutta. Jews are sitting around the table observing the Seder. They are dressed like Hindus, they look like Brahmins, and yet, they celebrate the Exodus from Egypt and recite "Next year in Jerusalem!"

I look further and I see that these assimilated Indian Jews, perhaps more assimilated than European or American Jews, have all the problems we are facing. The Torah is translated into Maharati, the language of Bengal, into Puno and Malayalam; there are prayers in Hindustani. And there is even a brochure in Maharati titled: "Why am I a Jew?" written by David Solomon Pezshavker in Bombay in 1895. The Jew of Bombay struggles with his history and must explain why he is a Jew, just as we do. He explains and does not know that no explanation is needed. He is simply what he is; a mystical force draws him, compels him, holds him and leads him. It leads him on roundabout ways to who knows where.

In Tatarland, in India, in Africa, where are Jews not to be found? They have assimilated everywhere, and they are always alone, always by themselves. They always speak two languages, Hebrew and Tataric, Hebrew and Malayalam, Hebrew and Chinese. And it became clear to me, once again, that this is the way it must be. There has recently been talk in Yiddishist circles of the holy Jewish language, of the only Jewish language." There is a desire for normality, for uniformity, and one forgets that the whole strength and beauty of Judaism lies in its duality and diversity.

Mr. Pezshavker of Bombay may also be preaching to the Jewish youth about the holiness and the uniqueness of the Jewish tongue, the Jewish-Maharti one. And why not? Had the Jews of India not spoken Maharati or Tamil or Malayalam or Puno from the time they came to settle? These were the words in which they poured out their longing, their joys and even their prayers.

Sephardi Jews have already initiated a movement toward a kind of Esperanto in Salonika, Sarajevo and the Balkans. Even Tunis and Morocco are struggling to formalize a singular Jewish language in Ladino. There is a growing literature in that language. There was, before the war, quite a large Ladino press, and who can tell how it will fare in the future. Yet above all these tongues, be it Chinese or Ladino, Malayalam or Tataric, there always hovers the ancient, uniting Hebrew language. It bridges two abysses: the abyss of the past and that of the future.

A small room. A few cases which contain so much energy, which are a source of strength, of assurances, of affirmation. How colorful are your tents, oh Jacob, and how adventure-filled!

Around the Center

A few years ago, when national passions reached a sizzling intensity, with every nation eager to manifest its greatness and its uniqueness in all areas, respected European thinkers joined the crowd, considering the question of what constituted a national spirit. William Wundt and Hermann Cohen resorted to an analysis of German philosophy in order to prove that it derived its profundity from being German. Their antagonists, among them Bergson in France and Santayana in America, also strove to prove the national character of the German philosophy and the close ties that bound Kant and Fichte to Bismarck and Hindenburg.

Now that the passions have cooled, the philosophers who yielded to following a political trend may be rather shamefaced, at least if they are genuinely dedicated to philosophy. But something has remained from that time, and that is the concept of a national philosophy or, rather, of an idiosyncratic national mentality; to wit, that a philosophical system, perforce, adapts itself to the general national culture of its people, to its given historical epoch and conditions. But it is only the form that adapts to changes, not the content. The content of all philosophy, no matter when or where, is always the same; it is the universe and the questions it raises, questions of life and death, of man's place in the world, about the present and the past, about our aims and our purpose. All these are the unalterable concerns of philosophy. This is the sum total of all intellectual energy, and it remains constant. What does change is the emphasis, and the form.

Imagine two people facing the same task. One approaches it from one angle, from one point of view, the other from a different one. And when they ultimately arrive at the same solution, it is often not recognized because the methods are so different. I am not saying that it is the task of philosophic inquiry to explore the nature of thinking, rather than thinking about the issues themselves. But when you leave the purely theoretical creative inquiry and start looking at the history of the inquiry, at the history of philosophy, then the psychological method is almost the only one possible. It is, at any rate, the most profound method, one that brings us closer to the source and motivation of thought. The history of philosophy becomes the history of the thought process, and the psychology of culture.

It is important for every community, for every people, to know how their culture has come about, the factors that determined their historic growth and development. It is a process of national self-knowledge and understanding. As important as this is for nations whose existence is tied to their land, how much more important is it for us, who are poised with one foot on Jacob's ladder.

Tradition tells us that "Israel and the Torah are one." Jews and the Torah, Jews and a view of the world, Jews and thought, are one entity. We cannot escape from it, however much we may want to. It is our fate. The question is: What is Torah? Or, what should it be? How did it come into being? What was its path? What strength has it retained, and what are its present potentials?

At the beginning of his recent book about Saadia Gaon, Dr. Henry Maltor cites a line from the Gaon's *The Book of Knowledge*: "God never leaves his people without a teacher whom he inspires and instructs, so that he should teach and lead his people and devote his life to it." This is highly characteristic of the entire Jewish view of life. Jewish life cannot sustain itself without a theoretical framework, without a fundamental idea. The idea, the philosophy, is at the center of its existence, and every era brings forth its own idea, creates its own center. But if the center changes with the times, with each generation, what form does it assume? The idea acquires ever-changing nuances, but what is its essence? Or, more precisely, what is the form of Jewish thought, and what path does it take?

There is a multitude of historians of Jewish philosophy, and there is an extensive literature on Jewish thinkers from Saadia Gaon, Yehuda Halevi, Shlomo Ibn Gabirol, and Maimonides — the greatest of them all — to the modern ones, who have completed and continued the work of those original thinkers. But the fundamental question has always remained unanswered: Were the Jewish thinkers philosophers in the true meaning of the word, i.e. free original thinkers, and not merely theologians, not merely defenders, interpreters of a dogma? Did Jewish thought have original concepts, or was it merely mediating between Moses and Greek philosophy, between Judaism and Plato and the Aristotelian system?

One of the latest and most competent scholars in this field, Professor David Naymark, has tried to answer this question. He has undertaken the task of demonstrating the force and originality of Jewish thought in his Hebrew book on the history of Jewish dogma, followed by his German work on the history of Jewish philosophy, and, lastly, by the first of a planned ten volumes on the history of Jewish philosophy. The first volume is an introduction, an overview of the basic ideas and their development.

It is not my intention to give a critical analysis of Professor Naymark's work, interesting as it may be to follow step by step the author's views and interpretations of the various Jewish philosophical systems. He is especially drawn to the Rambam, to whom he relates as a disciple would to his rabbi, allotting him the lion's share of space in his book. But this is not the main problem that the book poses, nor is it the main question that confronts us. What is most important is the fundamental question raised by Saadia Gaon: Since Jewish thought manifests itself differently in different times, how does it manifest itself in the time we live in? In other words: What is the fundamental motif of Jewish thought?

Naymark says that the innermost impulse, the root, the ur-motif of theoretical Judaism is the dogma of the spirit, of its absolute, undivided oneness. Its concern is neither with the question of creation and creator, nor with being and non-being, but with the question of unity versus division. And Naymark labors to show that since the time that Judaism has existed as a spiritual force, it has undergone an incessant struggle against dualism, against any diminution of spiritual wholeness, of universal unity. (He admits, however, that Judaism has contained leanings toward mythology, in its teaching of angels and in the creation story.) In every period Jewish thought was subject to an inner struggle: for instance, between Jeremiah, the pure monotheist, the absolute proponent of unity, and the mythologically attuned Ezekiel. And the concept of unity prevailed. The Mishnah remained free of all dualism, of all mythos. The Talmud fought for rationalism against mysticism. And mysticism, in the form of the Kabbalah, tried to adapt its mystical instinct to rationalism. But it, too, had to concede defeat. In the end, Jewish thought found its highest, purest philosophical expression in the strongly rational, anti-mythological Maimonides. This is, as it were, the completion and crystallization of Jewish thought.

According to Naymark, Jewish philosophy was neither Platonic nor Aristotelian. Ibn Gabirol and the Kabbalists had not merely carried over the Platonic concept of ideas into the Jewish field, nor had Maimonides simply followed Aristotle. Jewish philosophic inquiry had been a process of overcoming both systems and of combining the idealistic and realistic worldviews into an idiosyncratic rationalism.

Assuming that this is correct, that Jewish thought did follow this road and that rationalism is the source of Jewish spiritual history, the question remains: What is rationalism? What does this unification theory imply? What are its logical or psychological roots? Why are the Jews the only people in the world to adapt the unity motif? And is this, actually, its fundamental motif?

This is, perhaps, the most difficult problem. It is often said that the difference between Jewish and Greek thought lies in the fact that the Jew is always searching for ethical values, while the Greek searches for knowledge and understanding. Naymark inclines to this view, to a certain degree, but it is only one of the general ideas which cannot withstand closer analysis. When we take a closer look at Greek philosophy, and, especially, if we widen the field of study to include Indian and Chinese philosophy, we see that there, too, ethics is the primary motif. Ethics teaches us how to live, and this is of utmost importance. "First comes life, and then comes philosophy," as the saying goes. Knowledge is the second stage, one that evolves out of man's desire to relate to his surroundings. Understanding entails viewing life from a certain angle, but it is the degree of the angle that determines how life is viewed, that results in ethics.

Furthermore, is the struggle against myth and in favor of pure, rational thought an exclusively Jewish phenomenon? Is it not just as much a part of the Greek and the Indian mentality? Did not pre-Platonic Greek thinkers teach about the unity of nature? And then, what is this intellect that plays such a powerful role in Jewish thought? Is intellect pure logic? Thinking in words means thinking in images, and thinking in images is mythological. The concept of unity, if stated in a positive way, is a mythological concept; if propounded in a negative way, if it becomes nihilistic, an eternal "no," a sterile thought.

This is basic problem of Jewish thought and Jewish creativity. It is a problem which Naymark, his great learning notwithstanding, has not been able to solve. He has pointed to the center, but has failed to demonstrate its essence. He has shown the content of Jewish thought, but not its form. Thus the hope of Rabbi Saadia Gaon remains unfulfilled. We still do not know the full potential of Jewish thought, or what logical prerequisites and psychological conditions it needs in order to further its creative pursuits.

Leafing Through Graetz

I

The other day the mailman came bearing a gift, a new Hebrew edition of Hein-rich Graetz' *History of the Jews*, translated by Dr. S. L. Citron. And here I am, sit-ting for days on end, going through the work, not actually reading it, but leafing through it, page by page, chapter by chapter, all six volumes. One really cannot read history the usual way, especially when one is reasonably well versed in the flow of events, when one knows from the onset where it is heading and what stage it has reached. We must read it, then, in the way we reread, in our mature years, the great works we read in our youth. Then we consumed the pages, driven by our desire to discover the outcome. That was, after all, the aim of our reading. But now we do know how it ends. We are no longer in the grip of suspense; the content, the subject matter, demands less of our attention. And now, for the first time, we read the work slowly, we reenter it at the beginning, then switch to some event in the middle, eager to reread one remembered episode or another. The work acquires a new interest for us as we study its artistic truth and the ideas which inform it.

Years back, in my youth, I read Graetz' *History of the Jews*. It is an epic narra-tive about the Jewish people, perhaps the most griping story ever told. It is the story of Lazarus, the story of a people that again and again was buried and which, each time, arose from the grave. Exhausted and scarred from the struggle with death, the people soon regains its health and vitality…until the next catastrophe strikes. Another heavy stone dropped atop the disturbed grave, followed by another resurrection. One might, actually, call it a hunting story. Here they come, the hunters, astride their horses, resplendent in their red garb, gripping spears, swords or other weapons, sweeping through forests and fields in the pursuit of a small, weak fox or hare. As they corner their prey, teeth already ripping the flesh, the victim gathers all its strength into a desperate leap and escapes its tormentors. Until the next time and the next.…

I know this analogy may be a bit too modern. Jews do not like such allegories. We would rather recall something like "Judah was a young lion," the king of the forest. And maybe, considering the fierce reaction that Jews evoke in other people, considering the place that Jews occupy in history, maybe this really is a lion-hunt. This would, at least, make sense. But this is the tragic-comic element of life, that nothing makes any sense, that one expends more noise and greater effort in chasing a hare than in pursuing a lion. When we read the description of lion or tiger hunts in India or Africa, we are drawn into a quiet, mysterious, mystical mood; we are witnessing a battle of life and death. But what is the purpose of the two-thousand-year-old pursuit of Jews? Who benefits from it, and who derives any honors from it? Who, except, perhaps, the Jews?

As I leaf through the *History*, it seems to me that Heinrich Graetz is the only one who has given us a broad picture of world history as it is reflected in Jewish history. For Jewish history is a perception of the world, it is a mirror image — and often a very crooked one — of the life and thoughts, of the rise and fall, of world history, i.e. the history of Asia and Europe. As a crooked mirror it is therefore the best one, since it views life from a different angle, uncovering the other side of the coin. Jewish history is, in actuality, the only history written by those who were conquered, the only historical protest that has reached us. The dead keep silent. Peoples who have been destroyed and trodden into dust have disappeared, swallowed by the sands of time. They made peace with their fate, and submitted to the conqueror. Here and there was heard an outcry, like Cassandra's voice raised in sorrow as Troy was burning, but it remained a faraway, poetic lament, reverberating only in the imagination of the conqueror. The conquered people themselves were never heard from. And yet, this silence may be the most humanly gripping quality, the most interesting question, of all historical research. How does a people die? How does a culture become extinct? How do empires disintegrate?

Scholars excavate and find stones, graves, walls and ruins. They find stones covered with inscriptions, and each inscription is a memento to the lives and deeds of human beings. A closer look, however, shows us that these mementos were chiseled into stone at the time of the people's greatness and power, never at the time of their despair or after their downfall. Let us take the Hittites as an example. We know today that the Hittites had been a great, powerful people, that they had ruled Asia Minor, and that they had been a sort of Rome of ancient times. Of those times we do have some relics. Then the Hittites left the world stage and disappeared, and no one knows, no one will ever know, what the Hittites thought as they suffered through the agony of their extinction. Sometimes individuals leave a self-appraisal behind them, but a people never does, except for a people which from its very beginning has had to face a threat to its existence, and which, at all times, is aware of the knife at its throat, ready for self-appraisal: the Jewish people. What makes Jewish history such breathtaking reading is its being in a perpetual act of self-appraisal. This is also what makes it so difficult to understand, to rationalize, to "systematize": It presents us with events of the moment, with critical, dangerous moments, and not with the quiet, continuous, flow of life.

Greek, Roman or European history can be interpreted idealistically or materialistically. We can isolate key spiritual aspects, such as freedom, power, and creative energy. Or we can view it as a purely economic process. Theodore Mommsen, for example, portrayed Roman history as a people's march toward world domination, and made Julius Caesar into the central historical figure. Others, however, gave the central position in Roman history to the Gracchi, who fought for agrarian reform and the redistribution of public lands. Both are, of course, one-sided interpretations, yet each of them makes sense, makes Roman history intelligible. Jewish history, however, does not lend itself to interpretation. Do we choose an idealistic, that is a mystical, one? This would mean that an entire people suffered and struggled for the sake of an idea, a universal idea, and was rejected by the world for it. Mysticism does not appear to hold the key to the secret. Do we consider an economic, materialistic, Marxist interpretation? It might, perhaps, explain the motives for an attack here or a pogrom there, but it does not lead to an understanding of the attitude of other peoples, of all other peoples, to the Jews.

We are presented again and again with motivations of competition and jealousy, of money-economy versus barter, of town versus village. Is this not a transfer of our own concepts of the essence of nineteenth-century anti-Semitism to earlier generations? I specify the nineteenth-century, because the twentieth century has produced its own motivations, has put its own stamp on anti-Semitism. And if the nineteenth century cannot elucidate the twentieth, how then can we impute today's concepts to antiquity or the Middle Ages? All such scholarly for-ays into the realm of Jewish history that I am aware of have been, therefore, unsuccessful, more fiction than truth. The religio-cultural approach of Scheer and Kittle, as well as the anthropological, almost racially psychological approaches of Edward Maier, have been as wrong and fanciful as the very pene-trating, very astute socio-economic ones by Weber, in his religio-historic studies of ancient Judaism.

In the end, Jewish life cannot be understood; it can only be portrayed. And portrayal — genuine artistic perception — requires penetrating below the sur-face, seeing one's subject from the inside out. Yet this task is an impossible one. No one can achieve the kind of distance from a people that will enable him to perceive it as well as objectively judge it. Thus, being either objective or partial, how can he possibly sit in judgment? Yet where is it written that one must sit in judgment? Who says that we are owed an accounting of the deeds or suffering of the past? This is, perhaps, Graetz' greatest achievement: he does not look for too many secrets, causes, or hidden meanings. He paints the surfaces and does not try to dig too deeply. Historically speaking, this is a fault, but from a philosophical and artistic standpoint, it is a virtue, because it liberates history. Instead of dam-ming the river, Graetz opens the dikes, leaving each one to see in the stream what he wants.

Even the most gifted historian, the most brilliant stylist and the most learned scholar cannot capture the entire world from the distance of 3,000 years, in all its details. It is impossible to perceive with equal clarity Moab at the time of Ruth and Persia at the time of Esther; the Sea of Galilee at the time of Saul and Simon; the smell of Andalusia permeated with the smoke of Catholic *autos da fé*; or the odor of herring emanating from Amsterdam's Flachburg, where the Spanish Marranos settled.

A great amount of research and study will have to be accomplished before a second Graetz will arise and paint anew, with a modern brush, the thousand-fold diversity that is called Jewish history. It is a history as yet unfinished, a running stream still seeking its path. New rivulets join in, a rainstorm adds new power, and suddenly the stream takes a turn and we must follow it. It is difficult to be a Jewish historian, almost as difficult as being the bearer of Jewish history.

II

Achad Ha'am once posed a question, the cardinal question of Jewish history: Is it possible for the whole world to be guilty, and that we alone are the pure, the worthy, the just ones? He posed the question in connection with the blood libel against the Jews and his answer was: yes. It is possible, and the blood libel proves it. Oh, if only Achad Ha'am had been right! Then everything would have been worthwhile; even the blood libel would have been acceptable if it had resulted in a revelation that in a world filled with irrationality, chaos, and a hunger for life that can scarcely be contained, there exists a group of human beings who have conquered the beast within themselves. But this is easier stated than proven. And the great tragedy of modern man is his doubt in the validity of the idea of the "chosen people."

Those who have been engaged in tearing out roots have failed to understand that an idea, no matter what it may be, is merely an attitude; or, if I may borrow the terminology from the art of dance, a stance, a pose, a gesture. The Greeks adopted the stance of the thinker and the artist, the Romans that of a politician and a ruler, the French that of the rationalist, and the Russian that of a God-seeker. Whether the God in question is that of religion or social revolution, the evolution of the gesture remains the same: the stance becomes habit, and the habit becomes nature.

For so long Jews acted for history, and for themselves, in the role of the chosen people that it became a part, a basic element, of the Jewish rapport with life. More than that, it became a source of self-respect. The non-Jewish world also believed in the Jewish historical role or mission. It displeased them, they disliked the Jews, but they accepted the legitimacy of the claim. They accepted the Jew as an exception to the rule, as differing from all other two-legged creatures. And since being exceptional meant being privileged, the Jew had to bear the consequences of his status; he had to pay for it. As for the Jews themselves, no matter how hard and bitter their situation, morally, within the four walls of their homes or in their ghetto, they had been the masters of the world, the chosen ones, the aristocrats.

The emancipation, the widening of the horizon, however, deprived Jewish self-esteem of its innermost core. The Jew does not believe in himself anymore; he has lost his self-respect, has lost his reverence not only for his present but also for his past. Let us not fool ourselves. The most virulent anti-Semitism is not that spewed out by a Chamberlain, a Hitler, or a Polish rabble-rouser. Today's greatest anti-Semite is the Jew himself, especially the Jewishly-conscious one, the intellectual Jew. He has the greatest scorn for everything Jewish, be it language, culture, thought or tradition, and he passes his scorn down to the common man. Thus we find in the darkest recesses of Jewish folk-consciousness the same casual attitude, a quiet — and at times not so quiet — disdain towards Jews and Judaism. The foundation of their self-esteem had crumbled; they had lost their aristo-cratic self-assurance, an attitude that, then, trickled down to non-Jews. The Jews were no longer viewed as a persecuted aristocracy, as an exceptional people. We are on the way to becoming a *quantité négligible*, without any universal meaning.

Let's take Esau: active, passionate, a warrior. He traded his birthright for a pot of lentils and went on to build up the land. Yet when it was laid in ruins he con-tinued building up science, scholarship, philosophy, the arts. And Jacob? Jacob lay upon a stone and dreamt of angels coming down and going up a ladder. There comes to mind a lovely description I once read in an almost forgotten book, *The Microcosmos*, by an almost forgotten philosopher, Rudolph Hermann Lotze: "The ancient peoples pictured the Jew as one who goes around as in a day-dream, in a world of work and occupation." This is a perception by alien, unfriendly outsiders and, therefore, a very interesting one. How were the Jews actually perceived by an educated Greek or Roman? In Athens, Corinth and Rome life was filled with work. Work implies a purpose, and the purpose, of course, is life enhanced by comfort, pleasure, beauty, knowledge, and power. Such was the life enjoyed by Greek and Roman intellectuals as they strolled along the wide avenues. What a contrast to the Jewish Talmud scholar who hurries along, lost in thought! The manifold world around him holds not the least inter-est for him; he closes his eyes as he recites the eternal *Shema*; he sits in the Yeshi-vah and studies. What does he study? Laws and ethics and ancient sayings. Should a Jew try to understand the nature of sky and earth and study physics, he would be looked down on by the Talmudic scholar. Rabbi Johanan did not have a high opinion of Samuel, Mar Samuel of Nehardea, who was a mathematician and an astronomer, in addition to being a Torah scholar, because "...he was excessively erudite," because he may have been too involved with "alien books and alien philosophy" to be a true Talmud sage.

Thus came into being a remarkable paradox: Jews as individuals are the most practical people on earth, but as a people they were, or would become, dedicated to a dream. Individually, every Jew is endowed with common sense, is ready to compromise, to bow to necessity. But as a collective, Judaism is uncompromis-ing, which means without any rapport with the outside world. All of Jewish life is based on a dream, while its political goal has always been Jewish autonomy. Viewed realistically this is an irrational aspiration. Just as difficult to understand is why Jews have been unable either to maintain their identity the way the Greeks have, or else become assimilated, as have the Gauls in France and Spain.

I am leafing through Jewish history as seen by Graetz, and I am seeking, once again, to understand the meaning of *galut*, of exile. It is truly characteristic that for Jews the exile is not a politico-historical phenomenon, but a psychological one. Almost as many Jews were in exile before the destruction of Jerusalem as afterward. Masses of Jews were living in Egypt, Babylonia, and throughout Asia, as well as in Rome, Germany and Spain. There is a kernel of historical truth in the old legends of German and Spanish Jews. We are told that the first Jews came to Spain at the time of King Solomon, in the service of their master, and that Nehemiah sent a letter to the Jews of Worms asking for help rebuilding the Temple. Of course, these are legends, but they do indicate that the dispersion goes back to ancient times and that it precedes the destruction of Jerusalem. Yet it never occurred to Jews in Alexandria, Cappadocia, and Italy that they were "exiles," just as the Italians who settled in New York do not mourn their old home, do not yearn, day and night, for Rome. Only after Jerusalem had been laid to waste, after the sages had, as it were, officially declared a permanent exile, did a Jewish *galut* consciousness come into being. And Jerusalem, which had earlier been a remote, almost mystical image, became the focus of thought and of yearning.

We stand today, just as we stood 2,000 years ago, at the threshold of destruction, before a crisis requiring a decision and a solution. Never before have we had the same urgent need as we have right now for a philosophy of Jewish history. Furthermore, this is the first time that History has become of actual concern to us. It is not a matter of chance that, during the classical periods of Jewish life, Jews paid scant attention to their own history. The little material that they did gather was scattered and lost because Jews had no need of it. In this way the Jews resemble the Hindus, who lack a history and a sense of concrete reality. Their goal, too, is the world to come, which they call Nirvana, a world of nothingness that is formless and composed only of pure ideas. History, however, cannot exist among pure ideas and in the absence of all events. History begins when human activity becomes subject to change, when each period, when each individual life, becomes an end in itself, when each generation acquires its own merits and is, therefore, a challenge to itself.

Such a time came for India, in its own way; a time for political activity, for affirmation, for pushing aside Nirvana. And such a time has come for the Jewish community. Jewish history stands at the crossing of two roads: the road of acquiescence and the road of a new beginning. Up until now we have been following a road that wound its way between the world of dreams and the world of reality. We cannot follow this road anymore. We must make a choice.

The Third Pool of Light

In the course of difficult days, in moments darkened by a cloud of sorrow so dense that one could truly cut it with a knife, a sorrow for Jews who have become the target for all the heavy boots, I often find myself envying those who can settle in a nook with a volume of their choice (*angula cum bibula*) and derive consolation and courage from their reading.

I do not know whether this is a true story or a parable, but I was told of several well-known, highly learned men in Russia and elsewhere who, despairing of the world, had sought seclusion in a corner of a synagogue to study. Whether they studied the rituals concerning the cleansing of dead bodies, *The Zohar,* or anything else is quite unimportant; the importance lies in the act of studying, of turning away from daily life, and embracing seclusion. When the vanity of all action is recognized, then the *midrash*, the commentary, assumes a prime importance.

Actually, this constitutes the very purpose and the essential depth of Judaism. It gains its true dimension only when it loses its matter-of-fact aspects and assumes a symbolic dimension. Freedom from dogma transforms the ancient Hebrew words into pure poetry.

There is so much bitterness around us and within us. We feel bitter because we find ourselves helpless, humiliated and abandoned. Everyone is arrayed against us — from the east and the west, from the north and the south, flames of fire are advancing and poisonous darts are aimed. And there is no one willing to

314

understand us, no one reaching out to raise us out of the dust. Even our friends are of the condescending kind — they will "do us a favor," but they are ashamed to be seen with us. And if one cannot find refuge even in one's past, in the stream of light that once illumined our way, then what remains?

I know, of course, that the passage of time transforms the past into art, poetry, symbolism. But when reality is so starkly bare, it must cover its nakedness with a mantle of symbols. And so we are lucky to be able to turn to a bright ray of the erstwhile stream of light, the gripping poetry contained in an old *Midrash* (*Midrash Konan*): "And God opened the Torah and extracted from it three pools of light, one to lighten this world, one for the world to come, and one pool of light to serve the Torah."

It may well be that in any other circumstances, at any other time, I might well have passed by this ray of light without paying any attention to it, without feeling its cooling freshness, its majestic calm. But the days are coming when all other sources will grow dim and we must, willy-nilly, immerse ourselves in the last pool of light, in the third one. When one stands alone, one must live with oneself, one must concentrate upon oneself; and if one is prevented from reaching desired heights, then one must explore one's depths. As this world is sinking into darkness and the world to come seems scarcely more than a dream, we are left with only one vital element — with the light from the Torah.

However one may want to interpret the word and the concept of Torah, from whatever direction one may want to approach it, its ultimate, fundamental element is its vision of eternity, of timeless depths. And this is, actually, the only possible approach to the Torah, and to Judaism as a whole. Either we approach it from the inside out, or the entire matter loses all validity. Either we consider Judaism *sub specie aeternetatis* is, under the aspect of eternity, i.e. as a world-historical phenomenon which has not, as yet, played itself out, or else we are dealing with the history, customs, or — to use a word that has been rendered trite — the civilization of a small, incomprehensible and unessential splinter of the general world population, a splinter which Constantin Brunner, from his assimilatory vantage point, has dubbed a "non-people people," or, even worse, "non-human humans."

I do not know whether the historical accounts of other cultures, of the Greeks and Romans, are truly valid, but I do not believe that today's university professors are truly able to perceive, imagine and visualize the history of Athens and Corinth, to penetrate into the souls of Plato and Aeschylus, of Julius Caesar and Virgil. And yet, rendering an account of Greek or Roman history is an elementary task when compared to the task of interpreting the wondrous, variegated, incomprehensible Jewish history, whose origins recede into mythical clouds. How could Renan, for instance, have understood the history of Israel? He approached it the way an archaeologist approaches a piece of pottery. Studying his find, the archaeologist can perhaps determine the date on which the pottery was fashioned. With luck, he might even be able to decipher the inscription or uncover the artist's name, but what meaning does this knowledge have for us? Does it tell us anything about the man who fashioned the vase, about the life he led, and about the culture in which his creative impulses were rooted? Stone tablets remain mere stone if one does not sense the flames they contain, the black flames which follow the white ones. Still, Renan had been a man of artistic sensitivity, intuitive and even inclined to accord a measure of sympathy to the objects of his research.

Take, however, scholars such as Wellhausen or Maier, the German professors who are universally acclaimed as the High Priests of the study of Israel. As the historians of Judaism, how can they possibly sense or understand the essence of Judaism? Disliking Judaism, they have devoted their lives to the task of destroying its intrinsic worth. But understanding is a process of reconstruction and not one of destruction. For these scholars, the Torah is simply dead matter, forever arid, rather than a source which nourishes the living, a pool of light.

Only Jewish scholars can get at the very roots of Jewish life, and then only those who have emancipated themselves from the "wisdom" of the German professors, who refuse to be overawed by their academic learnedness, and who are willing to explore matters from inside out rather than merely from the outside. Such a scholar had been, in his time, A. H. Weiss, and in our time, Chaim Tchernowitz.

I am not a member of the guild of professional historians and consider myself a mere dabbler in the field of Jewish learning. But whenever I see a new book by Professor Tchernowitz, I experience an upsurge of warmth towards Judaism, and I feel that I have been led nearer to the source, with the ancient books acquiring a new meaning and a more vibrant vitality. I felt this in reading the first volume of *Toldot Halacha*, or *The History of Halacha*, and this feeling grew even stronger as I leafed through the second, just published volume.

At first glance the book deals with matters and problems of minimal importance to us: with Kohanim and Levites, Prophets and Kings, Sadducees, Pharisees and Judges, with the problems of religious observances and ancient jurisprudence. But then one finds oneself captivated by the style, an idiosyncratic style such as one rarely encounters these days anymore. Saturated with scholarship, steeped in the spirit of the past, it intertwines different eras so skillfully as to make one see the unrolling of a thread stretching back to primordial times.

Scripture, verses and parables, laws and commentaries, they all come to life under the Pygmalion-like touch of this Jewish historian. A scriptural verse from the Pentateuch is viewed in conjunction with a discussion in the *Gemarah*, a halachic ruling with an elucidation from the Rambam — and out of this veritable orchestration of erudition emerges not a compilation of petrified data, but a vibrant, gripping symphony. And this is due to Professor Tchernowitz's basic concept: *Am Israel chai*. The people of Israel is a living organism that has never stopped functioning, neither biologically nor spiritually. The whole tradition of Judaism, the quintessence of its precepts, is therefore to be found not in stone-engraved writings, but in an eternally self-renewing pool of light which illuminates the path of all generations.

Viewed in this manner, we find that the entire spectrum of Jewish history acquires a different meaning, that all of its questions, if not answered, are at least put into the framework of universal history and seen in a global perspective. There were the Priests and the Prophets, the Sadducees and the Pharisees, the written Torah and the oral commentaries — a struggle carried on for generations. But for what purpose? Historians, especially Protestant Christian ones, have treated this as a fruitless, merely theological, dispute, but Professor Tchernowitz treats it as a chapter of universal human history. This was a struggle between theology and life, between the letter and the spirit, between the priestly class and the people.

When we read, for instance, the chapter entitled *"Shaar Ha-Kitot,"* which deals with the Sadducees and the Pharisees, we perceive the life of the ancient Jews in a different light. We see the struggle between Ezekiel and Jeremiah as a struggle between the Prophet who is a member of the priestly caste and preaches the written theology, and the Prophet who comes from the people, who wants people to be part of the universal historical stream. On one side we have a historically determined nation, and on the other side a people which is a part of world history, or rather, a people which, for the first time in the history of mankind, had envisaged the concept of humanity and had presented us with the idea of world history.

The Sadducees, who adhered to their ancient religious precepts, cared only for religion and therefore assimilated into the surrounding civilization. The Pharisees were the bearers of the age-old tradition which embraces all humans — the pre-Hebraic ones, the ancient inhabitants of the East, the desert people, the tent dwellers, the villager and the city folk, and so on till the end of generations. The

Pharisees were the prophets of outreach, the priests who, starting from the distant onset of universal history, were heading into the timelessness of eternity.

In just such a perspective must we view Judaism, and only in this way can it, once again, become a pool of light for us. And — who knows — we have sunk so low in our own eyes, are so abased in the eyes of the world, that our pool of light may also have been dimmed by the enormous voltage of world-generated electricity. And yet, man can draw to a halt, sources of light can be obscured, darkness can come upon us — perhaps it has descended upon us already — and yet the pool of light can once again become a factor in world history. In a time of humiliation it is good to be proud. This is how our parents and our grandparents had saved themselves and their souls, and — perhaps — so will we.

The Petrified Branch

Almost all of Russia's nationalities were represented in our small student circle at St. Vladimir's University in Kiev. There were Russians, Jews, Poles, Germans, Georgians, Armenians and Tatars. And then there was a student who did not seem to be part of these nationalities. He was not a Crimean, surely not a Russian, yet he enjoyed all of their civil rights. His name was a strange combination of a Jewish first name and a Tatar family name. I tried several times to get him to tell me who he was and what religious faith he practiced. But he parried my queries with a counter-thrust: "What faith? Who believes in anything now? Of what use is faith in Russia?" And his ironic tone implied something more: "If you do practice your faith, was does it do for you but get you into trouble?"

For a long time I considered him to be an apostate because he so often spoke of Jews in quite bitter terms, which struck a dissonant note in our circle. I therefore asked my Armenian friend, Sarkis Pezavetovich Tapelianz: "Tell me, Sarkis, how can one be a Social Revolutionary and an anti-Semite? You come from the same region, tell me, who is he?" "Don't you know?" Sarkis had answered. "He is a Karaite."

This was the first Karaite I had ever encountered, the first living member of the apostate Jewish sect, of the small, secretive community that lives next to, yet apart from, the Jews, that is like a petrified branch on the trunk of a blooming tree. I tried to engage my Karaite co-student in conversation about his religion and observances, about Karaite history and traditions. But his response was angry: "Leave me alone with your mildewed theology. I hate them all, the Jews, the Karaites, and all of this old history. I know only that my forefathers had fought with your forefathers, and now the descendents of your forefathers are in deep trouble while we are doing quite well."

And thus it was. We, the descendants of the victors, the strong ones, the rabbis, as the Karaites call the Jews, have been persecuted and deprived of all rights. We have been herded into ghettoes and barred from universities. We had to be the first and best achievers in order to attain any position at all, while they, the rejected and discarded, were enjoying all of the civic rights and were able to become whatever they wanted. The government treated them benevolently, and society accepted them with open arms. They were Jewry's aristocrats.

Years passed, and I had lost sight of my classmate. I did not meet another Karaite until the trial in Paris of the poet Shalom Schwarzbard, accused of the 1926 assassination of the Ukrainian pogrom leader Petlyura. One of those who testified for the defense was the father of a pogrom victim. His son had belonged to a Kiev self-defense group and was shot by one of Petlyura's soldiers. The father, a merchant in his forties, had made his way to Vienna and had settled there. His fiery black eyes and round head were typically oriental features. Nobody, naturally, thought of asking who he was. What could the father of a pogrom victim be but a Jew? Who else could harbor such flaming hatred toward the murderer? But I soon noticed that his testimony on Petlyura differed somewhat from that of the others. His hatred was more burning, his accusations were more bitter, and his context seemed different. The other witnesses were less strident in their accusations and denunciations, but they expressed more forcefully their pride in their Jewishness and their solidarity with all Jews. The father spewed out only hatred and demonstrated no connection with the others.

The reason for this soon became clear to me. The father of the victim was not a Jew, but a Karaite. He was doubly bereaved. He had lost a son, and his death had been caused by an error. The bandits had not bothered to pay attention to the nuances of Jewish theology. They were unaware of the difference between the rabbis and the Karaites. They had never heard of Anan and of his teaching.

The young Karaite, for his part, had given his life for the Jewish people in disregard of the history of his group. The peril threatening Jewish life seemed to him to be tearing down the wall which history had erected between the Jewish factions.

How did the wall come to be erected? What was the historic event that caused the rift? And what was it that has kept the Karaites from returning to their roots, from rejoining the House of Israel? It is, after all, not the only Jewish sect to spring up. An Arab writer of the 10th century tells of seventy different Jewish sects existing in his time in Persia and in Babylon. This may be somewhat of an exaggeration, but it is true that Eastern Judaism never stopped changing and developing. It was a living organism, branching out in different directions, even in some anomalous ones. Mystical and rationalistic sects have continually argued with each other from ancient times, with their disagreements going back to *Eretz Yisrael* even before the national catastrophe.

In Babylon and in Persia Judaism had still been close to its source, still rooted in *Eretz Yisrael.* Jewish thought continued to grow, not yet having attained its final form. Jewish culture had been flexible, able to venture in various directions, trying out different manifestations. One sect after another came into being and dissolved. In times when politics and religion marched hand in hand, political parties had their own religious credos as well. There were the Messianic sects of Abu 'Isa al-Isfahani, of his disciple Yudghan al-Ra'i of Sherini, of David Alroy, and of the false messiah Shabbatai Tzvi. These were reverberations of the old Palestinian sects, echoes of the struggle between the Pharisees and the Sadducees, between Shammai and Hillel. It was the aftermath of the upheaval which ended up splitting Judaism in two, into Judaism and Christianity.

After this final, decisive split, all of the other sects lost their historical importance. They became embers, mere sparks without the power to erupt into roaring flames. The instinct of the Jewish people barred the sects from splitting up and frittering away the remnants of the cultural heritage that had survived the catastrophe. The sages, the scholarly rabbis, the *geonim* and the heads of the communities were leaders with the required spiritual authority to control the sects. They felt the need to erect a wall around the Jewish people, and this wall was the Talmud.

Fencing in a people's life force was a difficult, even a gigantic task, but there were occasional breakthroughs. The rabbis did not achieve their victory as easily as naive historians maintain. Reuben Fahn, who has studied the Karaite sect, mistakenly assumes that the prayer for the preservation and welfare of the political and spiritual leaders of Jewish autonomy is a spontaneous appeal by the people. Such prayers, such hymns of praise, never come from the people; they are dictated from above and imposed on the people. The rabbis won in the end, but on the eve of their decisive victory there arose one among the noblemen, Anan ben David, from the reign of the dynasty of David, and started a rebellion against the Talmud and the rabbis.

He was a legendary figure, as had been all of the rebels in Jewish history. Naive in its conception of historical processes, ancient Judaism did not make the slightest effort to give a realistic account of the opponents and of the struggle they were conducting. They simply wanted to overcome all opposition, to eradicate it and then to forget it. Thus they had dealt with nascent Christianity, and thus they dealt with the Karaites. Anan fought long and bitterly. He was not the first, nor was he the only one. He had not created the creed of the Karaites, of those who follow only the written Torah. His struggle, actually, was not so much against the principle that brought the Talmud into being, as against the way the rabbis were canonizing it. He wanted to counter the Talmud, the *Gemarah*, with a *Book of Commandments* of his own.

It has been pointed out more than once that the difference between Anan's *Book of Commandments* and rabbinical *Gemarah* is not as great as one assumes. Dr. Zvi Cohen, another student of the Karaite teachings, has shown that between the Karaites and the rabbis, i.e. the Jews, stands only a collection of fifty prayers; all other laws and observances are shared by both. Anan had stressed the divisions between the two communities, but subsequent Karaite leaders, among them Benjamin Nahawendi, sought to bring Karaite teachings closer to Jewish ones.

It is just a low wall that separates the two sides, yet it will soon be twelve hundred years that the two parts of the Jewish people have lived next to each other without any interaction. "The Karaites are not of this world." This witticism, coined by an 18th century rabbi and major communal leader, became the epitome of the attitude of the Jewish leadership toward the Karaites — a torn branch that cannot be reattached to its trunk.

As the years passed, the Karaites became more and more alienated, more uprooted, without any impetus for growth and development. This small group withdrew increasingly into its shell, locking itself into a ghetto — a ghetto within a ghetto — and becoming petrified.

I do not know whether Dr. Zvi Cohen is right in his assumption that at the outset the Karaites had been the "liberal and progressive opposition against rabbinic fundamentalism." Nor do I think that Reuben Fahn is doing justice to the Karaites when he accuses them of purposefully supporting the reactionary elements, of being "Judaism's fundamentalists." History as a whole cannot be expounded in theological terms, and neither can be the history of the Karaites. It is no more than a historical accident, a mere historical anomaly, such as occurs only rarely. Karaite history is Jewish stubbornness elevated to the nth degree.

Of greater interest than the story of their past, however, is the story of the current life of the Karaites. They are a few families scattered here and there — in Trakai, close to Vilna; in Halitch, in the Crimea; in Jerusalem and in Cairo. A small group of people, both Jewish and non-Jewish, lonely and lost. Very soon the last remnant will die out, the last spark will be extinguished. Mr. Fahn truly deserves our gratitude for preserving for future generations an image of the Karaites, of a part of Judaism that is about to expire: the old Krainduk; the pious Leo Shlomovitz who protects the law with his last breath; Samuel who yearns for the "Great House of Israel," and wants to come closer to Judaism, to fuse with it; the Tataric-speaking Karaites, with despair in their hearts. Nothing had availed them — neither making up to the Christians by honoring Jesus in whom they did not believe, nor the falsified documents brought forth in the mid-19th-century by their sage, Abraham Fikovitz, in order to prove that the Karaites had been living in the Crimea for the past 1800 years (thus bearing no guilt in the crucifixion). None of this had any effect.

"From day to day the flame grows weaker and weaker, and soon the sparks will be dispersed and the flame will be extinguished." Thus wrote one of their last thinkers, Samuel Figit, in his *The Story of the Wandering Samuel.* And the "soon" is almost here. The Karaite branch of the Jewish tree has become petrified, and now the stone is being ground into dust.

The Second Nation

It is difficult to imagine that there should still exist today, or, for that matter, for the last couple of thousand years, a group of Jews of the purest water, faithful souls sincerely devoted to their convictions which hold them together, living in seclusion, in the shadow of history for the last eleven hundred years, and yearning to draw close to the majority, to feel a part of its ancient roots.

Never a large group, they are even less numerous today — a handful in Jerusalem, a few in Egypt, with most of them in the Slavic and Tataric Eastern regions, in Turkey, in the small Galician town of Helitch, or in the Crimea. Alienated Jews, they communicate with each other for the most part in Tataric. They live by themselves, wrapped up in their past, sustained by their proud conviction that they, the Karaites, are the true Jews, passing on the unblemished Jewish tradition from generation to generation; a valiant minority opposing a confused, misled, rabbinic majority.

A minority is a minority, however, and the Jewish majority has shown them how a minority is to be treated. The Karaites tell a story which rings true to human nature. It happened in Pressburg [Bratslav], that pious Jewish city, ruled by a famous scribe who had led a bitter fight against the Haskalah, dead-set against permitting any free thought to find its way into his small Jewish empire.

One fine day two strangers arrived in Pressburg. The people wondered if they were agents from the Crimea bent on surveying the Jewish domain, or perhaps just two merchants passing through. They were soon discovered to be Karaites, and the holy assembly of Pressburg was in an uproar: How can these people be allowed to walk the streets of Pressburg, these people who are Jews but who have the impudence to interpret Judaism in their own fashion? How can one tolerate the idea that the Karaites might transmit some of their impurity to the citizens of Pressburg? Thus, young Jewish men began to follow their Karaite guests, dousing them with pails of water. After a while the visitors from Crimea decided to put a stop to it and lodged a complaint, not, God forbid, with the police but with the scribe. This luminary listened to them, smiled and answered: I really don't know what you are complaining about, for they pour water on you merely to purify you. How can I object to this since there is a special verse demanding the purification by water of all the extremities when performing a sacrifice, and you do believe in a literal interpretation, do you not? Thus did the scribe extricate himself with a joke, a joke about the Torah, and the poor Karaites cut short their visit and left town.

This Karaite version of the event may well contain more fact than fiction. Even though minorities, especially harassed ones, like to tell sentimental stories where they figure as pure lambs and their antagonists as evil wolves, these hyperboles tend, nevertheless, to contain a kernel of truth. Jewish history cannot deny the fact that Jews themselves had excommunicated a group and denied them all vestiges of Jewish peoplehood solely on the grounds that their ideas and their conception of Judaism ran counter to the established norm. Thus, as we complain of our fate, the fate of a minority, we might remember that our own hands are not entirely clean.

It was a small book by the well-known Jewish writer Dr. Zvi Cohen which recently appeared in English, *The Rise of the Karaite Sect*, which set in motion the above thoughts. It is, I think, a dissertation and as such lacks the stylistic finesse and historical thoroughness to be found in scholarly literature. It may also be that the author had taken on too heavy and too complex a task, since, notwithstanding the works on the Karaites published so far — Simcha Pinsker's *Likute Kadmaniut*, Dr. Firscht's *History of Karatism*, the works of Eliahu Harkavi and Dr. S. Poznansky, as well as the recent work of Dr. Jacob Mann — there still is a lack, to quote Dr. Mann, of a complete, good history of the Karaites, a history of this Jewish social organism whose roots reach to the very beginning of Judaism itself.

Actually, we have only a few factual historical data. In the year 860 the brothers Anan and Hananiah, scions of the highest Jewish aristocracy, the House of David, were living in Persia. Upon the death of the head of the exiles, Anan, the chief of the Jewish community, expressed the desire to assume this office, and the community was ready to grant it, on account of his illustrious lineage, or perhaps because of his great learning. But the rabbis of his time gave voice to their suspicions of him, suspicions that Anan was harboring revolutionary ideas, that he was rebelling against the Talmud, and this led to his being blackballed. The office was awarded to his younger brother Hananiah, and Anan departed in anger. It was this skirmish that gave rise to a split in the Jewish world, a split which could have become fatal had it not been for Anan's profound sense of honesty and integrity. Anan had, indeed, rebelled against the *Gemarah* and had called for a rebellion against the rabbis who had usurped all power over the Jewish community. Anan's rallying cry (which, in time, was to become the rallying cry of the Protestants against Rome) was: Back to the Torah, to the written word! There lies the final authority, and not with some preachers from Babylon, Persia and Syria, whose inept interpretations, sermons and *pilpuls* bar the way to the original source.

Unlike many of the fundamentalist Christian sects, however, Anan was neither sufficiently naive nor even so entirely bound to the written word as to barricade himself behind the Pentateuch and refuse to look beyond it. He instructed his pupils to study the Torah thoroughly and not simply accept his words, thus opening for his students the path of autonomous thought. From then on, any Karaite who had studied the Torah and had meditated on it had felt entitled to produce his own commentary and his own code of laws. Anan had shown the way with his *Sefer Ha-Mitzvot*. In following his example, his loyal successors have produced rather an overabundance of commentaries.

A first reading of Anan and his disciples (Benjamin Al-Nahawendi, Sahl Ibn Mazliah, Yafith Ibn Ali, et al.) seems to indicate that they had altogether abandoned the Jewish Talmudic norm and that their laws were radically different from those presented by Jewish orthodoxy. But scholars who have studied the Karaite texts (especially Eliahu Harkevy who has collected and published fragments of Anan's *Sefer Ha-Mitzvot*) have shown that the hue and cry unleashed by the rabbis against the Karaites had been quite unfounded, since Anan's departure from Jewish orthodoxy had been a very slight one. Dr. Zvi Cohen's thorough analysis of Anan's text and of the laws that he propounded in his *Sefer Ha-Mitzvot* shows that "ninety percent of Anan's laws are firmly grounded in the Talmud," thus confirming a thesis arrived at by the historian Jacob Kirkisani, who wrote the first history of the Karaites.

Does this mean, then, that the entire historic struggle, the splintering-off process was caused by the unjust treatment meted out to one man, and by the introduction of a few different rituals by the Karaites, such as Anan's decreeing that Friday nights must be spent in darkness? Is this what led one of Jewish leaders of the time, the Gaon Natrunia, to utter the bitter words with the finality of a death-sentence: "Anan has wanted to establish a second sect; he has established a second nation"? History is neither so simple nor so petty, especially not the history of a minority, of a people that had to struggle so hard and so bitterly for its own existence. The motives went deeper, the game was more hazardous. At stake were not merely a few laws but the center, the ultimate essence of Judaism.

Dr. Zvi Cohen compares the Talmudic laws and legends with those of the Parsees in order to prove that Anan was an enlightened man, a rationalist who had joined the Arab intelligentsia in their struggle against Persian mysticism, which had almost succeeded in swallowing up Jewish thought. I do not know if it was necessary to have recourse to Persian sources, since the lore of angels and demons, and a panoply of legends and myths has, undoubtedly, been a part of Jewish life from its earliest times. There is no nation without a mythology. The Messiah myth and the Christology which had its origin in purely Jewish soil attest to that. The Persians merely added their own names and embroidered the details, but the content was quintessentially Jewish.

The struggle against this Jewish mythology, on the other hand, was also entirely Jewish. In his dissertation on *The Halacha of the Karaim and the Halacha of Philo*, written in 1911, Dr. Bernard Revel analyzes with a considerable awareness of historical processes the original division between Alexandria and Jerusalem, between the Judaism of the philosophers and that of the people. The thinkers, the aristocrats — be they righteous men as the tradition claims or not — had wanted to cleanse Judaism, to protect it from all myths, to maintain it at the height of philosophical religious ideation. But the results they achieved were, all too often, negative ones. Jewish thought in its ultimate purity arrived at a negation of Judaism, in the same way that Anan's initial diversion grew into a rebellion against the basic tenets of all of Judaism — a rebellion of thought against dogma.

The most logical, the most consequential, of Anan's followers was Havi Hablachi, who went on to develop further Anan's concepts. Hablachi was the only Jewish thinker of the Middle Ages with the courage to follow Jewish religious thought to its end, to take monotheism, the spirituality of God, seriously, literally and without compromise. Orthodox Judaism found this intolerable, and Havi Hablachi was read out of Jewish peoplehood in the same way that Anan and the Karaites had been. We have always been masters of reading out and eradicating the memory of those we disagreed with. It is fortunate that Spinoza had written in Latin. Had he continued writing in Hebrew his memory would have been eradicated except, perhaps, for a few lines of invective such as were vouchsafed to Havi Hablachi or, at best, a sharp polemic as the one by Saadia Gaon against the

Karaites. Dr. Zvi Cohen now wants to revise the Karaite process and to join together the two parts of the people — the minority and the majority. He has my blessing for this endeavor, but he needs to obtain the blessing of the Agudah, and I am not at all sure that the rabbis even now will consent to it. Once Jews turn stubborn....

And Nathan Talks On

Somewhere far away, beyond the realms of space and time, the two great opponents are still continuing their dialogue. There is Saladin, seated upon his throne, a throne robbed of splendor, its golden ornaments replaced by brass and its ivory armrests by mere bone. But Saladin, himself, still looks the same — his head is crowned by a white turban and the sharp, bent sword of the Seljuks is at his side. Only his eyes, the perceptive, smiling eyes of old, have lost their youthful luster and express bitterness. And facing him, upon an old, torn pillow, sits Nathan, "Nathan the Wise," as Lessing called him. He is old and tired, his white beard almost yellowed with age, and his head too heavy for the withered body.

They are engaged in a game of chess, one of the endless games they have been playing for hundreds of years. Usually old Nathan is the better player, but when it comes to the final, victorious move, his glance falls on the bent sword, and, whether on purpose, or in an honest mistake, his move is deflected, allowing the sultan to win the game — or else leading to stalemate, thus letting both players win and lose at the same time. And between the games, the two players, who are friends as well as opponents, discourse on man and on the world, on the past and on the present.

"Do you remember, Nathan, the story you once told me, long long ago, about the three rings, a story which is said to have gained world renown? I have heard from men who have read the books of the non-believers that the story you told me traversed all of Europe, from Italy to Germany, and that a German called

Lessing had written it into a play and had given it your name. It is the story of the three rings which men have inherited, and of the way the three rings rolled about, and how their shape was changed in the process. You must remember it, Nathan, is the story still the same?"

Nathan slowly shakes his head. "Not quite the same, Saladin. A lot of water has flown down into the deep blue sea since I told you the story of the three rings. The world has changed since that day. Do you remember, Saladin, when Geoffrey of Boyan and Baudoin of Flanders led the Knights of Anjou, the warriors of the Christian world, against the unbelievers and stormed the gates of the Holy City? Then as now, those of my tribe are still caught between the millstones. When Christianity and Islam, Rome and Mecca, were mounting attacks against each other, we were the ones who were caught in the crossfire, we were the victims. Both the victor and the vanquished marched over our bodies. You ask about my story of the three rings. The story I told you then was of three rings that formed a single ring — Judaism, Christianity, and Islam. And I had preached tolerance. This, at any rate, is the way the world interpreted the story; this was perceived as the moral lesson to be drawn from my legend.

"I do not know how I would tell the story today. I have grown old, and my imagination has lost its vigor and its sparkle. I only know that my legend was too simplistic, too naive, that it lacked sufficient depth to penetrate to the essence of these three rings. So let me tell the same legend in a different way. It will, perhaps, lack the vitality of the earlier one, lack its freshness and imagination, but just because of that it may, perhaps, be closer to the truth.

"There once was a king who wore a golden ring on his finger. One day enemy hordes invaded his land, devastating it and setting fire to his castle. The king perished in the fire, his ring rolled off his burned finger, and the heat transformed it into a glob of gold. One day it was found and taken to a goldsmith who was told to refashion it into a ring. But the goldsmith could not find a finger to fit the great dimensions of the ring. The goldsmith then broke it up into smaller pieces of gold and fashioned a chain of smaller rings to fit smaller fingers. And these rings circled the earth, each a part of the great ring, brothers in gold, with each one claiming to be the true, the real ring, carrying the seal of the burned king. You remember these three which remained: Judaism, Christianity, and Islam, living side by side, steeped in a never-ending battle. Then a new conflagration erupted, and another fire spread around the world, engulfing the three rings and bringing them close together. They began to melt and slowly lose their shape, turning back into a glob of gold.

"So you see, Saladin, what has happened. Those knights of Anjou and Champagne and the monks of Rome thought that the world belonged to them, that theirs was the hand to wear the ring, and they thought that you and we were standing in their way, especially us. Their whole history has been a life and death struggle against us. Long ago, before you and I were born, the Bishop of Hippo in Africa, now called Saint Augustine, who had been one of their first, and best, leaders, said to the Christian community: We must bury the synagogue, in a decent fashion. And those who succeeded him followed his dictum, only their ways were not decent ones. They burned, hunted and killed us, inflicting all possible pain and suffering upon us. And they thought that once they succeeded in eliminating us from the face of the earth, both worlds would be theirs, the world of power and the world of the spirit. They did not know, they did not understand, that when we drop out of the game, the entire game will be finished, for them as well. And see what has happened.

"They now say, in the wide world beneath us, that Judaism is facing its greatest danger, perhaps its last hour. Yet they are beginning to understand that our last hour will be theirs also. If the synagogue will indeed be buried, either with honor or in shame, it will be followed by the collapse of the entire structure erected by Peter and Paul, of the Dome of the Vatican and the Basilica of Lateran. In Northern Europe, in the center of Europe, not only is the synagogue assailed but also the cathedral. And it is easier to tear down and destroy the 2000-year-old Christian Church than the age-old synagogue. We carry all that is ours within us. Be it in a cave, in the desert, or wandering along distant roads, we can get along without a building. It is good if we have tents, but if we must, we will manage beneath the starry sky. But they have laid down granite foundations and built upon them in stone, in marble and in gold. And should this be destroyed, should all this greatness and magnificence perish, then everything perishes. Two thousand years contain merely sixty generations, which means sixty people, each passing the ring to the next one, and this is not enough. On our side there stands, shoulder to shoulder, a row of generations, deeply rooted. They cannot be destroyed, not in a day, not in a year, not in a generation.

"It is already 200 years that they have been undermining Christianity; the ring of Peter no longer fits. The grandchildren of the Crusaders and the monks.... you are smiling Saladin, yes, of the monks, are once again assailing the Holy City, wanting to seize it, not in order to honor the grave of their redeemer, but in order to destroy and dismantle it, stone by stone. There are those who wonder: What is the cause of this sudden eruption of such a heated struggle against Christianity among the peoples of the earth? I wonder why this struggle still continues, since

Christianity collapsed long, long ago. A strange plant which blossoms in dark cellars and wilts in the bright light of the sun. The peoples of Europe have never really absorbed the great ideas, the essential aroma of Christianity, as it came to flower around the Sea of Galilee, as it spun out of the naive fantasies of the fisherman of Lake Kinneret and out of the overheated preachings of the Pharisee Saul. Neither the Slavs nor the Germans had the least intimation of the mysticism which had grown out of Judaism and had become caught up in a strange, alien world of ideas. For two thousand years people have been passionately working on deciphering the mysterious words graven into the ring, and they have failed.

"It is remarkable, a veritable historical irony, that, at the hour of greatest need, the hour of conflagration, two of the rings are approaching each other, coming closer to melting into each other. For are we not partners in sorrow and in struggle? How Torquemada would have rubbed his eyes if he had seen how Christian peoples persecute Jews and Catholics, Judaism and Christianity, at the same time and with the same hatred. Rome surely did not count on that; it never expected that a moment would come when Christians would have to hide together with us, undergo misfortune, and flee into exile.

"And your religion, Saladin, is also going awry. It once was a golden ornament, a delicate ring upon a proud finger. Today it is a black iron ring upon a coarse peasant hand. Worldly and spiritual power have both eroded, and there is no more Islamic culture, no world prominence as in the days of Averroës and of Avicenna. Today it is merely a political, nationalistic religion which lends itself to propaganda and to hatred. All three rings are in the fire. Perhaps they will all melt, and perhaps the goldsmith will cool the gold and fashion a new, a solitary ring. I do not know, but I believe that the Jewish ring will still remain, and that the true seal is really upon it, because it is still a ring not of power and force, but of free will and spirit."

Saladin's brow had drawn together, his eyes had grown hard, and his hand, with an instinctive gesture, had gripped the hilt of his sword. Nathan noticed it. "I have been expecting this, Saladin, and I am not afraid. I am too old, and your sword has also grown rusty."

"You are right, Nathan. Age does not protect me from foolishness or arrogance, and neither does it protect you. It is not good to be old. One knows too much, and one fools oneself. Let us continue our game of chess."

"*En remise*," Nathan said and smiled. "Let it rest for a while."

The Jewish Illusion

Esau was a hunter, and Jacob was a tent-dweller who went to school and studied Torah. We learned all this as children, and we pictured our Father Jacob as a well-behaved Jewish boy who attended *cheder*, studied the *Chumash* with Rashi, ruminated on *Gemarah*, and recited his lessons every Shabbat. We saw all of the Jewish past as a model, or rather, as a copy of our own small town life. We pictured Father Abraham as an old Jew with a long beard and a scull cap, and Sarah as a small, bent-over woman, her head covered by a kerchief, carrying a women's prayerbook. David, Solomon, the Prophets, the Sages, and all of the great, legendary figures of our history appeared to us in the guise of familiar, living Jews. And when we did come upon a picture showing a beturbaned Rambam, draped in a white Arabian burnoose, we felt that he was disguised, that he was playing a role.

It is this childish, naive way of seeing the past through the eyes of contemporary life that has, actually, bound us and the entire Jewish people to the past. We could not have survived any other way. Jewish life has derived its vitality from the great historical illusion that there is a tie between the past and the present.

Historical scholarship has destroyed, or at least weakened, this illusion for a part of the Jewish people. We now know, or we believe we know, that contemporary Western European Judaism has only a slight connection to the *ur*-Jews, to the people of Israel that lived in *Eretz Yisrael*. Anthropology teaches this, and history tells us to listen. They tell us that Russian Jews, at least those from South

333

Russia, are a product of the intermingling of several races and peoples. Among them are the Volga Khazars, many of whom had, at one time, converted to Judaism and mixed with Semitic Jews from the Byzantine Empire and from Germany.

There are those among us who are aware of these scientific claims but are, yet, unable to free themselves from the idea that we and the Jews of the time of the *Chumash* and the Mishnah, of the time of Moses and of Rabbi Akiba, are the links in one long, uninterrupted chain. In the final analysis it is not a matter of blood or race but of spiritual culture. Blood is thicker than water, but the spirit is thicker than blood. And it is this psychological illusion which sustains Judaism up to this day, which lives and works its spell within almost every one of us. However, not everyone has the courage to proclaim this with such matter of fact assuredness as does S. Z. Setzer in his new book *The Origin of Christianity*.

I can approach this book only from a psychological angle. Not only because the subject itself — the origin of Christianity, the birth of the Christian faith, and the life and the personality of Jesus — is shrouded in legendary twilight, but because the author views it in such a personal, subjective, I would almost say, lyrical way. In an outpouring of heartfelt bitterness, this modern Jew seeks to square accounts with Christendom, to free Judaism from any involvement with Christianity. He denies any familial ties. We are not hostile brothers, he tells us. We have nothing to do with each other. Leave us in peace as we are leaving you in peace. You say that Jesus was one of us and that we have killed him. But we do not claim him; he was never one of us, and we have not laid hands on him. The entire story is a legend, a myth. It is not a Jewish myth but a gentile one, from beginning to end. It had its origin in Rome and was carried to Jerusalem. We were not the ones to bring Christianity into the Western world, but they, Rome and the non-Jewish world, have laid this false accusation upon us. The whole Jesus legend, all of Christianity, is an enormous blood libel against the Jewish people, and we have not been able to free ourselves from it up to this very day.

This is, as I understand it, the basic idea of Setzer's Christology. It is, of course, not a new idea. Starting with the 18th century Rationalists, it made its way to David Friedrich Strauss, to Renan and to contemporary scholars, perhaps more Christian than Jewish ones. It became a timeworn assertion that Jesus, as depicted by the Evangelists, never existed, was a legend, created hundreds of years later than the official texts tell us. Furthermore, all of Christianity, as it has been shaped by history, is actually not Christian, not the teaching of Jesus, but rather that of Paul. And the dogma of the Apostle Paul is a combination, a fusion of two world views, namely the Jewish and the Greco-Roman one. Christian theology emerged out of the collapse of the ancient world. It is a condensation of all of the philosophical and religious teachings of the ancient world in a new mystical form.

Christian scholars, starting with Schleiermacher, have said all this better and more clearly than has S. Z. Setzer. They offered facts, which Setzer does not do. One can, if one so wishes, use historical methodology to question their historical assertions; one cannot do so with Setzer. They offer proofs culled from texts, while Setzer sweeps aside all historical methodology. He does not prove anything, nor does he want to prove anything. He does not treat historic assertions as science but merely as an assumption.

I do not want to go into the essence of the matter. It would be easy to marshal an army of texts and historical facts against a subjective assumption, but it is not necessary. Who would want to train a whole battery of historical criticism at, for instance, George Moore's famous Christ novel, *Brook Kerith*? And yet, this wonderful novel is more historical, more philosophical, than Renan's *The Life Of Jesus* or other so-called scholarly works. It might even have benefited Setzer to have read the brilliant assumption of George Moore before he began mounting his own assumption. Moore's hypothesis affirms the existence of Jesus and that he had undergone all the travails ascribed by the Evangelists, but to a lesser degree. He was a disciple of the Essenes, a young man with a gift of preaching, who stepped out into the wide world without any great ambition, merely one of the many preachers and agitators of the time. It was against his will and contrary to the real events in his life that he was placed into the mainstream of history. His missionary work was of but short duration. He was apprehended and punished in Jerusalem — and was forgotten. One of his friends, a Hellenist who harbored no hostile feelings against the Pharisees, the Torah or the law-abiding Jews, came upon him and brought him back to the mountains of Galilee, to the solitude and stillness of the Essenes, at the Brook of Kerith. There Jesus lived quietly for thirty years, having long forgotten about his mission and regretting the minor commotion he had created during the short time of his Jerusalem activity. Suddenly there appears Saul of Tarsus, the weaver. He comes to the Essenes and begins preaching a new Torah, the New Covenant, and in its center he places the figure of Jesus, acclaiming him as the Messiah who had been crucified and resurrected. His Jesus is a fusion of all of the legends, that of the Prophet Elijah, of the Greek Attis and of the Egyptian Osiris. He is the personification of all the religious fantasies and dreams of the East.

Yeshua, the real Jesus, listens and hears the legend that has sprung up about him and does not believe his ears. "Are you talking about me?" he asks in astonishment. And he tells the weaver Saul what had really happened in Jerusalem. He tells him about his simple, poor life, about the hopes of his youth and how they had come to naught. There they stand next to each other, the Messiah, an old, lamed shepherd from Galilee leaning on his shepherd's crook, looking out of age-dimmed eyes, and the disciple, the messenger, who goes out into the world spinning legends around the shepherd's name and weaving a crown of supernatural events to place on his head. And Jesus becomes frightened. It becomes clear to him how much misery this legend can cause in the world. He pleads with Saul to give up these fantasies; he tries to convince him, but Saul is in no mood for facts. He knows that Jesus is right so he flees from him into the world to preach about Jesus, in defiance of his will.

Such an assumption by a Catholic Christian is much more valuable, natural and moving than the one put forth by Setzer. Setzer postulates that Christianity was not passed on by Jews to the Gentiles but that it came into being in Rome, at the time of Nero's reign. Jesus was a social revolutionary, a kind of Bolshevik, agitating from within, having nothing to do with Judaism. The Roman rulers had, of course, suppressed the rebellion and killed its leader. But his message survived, became legend, and gradually spread throughout the world. At the time of the destruction of the Temple and the dispersal of the Jews, the revolutionary defeat came to blend into the Jewish tragedy. Jewish elements were fused with Christian ones. Thus, we Jews have really no connection with Christianity at all. Its spirit does not flow from our spirit; it is a coincidence, nothing more.

This assumption, as was said before, is not a very original one. It has been brought forth more than once, in one form or another. It is, furthermore, historically incorrect. Even though we have very few historical Jewish accounts about Jesus and his role in Jewish life, we still have sufficient indications and allusions in the Talmud, both Babylonian and Palestinian, to show that Jews of the time did concern themselves with Jesus, that they considered him a negative, destructive force and a branch that had broken away from the Jewish tree. Their constant warning against dissenters, against those who claim that there is a dual authority, all this proves that ur-Christians were part of Judaism. And after that, I recall only one mention in a later writing — "…we were taught that we do not accept him as a mediator…" — and it is this Christian dogma that has raised the most profound questions in Jewish religious thought.

Setzer portrays Jesus as a political, social revolutionary. Setzer is wrong. Least of all was he a communist or a Bolshevik. Evangelism, itself, proves it best. Once, an evangelical legend tells us, a woman came with a cruse of the finest olive oil and poured it on the feet of Jesus. The disciples were astounded and asked their rabbi why he had allowed her to waste the fruit of the earth; were there not poor people who could have made better use of it? And Jesus had answered: "The poor will always be with you, but you will not have me with you much longer." When Judas Iscariot, one of his best and dearest disciples, heard this, he left at once to report him to the Pharisees. One rarely dwells on this legend, but it is so characteristic of Jesus' personality and of his tragedy. "The poor will always be with you…." which means that Jesus did not come to solve social problems. This, though, is what Judas Iscariot had expected from him; this is what had attracted him to the rabbi of Galilee — and he was disappointed.

I do not want, however, to enter into any further historical debate or argumentation. What interests me in Setzer's book is the psychological aspect, the strange concept that Jews have of the past. Setzer is a typical example of those who identify Judaism, of whatever place and time it may be, with the form it has taken on in the last few centuries. He is typical of those who see the Jew as a man of reason, of clear intellect, keeping aloof from the wild, supernatural dreams of those who see the Jew as an anti-metaphysicist. He cannot at all imagine how a young Jew, even two thousand years ago, could indulge in such queer ideas, could be so illogical, so fanciful. And since he deems it to be psychologically impossible, he concludes that the whole story could never have happened. This is the psychological illusion about the unchangeable nature of the Jewish mentality. And there is the second psychological illusion: Assuming that Jesus is a purely gentile product, that he has no connection at all with Judaism, why has this connection been put at our doorstep? Setzer explains that the destruction of the Temple, this tragic chapter in Jewish history, was an event of such catastrophic, universal consequence, that it forced the *ur*-Christians to place the Christ legend within the Jewish framework.

How did he arrive at this? How does he know that the destruction of the Temple had been a tremendous universal catastrophe? We have no historic proofs of it. To the contrary, history tells us that the Romans and the Greeks had concerned themselves very little with the Jewish problem. Egypt, Persia, the Mid-Adriatic Armenia, Galicia, etc., have played a larger role than Jerusalem. The Jewish tragedy had been a mere episode, an event among many other events; it had not created any universal stir.

The Jew, however, places himself in the center of the world. He relates everything to himself and sincerely thinks that he is the focal point of world history. This belief has transferred itself to others as well. We have striven so long to be the center of the world that, to a certain degree, we have achieved it. What the world cannot forgive is that we take ourselves too seriously. What interests me so much in Setzer's book is that it is the Jewish illusion raised to the nth degree.

Still Older?

Harvard has been the subject of many vigorous complaints of anti-Semitism. But my complaint is directed at Yale and, especially, at Professor Albert T. Clay, professor of Semitic languages, who is highly knowledgeable in all the quirks of ancient Semitic scripts. Professor Clay has suddenly found out that the theory of the un-originality of the Bible, of its being, as it were, a hand-me-down, is wrong. He is flying in the face of the established scholarly dogma that the Biblical stories of Genesis, of Adam and Eve in the Garden of Eden being tempted by the serpent, of Noah and the Flood, all these stories that seemed so intrinsically Jewish, were not Jewish at all, but had been taken over from other peoples. This means that even when they were young, Jews had merely reworked and reorganized events; they had been merely middlemen.

According to conventional wisdom, there lived in Assur and in Babel men speaking a kind of Mongolian language, looking almost like Tartars. These were the Akkadians. It is not known exactly where they came from, and since it happened so long ago, it seemed hardly worth the trouble of exploring it. They had been an original and a creative people. They had given life to, or, perhaps, had inherited from someone else, old legends which then became the foundation for our entire contemporary culture. The Sumero-Akkadians, which is their official name, had only one fault — their language was so difficult, their scribbling on stone and clay so hard to decipher, that it required the patience of a Tartar and the lifespan of Methuselah to read their writing. The Assyrians, and the Semites who followed them, had then taken over the script and culture of their Mongolian neighbors, translating everything into Assyrian. And, once again, this would have remained unknown to the world had it not been for the Jews. They had taken over the script from the Canaanites and the Phoenicians and had rewritten, in a more readable script, the ancient stories left behind by the Sumero-Akkadians.

Now comes Professor Clay and brings forth an ancient book, written on clay, which now rests in the Pierpoint Morgan Library, and proves that the scholars are all wrong. It is true that the Sumerians existed and that they had their own legends, but they had nothing to do with either the Jews or the Bible. The clay book that he discovered (although its existence has already been known for twenty-five years), only no one had taken the trouble to read it) tells that 3,038 years ago, on the 28th of Shevat (February), an old Hebrew scribe called Iagiah, or something like that, had taken a couple of soft bricks and, with an iron or wooden pen, had copied from an ancient book, *The Story of the Flood*, that was already about 6,000 years old. He had, actually, written in the ancient rounded script, but the language was Hebrew. Professor Clay took the trouble to read the book, to photograph it and to translate it. It is the ancient flood legend, but much more detailed, with more moralizing and less poetry, using five lines to say what the Bible says in one. While Genesis limits itself to a hint, to just a few utterances, the writer of 6,000 years ago inundates us with a flood of words.

I will not concern myself here with the particulars of this discovery, since it requires the technical knowledge of a historian and a specialist in ancient Oriental philology. But even a cursory viewing of the lettering stimulates one to consider the development of Jewish writing. You find that the ideal Jewish form of expression has always been that of *tzimtzum*, of contraction, of discarding the superfluous. The fewer the words, the better the effect. Present the facts without elaboration and let the facts speak for themselves. This is what has preserved the freshness and naiveté of Jewish writing. Words and concepts grow old and moldy, but facts remain. The form changes, but the facts remain, and the story of the event always stays the same. It is Impressionism in its oldest form.

The most interesting and gripping aspect of Professor Clay's discovery is the fact that we are still older than we thought we were, still older than we want to be. I do not know whether age is such an advantage. I do not even know whether today's scientists are doing us such a favor in trying to prolong human life. One lives longer and eats more, but one has more worries and more heartache. And even the joys of life, how long do they last?

Actually, it is the brevity of life that is its greatest charm. One always has the feeling of not being ready, of the end coming too early. Life is interesting only as long as one has not accomplished everything one wants to. Imagine that you have done all that you desired. You have lived 200, 300 years already, have produced innumerable great-grandchildren, have satisfied all cravings, and have fulfilled all desires. What are you to do in the *next* 400 to 500 years? George Bernard Shaw tried to portray such a situation in his Methuselah play, but he did not succeed. When you see his old people carrying a load of several hundred years on their backs, you feel like throwing out all of the life-prolonging prescriptions, disregarding all the laws of hygiene and risking a young and quick death. Of course, we do not know what happens after death. We may be blown into the great beyond or we may turn into a flower in a garden. But the life we live is well-known to us, and to linger in it too long is much too boring.

Mankind has always disliked old age, has been afraid of it and in awe of it, and so has been unwilling to approach it too closely. Even today the primitive peoples of Australia and of Central America simply kill their old people. Old people know it and find it quite natural, having once done the same to their elders. And are not the Russian peasants waiting impatiently for the deaths of their parents and relatives who no longer have the strength to work, and who spend their days laying atop the broad stoves, waiting to be fed? A man is neither a beast nor a god to his fellow men, but simply a mouth that consumes food. And no one wants to work for anyone else, especially if the other one has nothing to offer you. It was necessary to include the commandment "Honor your father and your mother" in the moral code. And even then, to make this commandment acceptable to mankind, we were told that fulfilling that commandment would prolong one's own years.

Let us assume, however, that the aged one is not a father, not a relative, and not even one of your own people, but a stranger. Let us further assume that we are not talking about an individual, a man of flesh and blood whom one can pity, whom one can love and feel close to, but rather about an entire people, a group, a collective. All of the people of the earth are still so young or, at least, consider themselves young. The Italians and the Greeks are, perhaps, the oldest of all, but they acknowledge it only when it suits them, when they want to boast of their past. In their heart of hearts they know and feel that their link with the ancient Romans and Hellenes is as weak as that of the Russian peasants to their ancient bards. They are distant relatives; they are not sons but great-grandchildren. In fact, they want to be young. They want to believe that all possibilities are still open to them, that their wells have not yet run dry. The Russians are still clamoring to be the world's youngest people, believing that, as the saying goes, "the world belongs to the young."

Amidst these youthful nations, none more than 1,000-years-old, there walks an old people, a people of far-reaching experiences, smiling the mocking smile of those who know everything best. Nothing gives them great joy, and nothing surprises them, since there is nothing new under the sun. They have their own opinion about everything, points of view no other people can have. It is a people whose life is circumscribed by its memories. And do we not, as Jews, feel ourselves so very old? Wherever you turn, wherever you look, you encounter age. Everything we say has been already said by our grandfathers. They have used up all the words; we are simply following them. We are always turning backward, so that the newest idea is for us a mere repetition. If you talk of a societal renewal, you are harkening back to the ideals of the Prophets. If you dream of a national renaissance, you are up against a return to Zion, to the old mountain, the gray stones, to Abraham's cave of Machpelah. You always go back, never forward to new shores and new aims.

The Christians have better understood the tragedy of old age than have we. They have created the Ahaseurus legend, of Ahaseurus doomed to live and continue living. He pleads for death, but death will not come. He wants to rest from being always in the midst of life, but he cannot. He must go on living, always searching for something new but never finding it.

A noted Jewish sociologist recently said: "The greatest offense of the Jews is their stubborn clinging to live." He himself refused to commit this offence, and at the age of 70 he ended his life, together with his wife. But I console myself by asking: Are we really that old? Does the fact that the Greeks and the Romans have not known how to maintain their links to the past make us so aged? All right — 3,000, 4,000 years, is this so much? Our history began with our Father Abraham, which means 4,000 years ago. It is a considerable age, but not yet an overwhelming one. We still have ancestors; we are still grandchildren. But now comes Professor Clay and destroys this illusion. What ancestors? What 4,000 years? Iagiah had already in Abraham's time written a Hebrew document of events that had taken place 2,000 years earlier. And this original is also a copy of something written perhaps a couple of thousand years earlier, and we lose all count: 6,000, 8,000, 10,000 years. Did we never have a beginning? Are we, perhaps, leading an eternal life from the time the world began? A life without a beginning and without an end? Without a hope of being able to evolve into some other forms? Are we forever bound to the same language, the same motifs, even the same way of life? Were we, 6,000 years ago, already a pathetic, quirky, ethically stubborn people?

Old age shuffles on, steeped in its grayness, almost forgetting that it once was young. And those of us who want to regain once more the illusion of youth feel that we are drowning in the white foamy waves of time. Why did Professor Clay not break his newly discovered brick book? Why did he have to inflict this sorrow upon us? We know that we are old, but still older? The story is becoming too burdensome.

Moses

And no one knows where he is buried. Somewhere in the mountains, amid rocks, in the hot desert, he lies in solitude. He had led his people to the land that he had chosen for them, but had not himself entered. His people would leave the land again and return to it. They would spread his name across the seas and throughout many lands, singing his praises, fearing him, trembling in awe of him, rebelling against him and coming back to him with heads bowed in humble supplication. He towers like a mighty tree, his roots spreading from one corner of the earth to the other. He is the root, the source, the beginning; everything is contained in him. But he himself, who is he?

A prophet? But what kind of prophet? Isaiah was a prophet and so was Ezekiel; they were great prophets, full of pathos and passion. They preached and they chastised, they pleaded and they erupted in anger. They uttered words of despair and they brought forth trumpet sounds filled with joy and eternal felicity. But he, the prophet of prophets, the father of all who have spoken to their people and led them, he was devoid of passion and pathos. He was a quiet man and a modest one and he wondered uneasily: Who am I to come forth and speak in the name of God? Who am I to take upon myself the delivery of His message to the world? I am unable to make speeches. I am a simple man, not a hero. I am the man who fled into the desert, and there got scorched by the eternally burning thornbush.

This is how Moses viewed himself, and what he omitted to mention he omitted not out of pride but out of modesty, out of an inner necessity, since he saw himself not as a ruler of men but as a servant of God. He did not aspire to any mastery over men nor did he set out to be a leader; he only went ahead and the people followed him. He said what he was told to say and no more. He was a messenger, a teacher, not one who chastises, being sorely afraid to follow his own judgment, to demand more and to probe deeper than he had been commanded to do. And the people called him simply Moses ben Amram, accepting his presence without questioning, without attempting to lift the veil that was concealing him. It was a concealment which began in his childhood, spent at the court of Pharaoh, continued in the desert, enveloped him in the sweltering cloud covering Mount Sinai, and, finally settled over his grave…no one knows where.

And a doubt began to arise: Did he really exist? The doubt was not about Moses ben Amram of tradition, the miracle worker of Egypt, the legendary figure on Mount Sinai; that account was accepted as poetry. A broader question arose: Was there any kernel of historical reality hidden beneath that mythological, mystical veil? Or was the story of Moses like that of Job, one that "never was, never came to pass, was nothing but a fable," a collective fantasy, a remembrance of age-old legends, a mirroring of ancient historic perceptions? Is there a possibility, though, that there truly lived a man called Moses, who had been a leader, a lawmaker and a redeemer, one who had showed the way to his people? If so, when and where had he lived? And if not, why did Moses become a figure of world historical stature?

Ancient Jewish thinkers feared to pursue this question, and the Christian world of old did not have the courage to voice any doubts. But latter-day Christian theologians did. The Protestants were the first to remove the restraints and submit the Bible to analytical inquiry: If the church stories are mere legends, they asked, if the branch of a tree is nothing but an image and an allegory, how can its very roots be real? And scholars began to apply historical criticism to the Bible. Wellhausen and other German Bible scholars subjected it to relentless analysis, and, by dint of a great deal of insight and of even more imagination, they, bit by bit, tore down the entire historic reality of Moses, converting him into a mere symbol, into a mere historical synthesis of the birth of a people. And the greatest of all these scholars (the one most critical of all things Jewish), the historian Edward Maier, has striven to prove, with tremendous keenness and detailed analysis, that Moses had been nothing more than the personification of the ancient cultic desert god of Kidush (Marivah), located at the Southern border of *Eretz Yisrael*.

This meant that Moses had never been in Egypt, had nothing to do with the Exodus, had not been the historic founder of Judaism; that he had been, if in fact he had existed at all, a priest who had served the desert god, the God of Sinai. Subsequently, those who formulated and revised Jewish legend blended the figure of Moses, the servant of the Sinai cult, into another traditional tale, that of the Exodus from Egypt. This is both Maier's interpretation and that of most of the scholars of our time. And thus the burial place of Moses was shrouded in secrecy for a second time, with no one knowing who he had been.

But suddenly the ancient past sends out a ray of light that pierces the night. From under the rocks of Mount Sinai emerge testimonies, living testimonies of bygone times, testimonies which tell a story, tell it on stones covered with signs, with long forgotten characters, which had been waiting for thousands of years to be found. In 1905, the English archaeologist Flinders Petrie dug deep enough to find not only various papyrus sheets covered with Egyptian hieroglyphics, but also a few *Megillot*, written in a strange, unknown script. This script resembled the one used in the late historic Egyptian writings, yet the language was not Egyptian. No one was able to determine what language the writing represented or to fathom the meaning of the words, until the German scholar Professor Hubert Grimme solved the riddle in a book published in 1923, *Old Hebrew Inscriptions from Sinai*, in which he explained the origin of the strange *Megillot* and interpreted their meaning. He showed that the inscriptions were not Egyptian but Hebrew ones — the first Hebrew ones — the earliest original Hebrew documents we have. And one of the inscriptions says "I, the son of Hitshuhanimimon, overseer of the stonecutters and master of the Temple of Balat, Ichu and Sinai, and you, Hitsphishuhanmimon, beloved of Balat, have dealt well with me, you drew me out of the Nile and hid me in the antechamber of the Temple of Ablaut, which is in the Sinai."

Egyptian history tells us about this woman with the long name, and we find her listed among the rulers of Egypt. We know, furthermore, that the Egyptian King Thutmose III hated the very name of this queen and decreed the destruction of all the monuments erected in her honor; he persecuted all her relatives and followers in order to eradicate all remembrance of her reign. We also know that the goddess Balat named in the inscription is the Semitic translation of the Egyptian goddess Shaved, which in Egyptian was pronounced *Shadai*. From other inscriptions found in the Sinai we learn that the person appointed by the queen to be overseer of the Sinai stone quarries and the master of the Temple of Balat bore the name of Menasheh.

Now, in the Book of Judges we learn that Moses had also been born with the name of Menasheh, from the reference to "Jonathan ben Gershon ben Menasheh." All of these threads lead us to a remarkable, surprising historic fact: the actual existence of Moses Menasheh, as well as an illumination and affirmation of the entire ancient chronicle of Pharaoh's daughter drawing Moses out of the Nile, the affirmation of Sinai, of the desert and of the name Shadai. This name, which once had been a name of God, became, ultimately, the only name, the name which, expressed in four Hebrew characters, conquered the world. Faced with this affirmation, the historical criticism of Wellhausen, Maier and others falls by the wayside, and the entire critical process has to start all over again, according to Professor Grimme, in line with this interpretation of the oldest historic Jewish document.

This is not the place to enter into a further investigation of Professor Grimme's discovery. The general public has become aware of it only a few days ago from reports in the press. But the scholarly world has been working on this difficult matter for a number of years. Dr. Joseph Reiden is completely correct in stating in his very good recent article that for the time being one has to view the results of Grimme's interpretation very cautiously. One must take another look at the original Sinai findings, one must explore ever deeper until one can be perfectly sure of the ultimate truth, the truth about Moses. Yet even now a beam of light illuminates the grandiose figure of the world-renowned "engraver," as he arises out of his concealment as a living human being. We must continue to seek and search for a knowledge of our past and, who knows, we may be able to reach the very source of Judaism. We must dig, dig ever deeper, in the desert among the ruins, the ruins which contain the past, the present and the future.

About the Pillar of Gezer

In his book *Sidelights on Biblical Chronicles,* the noted archaeologist McAllister tells us about a very interesting monument that was found in the old Palestinian city of Gezer. It was a pillar of a house or of a temple, a pillar in Greek style, with Greek letters etched into it. Both sides were covered with letters, on one side a dedication or a prayer to the Greek half-god Heracles, and on the other side, in Greek, the *Shem*, the Hebrew name of God. On one side the West, on the other the East: Hellenism and Judaism in peace and harmony on a slab of marble.

It is a pity that only a fragment of the inscriptions has reached us and that the name of the pious soul who, in this manner, secured a place for himself in both worlds has been lost. He surely meant well, very well, this citizen of Gezer, who wanted to be a man of his time, yet did not want to abandon his roots. More than likely he had two names, Eliahu and Theopampus of Gabrielnikos, and wore a yellow Greek cloak, pinning to it a few strands of blue wool. Upon his head sat the Greek hat, the petasos, but beneath it he wore a phylactery, barely visible, but still…the eye that sees everything had seen that too, and it was sufficient.

Not far from Gezer, a few hours ride by donkey, was the village of Modin, a restless village, inhabited by conservative Hebrew peasants. And the village disliked Gezer, disliked the Greeks and their cult of beauty. Every week they used to gather in their town hall or temple, and one peasant would tell the others about the sinful city.

"The Greeks, the Syrians, the Gentiles, let them do what they want. They have their ways, and it is not up to us to make them change them. This is His worry, let Him take care of His name. And if these are His creatures and He allows them to do what they are doing, makes them strong and rich, and gives them power over us, then so it must be, it has a purpose, and it is forbidden to ask Him why. Neither can we reproach those Jews who have altogether left us. Let them be. There are so many Greeks, let there be a few more. Were we not promised that the children of Israel would be as numerous as the grains of sand on the seashore? What does it matter whether there are a few grains of sand more or less? Was he once called Simeon, the Son of Levi, and does he now call himself Socrates the son of Laius? Well and good. If he can fool the Greeks in Athens or even in Antiochus let him enjoy it.

"But what is inadmissible and not to be permitted, because it constitutes a dire peril, is when that Theopampus wants also to be called Eliahu, and when Gabriel adds a Nikos to his name. It is not the Temple of Zeus or of Heracles that profanes and defiles, weakens and sullies his home, but that very pillar which stands in Gezer and wants to serve both, affirming the God on Olympus and the God of Sinai."

Thus the village wise man argued, stirring up and inflaming passions until one fine day a band of strong, determined peasants, headed by Matityahu, marched toward Gezer and the surrounding cities, swinging their hatchets and chopping down all pillars with double inscriptions, all two-sided altars, all two-fronted temples. They thus put a sudden and sure end to the entire synthesis between the two worlds, Greek and Jewish. Olympus and Sinai each went their separate ways again.

But the pillar of Gezer escaped that fate and survived the Maccabees and the destruction of the Second Temple beneath layers and layers of earth, which protected it from the galloping, fanaticism-driven footsteps of the pursuers and from the trembling flight of the pursued. Jews left the land; others came in their stead. The earth resounded to the steps of other pursuers and other pursued, but the doubly inscribed pillar was lying quietly beneath the surface, waiting. It did not wait in vain, and the day came when it was discovered. And there are two sides again, there is a synthesis, Heracles on one side and *Ha-Shem* on the other.

Actually, what difference does it make whether one's name is Eliahu or Theopampus, or whether one calls oneself Haim Aaron Cohen or Alexander Cromwell Cowan? These are mere comedies, greater or smaller, and I do not begrudge anyone his happiness or his foolishness. I am also bothered little by the Heracles on the pillar. A child wants to believe in giants, in miracles, in legends

— why destroy its naiveté? And who needs the Exodus from Egypt? This is a heavy burden to carry on the road. And more than one battle was lost because there were too many soldiers. In spiritual accounting, less is often more.

One thing, however, affects me as if I myself had been standing among the Modin zealots. In one respect I identify completely with the fanatics who descended on Gezer. I am shocked by the so-called synthesis. I understand what is meant by "synthetic" threads, and I understand the possibilities of "synthetic food," but I cannot understand the meaning of "synthetic religion," or synthetic Judaism.

Even synthetic food still faces a great many questions. For years and years, starting with the famous experiments of the German chemist Berth in the 1930s, scientists have worked in their laboratories to produce synthetic, i.e. artificial food. Theoretically quite feasible, the formula exists; but when it comes to creating ersatz-nature, the work falters. And if they do succeed, would life become better or worse? There would no longer be the need to sow and to reap, our entire social structure would change, and man might not be able to stand it, he might become undone by too great a well-being. One might think, what is the difference? It is the same nature manifesting itself in one way or another. But evidently the "way" does matter. Dr. Faustus achieved his goal of bringing forth a homunculus, an artificial, scientific, synthetic man, but no recognizable human being would have emerged from the chemical pot.

It surely is one of the usual historical slanders and exaggerations when old chronicles tell us about the High Priest Jason who wanted to transform the synagogue into a temple of idolatry. Conquerors never show mercy to those they conquer, especially in religious wars. The Hellenists of the pre-Hasmonean time, the Jews who had imbibed Greek culture, had surely not really intended to introduce Greek polytheism into Jerusalem and convert the Jewish people. It is illogical, it is psychologically impossible that a High Priest, no matter how free-thinking or even heretical he might be, should be willing to deny the very essence of his faith, destroy its foundation, and wipe out the entire old tradition. This requires a religious genius, a revolutionary of the highest caliber, and it is evident that Jason and his followers had been neither geniuses nor great revolutionaries.

The intentions of the Jewish Hellenists were not as evil as the hot-blooded Jews of Modin assumed. They simply went along with their time, and that meant going along with the synthesis. The entire Eastern life at that time had been artificial and synthetic: one filled in the holes in the road with disparate stones rather than step over them; one heaped up old stones rather than construct new edifices. Greek philosophers, Egyptian folklore, Plato and Baal, Socrates and the Moloch, they had performed a remarkable, ingenious dance, a carnival. Both the Greek Syrian and the Jerusalemite who had turned Greek lost the passion of wholeness and, therefore, also the wholeness of passion. They visualized a comfortable world where all styles are represented, where every one, the wolf and the lamb, live in peace and smile at each other over a glass of wine. A kind of Noah's Ark in a sea of words.

But the sea had grown shallow and the Ark had run aground on dry land and the animals in the Ark had attacked each other with their sharp teeth. A breeze blows, and the entire synthetic culture vanishes without a trace, while the stone of Gezer has remained. The inscription changes; other names have replaced Heracles on the Greek side, while on the Jewish side there are still the four letters of the eternal name. There are those on the Jewish side who, like Jason, seek to find common ground, to smooth things over, to synthesize. One seeks to join Kant or some other thinker, another turns to modern science, and yet another looks to the Great Nothing, the spiritual void called culture, culture without the passion, without the will for distinction; a culture of ease.

On the market place of Athens stood an altar bearing the inscription: "To the unknown God." The altar still stands on all of Athens' market places but it bears a later, a Roman inscription: "I do not yearn for the unknown." And so may it remain. Let the mystery remain a mystery. We can get along without the Final Answer. This, then, is the new inscription on the Greek side. On the other side there are etched, for eternity, the four letters. Well, can this be synthesized? One can split it asunder, one can eradicate one inscription from the stone; one needs only an axe or a hammer to do that. But to connect, to unite, to establish peace? Poor Jason tried it and perished, leaving behind him only a stained name in a book, and the pillar of Gezer. And the old man of Modin still keeps watch; the stern elder is still guarding his borders.

Around the Sinai

First and foremost among the sciences awaiting their liberation from the bondage exerted by outdated theories and antiquated methods is history. In reality, of course, history is not yet a science, and it began as a simple narration of events, selectively chosen and, at times, purposefully falsified. The 19th century trend towards a rising preoccupation with narrative style, accompanied by a growing disinclination to ascertain the historical veracity of the data presented, can be laid at the doorsteps of German historians. It is difficult to find an example of a more unscholarly historical writing than that of Theodore Mommsen's famous *History of Rome*. Here everything reflects the author's own preferences, prejudices and moods. His interpretation of events is not that of a historian, i.e. an objective researcher, but that of a politician. Mommsen talks about Rome, but he means the German Empire.

The passage of years brought even worse in its wake. Modern historians have become so intent on validating their historical premises that they have completely lost their grip on actual facts. The sharp needle of reality has become lost in the haystack of hypothetical assumptions, as in the case of the Jewish people, whose history has been treated in a most fanciful manner not only by historical novelists but by historians as well, especially by Christian ones. I say especially, although this qualification may be redundant, since the study of Jewish history from ancient times until the destruction of the Second Temple has been the monopoly and primary concern of German Protestant scholars. They are the ones who laid out the path along which all of the others have followed. The books by Well-hausen and Edward Maier are still considered seminal works on ancient Jewish history. What unites these writers, in addition to their historical methodology, is a deep-seated animosity toward the Jews of their own times, an enmity which works its way into the past and shapes their approach to Jewish history. Well-hausen veils his sentiments, but Maier's anti-Semitism is stated openly and clearly; he makes no effort to disguise it, since his entire purpose is to minimize the achievements of ancient Judaism and thus justify the tragic history of the Jew-ish people. And one more thing emerges from all these works, a feeling of con-tempt for the people they write about. While authors writing about Greece and Rome approach their subject with love and admiration, historians of Judaism approach their task with an air of condescension. They make no effort to go below the surface, nor do they even want to broaden their knowledge.

Can anyone imagine a scholar of Greek history going no further than the time of Pericles, omitting to follow Greek history and literature until its dissolution in the Byzantine era? Or could a scholar possibly attempt to write a history of Rome without a command of Latin and its various dialects or a knowledge of Roman history in its manifold manifestations? Yet Wellhausen, Maier and many others have managed to become historians of Judaism without the slightest idea of what constitutes Judaism. They use one source, the Bible, only rarely reaching out to include the Mishnah, and this sparse material serves as the basis for their entire work. From this one historical fragment they evolve their theories. Take, for instance, the book of the German scholar Max Weber, *The Religious Sociology of Judaism*, where he presents the curious theory that "sociologically viewed, the Jews have always been a pariah people," pariah meaning isolated, shunned, treated with contempt. When you look for the data to support this strange and absurd thesis, you find only another analysis of Deuteronomy, Numbers and the Prophets, along with a superficial mention of the commentaries and rabbinical writing. Not knowing Hebrew, Weber was unable to read his source material in the original, choosing to derive his knowledge and understanding of his subject matter from second-hand, unsubstantiated opinions.

Now, however, the time has truly come for us to liberate Jewish history from its exile. Jewish historians steeped in knowledge of and about Judaism, Jewish scholars with open access to all phases of Jewish culture, must shoulder the task of becoming the historians of Judaism rather than continuing meekly to follow the line laid down by the German historians and Bible critics. This task requires a tremendous amount of knowledge of the philological and archeological aspects of Judaism as well as that of its daily life. One cannot deal with the political or spiritual history of Judaism without being familiar with Mishnah and *Gemarah*, the Torah and the commentaries; without being able to navigate securely through the crosscurrents of the Talmudic sea. All these things must not be treated merely as historical data, but must be experienced by the scholar from within, as his own. In addition, he must have a vast knowledge of the jurisprudence and culture of ancient times, be able to view them objectively, and, most importantly, must bring a new approach to his task.

Protestant theologians have looked upon Judaism as a mere religious sect and considered all of ancient Jewish literature to be nothing more than — in the words of the old Church Father Eusebius — a "*preparacia evangelica*," a laying of the ground for Evangelism. Jewish historians must develop a truly historical approach, a scientific one, studying the history of a people and not of a sect. One must not think of the Jews of Jerusalem, of Israel, as being totally immersed in religious observances, with no other interests than codifying religious laws. One must see the Jews of long ago as human beings, possessed, like all others, of all of the passions, faults and diversity of life. And one needs to listen to the sounds, the ancient melodies passed on from generation to generation, up to the present. This is the only scientific way to read and understand history, and it is beginning to come to the fore. Works of older Jewish historians, such as Nachman Krachmal, Isaac Hirsch, Zahariah Frankel and Abraham Geiger, their great achievements notwithstanding, are being viewed as old-fashioned and methodologically obsolete. They are being replaced by Jewish scholars using up-to-date methods to redeem the totality of the Jewish past and the Jewish spirit. Such is the work of Professor Louis Ginzburg, and the latest book by the grandmaster of Talmudic scholarship, Professor Chaim Tchernowitz's *Origins of Halacha*.

Professor Tchernowitz is known in the Jewish world as Rav Zair, this being the name with which he signed his articles on the history and methodology of the Talmud in Achad Ha'am's magazine *Ha-Shaliach*. A study of the Talmud must be part of any study of Jewish history because it is a completely idiosyncratic cultural phenomenon. Unlike the Hindu Sutra or the commentaries on the Koran, the Talmud is not a finished tractate, a compendium, or even, as it is frequently called, an encyclopedia. It is, to be sure, all of this, but it goes well beyond it; it is a workshop wherein the living Jewish spirit goes about the weaving and unfolding of its substance. Many generations have labored on it, each one leaving its own imprint, its own original thoughts and its own contradictions, all centering around one focal point — Judaism. It is a Judaism which comprises not only dogma, faith and ritual, but also the customs and the way of life of a long, drawn-out chain of interlinking generations, with Sinai as its center. From the desert mountain, Mount Sinai, there extends a line to the Babylonian Academies of Pumbedita and still further to Cairo, where the Rambam lived, and to the French city Lunel, where additions to the Talmud were developed. It is a zigzag line which cannot be geometrically defined; it is Judaism's spiritual lifeline. Thus the history of Halacha, as Dr. Tchernowitz explains philologically, is the path, the process, the way of life of the Jewish people.

Lack of space, as well as of competency, keep me from dwelling on the wealth of material which Rav Zair has packed into this volume, which is only the beginning of a much larger work. But I do want to bring out one point which, to me, is the heart of the work, and that is the question of what it is that sanctifies Jewish law. What forms the core of Jewish life, the precept or the people? Or, to put it differently, is it the written Torah, the law, or the oral Torah, the tradition? An old controversy, going back to a dispute between the Rambam and the Ramban. For the Rambam, the sanctity of the law derives from the written word, while the Ramban viewed the events at Sinai not as a beginning but as a crystallization of a long, prehistoric tradition. The opposing theories derive from opposing ways of viewing the universe. For Rambam, the rationalist, history proceeds in a straight line, deriving from immutable precepts. The Ramban leaned toward mysticism, and for him Judaism was to be found not encapsulated in a code of laws but in the living flow of the life experiences of the Jewish people. Rambam stressed the law; Ramban stressed history. Rav Zair sides with the Ramban, and thus with the modern view of the world. Judaism for him is not a mere intellectual process but an emotional experience, a way of life, and he, therefore, sees in the Halacha the reflection of the history — or rather, of the psychology — of the people.

Ancient traditions, age-old customs, political, social and religious values, philosophical themes, historical experiences — they all leave their imprint on the Halacha. And amid the swirling tides, there is an island — the written word, the Torah. It is not the totality of the Halacha but only a part, and, at that, not the most essential part. Other scholars have viewed the Torah as expressing the totality of Judaism, seeing the further development of the Halacha as merely interpreting and offering detailed instances of the general law. But Rav Zair holds the opposite view. Far from containing the totality of Judaism, the Torah stresses the details and lacks an overall perspective because it is, in reality, only a fragment of the great history of the Jewish spirit, a history which has anteceded Sinai, continued after it, and is preserved in the oral Torah. The oral Torah is older than the written one. Sinai is not a beginning but a continuation.

Modern historical research sides with Rav Zair. In the last few years new relics of ancient Middle Eastern life have been found, fragments of pre-Sinai documents, where we find reference to old laws and customs which were in force before the Jewish people codified its laws. Take, for instance, the ordinance "you shall not boil the kid in its mother's milk," which has been analyzed and discussed for centuries, and which now appears in a fragment of an ancient text. It appears that this law had been the custom prevailing in one of the ancient desert tribes which, at a later time, united with other desert tribes to form a new entity, that of the Jewish people. The further and the deeper research penetrates into the past, the greater the evidence that Judaism did not materialize on earth fully formed, like a meteor descending from the skies, but that it grew slowly, like a plant, following its own developmental laws, putting down roots and then branching out. This renders utterly ridiculous Wellhausen's, Maier's and Weber's discourses about Elohaists, Yahwists and a pariah people, those fantastic, unhistorical sandcastles built on a foundation of half-baked scholarship. And a little bit of knowledge is more pernicious than total ignorance because lack of comprehension leads to a fragmentation and misconception of the matter under study. It is insufficient knowledge which led Protestant theologians and anti-Semitic historians to dissect the living Jewish organism and to falsify the portent of Jewish history. The Jewish professor Tchernowitz, equipped with full knowledge, is restoring the Jewish spirit to its organic totality.

A Legend Destroyed

One more illusion has been destroyed. And the destroyer, as so often happens, is a persistent truth seeker who will settle for nothing less than the pure, shining truth. I have been under the illusion that the entire Purim story was truly just a story, a legend going back to an old Oriental myth, an old Persian holiday tradition of throwing lots, or to the tale of the Persian moon goddess Anareota which found its way to a Jewish cultic group and was assimilated by it. And this very fact was to me an indication of Jewish uniqueness, of the idiosyncrasy of the Jewish historic genius that subjects nature to a historic process and endows the universe and all its phenomena with a sense of morality. This epitomized to me the entire Jewish view of the world. Evolving out of natural history, it interprets brutal, factual events that have no meaning for us in a human, ethical way.

This development is quite clear for the holiday of Passover, an old spring festival that became a symbol of freedom and of liberation. The moment when the earth awakens and bursts into bloom is transformed into a historical spring, the onset of a historical era. It is also clear for the holiday of Purim. It is an old Persian story, taking place in the capital city of Shushan (Susa), ruled by a king whose name was not really a name but a nickname. The entire story was so fantastic, so improbable and unintelligible, that even in the olden days, the days of the Talmudists, the king was declared a "silly king," a fool, because he was so apolitical, so unworthy of being a link in the lineage of kings who had been leaders. And it is this very improbability that endows this holiday with charm. There is no greater joy than the celebration of events that have never happened. The enjoyment of unreality is the only thing in life that cannot be destroyed, that can be neither lessened nor increased, neither diminished nor exaggerated. It is the uniquely creative, artistic outreach of the human soul. But historians, the document-intoxicated bookworms, are engaged in an eternal struggle with art. They want to lead imagination back to reality. They want to transform it into the foundations of life, into the skin and bones of people who had once truly existed, thus reducing their meaning to the mere fact of their past existence.

A German historian has just written a book about Purim in which he tries to prove that the entire Purim story is actually true. Ahaseurus really existed, and he was in no way silly, but rather a great king whose realm extended over Persia and Media, from Hodu to Kush, from India to Ethiopia, and his name was Artaxerkes II, or Artakshashta in Persian. The historian shows that Haman, the son of Hammedatha, had in fact been a Persian satrap whose name has its roots in the Persian language, and that Mordecai had been a wealthy assimilated Jewish immigrant from Babylon, whose real name was Mordecai Belshinu (as he is also called in the *Megillah*). As to Esther-Hadassah, her real Babylonian name was Istarat Hodasa, which was the name of a Babylon goddess, etc., etc. Thus he turns all the players in the *Megillah* into living, historical figures. Even Ahaseurus' chamberlain, Harbona, of blessed memory, becomes a flesh and blood reality. He is, of course, a eunuch, but still a man, and a Jew at that, who had used his position at court and in the Harem for the benefit of his brethren.

The historian Jacob Hoschander demonstrates all of this, unmistakably and clearly, by dint of incisive, deeply probing analysis of the text itself and of all the scholars and critics who have studied and interpreted it. The picture we get is as follows: At the time of Artaxerxes II Jewish life in Persia could be likened to, let us say, present day Jewish life in England. The Court practiced Zoroastrianism, a magical, almost monotheistic religion. It is true, of course, that the god or goddess Ahura Mazda possessed an evil counterpart in Angra Mainyu, but the Jews of Persia were not sufficiently versed in theology to probe deep philosophical distinctions. As long as idolatry was not practiced, and as long as the unity of God was proclaimed, they could remain content. They could remain so to such an extent that the Persians were not even aware of the presence of Jews in Persia, and had there been some awareness of the "Hebrews" among them, they would have been viewed merely as a religious sect, not as a people. Jews spoke the language of the land, dressed like the natives, had both Persian and Babylonian names and were fully assimilated. Their life resembled the way Jews lived in England or in

America before the old Protestantism had raised its head and before the Jewish question assumed a national and racial character.

Suddenly, however, Persian politics changed. Haman assumed a purposeful role in the land, his mission being the consolidation and strengthening of the Empire. He wanted to fortify Persian power by providing it with a broader, more democratic base. The Zoroastrian religion had been the faith only of the aristocracy, while the masses had been more "Catholic," preferring icons and statues of the gods, incense, sacrifices and impressive processions. The people looked toward Babylon, just as the people in Protestant countries, up to today, have yearned for Rome and for Roman-Catholic magnificence. Haman worked out a compromise with democracy and wanted to make the mainstream religion more popular. The Persians themselves had no objection to that; they might actually have approved. But there was a puritanical group which did object, and among its members was an assimilated Babylonian Jew (who had concealed his Jewishness) named Mordecai Belshinu.

It may be that this was not merely a religious protest but also a struggle of the aristocracy against democracy. We have seen such struggles in the course of the Reformation in various countries. Whatever it origin may have been, Haman's entire struggle with his enemies was soon centered on Mordecai. And Haman prevailed. There being no lengthy court hearings in Persia, Mordecai would have been hanged had the harem not become involved. Queen Esther was drawn into the conflict, forced to intervene by Mordecai's threat to reveal her secret, i.e. her Jewishness. And she prevailed. Poor Haman's entire political program was discredited, and he was hanged together with his innocent son Vizatha. The city of Shushan rejoiced, and people from Jerusalem to New York City now gorge themselves on *hamentashen* and make noise with the *groggers*.

This is roughly the impression a reader carries away from Dr. Hoschander's learned historic interpretation of the *Megillah*, and of Purim in general. And, all at once, the entire charm and the meaning of the legend vanishes. Because in a legend — and only in a legend — a saint is a saint, and a sinner a sinner; only there do bright rays of light face shadows black as tar. In the legend everything was beautiful. Mordecai was a *tzadik*, one of the 36 righteous ones, a pious Jew who, undoubtedly, put on phylacteries twice a day, who was elevated to a high station in Persia and Media. Esther was a pious, devoted young Jewess, though not an impressive personality, to tell the truth. The *Gemarah* pictures her as being rather naive, but nevertheless a modest and intelligent woman. And as for Haman, he was the epitome of evil, the archetype of the bloodthirsty cruel villain who is not content to murder only one Jew. His cruelty was insatiable; he had to eliminate, kill and despoil all of Jewish life. The *Megillah* calls Haman the Haggagaite, a descendant of Hagai and of Amalek, while Mordecai is descended from Kish and from Benjamin. Two old enemies, Benjamin and Amalek, had met again. Two historical foes once more struggled with one another, and, once more, the saint prevailed over the sinner. Amalek was, once more, defeated.

Let us take a good look at the Amalek legend. It presents one of the most remarkable duels in world history, with a kind of age-old sense of guilt which does not allow the two opponents to rest, which hounds them and incites them to mutual pursuit. The enmity begins with Esau, the wronged one. Jewish history begins with enmity. And it is precisely the stronger one, the pursuer, who is initially fooled. In the final analysis, Esau really suffered an injustice. Jacob injured him, and Jewish historic imagination depicts the consequences of this original injustice. The one who is injured becomes the stronger one, the eternal enemy, sometimes in the guise of Amalek, other times in that of Rome or some other nation; the motif, though, is always the same. The enemy also has his moral motivation; he wants to correct a wrong, to avenge the lost blessing, the loss of the spiritual birthright that Jacob had taken from him. And Jacob defends himself, pushing off the final settlement until the time of universal peace.

But, once again, the scholar destroys the legend. He shows that the scribe made a mistake: The appellation should not have been Haggai but Baggai, which was a common Persian name. Haman's family name was Baggai; the Jewish author of the *Megillah* knew this and had written it so. But in later years, having lost touch with Persia and its language, the name had lost its historic content and instead was imbued with Jewish meaning. Legend became history, poetry became a prosaic chronicle. Imagination dies out and becomes a dry, not very instructive reality. Mordecai is no longer a *tzadik* but merely a rich assimilated bourgeois; Esther is no longer virtuous, but merely a beautiful harem woman; and Ahaseurus is no longer silly. What a shame! It is truly a pity that there is one less legendary figure in the royal gallery.

The entire miracle altogether loses its charm and its uniqueness, because within the historical realm there are many such stories and many more important events, stories and events of pious, legendary and miraculous tone that have taken place not only among Jews but among other nations as well. The elders evidently felt that the Esther story, be it imaginary or real, was not altogether Jewish, did not fit into their world view. The Midrash tells us that they had been unwilling to enter her into history and had agreed to it only after Queen Esther had informed them that her history was already recorded in the annals of Persia and Media. But their doubts persisted even after that. As it says in the *Gemarah*, "one may read the story of Esther, but one may not write it."

It is a good parable, a good legend, a good romantic story, but it loses its value when treated as history. It "evokes the envy of other nations," it does not fit into the Jewish mentality. History struck a compromise. Esther remained a legend until an historian placed her within the framework of history and robbed her of her last bit of beauty. I want to hope that the historian has made a mistake, since the collectors of facts and documents often do make great mistakes. Judaism has so few romantic stories, what a pity to rob us of any that we still possess.

Travels in Europe

Between Heaven and Water

On the water. Free. Between heaven and another sky. Heaven is far away and, therefore, calm, remote, still. The other sky, the one we call the sea, is right below me, with only a few planks of wood between us, and this very nearness subjects me to its unrest, forges a bond between us.

I have been taken to task, some time ago, for my critique of Joseph Conrad's *Sea-pictures.* It may be that my critique was a rather subjective one. Conrad's personality, his style, his anglicized Slavic hysteria, his supposed depth, all these are mere literary devices, and I do not like any of them. It may be that my critics were also subjectively motivated, that their sympathy for Poland had influenced their literary taste. But the more I watch the sea, the more certain I grow that it is not a fit subject for literature, since literature grows out of relationships, out of human connectedness. Literature is comparison and judgment, since what are description, analysis, portrayal, etc., if not acts of comparison? And we can only compare familiar events to those that are strange to us, which means that we ourselves are the touchstone of all comparisons. Yet the idiosyncratic, grandiose aspect of the phenomenon we call "the sea" is beyond all comparison. Its basic element is movement, just movement, nothing more; it has no purpose. The earth has a reason, and the skies play a purposeful role in our lives, but the sea exists only for its own sake; it does not concern itself with us, nor is it of concern to us. It is merely a course of passage and motion, and it brings forth an awakening.

Of what importance is all this to me — Conrad and literature, criticism and philosophizing about the sea and the earth, heavens and man? I am overcome by a remarkable feeling of freedom. Confined by four walls, by planks held together with iron screws, I still feel free. I cannot go anywhere, cannot span the distance that divides me from land, but neither do I want to. Suddenly all is complete; I do not need anything, and I do not think about anything. I am alone, a stranger to everyone, even to myself. I am disconnected.

The day before leaving New York I called the telephone company with the request to discontinue my phone service. The next day, a few hours before I boarded my ship, exactly at 12:00 noon, the phone rang in my apartment and a hoarse, far-away sounding voice announced: "You are disconnected," and silence fell. The telephone was still in its usual place, but it was dead. I do not know why the hoarse, rasping voice continued to echo in my ears and the word "disconnected" to reverberate in my mind. A moment ago I had been connected with the entire world; with a touch of my finger a network would extend — voice to voice, soul to soul. Love and anger, indifference and fascination, fatigue and determination, yearning, give and take — the gamut of life experiences vibrates along this web. No one sees those hidden threads, but they are stronger than steel cables; they are indestructible. And suddenly — cut off, quiet, alone. And thus, I imagine, it will be at one's last instant. One moment you are connected, enmeshed, bound, and then, suddenly, a voice from the other side, from the unknown — "you are disconnected" — and you are free and mute. We call this death. Is this an apt appellation?

I would just like to know whether that voice, that final voice, is also a hoarse, rasping one, or if its tones, as our imagination presents it to us, are sweet and melodious, like that of a harp mingling with the song of a psalmist? Even Sir Oliver Lodge, who is so well versed in things that pertain to the "beyond" and the "hereafter," has never revealed it to us. It appears that becoming disconnected means losing one's ability to distinguish tonal variations — everything sounds the same in the stillness of eternity.

Travel Pictures

According to the newspaper employing me, I am traveling in order to gather impressions and write about them, and when a newspaper prints it, it must be true. This, of course, is nothing new. It is not the first time and, surely, not the last, that people traverse the seven seas, climb the highest mountains, traipse over ice-covered steppes and make their way through sand-drenched, parched deserts in order to gather impressions and shape them into travel pictures. Even for me this is not the first and, I hope, not the last time.

Actually, I have been gathering impressions throughout my life, and this may hold true for all writers. One goes, as did Pierre Loti, to the land of the lotus and the land of the chrysanthemum, from country to country, from one adventure to the next, or by traveling in the manner of Xavier De Mestre's *Voyage autour de ma chambre*, taking trips around one's own room. Some hunt elephants and tigers, while others pursue thoughts and moods, which is a more difficult and perilous undertaking than a safari in an African jungle. And all of this — to what purpose?

A hunter risks his life to kill a tiger or an alligator; he skins it, mounts it and exhibits it in a museum in order that those who do not stir from their homes, who do not take any risks, who do not search for anything, in order that these calm and undisturbed ones may have the illusion of having taken part in an adventure. The botanist collects flowers and rare plants, cutting them off from their living roots and imprisoning them in a herbarium, in a book, so that others who lack their opportunities should be able to perceive the variety and colorfulness of life.

All those who roam the world, each one in his own fashion, collect impressions and transmit them to others as a gift. Giving someone a gift means, actually, giving someone a piece of oneself. Those who speak, write, or tell stories offer to others parts of themselves, dredged out of their own depth. And why not? In the final analysis, all of us give away more than we receive; we all produce *Mehr-wert*, surplus value — but who are the consumers? Must one apply Marxist dogma to the field of psychology, or should we look to the realm of metaphysics and Kabbalah in order to uncover the formula? Marx! He could not even find the right formula in such a simple field as economics! And who can?

According to my newspaper, I am setting out to write travel letters from countries I am familiar with and about people I know well, who have been a part of my life (and who are, just because of that, enigmatic strangers to me) and also to write about countries and people I have never seen before (and who, therefore, appear to me to be lucid and intelligible). The closer we come to a subject, the stranger it becomes; the further away we are from the thing we view, and the less we know about it, the simpler it becomes. The deepest incomprehension is the result of coming too close to a matter. It is only when we gain some distance that we begin to understand, if it is at all possible to understand anything in life. And so I want to try to gain distance from that which is close to me and to draw closer to the distant; it may yield a herbarium, dry leaves in an album, but with a reflection of sunlight still shimmering upon the dead leaves. They may yet awaken a yearning, and what other purpose does a writer have?

To the Dear Reader

The boat quivers, and my pen is sliding, yet I do not want to put it aside without saying a few words about the reader, a good reader. I rarely write to and for a reader; I never think about him. Why should I? No one writes for a reader — if, that is, he is a writer, if his writing has meaning for him. But no one writes for oneself alone. One writes for the sake of writing, just as one plays an instrument for the sake of playing. One sits down at the piano, and one improvises. Should someone be sitting nearby and like it, fine, and if he does not, well, it was not played for him. Still, the listener hears and shares, in his own way, the emotions expressed by the player, and a kinship comes into being; for a moment they blend with one another. One often yearns for such a listener, for such a good reader. As Montaigne says somewhere: "Greetings to the one who understands well."

A few of my readers have bestowed their blessings upon me before my departure, in letters resonating with responsiveness and devotion. Does this mean that there are a few who understand, who hear? A few soul mates? Does this mean that everything is not always in vain? The wind carries the seeds, and somewhere they take root and sprout — oh, that it may be so!

Legendary Prague

Prague is a town that has mastered the art of staying old, which, perhaps, requires more creative thought and sense of beauty than the art of staying young. Everybody grows older, but it is not given to all to know how to maintain the beauty, the maturity, the reveries of old age. Rome, the greatest city in the world, the city that has had the greatest impact upon the Western world, had not possessed this gift. Ancient Rome became transformed into a museum, an exhibit for strangers. And the new, young city looks with pity and contempt at its old grandmother who parades her deeply engraved wrinkles before the eyes of curious onlookers

Prague is the only unselfconsciously old city, accepting its age matter-of-factly, feeling no envy towards youth and making no effort to imitate it. Prague is a city enveloped by a web of legends. It is the city of Tycho Brahe, of Rudolf I, of the "gold-makers," of John Huss, of the Maharal and the Golem. It is a city of distinctive houses and streets, cloisters, towers and bridges and even of people, who appear as mirror images of the past.

I spent the entire morning wandering around the Old City, aimlessly and even without any curiosity as to historic events. I still vividly remembered the impression Prague made on me years ago, on my first visit. But now there was a change. A different language was spoken on the street, and a different atmosphere prevailed. At that time this was still Austria, and Prague had been the metropolis of the quaint, old, beautiful, song-filled Kingdom of Bohemia. The language spoken on the street of Prague then was German, a Viennese German, and you could feel the tension of suppressed anger. Though rooted in the past, in the Thirty Years War, the war between two races and two cultures, between the Slavs and the Germans, between Protestants and Catholics, the anger had still resonated in the ancient streets of Prague. But the tension was felt only by those who knew the history of the twisted and unquiet reign of the Hapsburg monarchy. Visitors, and those who are content to enjoy the surface that life presents to them, perceived Prague as a German town. The *Graben*, the widest street in the world, was bathed in light. Cafes and exquisite stores drew visitors to the Wenzeslaus Plaza, and the Jews of Prague were walking around proudly in their black Prince Alberts and their tall hats.

All this is gone today. Not a German word is heard, no German street signs are seen, and the *Graben* now bears the Czech name *Na Perekapu*. All streets display difficult-to-pronounce, un-melodious Czech names. Only Czech is spoken on the streets, and for a long time no one dared to utter a German word. And this feeling of constraint, of a conscious suppression of a culture and the imposition of a systematic, unrelenting nationalism, imparts a sense of sadness to the lively, joyous city of Prague. And Prague feels it.

I go from street to street, without a plan, without a goal. Crossing bridge after bridge, passing tower after tower, I enter a small street in the Old City. It is one of those old streets you find in not a few medieval cities of Europe. Narrow and crooked, it winds like a serpent, and you do not know where it will lead you. It takes you into some deep recesses, with houses guarded by black, iron gates, where generations had spent their lives, with streets impregnated with old, richly lived lives. In one of those recesses, next to such a gate, I saw a remarkable figure: an old man, with long white hair and a short white beard, dressed in a long black coat and wearing a brimless, skullcap-like, velvet hat. He was sitting on a bench, holding a fiddle in one hand and patting the head of a small boy with the other. A grandfather with his grandson; a street player. I stopped where I was, waiting for the old man to start playing. At first he seemed unaware of my presence. Then his eyes turned towards me for just a moment, and I read in his calm, disinterested look that this was a man who asks nothing of life, who looks only inward, who sees only his own world, a world we see as dead, but which still lives in him. His eyes turned from me and, smilingly, towards his grandson.

It was here that I saw a remnant of medieval Prague. This is the way the alchemists and the half-sorcerers lived in the stormy times of Kaiser Rudolf, 400 years ago. This is the way the Chief Rabbi Loew, the legendary creator of the Golem, may have looked, 400 years ago. What is this morsel of the past doing in the present time? How does all this political warfare — Czechs versus Germans,

Republic versus Monarchy, Masaryk versus the Hapsburgs — how does all this affect the old man in the velvet skullcap, who lives in a different world, a world which has nothing to do with political changes? He lives in the old, dead, and therefore beautiful city of Prague. He lives in a Prague that is no more a city, only a legend.

I stood for a long time looking at the old man. And when I came back, an hour later, to the same street, the old man was still sitting on the same bench. He was slowly, thoughtfully, playing an old song, a forgotten song of forgotten times — a song of quiet sorrow, of an old, age-old longing. The song of Prague.

I crossed the Karl Bridge into the Chradzin, the old fortress of Prague. Both walls of the stone-hewn bridge are adorned with statues of Christ, of the Apostles and of old heroes. There is a statue made of gold, of the gold extorted from Jewish coffers. About a hundred years ago, a Jew crossing the bridge neglected to bare his head when he reached the statue of Christ. The town magistrate imposed a fine, and the pious citizens of Prague used the money to erect a big, beautiful, golden Christ-statue — a motif which recurs everywhere any traces of medieval life can still be found. From the Titus Arch, built with money extracted from the defeated Jews as a permanent reminder of their subjugation, to the statue on the Karl Bridge, one path stretches ahead, one long path, the thorny path of the lonely Jew.

I climb higher, ever higher, along small streets and narrow bridges, and come to the Chradzin, a big square lined with palaces, which coalesce into one big palace, a monument to the Hapsburgs. An elderly guide, a Czech with a melodious German-Prague accent, takes me on a two-hour tour of cloisters and castles that date back at least 1,000 years, if not more. He leads me through rooms where each wall is covered with pictures of stormy, proud, heroic events of the time.

In the center of the palace stand the statues of Kaiser Rudolf and John Huss and a memorial to the Thirty Years War. A path leads from the palace to a short street, lined with small, almost dollhouse-like cottages. This is where the alchemists lived. It was here that the remarkable Kaiser Rudolf brought the alchemists, the gold makers, and forced them to work. My old guide now lives in one of these cottages and he invited me in. I saw two tiny rooms, the walls covered with alchemistic and Kabbalistic symbols. The bed, made out of old, red wood, stands in a corner, beneath a domed ceiling, and a bow window overlooks Prague, the green mountains, the Belvedere Castle, the palaces, cloisters and the green Moldau which winds like a ribbon below the bridges of the city.

Later on I was told that these cottages are sometimes rented to artists, painters and writers who are searching for the themes and moods they need to further their work, And this is, after all, the *raison d'être* of all of life, to be the soil and the climate in which new creation may flourish.

I was reluctant to leave that small cottage and the land of the gold makers, asking myself: Is it worthwhile to go on searching for new themes, to pursue new impressions, when in all of their thousands of variations they are leading us to the same end — to the impossible dream? I do not know how it came about that the tiny room of the gold maker was suddenly transposed before my eyes into the world of the living, into a noisy, young city of moneymakers — the city of New York. The small cottage was submerged in eternal sleep and quiet, while New York is always awake and noisy, yet money plays a crucial role in both places. But here in these secret cottages it was not merely money that was being made but also mystical signs, Kabbalistic laws and allusions. While Kaiser Rudolf had, in fact, actually needed the money he demanded from his alchemists, he was also seduced by a desire to catch a glimpse of universal mysteries, by a desire to lift the concealing veil. He used the money to erect an altar.

Someday, perhaps a hundred or a thousand years from now, a wanderer will walk the streets of New York, and an elderly guide will lead him over the broad, quiet, overgrown squares, along the still, sleep-immersed, petrified streets of New York, and will tell him the story of a generation which had sought money and had spun new symbols containing life-building substance. Narrow streets changing into broad avenues, small cottages transforming into tall mansions — the substance remains the same, and so does the mystery.

It was Sabbath. The Jewish community was at rest. The famous Altneu Synagogue was closed and so was the cemetery. I knocked at all the doors and appealed to all of the sextons, but the sextons in their tall hats all gave the same answer: "Today is the Sabbath, wait for tomorrow." But I could not wait, nor did I want to. The inside of a synagogue is not appealing, no matter what its age. Judaism is severe, stern and harsh. All synagogues have the same simple, abstract, cold greatness. The Altneu Synagogue is like all the others and had not appealed to me when I saw it the first time. It did not inspire a wish to return. The outside, however, is magnificent, because it is original, the most original synagogue you can imagine. It is built in the style of legendary times, the times of ancient ghettoes, of a closed-in, walled-in life. It is bent like an old Jew, with the strong, proud simplicity of Judaism. When you enter the synagogue you have to bend over and step over the threshold with your head bowed. But all of the beauty and enchantment vanish as soon as you are inside. Therein lies the tremendous power of Judaism: it remains eternally old.

I was not drawn to the cemetery either, but I approached the gate; and there, in the light of the setting sun, glimmered the wonderful words inscribed on the gate: "Reverence for old age, respect for property, repose for the dead." The entire philosophy of Judaism was inscribed on the gate of the Prague cemetery. How little do those understand the Jews who are ignorant of this eternal motto of the Jewish soul.

"You are walking around and around Judaism," said my companion, a noted Prague writer who is also looking for a key to the Jewish problem.

"Yes, I do follow a roundabout way, because I believe that this is the only way we can follow. Judaism is so overwhelmingly diverse that we are forced to create a roundabout way to encompass it."

With these words I parted from my companion and from the ancient, wonderful, legendary city of Prague. I had spent the day immersed in enchantment and mysticism and was returning to a world that has yet to arrive at its own enchantment. And, once again, the roundabout way is beckoning.

Old Nooks

There is a small town on the Rhine that is quite unknown to the world: a deserted nook. And this is also its name: Winkel. It was thus called 1,500 years ago, when today's reigning cities had been mere villages, or, perhaps, had not yet existed at all. Berlin, at that time, may have been simply an untended field, and Paris and London may have been just emerging from infancy. Only Rome was already old at that time, old and in ruins.

The passage of time brought forth new elements, old ways of life changed, and small villages grew into cities of millions. Only Winkel did not change. It remained a nook, a modest townlet, comfortable in its provincial narrowness as it nestled amid the grapes, on the shore of the Rhine — and thus it has remained.

There is a house in Winkel that has been there for over 1,200 years. It is the only old house on a small street and is surrounded by houses that are a mere 400 or 500 years old — a patriarch among inexperienced, impetuous youth. During the day the old man sleeps. The sun makes him tired, and the tempo and sounds of contemporary life confuse and frighten him. As old as Winkel is, the sun still shines on it and plays its games with old and young, with the living and the dead.

Daytime is devoted to the business of the passing day, and how seriously does the day take itself! And the shorter it grows, the more importance it assumes and the stronger grows its desire to go on, to succeed, to reach its goal. Daytime is the realm of today's German Republic, of the reverberations of the war, of hate and fanaticism, of determination and exertion.

But at night, when Winkel is sleeping? The young people grow tired and go to bed. Winkel's only lighted building, its movie house, is closed down, and the streets are empty; it is quiet. Only the Rhine is flowing, and all is idyllic, as Heine tells us in his "Lorelei." Now is the time when the old man awakens. Now forty generations are recalling their past. Twelve hundred years — or perhaps more? — of human nothingness and of human godliness, of dreams and of achievements, of failures and of ecstasies.

A bed stands in a corner, against the wall. It was there that Rabanus Maurus died 1,160 years ago. At this very place, where so many other beds had stood, and so many other people had died. Rabanus Maurus, whose name alone has such a romantic, medieval sound, indicating a truly monastic monk, was born in the ancient city of Mainz and lived at the court of Charlemagne. He was a scholar, one of the few enlightened men of that strange, incomprehensible, legendary time. He was a pedagogue, one of the first to give thought to the art of education. He was pious, searching, naive. All day long he taught children as well as adults, searching for ways to free man from the grip of his animal nature, to clip the claws of the bear, the German bear. At night he sang hymns and songs of yearning, monastic yearning. During the late hours of the night, more than once his neighbors at Winkel must have heard the learned monk singing a strangely sad song, a song which is still sung today: "*Veni, Creator Spiritus.*"

Old yellow notebooks filled with just a few simple words of yearning, of sad wisdom, an old melody and a few names are the only remnants of a life and of its time. And the ensuing twelve centuries have rolled over Winkel, over Winkel's way of life, the way of life that had been lived in every nook.

The death of Rabanus Maurus left Winkel without any claim to fame. We do not know who lived in the old house after him. But the names are not important. They were people who were carrying on the old monk's educational endeavors, teaching students, who, in turn, taught others, forming a chain of gradually rusting links, up to the fortieth generation. And why not? Why should the house in Winkel not stand for twelve more centuries? Berlin and Paris will, perhaps, also become legends, the entire face of the earth will change, but Winkel will remain and preserve all of the echoes of stormy generations, all of the vibrations of millions of lives. This, really, is all that can be preserved. Life's final purpose, after all, is to bring forth resonances. Happy are those who can hear it, who can transmit its message to the oncoming generations, thus filling them with hope of being able to create a resonance of their own. This, truly, is Europe — not today's Europe, but the old one. Not the boulevard, but the nook. Not the newspaper, the psychological novel, the dramas, the art forms, but Rabanus Maurus and the old notebooks. Culture is to build a nook and to live in a nook, an art that is being lost more and more.

Europe finds itself caught between two extremes: Russia and America. America destroys the nooks and builds up boulevards. Russia destroys and does not build anything, leaving barren fields and flat spaces. America does not understand the meaning of a nook because it follows a simple straight line. Russia hates the nook because it sees in it a prison and a pit of poverty and suffering. In Russia a nook means the "underground." Leo Shestov sought to shed light on the spirit of Dostoevsky and, through him, on the Russian spirit as a whole, by interpreting the meaning of his "underground." It is not, as some naive interpreters claim, an underworld, a world of instincts, of passion and of crime, a world that has broken off all ties with society; it is not an anti-social world.

The underground of Dostoevsky, and that of Russia, is merely a nook-life. The normal, quiet, banal life led by generation after generation. It is neither anti-social nor anti-societal; it is, merely, a-social, not yet having reached the societal rung of the ladder. Life is still chaotic. The dwellers of the Russian nooks hate themselves and the walls that enclose them, and from these walls their hatred extends to all borders and all limits. And from their nooks issues a song of hatred, a song invoking general destruction. And this is the idiosyncrasy of our time: We put nook in the place of underground, and struggle against the nook. We tear down all walls, break all pillars, but the pillars do not fall; the Philistines are not perishing. It is, instead, our soul, our innermost self, the stillness and the yearning that are dying. We are searching for a nook wherein to hide, and we do not find it anymore. The space is occupied, built over, crowded.

From time to time a sigh reaches us: "*Veni, Creator Spiritus*!" Come Creator! There has been enough destruction, enough chaos. We want to erect a structure, even if it were narrow, as narrow as the world we live in. We will broaden it ourselves. Did not Rabanus Maurus from his narrow Winkel perceive a broad, endless universe, with angels and seraphim? Was the soul of the medieval monk not as encompassing as ours and, at the same time, perhaps more so? He allowed himself to believe and to dream. We cannot allow ourselves to do so; we are too clever, and we know too much, or too little. The vaster our knowledge, the less we know. We lack nooks, nooks where the soul can meditate, can rest, can bring forth out of its depth the pure, ecstatic hymn: Come, Creator! And when He is called upon, He comes. But He cannot be called upon from any place. We need temples, and we have destroyed them. We need an inner sanctum, and we have opened all the doors and all the gates. We need intimacy, silence, self-appraisal; our world is so public, there is too much light.

"More light!" This was Goethe's command to modern man. And his command has been fulfilled. Light is shining upon us from all sides; we are bathed in a sea of light. A little less light would have been better, a bit more shadow, more half-tones. We need more nooks, nooks like the Winkel in which Rabanus Maurus, the educator and monk, had dwelled. Or are, perhaps, all lines straightened out already, and all nooks unbent? Has the world become flat, straight, without a curve, and without corners? Can there be buildings without corners? Or are we in need of new architects? And, once again, we hear an echo from the hymn that resounded from Winkel: "*Veni, Creator Spiritus.*"

Among Old Houses

On one shore of the Rhine are the German mountains, and on the other shore is Switzerland. Between them flows the broad, quiet, green Rhine. Both shores are almost alike, except that on the Swiss shore you can see, in the distance, silhouette-like spines of the mountains. The Alps are already behind us; we are in a valley that is not a real valley, but an undulating, rising and descending plane. It is a quiet, idyllic place, so quiet that the only sound to be heard comes from the lapping of the waves against the hull of passing boats. It is so idyllic that it is hard to believe that there exists somewhere a world filled with noise and happenings, that somewhere people are building skyscrapers and flying airplanes, that people are courting risks, creating things, and, more often, destroying them.

Such a small town on a Swiss mountainside has captivated me. It does not matter at all to me what the townlet is called, be it Rhein or Rheinfeld or any other name. It consists of a few hundred old stone houses, with red-tiled roofs, lining narrow, shady lanes overgrown with grass. You see almost no people. And when you do see someone coming towards you it is as if an old tree or a rock was slowly moving along, as if he were an outgrowth of the soil, a pebble off the mountain.

Where are the people? It is strange; the smaller the place that I come to, the fewer people I see, which is just the opposite of the townlets in my native Russia. There you also have nature and enclosed spaces, you have rivers meandering through towns, you have trees and gardens, but you also have a feeling of being in a town, and you see people everywhere. Storekeepers are standing outside their shops, children are engaged in noisy play, Jews are peddling their wares, peasants are driving their carts filled with the fruits of their fields; there is a hustle and bustle of life, and people are gladly taking part in it. This holds true not only in the townlets of the Jewish pale, but also deep inside Russia. The townlets, no matter how small, are centers of activity. Then there is a still smaller social unit — the village.

Western Europe has, really, no more villages; they have become almost indistinguishable from small towns. The distinction now is between small town and big cities. It is in the big city that all of life's tumult is being enacted, that life expends its energy. And it is in the small towns that this energy is harvested, or created. The small city is not only quieter, it is also more profound, more thoughtful, more philosophical. And it remembers more.

I walk along the streets of the small Swiss town. My eyes fall on an old house, built in the style of the 15th century, with small turrets and ornaments, with walls covered with paintings. The figures are no longer wholly visible, the colors have faded, but you can still discern their poses, and here and there you can see a head or a foot. The roof cornice bears a wood carving of a figure clad in the garments of a knight or a soldier: a broad vest with padded sleeves and broad shoulders, a sword and a hat with feathers in its band. And atop the high, black wall is an inscription in old German:

> This is my house.
> Yet it is not mine.
> The one who came before me —
> It wasn't his either.
> You pass from one to the other,
> And after my death
> You will do so again.

This is neither profound philosophy, nor great poetry. But from these simple, childlike words, penned by an unknown writer who died 400 or 500 years ago, there emanated so much historic truth, such human suffering, such a strong echo of Kohelet, that I could not tear myself away from the house, forgetting about my travel schedule and the time of departure. I wandered for hours through the town, only to return again and yet again to the old house, and to read the remarkable inscription. Mine and yet not mine. And whoever thinks that something is his, fools himself. Thus it has been, thus it is, and thus it will always be, as long as the mountains stand, and even longer.

The people of long ago had a remarkably acute sense of death. "In the midst of life we are dead," sang the pious monk Natker, a local celebrity. Holbein in Germany and Orcagna in Italy had each painted the "Dance of Death," death being the dance master and humans the foolish dancers. Each dancer seeks to attain his goal in life: the emperor reaches for his crown, the beggar for a crust of bread, the maiden for her lover. A dance of death, or, as Holbein had titled one of his wonderful woodcuts, a dance of instruction. The older, the more remote the culture, the stronger the aura of death. Except, perhaps, in Jewish culture, where the concern for life has always outweighed thoughts of death, where the main problem was survival and not preoccupation with death. All other cultures, even the most sophisticated Greek one, idealized the dying hero. It was the Stoics whose aim in life was epitomized by the word euthanasia, meaning good dying, a beautiful death. The Jewish aim has always been a heroic life, which means not living as a hero, but living heroically; not being a predator, but being strong. And then "death overtook the Philistines...." And on and on, without end.

I spent the entire day walking along the old gray houses, until the whistle of the last motorboat going from Schaffhausen to Konstanz, from Switzerland to Germany, from the Rhine to Lake Boden, recalled me to my travel schedule and reminded me that this townlet on the Rhine was not my final destination. And yet, why not? And what is one's final destination? Where can one, and where should one, stop? Here and there everything is mine and yet not mine, and after my death it will go on like this. The gray stones will stand, looking out on the Rhine, until they too will crumble and fall into the river.

Just as well that I have to continue on my trip. My thoughts are growing too cumbersome. "We do not need to live — we need to journey." They were clever, the old Romans who coined this adage. They knew that the only purpose of life is — to journey.

The Sage

Weimar — a fortune-favored city that will forever be enshrined in the annals of German, of European, and of world history. It was in Weimar, following two historic disasters, that the words that saved Germany were spoken.

It was not long ago, before our very eyes, following Germany's post-World War collapse, that the Weimar City Theater was the scene of a re-casting of German life. The representatives of the German people had gathered there, forming a Founding Commission that had turned broken-down Germany into a Republic. A Jewish professor wrote the constitution, and a Jew presided when Germany's fate was being decided. It was a new point of departure, the beginning of historic epoch.

Many cities wanted and sought this honor, but little Weimar won out, due to its ancestral lineage. Germany's strong feeling for continuity helped it understand that only in the city where the greatest and freest man that the German people had brought forth, in the city where the greatest, if not the only, European and universal man had lived and created, that only in the city where Goethe had breathed, could Germany begin to breathe freely. The place where German wisdom came into being had also to be the birthplace of German freedom.

Germany had been truly fortunate. Not all nations are so favored. There are many that live out their histories without bringing forth one single great personage, while others do produce great men, but of unequal greatness. Italy has Dante — surely one of the greatest poets who ever lived, but Dante was just a poet and, furthermore, one whose medieval poetry is unintelligible to contemporary readers, and who has thus become more of a legend than reality. England's one truly great achievement is Shakespeare, but only the writer, not the man. Hamlet lives, Macbeth and Othello still wander among us, but of their father, of William Shakespeare, we know nothing at all; he is lost to us; he has vanished. The Germans, however, are the only nation whose great personage is both an ideal human being and a real person: Goethe.

Goethe was a poet, an artist, a scholar, a statesman and a thinker. He was also a man with all of the weaknesses and shortcomings, as well as all of the blessings, with which a human being can be gifted. I do not have with me Emerson's famous essay on "representative men," and I do not remembered how he classified Goethe, but I am sure that he tagged him as The Poet. And this is, surely, true. Because no matter what we may say about Goethe, by whatever title we may call him, it will be an appropriate one. The poet — surely there are few poets in the world who are his equals, and still fewer who are superior to him. Artist. Scholar. Explorer. He has claim to all of these appellations, which still do not suffice to get to the bottom of the tremendously varied, rich inner life of this unique human being. I find labeling people a rather narrow-minded and shallow thing to do, but if I were called upon to pin a label upon Goethe, it would be The Sage. Nothing more and nothing less.

I spent some hours in the laboratory where he made his physics and chemistry experiments, looking at his mineral collection and his remarkable tools. I saw the books he studied, his experiments with colors, with plant development and with human anatomy; and the more I saw, the greater grew my reverence for this magnificent mind. It was not so much his genius that awed me, because genius is a gift of God, but his diligence and his perseverance. Yet maybe this, too, was part of his genius? Because such diligence and perseverance requires an understanding of the meaning and the purpose of one's work. Only those who know what they are looking for persist in their search.

From the laboratory, from the library, from the writing room where the great artist created his Faust, leads a hallway to a small room containing an old, narrow bedstead — the place where the sage had died. There he had spoken his last words, words that have become a classic quotation: "More light!" He was 82 years old, the last one of his generation. He had outlived all of his friends, his loved ones, his wife and his son. Having remained alone in a world grown alien, the great old man, lying in his small dark room, had asked for some more light before departing.

Maybe this also is a legend. Perhaps he did not say anything, or just the kind of words a person usually says when he is nearing his end. But this is, really, the hallmark of genius, that it keeps on creating, that it infuses even trite words with fresh meaning. And while standing in the room of Goethe's death, I remembered a line from a poem a minor Russian poet had written upon Goethe's death: "He was one of those who had heard the grass grow." He was one of the few people in the world who was attuned to the most mysterious and the most basic processes of nature. He was one of the very few who understood the abyss-deep concept of the unity of nature posited by, as he had called him, the "sainted Spinoza." Spinoza thought this concept through to its conclusion, but he had derived it from his philosophical and ethical quests. Goethe arrived at the unity of nature by looking at it. His eyes were the lenses where all of the rays came together.

The museum curator is ringing his bell. It is time to leave the hallowed house on Weimar's small street, time to take leave of Goethe and return to everyday life. And now my imagination shows me this same street a hundred years ago, with an elderly, stooped gentleman, the Geheimrat von Goethe, making his way to the White Swan, to drink wine, eat sausages and converse with his neighbors in his broad, slightly comical, Frankfurt accent. A disguised spirit, assuming various forms, is traveling around the world, a wanderer following his whims. A strange whim leads him to the Germans who, surely, do not deserve him.

The Iron Maiden

I recently visited the city of Nuremberg, not so much because of an interest in the historical aspects of the city, but rather a desire to see the small statue of the Goose Man which stands on its market place, and to visit the town of Zirndorf, near the much more vital Jewish city of Furth. My interest in both these sites was due to Jacob Wassermann. *The Jews of Zirndorf,* Jacob Wassermann's first literary venture, exudes a mood of youthfulness and new beginnings. His novel *The Goose Man* is the work of a mature, aging, writer who puts too much meaning into the old, naive Nuremberg legend, imbuing it with a profoundly pessimistic philosophy and elevating it to a universal symbol.

I came to Nuremberg to find the sources of a writer's inspiration, but I soon gave it up as a futile endeavor. The Goose Man turned out to be quite an ordinary bronze statuette, such as I had seen in a number of southern German cities. Zirndorf, and even Furth, were merely small cities, without any distinguishing atmosphere. But Nuremberg itself did make a powerful impression on me. Nuremberg is one of the few European cities that have retained its genuinely medieval character in a most natural, unforced, almost unbelievable way. It gives you the kind of feeling you have when you enter the city of Pompeii, a city that has remained as it was two thousand years ago.

Streets, houses, temples, everything there is as it was before the city was buried in ashes, except for the absence of roofs, except for the absence of life, of human beings who care not for the past but are the creatures of the present, with today's worries and joys, filled with the hopes of the passing hour. Pompeii is a museum, but Nuremberg is a living city. And no one seems to give a thought to the fact of living in the shadow of at least eight centuries, in the most medieval city of Germany and, maybe, of all Europe.

These thoughts occupy only a few historians and archive scholars, as well as the guides who accompany foreign tourist groups and who lecture enthusiastically — "Four marks a tour, please" — about German emperors who made the Kaiserstadt Nuremberg the seat of their rule. They tell about the fortress that is at least six hundred years old, about the House of Hohenzollerns, the dynasty which made Germany great and which had, in the end, ruined it. They tell about Albrecht Dürer, the painter, who is said to have been as knowledgeable, profound and searching as Leonardo da Vinci, only more ponderous, more naive, of rather smaller artistic stature. And then the guide tells you about the shoemaker Hans Sachs, who had also been a poet, one of the *Meistersinger* immortalized by Richard Wagner. He goes on to describe the old houses where the Nuremberg patricians lived, meaning the wealthy merchants who, as in all old cities, had exerted the main influence on their city's government.

The guide, of course, forgets to mention that the city's very beautiful main cathedral, the Frauenkirche is located in an area that once was the Jewish Ghetto. It was here, in the year 1389, that the great Nuremberg slaughter took place, when all of the Jews who had been unable to leave the city were burned. Neither does the guide remember that in the old city had stood a synagogue headed by Rabbi Jacob Polack, the formulator of the Talmudic *pilpul*, which has exerted a remarkable influence on all of Eastern Judaism, injecting a greater acuity as well as greater flexibility into its study process.

All of this, surely, is of no interest to the German guides who lead us through the streets of Nuremberg, and even to the Jews who live in the city. They are, as everywhere in Germany, successful businessmen, bankers, liberals, and they do not want to be reminded of their sad, pathetic past. Neither is Rabbi Jacob Polack and his *pilpul* of any interest to them, since they no longer know any Hebrew, and even their closest neighbor in time and space, Jacob Wassermann, is also too difficult, too complicated for them.

There is one historic relic, however, that the German guides of Nuremberg remember to call to the visitors' attention, completely unaware of the sharp criticism and accusation that it sends forth, condemning them, their culture and the entire Christian world. The guides lead us to the Iron Maiden.

In the great tower, Nuremberg's oldest structure, a massive building which fifteen hundred years ago was already called Old Nuremberg, there is a small room, and our blond young female guide tells us, in a soft, even voice, of the things that took place between those stone walls. It is not difficult to visualize the things she explains, for the evidence is still in place: the handcuffs, the needles used to blind the prisoners, the iron-studded cots and other tools of torture. This was the room where the executioner tortured those unfortunates who had fallen afoul of Nuremberg justice, and who were usually not serious criminals, but run-of-the mill transgressors. As one used to say in Old Nuremberg, "One hangs the small thieves, the big ones one lets go free." But they had not been content merely to hang the small thieves; they had first to torture them in the cruelest way.

And now we come to the nub of the entire torture process, to the Iron Maiden. At first glance it is only an iron statue of a maiden dressed in a medieval dress, with a sweet, pious smile illuminating her face. But then the statue opens up and what you see could have been thought up only by the most sadistic imagination. The Maiden's interior is completely filled with iron spikes, which were heated before the condemned was put inside and the two parts were closed, slowly, to prolong the torture. Afterwards the Iron Maiden would resume her sweet, illuminating smile, and the assembled populace, the monks and the judges of the Free City of Nuremberg, would disperse. The monks would return to their cloisters to sing Ave Marias in honor of the "Heavenly Maiden," while others would gather in taverns or, perhaps, drop in on Master Dürer or Master Hans Sachs to admire their art and to join them in the traditional *Minnelieder*, the songs of love and of beauty.

The pale young woman smiles sweetly as she retells all those horrible details, and the young visiting brides on their honeymoon trip (the only time a German travels anywhere with his wife) sigh sentimentally: "How horrible, my God, what cruel times those were!" These naive souls do not know, do not sense that life is a continuous process. The fact that the Iron Maiden could have been linked to the Madonna, to "Christian love," and that such cruelty could have been perpetrated quite casually, without even the religious fervor such as brought forth by the Spanish Inquisition, implicates all of their culture and raises the question of whether their inheritance is as pure as the Germans, as the Europeans, as all of the Christian world consider it to be. They do not understand this, or else they would not have moved the Iron Maiden out of the dark cellar where it had once stood within the tower, the five-cornered tower with the colorful windows, the tower which was then and which is still called Old Cruelty.

Perhaps it is this very lack of understanding that is at the root of their strength. Only thus can a rich and powerful culture come into being, out of contradictions, out of eternal suffering, out of blood and cruelty. They had to evoke the vision of a Heavenly Maiden in order to bring into being the Iron Maiden. And the Heavenly Maiden had withheld redemption.

The Loyal Ones

It appears that the size of a country stands in direct opposition to the degree of patriotism it inspires — the larger the country, the less affection it evokes. The opposite, at any rate, is surely true: the smaller the country, the less land it covers, the warmer, stronger, more intimate is the relationship of the individual to his country. A closeness is created between man and earth, a rootedness. In a large country, only the few, the elite, those who think and work on behalf of the people, are the ones who relate to the country as a whole. The simple, ordinary, unconcerned man of the people has, at best, only a dim mental picture of it. What meaning does the word "Russia" (or whatever it is called now) have for a Russian? Pushkin could easily say: "From the cold streams of Finland to the hot lime pits...from the Ural to the Altai...." He knew what he meant; he had traversed the length and breadth of the land. For him, for the poets, the thinkers, the politicians, Russia was truly one. But for the man from Poltawa or Ryazan, for the peasant from Irkutsk, what meaning did "Russia" have for him? He cannot even visualize it, he cannot hold in his mind the immense stretches, and he remains all his life a man from Poltawa or Irkutsk, and the same holds true for America.

The entire inner rift of contemporary America derives from the fact that the individual whose concrete, personal experiences are rooted in his particular corner of the land, finds it difficult to relate to the political image created by his culture. The man from Iowa or New Mexico cannot see — and that means understand — the tremendous complexity of America; between Albuquerque and New York City lies a psychological abyss. That is why the new American patriotism sounds almost hysterical, because it is not in step with personal feelings; because it is willed and not rooted; because it is political and nationalistic, not intimate, not part of one's spiritual life. Is it possible to have spontaneous, intensive patriotism in America, Russia or any large country?

It is early fall, and we are crossing the Vierwaldstaedtersee. The sky is overcast; it is drizzling, and at times you do not know whether you are being rained on from above or sprayed on by the waves created by the boat. We follow the shoreline, much eroded, which stretches out between the mountains, and anchor at the foot of the Ritli Mountain, sacred to the Swiss. Some 600 years ago Switzerland's freedom was forged here. It was here that three cantons — Uri, Unterwalden and Switz — had formed the *Bund* and sworn to throw off the yolk of Austrian domination. It was here that the men had gathered in the dark of the night to swear the historic oath, the Ritli Oath.

Switzerland became free, its old enemies were vanquished, and it became almost the most secure country in Europe — yet it still remembers. There is a tavern on the mountain, and ten or twelve old Swiss men are sitting around a table, drinking beer out of large steins. Gray-haired, red-nosed, pot-bellied old men, wearing dress-suits and top hats, drink their beer and sing the Ritli song:

> We want to be a united peaceful people
> And not break up in times of peril or need.
> We want to be free, as were our forefathers.
> We would rather die than live in servitude.

The basso voices of the old men are strong and far-reaching. The singers hold their glasses high, their faces are red, and they look at you very seriously. The *Verein* sings, and the stout innkeeper in the white apron and the waiter in his too-short jacket sing. Then the captain of our boat joins the choir and soon all of the Swiss boat passengers start singing along.

Switzerland sings anew her Ritli oath, and she sings it with feeling, because she remembers; because for her it is the only reality; because she is so touchingly small and so hard and stony. Men had to perform backbreaking work in order to hew their homesteads out of the mighty stones. And they are grateful. We love only what we attain in anguish, what is born in pain. We remember it because the strongest memory is that of suffering.

We continue on our way to the Valley Plateau, to the rock from which William Tell, the hero of Switzerland, jumped into the water when captured by his enemies. And this is one of the most remarkable legends told in Switzerland about William Tell the mountain dweller, the best marksman in the land, whose arrow had shot an apple from the head of his son and who afterwards aimed his arrow at the heart of the Austrian tyrant Gessler. In the townlet of Altdorf stands Tell's statue with the inscription: "He will be remembered as long as the mountains stand." Each year Tell-plays are staged in a beautiful theater, re-enacting the entire legend. Statues, songs, plays — yet Tell himself never existed. None of the events related have ever taken place, or at least not in the way it is being told.

A legend out of the faraway past, out of the ancient Orient, a legend spun by hunting tribes, by sun-worshippers, had reached the people of the North and was taken up by a German king who kept annals in which he recounted small miracles and traditions. The Swiss took over this piece of literature and adapted it to their own time and land. They interwove it into their own folk legend of the *Tell*, which means the fool, akin to the simpleton of the Russian folk legend: the foolish man who, in essence, is smarter than the clever ones, who becomes a hero in time of need. This is also an old folk motif, a kind of folk philosophy, which was crystallized in stories, and out of the fusion of these legends a new one emerged, and a hero was born. A poet, Friedrich Schiller, picked up the legend, looked at it with new eyes, infused it with new content and meaning, and brought it to life. And once again, Switzerland acquired her national hero by way of literature. Georg Brandes once said: "The only Dane who is world famous is Hamlet, and he is a mere figment of imagination." But who knows? Perhaps this is the way all folk traditions have come into being. A tradition most treasured by a people as its very own comes from abroad; that which is most sacred is borrowed, and the folksiest tales are, in fact, literature.

Then there is Lucerne, an old city, with streets whose stones date back to the Middle Ages, with wooden bridges that resound with the steps of generations. In Lucerne there is a wall cut out of the mountain, and a statue has been hewn out of the wall, that of a lion. It was the great Danish sculptor Thorvaldson who carried out the desire of the Swiss to honor the memory of their sons who had made the supreme sacrifice. And do you know who these sons were? Do you know who the Swiss, the free citizens of a republic, the Ritli confederates, have thus eternalized in stone? Not freedom fighters, not revolutionaries, but Swiss soldiers who protected Louis XVI at the outbreak of the French Revolution. This is the famous Swiss Guard, which "dies but does not submit." France had denounced them. In all of Europe, and throughout the whole world their name came to symbolize servitude and ferocity, to describe mercenaries who kill freedom for pay. But the free citizens of Switzerland have not forgotten them; they were their sons, Rítli men who had swore the oath. The Swiss had sworn to protect the French crown, and they had kept their oath, sacrificing themselves, even though the sacrifice was a futile one.

To be loyal — is this the highest attainment, or is it the most severe form of servitude? Where is the boundary between the two? The Lion of Lucerne sleeps with his head on the shield, loyally guarding it. Monuments, after all, are made out of stone, and stones are devoid of moral considerations. Stones are what they must be. Sometimes they pave a road to the top, and sometimes a road to an abyss. Sometimes they form a path, and other times they create a wall.

Mountains, Cities, and Men

Reading Count Keyserling's *A Philosopher's Travel Book* has left me with a reluctance to come forth with any traveling impressions of my own. Not because this may lead to too close comparisons, nor because of too great a modesty on my part. It is, rather, because Count Keyserling's book has proven to me that only an artist can truly approach nature, and being an artist means being able to reproduce with a few brush-strokes, colors, and lines the manifold impressions we gain from the outside world. One cannot describe nature, and one cannot recount it. One can only "paint" it. And to paint with words is an impossible task, because no matter how well rounded, colorful and meaningful words may be, they ultimately miss the heart of the matter. They tell us only of things as they are, and this means as they are at a certain brief moment in time when the writer's eye alights upon them — and this tells us very little.

The "impressionists," the professional collectors of impressions, write this way. But if this proves insufficient, if the viewer tires of circling around his object, tires of performing acrobatic feats, of dancing around the inexhaustible reality, then the Keyserling way emerges, and nature, the visible and the hidden, becomes the key to everything in the world — except to that which is really in front of him. Keyserling views an Italian landscape and recalls socialism and the philosophy of the art and paintings he has once seen in a museum. He comes to California and beholds prehistoric natural wonders, which evoke in him musings about American psychology and comparisons between the old and the new worlds. Soon both he and the reader forget about California, losing themselves in inquiries, ideas, meditations.

Painting! Painting is the blessed art with which a movement of the hand creates an illusion of reality, recasting and recreating it in a way that would travel from eye to eye.

If only I could do that. If only I could transmit to paper in a way that would travel from eye to eye, rather than from eye to brain, the wonderful scenery that has opened up before me at the Wengern and Berner Alps, in the German part of Switzerland.

Wengern Alp is just a few hours from Bern, the most Swiss of all Swiss cities, the only city in Switzerland which is not German, as are Basle and Zürich; not French, as is Geneva; and not international, as are Interlaken and Lucerne. Bern is pure Swiss, with all the originality and character imprinted on it by an independent people which is older than all other European nations, a remnant of ancient tribes who have left no historical heritage except for some names, a few legends and…an accent. You think they are speaking German, but it is not German, not even a dialect. It may be difficult to understand the German spoken by a Bavarian, a Saxon, or even an Austrian, and you may wonder how the German language has come to assume so many different forms; but throughout it all you can still recognize the German cadence. But when a Berner Swiss says to another in his native accent: "Look, the sun is coming out," you may well make the mistake of thinking you have heard one Chinese addressing another. The hard consonants, the swallowed vowels, but most of all the wooden, I would almost say cavernous, tone, all these turn the Berner *Deutsch* into a language of its own. It contains the echo of a language that once lived and was spoken in just that one place, amidst the mountains: a dead language that has bequeathed to its heirs its sound and its cadence. Thus it is that a Jew from Grodno or Berdichev, who in literate Berlin or Vienna has been rather angry at his forefathers for "spoiling" the German language, can in Bern feel relaxed and superior since the Swiss speak even worse, and since the German spoken in the canton of Berdichev is closer to the tongue of Goethe and Schiller than the language spoken in Bern.

As the language, so the people, a people of ancient origin, remnants of a race that has died out, of a tribe that surely was very powerful, but with as little esthetic sense, refinement and polish as the stones on the steep mountains — stones among stones. They are a race as strong and natural as the bears in the Berner Stadt Graben, which itself is a reminder of ancient times and dead beliefs.

While in Bern I admired the bears, fed them red carrots, and wandered around town, following old footsteps, the steps of our youth. It seems that it was not long ago that we were all sitting here, the Russian-Jewish intelligentsia, the seething, revolutionary youth. We were sitting in the cafés, walking late at night through the city talking and arguing about God and the world that we wanted to create, that we had to create. Bundists had fought with the Zionists, Socialists with the Nationalists, and each of the groups had their own internal struggles. The reading of reports stretched over a week and late into the night. Young, starry-eyed girls, filled with enthusiasm and admiration, were falling in love. Theories were built up and torn down. This was the laboratory of the Russian revolutionary movement, Russia's youth in its youth. Children were playing with the Russian bear, and, strangely enough, in the end they had conquered it.

The children of long ago are now scattered. Some of them have joined the bears, and others still circle the moats of the park, teasing the bears and being frightened by them. Youth has gone, but the play continues, a tragic, too-serious play. And there is no way leading back to youth. "He had known that one cannot reach the past by crossing the new bridge," says the noted Anglo-Jewish novelist Merrick in his novel *Konrad Seeks His Youth*. One cannot reach the past by crossing a new bridge, nor an old one, nor the moat of the bear garden. I, too, knew that, and the knowledge has stayed with me.

I go to Interlaken, the tourist town, with the big, imposing hotels that cater to wealthy patrons, trysting lovers, eccentric Englishmen and practical Americans. Situated on the shores of the sunny, blue-green Tuner Lake, Interlaken spreads out between the mountains in a calm, idyllic, serene beauty. And then I continue in the sun and freshness of an early morning, along mountainous, stony roads, leading from one mountain to another, towards the Jungfrau, towards snow and ice.

The first stop on the way to Jungfrau is Wengern Alp. We are not yet standing amid the snow on top of the mountain; that is where its beauty is so close that it loses its picturesque charm. You can see the white snow-covered mountains before you, your eyes drink in the shimmering lights and the mountains open themselves up to you, but still within perspective. Your eye is still free; it can smooth out imperfections and disguise them. A tunnel leads up from Wengern Alps to the top, where the snow and the ice are no longer picturesque but shockingly real, and the beauty is gone. There you see all the knobs and wrinkles of age; there the "Maiden" is old and ravaged, and even its whiteness loses its shine, turning to grey; there you feel the harshness of the elements, the harshness of reality.

If you come too close to a picture it loses its effect. You see only dabs of colors laid one next to the other, blue and green and red; you see the picture in its evolution. You have to step back at quite a distance from the picture in order to see the way the painter wanted it to be, the way the painter had envisioned it. Then the splashes of color assume contours, come together, form a symphony. The lesson is to view everything from a distance. And, maybe, this is why we truly love what is "closest" to us, because without love we could not bear it. We are enamored of the faraway, whether it is the messianic ideal, God, or the "faraway Princess" of Rostand's dramatic legend. We accept what is close to us with pain, and even our love for it is filled with suffering.

A trio is facing me: the three white, snow-enveloped figures called the Eiger, the Monarch, and the Jungfrau, their snow-covered shapes topped by icicles that glitter in the sun. It is quiet. From time to time a tourist stops for a while to take in the view, then straightens his shoulders and walks on. From somewhere comes the sound of thunder, or rather, the echo of some faraway thunder. Somewhere snow is falling from the white tops onto the stony sides, drawn further down into the valley, becoming pulverized on its descent, except when it is caught in strong crevices and turns to ice.

And you feel that everything is in motion, that there is no rest, no final destination. Snow is falling, and the glaciers are moving, crumbling from within. The rocks may move in century-long intervals, but what matters is that they continue to move. We, the mountains, the earth, the sea, everything is moving forward. And somewhere everything meets — there where everything begins, there where everything ceases. Above me the white mountains; below, the green valley. White and green, fresh as youth, too beautiful. It is impossible to endure such touching beauty for long.

We go on, rise higher, cross a glacier, follow a narrow path, go through tunnels, up to the eternal snow, to a cold, restless, grandiose scene. It is so cold and so monumental that words freeze on your lips. And one would have liked to show in one line, in one stroke of the brush, the final, the only possible vision. And this is impossible. What good would it do? The mountains cry out for solitude, for stillness and reverence. There is no way to approach them; they do not want it. I look, I freeze, and I remain silent.

Amid the Fog

It is Sunday. The streets are quiet, empty, and only now and then does someone cross your path. I am walking along the streets of Vienna, and ahead of me, all around me, is a gray, dense fog. It descends upon Vienna like a dark silken veil, enveloping it and concealing its face. A remarkable sight! You can actually see it coming down like a hand, like the hand of a woman who is slowly and flirtatiously veiling her face. A gesture out of the past, when the veil would cover a young, blooming beauty, being replayed at a time when only traces of former loveliness remain.

There are cities that are beautiful and interesting only when they are bright and gay, rich and young. But should a mishap befall them, should the sun hide their face, should the skies turn gray and the air drip with dampness, these cities turn dour and dreary. There are cities, as there are human beings, which cannot endure sorrow. And then there are cities, as there are human beings, which achieve full stature only when sorrow befalls them. Berlin, for one, is truly insufferable when it is quiet and gloomy, when the streets are deserted. The houses all look alike; the streets and the people so commonplace and morose.

Venice, on the other hand, is most beautiful when big raindrops fall into the canals, when the waters in the lagoons reflect the trembling flames of the lanterns. Then one can see old Venice come to life again: Shylock, Jessica and Antonio are crossing the Rialto Bridge, and on the Piazza San Marco a white-haired nobleman is sitting with his young, beautiful wife. The present withdraws, and the past accompanies you across the bridges of Venice — the multitude of days already passed pushing aside the present moment. The French call it "evocation." This has always been Vienna's distinctive trait as well, and you feel it now more than ever. You feel that your are conjuring up the past, just as Saul, coming upon the witch of Endor, used the flickering light of his torch to conjure the vision of Samuel. The fog follows me, and in the fog there materializes all of Vienna, all of Austria, a world which seems legendary and yet was real.

Was it really so long ago that I was walking along the same streets of Vienna, a time when so much was being built and so much destroyed? Actually a mere twenty years have passed. Austria was then at the height of its power. It was performing its final dance, its heroic gesture. The Hapsburgs annexed Bosnia-Herzegovina, Russia became agitated, Serbia began to hold maneuvers at its Romanian border, and Italy protested. Austria smiled, bowed with a ceremonial kiss of the hand, with the bravura befitting Austrian nobility. Officers carried the Hungarian emblem boldly on their regimental uniforms, the Viennese sang "Servus my master, did she say to me…." Vienna was singing, sitting in cafes, reading the papers, playing cards. Vienna felt at ease.

But the ease prevailed only in the cafes. Journalists and politicians were struggling with the question: "What is going to happen? Will Austria manage to reach the top of the mountain or will it come crashing down? Is this a new beginning or the beginning of the end?" Because all of us were feeling then that this was the beginning of a new chapter. Either Austria had to swallow its smaller neighbors and become the great Danube Federation, including Serbia and Romania, reaching as far as Constantinople, thus forming, as it were, a Slavic-Hungarian-German-Romanian league of nations, or else Austria would be the one to be gobbled up.

The old Emperor was sitting in his "Burg," combing his sideburns, nodding his head, saying only: "Everything is fine, I am very pleased…" Archduke Ferdinand was sharpening his great sword in a smithy in Schwarzenberg, making plans for a new empire, while Archduke Otto was roaming through the Hotel Zachar, often wearing nothing but his sword.

Wise men in editorial offices were propounding that "political chemistry demanded that Austria and Hungary fuse into a 'new state.' In their cafes, the Serbs, Croats and Italians opted for a "federation" while autonomy was preached in yet others. And what is being said today?

Sitting in a cafe over my cup of coffee with the morning newspapers, I had seen the same lengthy articles, the same terminology, the same pages of literary criticism. It was as if nothing had changed, as if everything was as it had been.

But only as long as you were sitting in a cafe, reading the newspaper. You had only to glance outside to see the tremendous change that has occurred.

I walk amid the fog, and Vienna walks with me. There is the Parliament, as grandiose a palace as can be seen anywhere in the world: tall, broad and massive, lavishly built for generations to come by a great power aspiring to ever-greater might. I enter the building, into a broad, eighteen-columned corridor. And my mind pictures the people who have wandered around there, gesticulating, arguing, exchanging barbed words, and matching wits. There is Professor Masaryk with his pointed goatee and with "idealism" etched into his face. And here comes running a greatly agitated Czech nationalist who had just pounded the podium in the conference room and screamed "Shame!" when the German representative from Bohemia had begun to speak. Biankin, the white-haired, black-robed priest from Dalmatia, is conferring with Father Schmid, the anti-Semitic priest from Nether-Austria, as they pass the hook-nosed Jewish Deputy Kuranza, talking to the Slavic-looking Zionist representative from Lemberg. Here are Slovenians, Czechs, Italians, Germans, Ruthenians, Romanians from Tchernowitz, Poles from Galicia, Jews from anywhere, speaking all of the languages of Eastern and Northern Europe. And above the clamor of all of the languages hovers the golden, soft, Viennese humor. Vienna stood by, looking on quizzically, good-humoredly shrugging its shoulders as if to say: "This is what we are."

"Where does Parliament meet these days?" I asked the lonely, sad old waiter. "In the small assembly hall in the Herrenhaus, where influential magnates once used to meet," he answered. The magnates are no more, their empty seats amply accommodate the remnant of the Austrian Parliament. Its former members are all scattered now, each returned to his own home, to his own special concerns. Do any of them miss the old Viennese Parliament where the course of history had been debated, where one struggled with imponderable forces, the way Don Quixote had fought with the windmills?

The chaos, after all, had had its romantic aspect, whereas today everything is so realistic, so matter-of-fact. And it had been, precisely, the illogical and unintelligible traits that had rendered Vienna so beautiful and unique, endowing it with depth and with a higher purpose — it had been a utopia struggling to fulfill itself. It had failed to do so. But it seems that only strangers, or, if you will, "intimate strangers," can feel the meaning and the profound historic essence of a town's culture.

This is, perhaps, why Jews are the best interpreters and the most loyal adherents of all of the cultures that come their way. And this is why they are so hated, because people do not like being understood. The world is like the goddess Isis who demanded to be admired while draped in a veil, and woe to those who presumed to lift it; they were turned to stone. This is the punishment meted out by the veiled world to those trying to pierce the veil.

Vienna had drawn the veil of fog more tightly around itself, with only some single rays of light escaping here and there. And I followed the trembling lights over the lonely bridges of Vienna, along the paths of my obliterated youth.

Sights of Paris

I

Day after day, until late into the night, I walk, I roam, I am driven around Paris. I walk along big, busy streets with tall houses, American advertisements and all of the noise. On every step someone stops me — a haggard South American, a seedy-looking Frenchman — whispering into my ear in Spanish or French, offering me their guidance to all "the wonders of Paris," the special movies, massage parlors and other Parisian attractions. I really do not know how they spot me as an American, unless the very air of America has an almost physical ability that puts its stamp on one's features.

I leave the grand avenues and enter the old, narrow, quiet, unplanned, ubiquitous side streets. Each street bears a name that is significant, that tells a story, that is a piece of cultural history etched into stone. I am reminded of a book that held me spellbound as a boy. It was an old French book, printed about 60 years earlier, by the Parisian historian Marcus de Cass. The hard, parchment-like pages of the Bible-sized tome were filled with wonderful illustrations of old Paris. You were led along from street to street, and even the smallest one was granted a biographical sketch. It is hard to believe what stories these small streets had to tell, these narrow passages between old, dark-gray houses, these Parisian ribbons which run alongside each other, then interlace, separate and suddenly join together someplace else, forming a circle.

There are lanes that remember the times when Caesar came to *Lutetia Parisianum*, as Paris was once called. There are streets that can reveal what happened when Attila the Hun was at the gates of Paris, and how St. Genevieve encouraged and comforted the citizens of Paris. All this happened a long time ago, but the stones remember; for them it all happened yesterday. Still others remember Saint Louis, and the Crusades. They had seen the white-robed knights setting out on their way to Jerusalem, and they had witnessed the famous Children's Crusade, when small feet, pressed into wooden shoes, clattered along the stones on their way to Zion — and death. And further on, picture after picture, a panorama unlike that of any other city in the world: Louis XIV, Louis XVI, the Revolution, the shadow of Danton, the mask of Robespierre, followed by the Eagle, France's miracle and Europe's legend, Napoleon. And on to today, to…to what future?

I do not know. I cannot visualize what the future will be, where Paris is heading to in times to come. I cannot perceive the path it will follow. When leafing through the book as a young boy, my imagination presented me with wonders. As I matured, Paris turned into an enigma, and I began to search among its stones for the key to its essence and meaning. Paris is called the City of Light. This may have been true once, but not anymore, since the best-lighted Paris avenue pales when compared to Times Square, and the Place de l'Opéra dims when compared to Piccadilly Circus.

Paris as City of the Spirit? Yes, there is spiritual life in Paris, intellectual life; there are intense mental processes, which began when the Rue du Ecoles, when the small streets around the Sorbonne, resounded with the melodious voice of Peter Abelard, and which came to an end with Ernest Renan and Anatole France, and…and…who else? Everybody knows them, the earth is filled with the sound of their voices, and yet, the spirit claims other centers as well. Paris is no more its capital, its only residence, and, perhaps, it comes to Paris only to rest, to relax?

The City of Pleasure? Of course. Paris awaits the idlers, those eager to bring out the best in themselves, those panting to subject their egos to searching adventures. Paris embraces them, takes their measure and smiles kindly and knowingly at their naiveté. Paris is all of this, and it more than fulfills our expectations. Yet Paris also withholds parts of itself from us.

What is it, actually, that drives me, day after day, late into the night, to walk around Paris, to go from museum to museum, from play to play, from church to café, and from café to cabaret, never getting sated or even tired? I ask myself this question every time I come to Paris, and every time the answer is a different one — a natural procedure for a thinking man in search of a key to himself. This time the answer was: Notre Dame de Paris. The cathedral has been subjected to so much descriptive and definitive appraisal that I will forego adding to it, except to say that it is the miracle of Paris. Nowhere in the world, not even in Rome, has Christianity risen to such a profoundly thoughtful symbolism as in the cathedral of Notre Dame de Paris. And small wonder, since nowhere in the world has Christianity undergone such a tragic history as in France, as in Paris.

France was once called "the most loyal daughter of the Church." It was the loyalty of a very loving woman. Not the blind, fanatic, cruel loyalty of Spain, or the extreme monasticism of Italy, but a vital relationship between the idea and its actualization, an eternal questing: Why? To what purpose? What is the goal? The Italians took on Christianity the way one acquires a new garment, adjusting it to one's size and girth. The Spaniards wear Christianity like a shroud. But France does not wear its Christianity; to France, Christianity is a picture to be hung on a wall, a statue, a book, a song; it is — art. And here we find that the French imagination has adorned its most artistic expression of religiosity, the Notre Dame de Paris, with a paradox.

The Saints are inside the church, guarding the doors, and between them, on the main door, stands Jesus, extending two fingers in blessing the world. But overhead, on the cornices, on any open outlook point, stand strange figures, leaning out, looking at Paris. Half-human, half-beast, they are fantastic, legendary beasts out of a medieval, Dante-esque, apocalyptic, Ezekelian zoology: a goat with a human head, a human head with the body of a tiger, serpents and lizards with wings — and all the wide-eyed chimeras, smiling cynically as they bite into human flesh, sucking its blood. One is holding a human head between its terrifying teeth, a second one is gobbling up a hand, a third…and so it goes, one chimera following another, an entire army, bigger and stronger than the Saints that have been etched and sculpted on the doors and walls of Notre Dame, and who cling to the one who is blessing the world with two fingers.

And I think: This is Paris. A city of chimeras. The only city in the world where man himself is perceived as a wonder, as an enigma. A city where man views life ironically, seriously, but not tragically; honestly, but not cynically. The only city that is quite free of cynicism. The greatest cynic is, actually, the ascetic; not the Nazarite, not the one who afflicts his flesh, but the devout one who is afraid, every hour of his life, of committing a sin. He is afraid of sin because of its overpowering strength, so that, should he yield for just a moment, he will be lost, pulled into the abyss. Paris, however, is not afraid of sin; it denies the whole matter; it frees itself of sin in affirming everything that the body desires. A load is lifted off the shoulders of the individual and becomes a load shared by all humans. Equality, liberty, brotherhood, and — sisterhood. Does this hold true politically, socially? Perhaps not. Perhaps America and England are more democratic, perhaps even freer, and surely more egalitarian, more uniform. But brotherhood and sisterhood are in Paris, are in France, and only there.

The greatest chimera of all, the most mysterious but also the most fertile, is man. He gave birth to the French Revolution with all of its consequences; he is the foundation on which France rests. Out of the love for man comes respect for man, comes the desire to please and impress him, the yearning for fame and glory. This is not the Nietzschean will to power, the will to dominate, to be stronger, bigger, mightier. To assume power is to distance oneself from others, while fame and glory lead to a blending in with others, uniting not only with one's contemporaries, but also with those yet to come, with future generations. It is the national cult that is the religion of France.

◆   ◆   ◆

I had not intended to get caught up in philosophical ruminations. I only meant to relate and to describe. But a few hours ago I was standing on the Pont Neuf, where Pascal had his divine revelation, where he had seen the abyss. It was here that France's deepest thought had come into being, the thought that life is a dance between two abysses, that to live is to dance upon a rope which spans two eternities. And what a beautiful dance it is, with the dancers cautiously maintaining their balance, in a pliant, graceful way. But Pascal's vision had lasted just a moment. Because Paris does not allow a serious mood to linger, to turn into sorrow. Paris laughs, and you feel light-hearted, and the dance continues, the dance upon the rope.

II

It is hot — a broiling, massive, exhausting heat. And this time Paris does not smile at me. Its former joyful, carefree graciousness is gone. Paris is greatly worried; dark clouds are gathering on its horizon.

In former years you came to Paris to enjoy a rest after having toiled in New York, after an intoxicating but exhausting time in London, studying profound thoughts and penetrating words. You come to Paris to relax, to experience the joy of simply being alive. This is, perhaps, a paradox, since serious, virtuous people claim that Paris is a bottomless pit, giving rise to a greed that can never be satisfied, that Paris seduces and leads us away from the straight and narrow. But must the way always lead us uphill and into the distance? May we not stay where we are? And why this concern with tomorrow and the day after tomorrow, and not with today and with the present? "Let us eat and drink for tomorrow we die" — the prophets laugh and mock us. Yet they were right. "Tomorrow" is the most legendary of all words. "Yesterday," though filled with deep yearning, though floating like a dense fog above the mountains, is still something we can grasp. But "tomorrow" is an act of faith and the greatest of all illusions.

Paris is a gathering place of ghosts. Yesterday's rule of satire has given way to a skeptical smile. Yet Paris is the apotheosis of "today," of the present hour that is granted us. And the greatest accomplishment of Paris, the very essence of France is the art of slowly drinking from the goblet of life. And all sages, all profound thinkers arrive, sooner or later, at the same philosophy of life.

Not long ago I was reading a wonderful booklet, the work of one whose life was ebbing away, who was preparing himself for the unavoidability of death. The writer was D. H. Lawrence, and I rather regretted the harsh words I wrote right after his death, suspecting that I may not have given him his due, that I had failed to perceive his profoundly human assessment of life that underlies his over-heated, strained eroticism. The small book bears the title *The Man Who Died*. It is the story of Jesus after his "death." He had still been alive when removed from the cross and put into his cold grave. For a while he remained dead, undergoing all of the proper burial procedures. Afterwards he arose and came back to life. He then understood that his life had been a failure, his sacrifice meaningless. He had wanted to teach people how to conduct their lives, yet did not know himself how to live. Because there is only one life: the small, narrow, personal one; because the only purpose of life is to live it. Jesus throws off the mantle of the teacher, the role of the redeemer of the world. He becomes a man among men, a wanderer who exults in the delights of an eternally young world. "Tomorrow is also a day!" Thus ends the book written by a man who had no more hope for his own tomorrow.

◆   ◆   ◆

I know that all of this seems rather far removed from Paris and the grave problems that concern it, the great apprehensions that make its blood run cold. But is it really so far-removed? Let me focus on one event, then, on the Congress of the French Socialist Party. I have, undoubtedly, arrived too late. Wires have carried reports far and wide, and the news about the struggle between its three factions has already been forgotten, especially in America. This is a French internal party struggle, which is almost incomprehensible to an outsider, to a foreigner. But even the Frenchmen do not rightly understand it. The common people, but also many intellectuals, have taken up the phrase National Socialism. The reactionaries, prompted by either interest or mere curiosity, enjoy hearing some discontented socialists using a language that is almost fascistic: national idiosyncrasy, bankruptcy of internationalism, socialism adapted to France. They enjoy hearing these echoes of Hitler and Mussolini. And, since nothing succeeds like success, the success of Hitler and of Mussolini is casting its spell on French youth. They, too, have dreams and are looking for a leader within the Socialist Party.

The extreme right and the extreme left are confronting each other. While the leaders of the neo-socialists are leaning toward fascism, Jean Jeromsky, the leader of the left, is turning eastward and is smiling at the communists. There he is on the podium, pounding on it with his fist, as if he were striking a drum, drumming out a battle song, the battle song of universal liberation. But then Léon Blum, the leader of the center, ascends to the podium. Compared to the bearded Renalde in his theatrical beret, to the massive, coarse-looking Jeromsky, Léon Blum makes the impression of an aristocrat addressing the common people. He is tall, thin, of slightly bent stature, with finely etched facial features, intelligent, sad eyes, and a voice…so calm yet with a controlled passion vibrating in his lower tones.

Blum talks about ideas. Blum talks about the spiritual essence not only of socialism, but also of France, of the ancient, profoundly human culture that it has produced. He speaks in political terms, but those who really listen know that he means culture. Culture is the guiding principle of an organization, of a humane way of life. And he says: "Tomorrow is also a day." Be patient, do not attempt to solve all of the problems at once, do not set your sights on redeeming the whole world. One must only understand and love. The present day, the present hours, will pass, so use it to the fullest, make it beautiful and abundant. Nietzsche, Mussolini and all those who propagate the dogma of bringing back the past, say to you: Live dangerously. To this the socialist Blum answers: Live wisely, live humanely.

He did not, of course, say all of this. He had talked about Marxism, the dangers of nationalism, etc., but the assembly sensed the underlying meaning, and Blum won out. And this reminds me of another Jewish intellectual, from an opposing camp, Julian Brenda, who is an anti-socialist because he is an anti-Marxist. He opposes Marx because he equates him with Hegel, i.e. with a doctrine that propounds motion, that teaches that values have no eternal validity. And because he opposes a philosophy of motion he is, also, a bitter foe of Bergson, whom he holds responsible for all of the troubles of today's world. Julian

Brenda demands internationalism, or, as he terms it, a new European culture, led by reason and ruled by France. He says France, but he means Plato and Spinoza. He means a value system that should be as firm as the values of ancient religions. He says France, but, in the final analysis, he means Judaism. And beneath all of the disguises and aliases, there is the eternal struggle between two world views, between two spiritual spheres, between the will and the law, between the temporary and the eternal.

This is the struggle that goes on today and that will continue until the final sunset. But men are willing to deal only with the surface; they are afraid of the abysses.

◆　　　◆　　　◆

Will it come, or will it pass us by? Will the wave of fascism inundate France? This is the disquieting question Paris is asking itself. Paris is worried, but it is also ready to fight, to resist. I do not know how long and in what shape democracy will survive in France. But even in the worst case, even in defeat, Paris will know the art of a beautiful death, of dying with a kiss. And should it come to an armistice, to a compromise between the two hostile systems — the one advocating universal redemption, and the other the "small," individual, and, therefore, unique life — Paris will know how to create a synthesis, or so I hope.

On the Island of Love:
A Leaf from Cyprus

The sun is shining so brightly, the sea is so blue, everything is wreathed in a festive smile — is it any wonder that it was here that she emerged from the foam of the sea, on the shore of this island? She, the one with a thousand names: the "all-seeing," the "disturbing," the "savior of men," Ishtar, Astarte, Bel, Venus, Aphrodite. The name Aphrodite is an incorrect, but nonetheless beautiful, tender, artistic interpretation of the phrase "The one who has come out of the foam." And it is told that she was born right here, where a small covered boat is taking me from a ship to the shore of Cyprus, the island of love. It is here that she suddenly emerged from the foam and laughed in the sun. I am on my way to the island where love was born.

I am one of a group of passengers: three black-bearded Greek priests; a Englishman in his sixties with his bare feet stuck in sandals, tall, thin, and youthful; a Zionist from New York; and two ladies. One of them is petite and wears glasses; the other one is a nurse from Vienna, with the firm, assured, competent step of the medical profession. I am asking my boat mates why they are going to Cyprus, what is it that interests them most? The Zionist answers that he remembers the "number plan" of Tritsch, and he wants to see why this plan had failed. The sandal-clad Englishman has business in the colony and wants to enjoy a breath of "his homeland." The two ladies do not know why they are going, but

405

something draws them to the island. The one born out of the foam is calling them, although they do not know whose voice it is.

Larnaka is the first Cypriot port. Narrow streets, airy, quiet, neat, more like a postcard picture than a real town. Nowhere in all of the East, nor, perhaps, in the West, are to be seen such clean streets, courts, stores and houses as in Larnaka. And it is so quiet, just as if all life had stopped, just as if the town were dreaming — and it does have a great deal to dream about.

I quickly manage to lose the Zionist, but the two ladies, the one with the glasses and the nurse from Vienna, want a guide, and this lot has fallen to me. I do exact my revenge by leading them into the old Greek cloister of St. Lazarus, among others, forcing them to listen to the museum curator pelt them with ancient Greek references — and modern discoveries — about the origins of Cyprus. It is to no avail. Female patience knows no limits; they suffer but they do not leave my side. Thus the three of us walk along the streets of Larnaka.

"Do you know, ladies, what it is you are now seeing?" I ask. And before either of them could recite any of the foolish things from the illustrated travel guide, I tell them about the past greatness of Cyprus and of the opposing elements that had confronted each other on the island: the stoic philosophy of Zeno and the advocacy of love by the beautiful, rosy-fingered, golden-haired Aphrodite.

The ladies, their eyes wide open, implore: "Tell us about it."

"About what? Shall we talk about love, ladies, shall we talk about Aphrodite on the island where she was born?"

The bespectacled lady says: "No, tells us about Zeno."

"Right here where we are walking, 2,500 years ago, was a Phoenician town, called Kitim, or, even earlier, New Carthage, the new city, i.e. the renewed city, because before the Phoenicians had come, Cyprus had already had its old, over-ripe culture. Hittites had lived there, the same Hittites who were so closely linked to Jews by marriage, and who were, perhaps, even their ancestors. You may remember that on every step of ancient Jewish history we stumble over the Hittites. Hebron was a city of the Hittites, Jerusalem a Hittite fortress. And the Prophet Ezekiel had called out: 'Your mother was a Hittite, oh Jerusalem!' And these, our maternal ancestors, left us an enduring heritage — our face. Do you want to know what a Hittite looked like? Look at a German Jew of "pure race." Just so are Hittites depicted on ancient monuments in Boghazekini, the capital of the Hittite land. And thus you see them on the stones in the British Museum: the crooked noses, thick lips, all the negatives come from the Hittites. And the most remarkable thing is that the Hittites were not Semites but pure "Aryans" in their origin and their language. Recent scholars have proven that the Hittite language has strong ties to Greek and to Latin. The joke that history is playing on us is that we, the grandchildren of the Hittites, are being persecuted for our Semitism.

"Be that as it may, I am not pursuing philology or politics now; I am concerned with the Phoenician merchant Zeno, from the city of Kitim, who, at the age of 40, had sold his business and moved to Athens. His business may have included acquiring copper from the island of Cyprus, the richest lode of copper in the ancient world (hence the name of the metal), and trading in perfume, extracted from the lovely smelling flowers which to this day grow on this island. Zeno went to Athens and had forgotten to return. The Canaanite man of business became enraptured by the beauty of Athens. He went to the philosophers and listened to their teaching. He weighed and analyzed their arguments, subjected them to the searchlight of reason and perspective, compared his old, Cypriot world view to the new Greek one and rejected them both.

He remembered his native island Cyprus which functioned as a bridge between East and West, yet always maintained its own way of life. It had taken things from the West and had drawn sustenance from Asia Minor, without becoming engulfed by either. Following this model, Zeno became a mediator between East and West, between the faith of the East and the beauty of Greece. He settled in Athens, assembled scholars around the "colorful columns," and laid the groundwork for a new academy, a new teaching, and a philosophic system that would transform the world. Zeno the Stoic became the father of the philosophy of Stoicism, the philosophy of measure and of moderation. And the teaching that life should be conducted according to moral principles had, in the end, prevailed in Greece. Without Zeno, the Cypriot, Christianity could not have taken root in Greece. Zeno had prepared the ground; he was the first messenger from the East to the West."

"Tell us about love on the island of love," interrupts the lady with glasses.

"About love? This is what I have been talking about all along. Oh, I forgot, I have been calling it philosophy, the moral philosophy of Zeno the Stoic. But you see, ladies, this is actually one and the same. No matter what you may be talking about, Eros — love — follows you. You may remember Antigone's song: '*Eros, Eros, anikatat*' — Eros, the love which one cannot conquer. Those who attempt to prevail over it are the ones who become its slaves. And the intent of all philosophies is to gain access to love, be it the philosophy of Socrates, Plato or any of the others, even if they are unaware of it. Philosophy wants only to spread and to interpret love, to find its spirit and its body, to bring fervor and passion into every breath we take.

"Look over there, you can see, in the distance, the mountain where Papho stood, the temple of Aphrodite, the young, the eternally beautiful, as if just arisen out of the foam of the sea, with a smile on her lips, her golden hair still damp. And Cyprus accepted the mountain temple, knelt before it, and placed wreathes on her exquisite head. But do not think, ladies, that this was so easy for the Cypriots of the past. They, too, along with the entire ancient world, had different views of love. They, too, regarded it as a purely biological phenomenon, as motherhood, birthgiver, as more frightening than beautiful, and deeply mysterious. You see, before there was an Aphrodite, there was in Cyprus a temple for Aphroditos, a statue of a god half-man and half-woman. The woman was bearded, ugly, and cruel, as were the love goddesses of the ancient world, as was Ishtar, as was Kali of India. Love was depicted as a sacrifice. But then the blue sea waves brought Cyprus a gift: Aphrodite, the love that is no more a sacrifice but a gift, a sweet sigh, a perfumed smile, an unreachable dream. Aphrodite, the eternally young, eternally beautiful charmer. And an old legend tells us that if a man spends an hour sleeping on Cypriot soil, his entire life will be permeated with the aroma of love and throughout all of his life he will be unable to free himself from it. Like Horace the poet he will plead: 'Oh Venus, queen of Cinidid and Papho, leave your beloved Cyprus, leave it and come into our temples, there where men live and where hearts are yearning — come make your home there.'"

"Better tell us more about philosophy," the nurse from Vienna interrupts my outpourings. "Because love is too beautiful, too Cypriot. It demands too much from us women."

"This is just what I am doing. I have been talking all the time about philosophy. But 'love is the preamble to all science,' a poet once said, or maybe it was a philosopher. I do not know myself where the division lies."

It is so easy to let one's thoughts roam here, the air is filled with yearning, yearning for everything that is beautiful, good and eternal on the island of love. And you yearn not to have to leave it. But you must. From the sea comes a whistle; the ship is calling. I say goodbye to Zeno and to Aphrodite, to the foam of the blue waves, the waves of time, the waves that never reverse their flow....

Stromboli

It was late at night when the old sailor knocked at the door of my cabin: "*Monsieur, on le voit* — you can see it now, sir." I had requested this service, as is customary on ships traveling on this Eastward route from Europe to Egypt. If you pass the Stromboli volcano at night, a sailor will awaken all the passengers who had expressed an interest in this matter. Because on a voyage like this even a living, fire-spewing volcano is an attraction, an extravagance, and not everybody who makes long sea journeys is open to such extravagances, not everybody is willing to give up an uninterrupted good night's sleep to look at a fire in the midst of the sea. A fire on land, a fire that one could extinguish, a fire that one could control, this might have been considered an exciting addition to their trip. But a fire in the midst of the sea, a fire that water cannot extinguish? "What can I do about it?" the traveler asks. "How does this concern me?" And turning on his left side, he goes back to sleep.

Bleak are the southern summer nights at sea, as well as on land — unsentimental, lacking all atmosphere, as is the way of southern art, as are the people living in the lands of straight lines and transparent air. There is little atmosphere here, just a formidable horizon. On the North or Baltic Seas you have only atmosphere: a gray fog which, you imagine, is hiding some deep mysteries, a whole world of unknown shapes and colors. Your imagination assumes full reign, and only the extensive, knowledgeable traveler knows that beneath the gray pearls of water that condense into sheets of fog there is more water, and that further on, at

409

the shore, you will find a very prosaic, ordinary land. But how many travelers can be so well-versed, how many had the chance of an all-encompassing tour of the world? Thus the North dupes us and catches us in its mood of a magical surrealism. The South does not trick us. It shows us its true form and is content to leave it alone, and so are we. Because its form is beautiful. All we see are the wide horizons that do not deceive us, because we know, we sense, that in the distance is just more blueness and light, sun and more sun.

The southern night is bleak and clear; the stars are fixed like lanterns, like glowing embers of coal. They do not evoke your tears and sighs. Their twinkle contains a kind of laughing realism that discourages the lyrical effusions and dreamy songs of the North; they merely light your way. Yet out of the clear, warm, sober Southern night there rises a shadow. At first it looks like a cloud, a kind of dark, opal-gray ribbon extending along the horizon; like a hem of a gray garment, criss-crossed with red threads.

The ship comes closer, and the cloud becomes a line, the line acquires a contour, and the contour forms a shape. There, in the middle of the sea, stands a fiery mountain surrounded, on all sides, by rivers of flame, fed every five minutes by eruptions. From somewhere on the mountaintop, which cannot be seen from the distance, there emerges a fountain of sparks, waves of fiery splashes, forming streams of flames pouring slowly down the sides of the mountain, shedding in their descent a red glow on the black-blue waves before disappearing into the depth of the sea. Stromboli, the volcano, is working day and night, without stopping. A five-minute pause is followed by another explosion, a small interruption, and the fire resumes its descent into the waves. Water and fire were linked together at this spot at the creation of the earth, and have remained engaged in an eternal dialogue.

It is dark; I am unable to see anything except the black contours of the mountain and the red threads, and, as usual, my imagination takes over. A desert of volcanoes, solitary and empty, an area designed for combat between elemental forces, not for puny, human disputes. Fire and water, flame and stone, in a gigantic duel — destruction versus creation. Man with his so-called achievements and struggles appears like a fly on the nose of a jungle elephant. Imagination has presented me with a Byronic picture, an Ezekiel poem.

◆   ◆   ◆

It is now another morning, a month after my first encounter with Stromboli, and I am returning from the East to Europe. Very early on this wonderfully clear, sapphire-blue morning, we pass the shores of Sicily, close enough to see the city of Messina. We see a green mountain, white, serpentine mountain paths, red roofs on white-yellowish houses. It is quiet, but in the early morning stillness you can hear the first sounds of a freshly beginning day, the first notes of the eternal song of universal life. Not long ago, almost before our very eyes, there was volcanic destruction. The stones crumbled, the mountain collapsed and wiped out the little bit of life that had attached itself to its strong walls. Not long ago this had not been a song, not a psalm of praise, but a roaring storm, with its own tonal palette.

The storm has passed and, once again, life is optimistically clinging to the rocks. Once again Messina sleeps and awakens afresh, just as it had done before the catastrophe, not thinking about the flaming forces deep within the earth, waiting their hour. And even if Messina thinks, even if it knows, that a new eruption must come someday — well, as long as it will not come today or tomorrow, but someday — who knows? Perhaps it will not be until the end of days. And is all of life not lived "in the meantime"? This is, actually, the only possible way of going on living.

The ship continues on its way, and there stands before me my nocturnal companion, the volcano Stromboli. In the daylight it looks dignified, not mystical anymore, neither Byronic or apocalyptic, but as real as myself, as the wooden ship on which I am sailing, or as the barefoot sailor on the deck. Nor is it terrifying any more. It is merely a mountain in the sea, worn down and torn asunder. The fire that sent its flames into the night was now concealing itself deep within, and only strands of smoke emerge from the chimney high on top. Smoke produced in a smithy, a workshop, or, perhaps, a kitchen deep below, has become, once again, mere wisps of fire in the clean, blue air. The mountain is bare and desolate except for a narrow ribbon, right at the seashore, harboring rows of white houses with thin strands of smoke emerging from their chimneys. Smoke from atop the mountain spells destruction and death. Smoke from the chimneys below means comfort, peace and enjoyment — life.

Those of us standing on deck were startled to see that people were living on this eternally burning mountain, alongside rivers of lava. How horrible must it be always to have the earth-splitting roar in your ears, always to be filled with terror of what the next hour may bring — to live here! Having been stranded on the stormiest place in the whole, wide world, people had decided to settle here, being content to stay. They must, of course, have been motivated by necessity, perhaps also by inertia. Having been born there, people grew roots. And where else should they go, these poor fishermen from Stromboli? What would they be doing somewhere else, these people from the fiery rock?

One can thus understand and explain their staying. But these explanations neither go far nor deep enough; they do not fully account for the phenomenon. Surely there would have been room, somewhere on this earth, for a few hundred people from the volcano. And if one truly must escape, one does not stop to think of what may be waiting somewhere else. So is there, perhaps, another reason? Is it, perhaps, the very fact that a volcano is so perilous, that the earth beneath their feet is afire, that lends their life the allure of adventure? Living close to fire, to the earth tremors, always facing another eruption of the fiery lava, always just a step away from final destruction, is this not one of life's component elements and, perhaps, its most compelling one?

The group of passengers on deck this early morning is comprised of some Frenchmen, some Americans and some Jews from Palestine. One of the Americans is from Texas, the largest, earthiest of all American states. Another one is from Iowa. Both are accustomed to wide expanses of yellow cornfields, of stillness, and of a matter-of-fact certainty of the continuity of their easy existence. We have been conducting, for several days, a discussion about Europe and the Old World. "How can anyone stand living in Europe?" the man from Texas wonders. "Paris is, of course, beautiful, but just for a few days and nights. One can go there for some enjoyment, some interesting experiences, but not to live there. You can see that the old world is seething in turmoil. Take a look at the passengers on our ship. There are French soldiers and officers coming from Syria where they face uprisings, wars, struggles for power. And the English civil servant talking to the captain comes from the Sudan. His life is dedicated to the task of keeping a lid on the jealousies and intense hatred among the Arabs and the Sudanese Negroes — a fire that resists all efforts to extinguish it. Wherever you go, wherever you look, there is destruction. The whole world is a potential volcano, so why would someone live near a real one?"

I find it difficult to answer this question or the question of how people can live in the vicinity of a volcano. How can one rationally explain it? This early morning, on the blue sea, we take up this question again. And the Texan answers it himself. "Look at the houses at the foot of the volcano; fire and smoke come from above, and smoke and water come from below. People live there, and, who knows, such a life on Stromboli may be more exciting, more stimulating, more creative than life on the broad plains of Texas!"

Life, in the final analysis, does not follow only the sensible, clever, cautious path laid out by Epimetheus. Life also follows the daring path of his brother

Prometheus, the path of fire and flames, of eruptions and defiance, the path of a gauntlet eternally thrown in the face of the world. "You want me to follow you. Why?" asks Prometheus of his brother, in Goethe's wonderful poem. "You want that I should follow you, you who are the world, who are life, who are necessity, who are reality. Why should I? You say you are more powerful than I; if I oppose you, you will prevail — so be it. Is this all? You may say whatever you can, whatever it is you must say. I will oppose you because I can, because I will, because I must."

The ship continues on its way. Stromboli soon vanishes from the horizon, and the sea, once more, takes on its bluish coloration. The smoke and fire of Stromboli have receded into the distance, once more becoming a legend. And, for a moment, the doubt arises: Can people, possibly, live at the foot of a fiery volcano? And yet...and still...Stromboli is a reality; it exists.

Travels in the Americas

In Wondrous Bimini:
Impressions of Florida

I

I set out without a destination, without a watch in my pocket. What difference does it make what time it is? I am in no hurry; I have time. I want to have time; I want to forget everything for a while, all the noise and commotion of New York, its cramped, anxiety-ridden East Broadway shouldering the woes of all Jewry — a symbol of petrified Jewish suffering, only on a smaller scale.

I know that this is an exaggeration, one that we have manufactured for ourselves. Like the rooster Chanteclair, we too have come to believe that the sun rises when we crow, and that it is the strength and melodiousness of our crowing which determines whether a day will turn out to be bright or gloomy. This being the case, Chanteclair felt that he was carrying the weight of responsibility for the entire world, until he grew tired. And suddenly he realized that it was not his doing if it was raining and storming, if worlds were being destroyed and new ones were about to be born, for he was only passing through.

I have often thought that everyone should experience, once in his life, a phase which, in psychiatric parlance, is called amnesia: a phase in which one forgets about oneself, separates from oneself, forgets even the name one received in one's cradle and that follows one to one's grave; a phase during which one throws off

417

all of one's past and begins life anew. A life that starts in the middle, without a childhood, without growth, when we simply leave one personality, enter another one and then return. To be able to spend some time experiencing various fates, not always be wedded to one's own.

This is a fantasy. I know that those who suffer from amnesia are sick. Man wants to wander, even to stray, but he does not want to get lost, hoping always to find the way back to himself. He wants to be able to forget and, at the same time, to remember — and this is the function of artistic creativity, to allow a man to step out of his own frame and still remain himself.

Modern technology, it seems to me, is leading contemporary life back into the past. In all areas, at least politically, we are retreating ever deeper into the medieval concept of life. Fascism reaches back to Platonic despotism; communism returns to the ideals of Turgot and the Physiocrats; and our present Hooverized America is reaching out to the Enlightenment of the 18th century. And I am going, or rather, riding, with the time. The railroad is already too old, too archaic, too complicated — it is still the 19th century. And like 19th century philosophy, the railroad has equalized everything: The roads are all leveled, mountains are split, valleys are raised, and paths interlace the earth. And with everyone — be they rich or poor, imposing or simple — you see the same arrangement, the same style.

The airplane, for its part, does away with distance and concrete reality, making distant locations into mere dots on the map. They become just points of departure and points of arrival; and everything in between vanishes. All of the real, seething, blood-red life in the fields, forests and rivers, all of the human dwellings and all of the signs of human habitation, the smoking chimneys at dawn and the small fires in the gardens in the early evenings, all of this disappears. There is a beginning, and there is an end, and in the middle there is emptiness, is air. This is perhaps the way the world will be someday, a few large centers filled with people, and nothing more. Technology and science are leading us to it with an iron grip. But in the meantime there is still earth, earth and green fields, and I am traveling across America the way people used to travel, in an autobus. The passengers slowly make their way to their stations. The driver sings a song while he works late into the night. Every two to three hours the bus stops at an inn for meals. The passengers are sitting close to each other. It is not very comfortable, yet everyone is quite friendly. People talk, tell stories, sing songs, and step on each other's toes.

The road leads through fields, through forests, over hills and vales. Sometimes the road is smooth as ice, at other times the bus jumps over hard clay and you are shaken to pieces. The driver is bent over the wheel with a pipe in his mouth, and as the engine runs and dances up a storm, your pulse beat faster, your heart beats more strongly, and you can feel the surge of your blood. Suddenly the road is blocked by large vans filled with merchandise, followed by a long row of cars. We are now progressing as slowly as New Yorkers do on 5th Avenue, at rush hour. Moving step by step, we could have done it more quickly on foot.

◆   ◆   ◆

Half a day's travel from New York has brought us to the narrow streets of Philadelphia and out again onto the open road. In a few hours it has brought us to the spot of America's highest aspiration: Gettysburg. It is a small town, but one of epochal significance for America. It was here, on the field of battle, where the fateful question was decided whether the young American republic would remain united or be split asunder. It was here that Lincoln gave the most magnificent speech of the 19th century, the greatest speech America has ever heard. It is studied in schools, and pupils learn it by heart. "…The world will little note, nor long remember what we say here, but it can never forget what they did here…." "They" means the fighters who had fallen on the battlefield of Gettysburg, in the defense of human freedom. "…We here highly resolve that these dead shall not have died in vain, that this nation, under God, shall have a new birth of freedom, and that government of the people, by the people, for the people, shall not perish from the earth."

And here I am, standing on the former battlefield that is now the Gettysburg National Park. All around are monuments, guns, gravestones, and, amidst them, the tall, pathetic, awe-inspiring figure of Lincoln, the greatest American that has ever lived. The only one who had been seriously committed to what he was fighting for. The only and, perhaps, the last one.

"Of the people, by the people, and for the people": Lincoln worded the basic American idea in the shortest, simplest, most definitive form, and it calmed America. Gettysburg was the highest peak that America had ascended, and after that began the descent. Today Gettysburg is as much a legend as the *"Liberté, Egalité, Fraternité"* of France, or Russia's "The Republic of Free Workers." These were once living forces, and they have become stones in a park, exhibits in a museum — they have become legends.

◆   ◆   ◆

We pass through smoke-filled, overcast Pittsburgh, with its black factories whose chimneys are eternally spewing out fire, and where work never stops. America is working day and night; this is what makes it a world power. Wherever you look in Pittsburgh you see Westinghouse, its compound visible from miles away, a city in itself. It is more imposing than Ford's factories in Detroit. One feels its solidity, its strength and its self-assurance. This is manifested not by way of advertisement or media aggrandizement, but by a proud, mature, strong and steely conviction in the meeting of a need. It follows German tradition. It is Essen and Dortsmund and Elberfeld on American soil. It is still Europe, albeit transported into a new land. It is vastly different from Ford, symbol of the rootless and unbound new American man.

We have reached Cincinnati, the only American city where Jews are treated with respect, the only city where they are not regarded as strangers and outsiders. The mayor is a Jew, and Jews occupy other high positions in the City Council. In New York, the worlds largest "Jewish city," Jews are elated if they manage to assume a minor position in the city management and do not even dare to dream of a Jewish mayor. But in Cincinnati, with its small Jewish population, Jews play a leading role. It is the cradle of Reform Judaism in America. And it is due to its being "reformed" that its Jewish community is so intensely Jewish. "Synagogue news" is considered here to be an important matter. They tried to share some with me, but my bored smile soon discouraged their effusions. Religious disputations have stopped being a matter of concern to me. I cannot muster the slightest interest in religious affairs and institutions. And the more reformed they grow, the less interesting they become. Religion is a grand gesture, or, rather, a chain of ritual observances, which acquire significance and charm when they become very old. Such are the religious dances in Japan, where even the smallest gesture is prescribed by tradition, where everything arises out of its past.

It may be that, a thousand years from now, even Reform Judaism will have acquired beauty and a degree of sanctity. But in the meantime it is Cincinnati versus Safed, Dr. Isaac Mayer Wise versus the chain of past generations, the modern rabbi versus the stern, archaic, petrified yet still virile old Judaism. But the binding thread is becoming thinner and thinner; it is losing its power to bind.

II

I am in Jacksonville, Florida, sitting on a park bench beneath the palm trees. The strange-looking man sitting beside me on the bench begins to talk. His high, musical voice rises and falls, like a song. His English sounds archaic, rich and finely nuanced, an English rarely heard now, the kind one used to read generations ago. He tells about evenings spent among Florida's palms and tropical flowers, about his trip on the boat Aseala along a river with the sonorous Indian name Akaava. He tells about how he tore himself away from the sober newspaper-dominated reality, and came to the bright South, the tropical forests, to the land of romantic dreamers, where Spanish caballeros had serenaded black-eyed beauties, and he sighs the old musical sigh of the Spanish romances "*ai de mi alma*" — woe to my soul!

He talks about everything, about past grandeur, about a world of wild beauty that is gone. He tells about the serene forests and the tropical birds that sing their "tia tia" songs at night, amid the tree branches. He talks about his yearning for the South and the Orient, for the sun, for slow, rhythmic movements, for temples where incense is burned, and for a way of life that has vanished into dreams. And I find myself wondering: How did this physically unattractive man acquire the remarkable ability to endow his speech with such graphic beauty?

"Well?" I am addressed by a voice that has suddenly become quite prosaic, and I see my homely, half-blind neighbor looking at me. "Well, what?" I ask, "What do you want me to say?" My neighbor begins to explain, and after a moment of not understanding a light begins to glimmer. He wants money; he is just a beggar. Looking at him again I suddenly understand my strange mistake. It seems that my first whiff of Florida's air had intoxicated me and affected me like a narcotic, bringing forth a kind of hallucination. The one-eyed man had, accidentally, evoked a vision that, in turn, carried verbal associations with once read and long forgotten words, bringing them out of hiding. The vision was of the remarkable American writer Lafcadio Hearn, the half-American, half-Greek stylist, who began his career as a reporter in St. Louis and New Orleans, and ended his life in Japan. And the words ringing in my ears were those of his long forgotten description of Florida, the *Floridian Revelries*, written, yes, written at a time when I was just born.

"Oh, well, how much do you want?" I ask the beggar. He names quite a small sum, though he really needs more, but, if needs be, he will be content with half a dollar. I press a dollar into his palm and shake his hand. He does not understand why I am so satisfied, nor why I am smiling so happily. I can see his one eye plainly expressing his regret over not having asked for more. He does not know that he has, accidentally, opened in me a source of melodious words, has brought to life for me old, forgotten vistas, and has placed my present experiences into a broad, golden frame.

Evening is approaching, the sky is purple, and colorful clouds are retreating, giving way to a silvery light. I raise my head and, to my right, I see big gleaming letters spelling out the name Cohen, the name of the biggest store in Jacksonville, a white stone building, located between two city parks — a big and prosperous store. And I am rejoicing that at the gate of what was once *Reinado de Florida y Bimini*, the Kingdom of Florida and Bimini, as it is called in old Spanish documents, you are greeted by the name Cohen. A historic irony — or revenge — whichever way you want.

◆   ◆   ◆

The year was 1512, and the place was Puerto Rico's capital, San Juan de Puerto Rico. The man occupying the governmental palace was 52 years old, short, starkly darkened by the sun, and burned out by his passions. He had climbed as high as he could, but not as high as he had aspired to. He was the master and ruler of the rich island of Puerto Rico as the representative of his Catholic Majesty, the King of Spain. He was rich in gold, and what more could a Spanish caballero want? He could have all the women he wanted, white ones and brown Indian ones, and, in due time, he could return to his native Seville. There he could, perhaps, become a Grandee of the Kingdom and almost an equal to the proud courtier whom he, Juan Ponce de León, had served in his youth as a page and armor bearer. But Juan Ponce de León wanted more and dreamed of greater things than gold and power; these meant little to him. What he wanted was freedom. He did not want to be a representative anymore, to rule by the grace of the King of Spain. He wanted to be king, a ruler, a discoverer in his own right. And old Indians were telling him stories. The old Indian woman Naka, the brown witch who paddled a canoe from island to island, told him that somewhere, far away, somewhere out East, there was a great, wide country rich in gold and spices, and that it also had a fountain that could make you young again. Swallowing some of its water would make the years fall away like leaves off a tree. People on that island live a life of eternal youth and eternal bliss. "What is the name of this island, Naka?" "In our language it is called Bimini."

Juan Ponce de León returned to Spain and told the royal court about the wonderful island of Bimini and its fountain of youth. The king granted him the rule of this new land that had yet to be discovered and the title of *Adelantodore de Bimini*, the ruler of the island of Bimini. He equipped a few ships with men and weapons and started looking for the fountain of youth. And one day he came to a shore and found the fountain. He planted a Spanish banner and called the land *Florida*, the flowering one, and he became the *Adelantodore* of Florida and Bimini. Ponce de León drank from the fountain of youth and waited for the miracle. But no miracle occurred. He did not grow younger. As Heine describes it in his fragment *Bimini*, he had searched for youth but had grown older and older, more and more bowed down and worn out.

Juan Ponce de León grew older and more fragile. He saw before him a wonderful land, a new kingdom, but he also felt this land required the tremendous energy of a Hernando Cortez or a Pizarro, the conquistadors who had conquered Mexico and Peru. He felt that he lacked the energy; he was tired, worn out. Wounded by an Indian arrow, he went to Cuba and soon died there. But Florida remained, and its fountain of youth is in America's oldest city, St. Augustine. I also drink from the fountain — at 25 cents a cup. Was it worthwhile? Have I grown younger? Perhaps, as Strindberg used to say, "Age is merely a prejudice." Perhaps youth as well? At any rate, you cannot expect much from 25 cents worth of water.

◆   ◆   ◆

I am traveling across Florida, through forests of palm trees and plantations of orange and coconut trees. The latter are remarkably proud trees, plump at the base and growing ever slimmer as they gain height, somewhat like a pregnant Modigliani woman, reclining amidst tropical flora, dreaming about Napoleon.

Historians acclaim him as an eagle-eyed politician of genius, and look at the chance he let slip by. Florida had been Spanish and then became French. But neither Spain nor France had been able to keep its hold on the land. And France, in the end, gave Florida up and sold it, together with Louisiana, to America. Napoleon failed to understand the course of history. He chose to fight England in India and waged war in Egypt and in Europe. But he overlooked the only empire France could have established, the one in tropical America.

Actually, neither the Anglo-Saxon way of life, nor, even, the tonality of the English language, are well suited to this hot, tropical land. The Floridians feel it themselves, and they bedeck themselves with Spanish feathers. Wherever you go, you see Spanish names, a Spanish style. Close to my St. Augustine hotel, called Alhambra, on a street called Granada, is a palm-lined boulevard leading to a villa bearing the name Zaraadia. This is the name of a Spanish Arabic romance, which recalls Granada, the beautiful, and where the heroine sighs for Baabdi, the last king of the Moors. The house is in a more Spanish and Arabic style than may, today, be found in old Spain. But the house stands empty until the tourist season arrives, and then the Zaaradia who greets them is apt to be a Mrs. Smith or a Mrs. Blumenfeld, and the love-stricken Don is likely to be a businessman from Brooklyn.

Thus it goes through all of Florida. Everything is romantic allusion, a mere carnival mask. And everything is built on sand. "What is the truth about Florida? The truth is — a lie." This is a sentence I read in a book about Florida, published by the Chamber of Commerce. This is the only truth that has been said about this state; everything else is advertisement and the desire to get the better of California. But the advertisers are forgetting the basic principle of economics; it is not the sky and the air that make a country prosperous, but human imagination. California might, perhaps, have remained a sandy desert if gold had not been found there. But Florida has no gold, only the everglades, wetlands, palms and the sun, traversing the Tropic of Cancer. Florida's future is, perhaps, nothing more than a mirage.

Among the various wonders of Florida are the millionaire quarters of Palm Beach and the gardens in Miami, where one can point with reverence to the houses of Firestone, Rockefeller and one foreign ruler or another. And among all these wonders, the millionaire's villas, the crocodiles and the ostriches, one is also shown the Indian Village, the village of those who once ruled this land, the Seminole Indians. In a dirty yard, on a long wooden bench, sit some Indian women dressed in their historic garb — long black robes and a mass of ornaments around their necks and on their heads — sitting and spinning. The last ones of their people, of a great, strong people, with its own culture, a people that had been unable to withstand the white man. Why? How did it come about that the Indians had been vanquished so quickly? Was it merely the number of white men, or their cruelty?

Or are there deeper causes? An old Seminole legend gives the answer in the *Story of the Three Small Boxes*, told by the Seminole leader Geamalto: "The Great Spirit fashioned three small boxes. Into one he put ink, paper and a compass and gave it to the white men. Into the second one he put a shovel and an axe and gave it to the black men. But into the third box, which he gave to his favorites, the red men, he put the tomahawk, the Indian war axe. And each box contained their fates." The Indians of old perished because of their predilection for the tomahawk, because of their adherence to the entire aristocratic-militaristic view of life.

Work was for other people, as was knowledge; the red people preferred the noble gesture. And ink and paper prevailed over the aristocratic tomahawk. Today the red people sit in the Seminole Village in Miami, spinning linen for half a dollar a day, in order for white tourists to have something to look at.

It may be that the story of the three small boxes is a key to all of history, and that Geamalto had been, in his own way, a philosopher of history. It may be…

The sun is burning; it lures you to the ocean, to the island of Cuba, and I am responding to the lure.

On the Road

It is difficult to write on the road. Difficult, because it is too easy. Unsought, unpursued, impressions are crowding in on me, picture after picture, thought after thought. They, too, are on the road, traveling. And they are taking themselves so seriously, as if in pursuit of life's true essence. On the surface this is merely an outing, a few weeks respite from the ordinariness and triteness of a familiar environment; it is just a pause. But my innermost world has set out on a long, far-reaching, serious journey.

For days, weeks, months, we may succeed in keeping our deepest thoughts under lock and key, forcing them to follow the straight and narrow. They go along, obeying our direction until, suddenly, they erupt, forsaking the beaten path, abandoning all purposeful pursuit. They dwell no more in our world, in our time, but in their own, in the world of our imprisoned, fettered soul. They roam without an aim, without a focus, following only their own impetus. On the surface they seems like pure whimsy, like accidental gifts of the moment. They are like the clouds in the sky, constantly changing, forming new shapes. Poetic constellations change into comical ones, a lion is transformed into a two-humped camel and then becomes a giant whose outstretched arms encircle the sky. The clouds are all of this, and they are nothing. For us they are what we can see; in themselves they are mere movement, mere being.

When we want to capture our wandering thoughts and visions on their return, they retreat and refuse to be put into words, refusing to yield their secrets. They are like the sea that I observe from my window on Cape Cod's Provincetown. It is a remarkable sea; rarely do we see such a precisely executed transformation. One moment ago this was an energetic, exuberant, roaring sea, steel-blue when the sun is shining, steel-gray when the sky is overcast. The inn I am staying in is right on the shore, and as I look out of the window I feel like I am on a ship, so close is the water. In the distance I can see the white sails of the fishing boats. The air is filled with shimmering blues and whites, and a festive atmosphere prevails; an adventurous distance and a warm closeness seem to embrace both life and work. A few hours later, I return from my walk along the narrow streets of the old, curious small city and turn towards the sea — and it is gone! Beneath my window are grimy dunes, yellowish with dirty green or black spots. Here and there are pools of water, and dead fish lie on the sand. Black and gray cats roam around, and children play in the wet sand. Somewhere far away, it seems at the very horizon, the sea starts anew.

This may be the spot that best symbolizes Provincetown, New England, and all of America. I am standing here, as it were, at the very source. It is here, on this rough shore, that America had its beginning. It was here, on the very rocks I am sitting on, that 350 years ago fifty Englishmen had laid the foundation for the most magnificent historic experiment that has ever been undertaken: creating a country based on purpose and faith. Nowadays, of course, when the Pilgrim Fathers are being considered as the first aristocrats, as a beginning of a new aristocracy with all of it deceptions and pretensions, one tends to take less of a historical, less of a romantic view of the Mayflower.

But here in Provincetown, Plymouth, and the small cities and towns of Massachusetts, on Cape Cod, in Arlington and Concord, the names of the Pilgrims acquire an unfamiliar sound, and all of America is transplanted into quite a different atmosphere. You now see America in a historical perspective. Actually, what difference should it make to us, living today, whether the events of the past had taken place yesterday or a hundred or a thousand years ago? The recent past is as dead as the historic events of ancient times.

History imposes an ending, an unquestioning acceptance of events as resulting from natural necessity. Yet the closer we are to the events, the less willing we are to honor such an acceptance. We are willing to accept the yoke of a distant past, but not of a recent one. It is just because we are seeing the process unroll before our eyes, because we are standing within the workshop and witnessing the creation of history, that America elicits such strong controversy, that its achievements command so little respect. Only in New England do we experience respect for America, not just for its breadth, its wealth, and its wonderful roads — leading who knows where — but also for its spirit. I was standing in Provincetown in front of a monument with the words of America's first constitution etched in bronze. And, for the first time, I understood that the greatness and the essence of America lie in its spiritual foundation.

I wondered: Why had no one before managed to create such a society? Greece had its chance, and so had Rome. But their attempts had resulted in new barbarism, causing much suffering and requiring great efforts to achieve some slight refinement. Rome colonized Romania, and what is Romania today, 2,000 years after Trajan? The same barbarism that Ovid had described is still reigning, albeit covered up with a bit of French gloss. And what has become of the Greek colonies on Ephesus and in the Ukraine? Tartars live there now, and barbarians. Plato's spirit is not hovering over Melitopol or Odessa.

But the spirit of Milton and Shakespeare, of Wakefield and Chaucer, of the entire Anglo-European culture is floating above the dunes and hills of New England. While Alexander of Macedon and Trajan, Germanicus and all of the Greek and Roman colonizers, founded their rule on force, the Pilgrims who had come from England — the Winslows, Bredfords, Whites and all of the others who had signed the first Freedom Declaration — did not want to conquer and to colonize; they merely wanted to live according to their ideals. They wanted to make room for the most exalted cultural achievements of the European mind.

There is another American characteristic that is derived from the pilgrims who had been wanderers: the fact that Americans are not inextricably bound to a given piece of land, its stones and vegetation. In France and in Germany you can see villages that are more than a thousand years old, and peasants tilling land and preserving a life passed on to them by forefathers going back to the time of Charlemagne. Had Provincetown been a French or German city rather than an American one, it would, certainly, have been turned into a national museum, fenced in and closed up, to keep any strangers from settling there. But in the depth of the American unconscious the flame of the wandering spirit still flickers.

Only in America could Provincetown have become a predominantly Portuguese city. Except for a few visitors and tourists, the streets, or, rather, the street, of Provincetown plays host to two groups. On one side, the one facing the sea, there is a group of colorfully garbed men and women (more women than men) standing in front of easels, covering canvases with paint, daubing rather than painting. It seems to me that the red, blue, yellow and green smocks harbor no true talent, at least to judge from the results. But the painters are enjoying themselves; they strike artistic poses along with the satisfaction of being hard at work. Being surrounded by curious onlookers adds to their feeling of consequence.

Thus everybody is content, the artists because having this free exhibit saves them from the necessity of hiring a hall, and the onlookers, because nothing tickles one's funny bone more than witnessing the pretensions of talentless people.

On the opposite side of the street, the one facing inland, you see a different, quite un-American looking crowd — people of almost black or yellowish complexion, with black-bluish hair, sparkling eyes and profiles as if etched in bronze. And this side of the Provincetown street resounds with rapid, melodious talk. These are the Portuguese. Seventy-five years ago some Portuguese fishermen had settled here, and today, most of the city and its surrounding countryside are inhabited almost exclusively by Portuguese, by the Pereiras and Venestas, Olivereiras and Espinolas.

"The Yankees are dying out or are moving away," one of the Portuguese fishermen explained. The descendents of the Pilgrims no longer feel bound to the sand dunes of Cape Cod; they have spread out over the entire land. They are wandering.

"And you?" I ask the almost chocolate-brown fisherman, "Do you still feel like a Portuguese?"

"No, sir!" he proudly replied. "I am an American. This is my country, I was born here and this is my home." He speaks only Portuguese, but he is already a full-fledged American, except for his expressive Southern eyes. And this, too, is America. It covers with sand everything that the wind brings in, and the sand links it together, absorbs it, lets it grow roots.

I proceed to Boston, and on to the heart of New England, to the green fields of Arlington, where the first shot was heard, the shot that had opened a new chapter of human history. I go on to the bridge where a few American farmers had, for the first time, defeated British soldiers. Wherever you look there is history, and once again, it is the history of the achievements of the mind. Emerson, Hawthorne, Alcott, Thoreau, these are all names of thinkers, albeit perhaps not as great as they are, or were, reputed to be. Emerson was, surely, not a deep thinker, nor was Hawthorne a great writer; his books have little to say to us today. Even Thoreau, the most original and the greatest representative of the entire New England school, strikes us as being mediocre. But this is not important. What is important is the respect accorded them by their contemporaries. What is important is that these outstanding creators of culture bear all the hallmarks of the environment from which they came: goodness, mildness, gentleness. They were the product of a long, rich — too rich — past and, therefore, found themselves cut off, estranged from the new American world. They had to retreat; they had to wilt, in order to allow fresh seedlings to flourish.

Jonathan Edwards, John Cotton, Cotton Mather, the theologians, the thinkers, the puritans, the religious seekers, Emerson, Longfellow — they all had to exist to make it possible for the new blood and old barbarism brought to their shores by the Portuguese fishermen to flourish. Both elements, the old and the new, barbarism and culture, had to join together to build a new edifice.

The usual course of history has been first barbarism, then culture. America is the only country where the course has been reversed. It is a country of paradoxes, a country of antipodes.

Desert

Earth — uncultivated, uninhabited land, sand, skies and hot winds. A frightening world, familiar to all of us from our childhood years. For thousands of years a people has been telling the story of its greatest experience — the forty years of its sojourn in the desert. They perceived a world that was filled with miracles, as no other people had seen it. But it was the suffering endured in their years in the desert that had retained its strongest grip on the people's memory.

Each one of us is likely to have experienced, at least once in our life, a strong yearning for the desert, a desire to relive the story personally. The legend tells us that we were called on to shoulder the heaviest burden, that of being cut off from everyone else in the world, of being absolutely alone. Each one experiences this in his own way, some in the mountains, others in some forsaken corner of the earth, still others within a large city. And truly, it is the stony cities; teeming with people, that harbor the greatest loneliness, which come closest to resembling the solitude of the desert. One has, however, to be completely wrapped up in oneself not to notice and be caught up in the city life around you. No matter how alone you may feel, your ears and your eyes cannot help but be filled with the sounds and sights of life. It becomes more difficult to evoke complete solitude, and we begin to forget how we came to experience it and why. The only place where we may recapture the feeling of absolute solitude is the desert and, even then, for only a moment. But the soul does not measure its experiences by time, and one moment may have a greater impact than many long years.

My heart skipped a beat the first time I saw a desert. I never had a chance to do so in Europe, which only has a few uninhabited, uncultivated stretches of land: the Limberg Heath in Germany, the Belawest wilderness in White Russia. But these are not deserts, just infertile soil, and they do not evoke a desert mood or vision. Nor does the Siberian taiga, where, day after day you pass long stretches of land, densely covered with small black trees, which seem like a black cloud, spreading gloom over the earth. The gray sky is bleak, and you are gripped by a feeling of disquiet and sadness. Such cold, barren wastelands cannot bring forth sunny thoughts, cannot ignite human imagination.

But at this moment I am in a true desert. It begins the moment you cross from Colorado into Utah. Here are mountains of bare rocks; here is bare earth and limitless sky. The solitude and the silence are interrupted from time to time. A tall chimney comes suddenly into view, as if arising out of the depths of the earth, as well as a shaft, all part of the iron works, oil fields and naphtha sources. Nearby is a small town, and further down, a ranch.

The mountains lie beneath waves of velvety soft bushes. Flocks of animals criss-cross the lean earth in search of food. Here and there you see a herd of horses steered by a rider sporting a broad hat and a kerchief around his neck. It is a bare living, but men have not given up yet; they still extract from the earth whatever they can. They have not yet bowed in submission to the desert.

Now we are traversing the remarkable fifteen-mile-long bridge over the Great Salt Lake, a wondrously engineered short cut, and soon we arrive in Nevada. The Sierra Nevada Mountains bear old Spanish, romantic names. The white capped Sangre de Cristo, the blood of Christ, is looking down upon us. It is a relatively later mountain formation, not too tall, and not oppressively majestic. It is closer to us, more human and, therefore, imbued with a dreamy sadness, with a strange yearning.

The mountains do not hide the horizon. Everything is wide open, both the earth and the skies. The earth spreads out before us, bare and still. You see no trees, no human beings, no animals, nothing but clumps of gray-brown sage-brush covering the earth. It makes you feel as if the poor earth, ashamed of its nakedness, is covering its old limbs with rags. They uncover more than they cover, but still, the rags give the illusion of a garment.

The Nevada desert. It was named a desert and so it has remained, since every-thing is determined by the way people perceive a given thing. Having agreed to call it a desert, it became a desert, and no one has tried to cultivate it, to release it from its imprisonment, to free it from its wildness and loneliness. The American explorer and Arctic traveler William Stevenson said, not long ago, that "Men have decided that the Sahara or the Gobi, the greatest deserts in the world, are condemned to be deserts, and they will not even bother to find out whether this is truly the case." In Nevada some tried, but unsuccessfully. The few silver and iron mines found there were soon exhausted. The few cities which were founded there are emptying out, like the city of Goldfield, which had at one point about 20,000 inhabitants, and now has, it seems, only a few hundred. The population does not grow; its number diminishes as people leave. Men do not want, are not able, to fight the desert.

From time to time we pass through a small town, next to a small stream. All small streams here are considered rivers, and all of them bear the name Humboldt. The name of the great Count Alexander von Humboldt, whom the world has almost forgotten, suddenly reappears as a living reality — as Humboldt rivers, Humboldt mountains. The name brings back to mind the beauty of Humboldt's description of nature and evokes nostalgic memories of my youth, and I find myself engulfed by a dream: The train, the comfortable Pullman car, has vanished. I am now wandering through a wide, flat, mysterious land, unknown and undiscovered, bearing names such as Nevada and the Cordilleras. These old Spanish names acquire a new charm, almost like mirages in a desert. Along the mountain ridges I see Spanish priests, the *padres*, missionaries riding on their mules, followed by Shoshana Indians, adorned with feathers and red scarves. A bit further away is a caravan, led by a German, sitting tall on his horse, wearing short pants, long white socks, silver buckled shoes, his head covered by a wig. Alexander von Humboldt is on one of his exploratory trips. It may be that in those times the desert itself looked different, crueler, more magnificent, more solitary, its very poverty making it richer. It had, at that time, a purposeful existence of its own; it was not a mere path to travel along.

◆   ◆   ◆

Another desert — intense, shimmering reddish-yellow sand and a searing sun. The Arizona Mojave Desert lies between Southern California and New Mexico. You barely leave Los Angeles and the San Bernardino Mountains and you are in the desert, but one very different from the Nevada desert. This is a southern desert. This is what the desert of the forty years of wandering must have looked like. This is the kind of desert the holy men and the prophets of the time had retreated to. And it was in such a desert that the thorn bush of faith had burned, setting all the earth aflame.

While the Nevada desert is ashamed of its nakedness and covers itself with rags, the Arizona desert is unashamedly naked; there is not a tuft of grass, not even a thorn bush, just sand, hot, reddish-yellow sand stretching out freely toward the horizon. Wherever you look, you see the sky and a shimmering, yellow expanse by day, and a deep, star-lit blackness by night. Nowhere have I seen a night sky as I saw in the Mojave Desert. It is neither blue nor gentle, but black as tar, forming a black dome, and the stars are bigger and closer than anything you will see elsewhere. Emmanuel Kant must truly have had a powerful imagination to be able to envision a desert night and to utter the famous words: "The stars above me and the moral imperative within me." Because above his city of Königsberg he could see only faraway pale stars in a gray-blue, melancholy sky. Only in the desert do the words "the stars above" acquire a meaning; only in the desert do they become a living reality. This is why the people of the desert had been under the spell of the stars. It could not have been otherwise. On that night, traveling through the Mojave Desert, I myself nearly fell under their spell.

It is said that mirages occur in the Arizona desert. Before your eyes there suddenly arise oases, cities, blue rivers, riders and ships. I did not see any. One does not have to go into the desert to see mirages. We see them day-in, day-out, we only call them by different names; we call them art, literature, philosophy — or love. But what I did see in the yellow desert was not less unique than the most beautiful mirage. I saw nature at play, amusing itself. It had taken a sandy desert and transformed it into a remarkable museum. It had adorned and painted the desert plains, and America calls it the Painted Desert, as it had been called already by the Indians of the region, the Hopi, the Suni and the Navajo. Red stones stretch out along the sides like shelves, with pieces of flat, rounded rocks rising out of the earth and dispersed like small altars throughout the tremendously long plain. Each rock is differently shaped, differently colored, the basic color being red, but here and there an admixture of various colors, a veritable orgy of color.

I would have liked to stop at some of these red altars, to prolong the experience of being witness to a long-gone state of existence. But life was summoning me: contemporary, quick, bustling life. From one desert my way led to another. From the Painted Desert, covered with red altars, beneath a star-studded firmament, to another desert, the one with stone walls and a pale sky, one filled with smoke and sadness. And in both deserts the same voice is heard, the voice of the wilderness, the beckoning voice of solitude.

Mitzpah

I

Surrounded by oceans, traversed by mountains, gifted and burdened with everything nature has to offer — abundance and dearth, fertility and waste, the tropical and the arctic, the eddying of a whirlpool and the stillness of a cave, the seething of an erupting geyser and the iciness of eternal snow — this is the remarkable, unique land that is called America.

It is a country that was destined to become a gathering place of peoples from the various corners of the world, a kind of museum of universal mankind. The Indians called it the Land of the Seven Tribes, but it became the land of seven times seven, and not just tribes, but of physically, mentally, culturally and linguistically disparate groups of people. And it proceeded to transform them into one people, one language, one way of life. Its beginnings were raucous, full of legendary achievements and adventures, but the passage of time transformed it into a land of suppressed instincts and of a soberly, conforming bearing. And this is, perhaps, what strikes one most in America, and what makes it truly worthwhile to follow the boisterous and colorful admonitions of all of the tourist and traveling agencies: "You have to see America!" "To see America" means to see the incredibly colorful, variegated world which is hidden by a gray veil of a humdrum human existence. To see America means to observe the wonderful struggle men conduct against nature — how they emerge victorious or how they are defeated.

◆   ◆   ◆

It is said: "New York is not America." Maybe so. At least that is what the out-of-towners say. They say it with envy, secretly wishing they could come to this "un-American" city, but also with hostility toward the Eastern giant who has put his golden heel upon American economy. This may be true, although one apparently has to live a long time in "the real America" in order to understand what America actually stands for. And if one has lived a long time there, one tends to become so petrified, so small-townish, so provincial, that one loses all concept of America's greatness and vastness. Because there is, in the final analysis, no disparity of temperaments or striving in America, no distinct traditions or historical reminiscences, no opposing pulls, such as occur in Germany, where Bavaria and Prussia have deep-seated tribal differences, or in France whose North and South differ in everything, even in their language.

In America it is only the big cities that differ from the small ones, a difference in degree rather than in essence, a quantitative rather than a qualitative one. It may be that this will change some day. It may be that two generations from now, people in Nevada or Montana, in California or New Mexico, will be altogether different from the people in Philadelphia, Chicago or New York. But at the present time these states are still in a colonial phase, as it were. Every "westerner" still remembers his origin, his former home — remembers it from his own experience or from his mother's or grandmother's tales. He is still a mere guest in the vast solitudes of America.

Solitudes. In America you come upon them quite suddenly, almost without any transition, just like nightfall in a tropical land, or a city on the rim of a desert. Actually, though, they begin as you leave Chicago. You can travel the long stretch from New York to Chicago with your eyes closed, as one is apt to do on crossing the ocean, when one wave follows the other, each as gray as the next. Every once in a while, one wave will noisily top another, only to be swallowed up, letting monotony reign again. And Chicago itself? No matter how many times I have been there, it always remains the same — long, dreary streets, houses with smoking chimneys, work-a-day people wearing drab work-a-day clothes, topped by gloomy skies. It remains the same even though new streets are laid out, new houses, both pretty and ugly, are being built for the influx of new people, and it stretches further and further into the distance. And I am seized by a sad, oppressive mood. What are people doing in this anthill? Nowhere in the world have I been struck so forcefully by the meaningless routine, the ant-like aspects of life, as in Chicago. New York, at least, has the ocean, hills, whimsicality. Chicago is so business-like, so down-to-earth.

A great plain stretches out endlessly. On all sides are fields filled with waves of green and yellow corn. Here and there stands a house, shimmering silvery white in the moonlit night and dull grayish-white by day. We are leaving the industrial world and entering the rural idylls of Iowa and Nebraska. It is impossible to tell by sight where Illinois or Iowa or Nebraska begins or ends. And it really does not matter. What is in a name? It may, of course, have meaning for political candidates running for Congress, but to an outsider, it all seems the same — one simply sees earth, wide fertile earth.

There are steppes here, but without the aura of the Russian steppes. I do not know why those come across as less vibrant, why they project a different mood, a different smell. The Russian steppes are poorer but more pleasant. The train there crosses them at a slow pace, and the men in the field also move slowly. At the sides of the black or yellow fields stand heavy wagons drawn by teams of oxen. In the distance is heard a sad song, and a wisp of smoke rises out of a chimney — nothing but a brief stroke of the brush, a hint, but you feel that they arise out of an ancient, deeply buried world. The earth there has its own mystique.

You do not see any oxen in Iowa or Nebraska, nor do you see peasants in cotton shirts. Fords are driving in between the fields, and the houses are electrically lit at night. Here and there we pass small towns, sporting the same advertisements as New York City or Boston: Wrigley chewing gum, cigarettes, underwear and whatnot. And you come to feel that the earth is merely a workshop where one works a certain number of hours a day to produce needed goods. The earth here is not a terrifying master who entices man to enter his service and holds him captive in a magic spell.

We proceed westward, and suddenly you see, on the distant horizon, dimly discernable dark silhouettes of a broken chain of rambling mountaintops. Your eyes follow the line until they close, overtaken by fatigue. And when, at the end of the night, you open them again you no longer see silhouettes, but a substantial and magnificent mountain range. You see the Rockies.

◆   ◆   ◆

The first thing that catches your eye as you arrive in Denver, Colorado, is the tall arch in front of the railroad station, carrying the strange inscription: MITZ-PAH. "This is a Hebrew word that means welcome," the elderly woman at the information desk is explaining to an American traveler wanting to know the meaning of the word. The lady is, actually, not very well versed in Hebrew, since the word is closer to "you are being watched over." But she is not to be blamed. It is not her fault that today's inhabitants of Denver have already forgotten the meaning and the symbolism contained in the ancient Hebrew word *mitzpah*. They do not understand why their ancestors had chosen it as a symbol of welcome. "May God look after us, when we lose sight of each other," was once intoned in the solitary stretches of the West — the gate to the solitudes, the entry to the mountains, where man is alone with himself and with silent, magnificent nature. Every man is on his own, in a constant struggle with danger. But among those solitary men, each climbing the mountains on his own, dwells God's watchful presence.

It is a beautiful vision, strong and intimate, but what has remained of it is only a word, a word that has already lost its source and its meaning. In a short time men forgot the meaning of *mitzpah*, and what remained is just a memory of a time, a time which came to an end before it reached maturity. It is a gate to romantic America, where romance is now seeking refuge in cheap novels and in penny movies. Yet the gate to the country's true romance opens onto the road into the mountains.

Before I was free to see the mountains that strong men climb, I had to see the mountain where sick people dwell. It was a promise I had made to Dr. Spivak of the Denver Sanitarium. Thus, propelled in equal measures by feelings of good will and of guilt, I began my visit to the Colorado mountains at the abode of tubercular patients. It is like a small city, a very clean and quiet one, equipped with kitchens, libraries, a chapel, even workshops. There are few indications that the people you see are patients, yet the experienced observer will note the too bright eyes and too red cheeks, and will know that these are people who are fighting for their lives. Perhaps it was due to the crisp air and the bright sunlight that I did not succumb to the feeling of pain and sadness that usually grips me whenever I enter a hospital. Or perhaps it was due to the fact that the patients seemed to feel stronger and more optimistic, had more faith. The place felt more like a camp than a hospital, and the hospital, in turn, makes every effort to maintain this camp-like atmosphere. If only the patients could spend the rest of their lives here, if only they did not have to return to the damp streets of their cities! This, I was told by the Sanitarium directors, is their main problem. They know that the patients ought not to return to their old environment, but there is nothing they can do to prevent it. The number of patients is growing, while their budget is not, and the means at their disposal are barely keeping up with their needs.

I talked with the patients, listened to the administrators, and having, done my duty, took leave of them with a clear conscience. I started on my way to the solitudes of the free mountains, to Colorado Springs and Pikes Peak, the mountain of the eternal snow. Here stillness prevails, and a holiday feeling is in the air. You sense a primordial silence, and you would like it to stay that way. At least for a while....

II

What is it that draws men to the mountains? Why do they risk their lives climbing high, icy-cold mountains where the eternal snow shimmers in the sun? One after another, adventure-seekers come to scale Mount Everest, the highest Alpine ranges, the Chimborazo — wherever the greatest danger, perhaps even death, awaits them.

In Switzerland you can see multitudes of tourists, risking their lives as they drag themselves up Mont Blanc and the Chamineau, these tall giants covered in ice and snow, each tied to the other with ropes and all of them to the mountain guide. They get exhausted, breathing requires an effort, and they labor at getting ahead with a hard and bitter determination. And I always ask myself: What for? Why do they need to do this? Is it not easier and more pleasant to sit on a balcony in Montreux, or the green Rhone valley, where breathing is so easy, where the smell of flowers is intoxicating, where the earth sings and the river answers? What is it one sees up on the tall mountains? What can one see except snow, except a harsh, stern, almost dead nature?

Everyone knows this, the explorers, the geologists, as well as the ordinary tourists, and yet, they are drawn to the mountains as if by a magnet. According to a statement by the British Alpinist Club, "There develops a feeling of camaraderie among all those who have undertaken the task of climbing a mountain, who have experienced the same pleasure, exerted the same effort, faced the same danger." Pleasure? Climbing a mountain is not, in itself, a pleasure. On a hard, difficult ascent you breathe more heavily, and your heart beats faster the higher you get. You get dizzy as you look down, and your blood sings in your ears. You think: Enough! You are high enough, what else is there to see? A few more rocks, more vastness, and an angry, oppressive, superhuman greatness. You are tired. All of your body clamors to return to the familiar valley. But deep inside you a voice commands: higher, higher, up to the highest top!

The eye is always drawn upwards, and the greater the danger, the greater the appeal, the stronger the attraction. I did, one summer night, climb a mountain in the Swiss Alps, although it was not a very tall one and can be ascended on foot in about 5 or 6 hours. I walked, all alone, through the entire night, in the quiet, strange, oppressive solitude, in order to see the sunrise. And throughout the night, as tired as I was getting, I was led by the desire to reach the top. I lost my way in the dark, missed the path, had to climb over rocks, over fallen trees, had to hold on to thorny branches and to perform all kind of acrobatic feats in order to maintain my balance. I could not understand from where such agility came to me, such an ability to adapt to the demands of the hour, but I was led by instinct, and it was my instinct that did not allow me to turn back. Higher, higher, a voice inside me was singing, and I followed the song.

It may, perhaps, be more than wanderlust alone, more than the lure that all danger extends; it may be a love for the superfluous, for the useless. Of what use are they, these naked rocks? What do they offer us? And the things they sometimes do offer, the gold and silver, iron and copper, these offerings have to come to us at a high cost of toil and of sacrifices. And yet, it is just because these mountains do not serve any purpose, just because they exist without any ties to our human needs, that we find ourselves drawn to them, just as we are drawn to everything that is incomprehensible, to everything that is more powerful than we are.

◆　　　◆　　　◆

On this trip I did not have the chance I had in Switzerland to make the climb by myself, at my own risk and by the grace of God, and to encounter the mountain by myself. I did not have the time, being caught up in the tempo of American life, in its resolve to experience everything, even mountain solitude, in a socially organized, hurried way. I was among a group of tourists in Colorado Springs, a wonderful small town with well-kept streets, pure mountain air and crystal-clear water. We were scheduled to take a bus which would drive us to Pikes Peak, at the very top of the Rockies.

How I envied old Zebulon Pike, who was the first to "discover" the mountaintop, the first to have had the courage to climb up to the snow-covered peak. I could just picture it. It was in the early morning hours of a day just like the one I was viewing from my comfortable tour bus — a pure blue sky shining above the sparkling green earth below — when Zebulon left Colorado Springs atop his mule. After a few hours he came to the Indian village of Manioto nestling among the rocks. These are red, strangely formed, fantastically shaped stones, as if deliberately carved out. A stone wall has the look of the walls of an Assyrian palace.

Waterfalls have etched in figures that look like hieroglyphics, animals and painted figures. And here is a cave blown out by the winds, a labyrinth, a tunnel in the mountains. And in the cave are the most wondrous shapes, stones emerging from above and from below, stalactites and stalagmites, like a garden of stones, bedecked and adorned. From a ceiling descends something like a lantern, hard, glittering, notched. In a corner, out of a damp stone, comes a branch of red and green stone. This is truly a catacomb, but a catacomb of life. The earth here is leading its own existence; it develops on its own, indulging in its own idiosyn-cratic, artistic play. On the surface of the earth, everything has its purpose, every blade of grass has its use. Beneath the surface, the earth allows itself the luxury of being useless, of simply being an existence without a purpose.

We leave the cave and follow the path between the rocks. We enter the Park of Stones — red stones. Two red rocks form a gate. The stones are red, the sky is blue, the earth is green. We are surrounded by red shapes, one more fantastic than the next. One looks like a bear, another like an eagle, yet others like heads of animals and humans. The Indians named this stone park The Garden of the Gods. This, at least, is one of the many stories imaginative white folks tell about Indians. But, even if only imagined, it is still true. This kind of garden seems worthy of being dedicated to the gods of the Indians.

We climb higher. The mountains open up and close behind us. We have to search for the Utah Path, which the Indians laid out sometime in the distant past. Among the rocks, from the top of the mountain, runs a stream. It runs and sings playfully, and in one spot it falls with a joyous splatter, creating a spray which takes on the colors of the rainbow. Quiet reigns; there is not even a rustle to be heard. From time to time a gray mountain squirrel with a long tail and large, curious-looking ears emerges from a crack in the rocks and flits, shadowlike, across our path, only to disappear into another crevice.

It is quiet, but something like a song is coming from somewhere. Something is calling. Is it the mountain? Is it a pounding in my ears? We move higher and higher, and the climbing is getting more difficult. The path is becoming nar-rower, winding like a stony serpent. Your steps now resound in the still air and are brought back by an echo. We have already reached the Feet of Bartholomew, 11,500 feet up. You feel dizzy. You are drawn downward, feeling that if you let yourself fall, you would fly down as on wings. You have to close your eyes and make an effort to tear yourself away from the pull of the depth below.

You go on climbing higher. It is getting colder and colder; the air is harsh, the earth frozen and snow is all around. And here, at an altitude of 14,100 feet, is Pikes Peak. Snow and ice. The earth below is barely visible. You see only other mountains, walls of stones and peaks. It takes your breath away; your heart beats like a hammer, and you are gripped by fatigue. It is time to descend into the valley. It is difficult to linger on the heights.

◆   ◆   ◆

I was envious of Old Zebulon. He followed the lure of danger; he risked, and he discovered. I followed the same way so comfortably, so prosaically, so hurriedly. But one consolation remains: I have seen the same things that Zebulon did. He could not have experienced anything more, only at a slower pace; not more intensively, only at greater peril. But maybe not even that. Old Zebulon had surely not known anything of the perils of being driven by a speeding bus driver along narrow roads winding between abysses. Each age has its adventures. And who knows who had the greater ones, we or those we have hailed in song and ballads? There may be more poetry in prose than in romances. There is, at any rate, a stronger cadence, the cadence of nature's striving to maintain its wildness.

The Damp Cellars of the Inquisition and the Swimming Island of Song

The rain is falling in buckets, although it is a bit too early in the season. It is just my bad luck that the rain is in a hurry. But rain or shine, one has to venture out into the environs of Mexico City to see the land. My first trip is to the Desierta de Leones, the desert of the lions. In truth, I do not really understand how the lions got here, at any rate the kind of lions we see in our zoos. Mexico does not have many of our animals. There are no bears — Indians do not even have a name for them — and there were no native horses. The first time the Aztecs saw a horse was when Cortez arrived with his soldiers. At first, they thought that horse and rider were one creature. Neither are there lions, only pumas, animals resembling lions, but a lot smaller and more feline. Whatever the animals are that populate this desert, they are tame and domesticated.

The present-day Desierta de Leones, however, is quite unpretentious. It is a small Indian village with its barefoot Indians, a few poor peasant huts and a small restaurant for tourists. It is strange being merely an hour and a half from the capital, from the ambitious Districto Federale, yet we seem to be in a faraway, primitive country, unpopulated and uncultivated. Is this, perhaps, the effect of the rain that imposes such a dark coloration on the landscape and the people? Or

443

maybe the shadows of the black, bluish mountains that darken the road? But everything is two to three degrees darker, browner or blacker than in Mexico City, even the Indians. In the city, most of them also go barefoot, but they seem to be a part of the street, of the market and the taverns. In the city they are simply poor people in tattered clothes and without shoes. But here, in the open fields, among the mountains, in the desert, they are genuine residents. They are where they belong, the only ones connected to the mountains and the fields, to Mexico's holy cactus tree and cypress. They are both darker and sadder than the Indians in the city. I see them walking in goose formation, according to Indian custom, one following the other. The women, carrying loads on their heads, lead the way, with the men following. Their way of walking is more like running, taking small, rapid steps, with their torsos thrust forward, and they seem to be bent on escaping pursuit. Their walk lacks the slow, graceful dignity of the Near East and more closely resembles the Chinese way. The Chinese, Koreans, and Mongolians all walk this way. Is this a racial characteristic, or the historic imprint of 400 years of enslavement, of dodging the whip of harsh masters; 400 years of fleeing and of fear? Or does this go back even further, into the ancient past, when the Indians themselves had been strangers in the land of Arawak?

We arrive at the Desierta, an old French monastery, partially in ruins, but the surrounding fence and the church walls have still preserved their iron-like solidity. The Spaniards did not know how to erect beautiful and comfortable buildings, but they did know how to build walls strong enough to protect them. And in the end, the lion desert is nothing more than the former prison camp of the Inquisition — the "Holy Brotherhood."

Our official guide is a thin, bow-legged boy who looks ten years old but claims to be twelve. "What is your name?" I ask him. "Savario Tiburso Suarez, at your service, Señor." The latter part of the sentence is a mandatory part of the answer every properly brought-up Spanish child must use when asked a question. And bow-legged Savario Tiburso is well educated and versed in the art of guiding tourists. He holds a candle in his hand and gives me one too as we walk into the dark, damp underground tunnels of the inquisitorial prison. The cells built into the tunnel are so narrow that an average-size person can barely squeeze through, so low that you must bow your head in order not to hit the ceiling. Water drips through the cracks in the stones. Two small holes in the wall, at waist level, serve as windows. An adult can barely stand upright. The unfortunate victims of the Inquisition were chained to the wall. Chunks of bread and cups of water pushed through the windows were their only nourishment. Thus they had to exist for years until they were removed from the dark dampness and led to the red-hot glare of the stake. Following periodic visits from the inquisitor, the "infidel," i.e. the Jew or the New Christian, was led into the torture chamber, and afterwards returned, broken in body and spirit, to his cell, to the dark, wet, lonely night. Only rarely, very rarely, was a prisoner released into "freedom."

Savario Tiburso tells all this in a childish, matter-of-fact tone of voice, the voice of an experienced guide, without showing any understanding of the terrible, cruel tale he is telling. "Do you know what the Inquisition was, Savario Tiburso?" My candle has burned out, and I can barely see him. "Of course, this was the religion of the monks. I am at your service, señor." And you can hear religious indoctrination in these innocent words. I do not pursue any further conversation with the young Indian.

It is wet and slippery; raindrops are falling from the walls, like immured sighs of the past. I take a deep breath as we emerge into open air. I come from the line of those who once were tortured here, and Savario is the small great-grandson of the fallen, conquered and enslaved Indians. Maybe our great-grandchildren will someday look with compassion and sorrow at the ruins of our present-day inquisitory cellars, and another young Tiburso will, perhaps, explain that "this was the religion of those days." This is the Utopian picture Romantics paint for us, and it may possibly come to pass. Every generation inherits its past and fails to understand the sorrows and sufferings the previous generation experienced. Human beings forget. This is their good fortune.

◆   ◆   ◆

"Soldiers of France, forty centuries are looking down on you!" I tried to recite the famous, legendary speech Napoleon delivered standing in front of the pyramids of Egypt. But I did not get any further. My group, a couple of young Mexicans and a social worker from Philadelphia, remained unresponsive. It did not grab them. I suspect that the French soldiers had also not been greatly impressed by Napoleon's flowery speech — if he had, indeed, uttered these sonorous words, which is actually quite doubtful. Yet the pyramids of Egypt are proper sermon material. It suits them; it is a part of the whole scene: white desert sand, distant rows of palms beneath the burning desert sun, two gigantic black-gray stones rising like mountains, and between them the Sphinxes, the last traces of a long-gone, mysterious world, of a dead culture.

But in San Juan Teruvacan, the Mexican pyramids stand mutely — stones, tablets, and nothing more. And the tablets contain alien names, names I cannot relate to. They are called pyramids only because people like to affix familiar names to things. Actually, these are not pyramids and do not bear the slightest resemblance to the Egyptian monuments. These *mesas* are gigantic mountainous plateaus, paved with stones and bricks, as are the surrounding terraces. The pyramids of Gizah, the Egyptian pyramids, are symbols cast in stone, symbolizing human labor, suffering and death. The pyramids of Teotihacan are giant altars to gods whose names are too difficult to pronounce, to gods with an undetermined function in the world.

It is remarkable how complex were the manifestations of primitive man. The richer a culture, the simpler and clearer its expressions. Greek mythology is crystal clear and easy to grasp, and even Egyptian mythology can be elucidated in words and in pictures. But it is almost impossible to take hold of Mexican mythology, to understand its symbols in the context of their religion. Eagles, serpents, human heads with snakes in their hair, fantastic beasts, and everything in such an exaggerated scale. It is a religion of fear, of childish terror, a religion without any intimacy.

I walk up the steps of the main pyramid. The 300 steps are getting smaller and more slippery as they rise to ever-giddier heights. The story is told about priests of the god Vishtilishtil ascending these steps in their picturesque, feather adorned robes, followed by soldiers leading the "offering" — prisoners to be sacrificed to the bloodthirsty god. On the top stands a stone table, the altar, with a knife of black mountain glass. The prisoner is put on the altar, and the priest cuts out the victim's beating heart and sacrifices it to the god. At the foot of the ladder Indians sang their sad songs, played their instruments, clapped their hands and danced their wild dance, wearing masks of the ancient, fantastic animal faces on their heads.

I open my archeological guidebook and read what it says about the Taltecs, the builders of these pyramids. I see barbaric sounding names and incomprehensible symbols, and I close the book. These names do not tell me anything, and the symbols are of no interest to me. The past is meaningful only when it passes on a heritage, when it contains a linking thread to the present. But there is no bridge linking me to the Taltecs or the Tchimics; there is no point of contact. These are stories that do not remind me of anything.

I make my way to the highest plateau, at the end of the 300 steps. The air here is fresh and soft, permeated with sweet, intoxicating smells rising from the valley. The horizon stops at the mountaintops, at the chain of the Cordilleras. In the distance you can see the white domes of Mexico City. Everything is still and dead. And I am overcome by a feeling of remoteness and of estrangement. Remote from everything that is "now," and estranged from everything that is human. It seems to me that I am standing on a plateau in a world that was completely different, without any connection to any history, to any possible reality.

I sit down on a step and rest. In my hand is the small, thin booklet written by an Indian named Abraham Lopez, titled *The Men from the East*, a legend of Mexico. He cites an ancient Indian manuscript, the so-called "Lambian Codex," describing the arrival of ancient Mexicans from some faraway Eastern countries. He tells of their struggles and sufferings, of the mysterious land of Nasabi, of kings and priests and the ancient traditions of a people that does not know where it came from. He tells of a people yearning to find its roots somewhere in the abyss of the past, and being unable to find them.

"Isn't it remarkable," a member of the group asks me, "that the ancient Indian name for god was the same as Greek, 'Theo'?" And note that the word *calle* recalls the Hebrew word *hekhal*, which in turn comes from the Sumerians, a people that lived in Babylon before the Semites. Is there perhaps a connection between our East and the East of the Nasabis? I cannot answer this question. The science of etymology is still in its infancy. So far it is impossible to find any connection, any similarity between the ancient languages of Mexico and the dead languages of the East. But who knows, someday one may reach the secret of history and rediscover the way men have walked over the earth, in an eternally restless pursuit of an illusion. We have, once, all been connected and enmeshed. We only are unable to untie the knots — at least not yet.

◆   ◆   ◆

We return to the city. In the distance a white cloud is visible, Mexico City's dust cloud. It occurs almost daily. At a certain hour of the day, there arises from the surrounding valleys a cloud of white dust, which stays for a couple of hours and then dissolves. There is always some storm over Mexico City, even if it is only a dust storm. Coming into the city we stop at the famous church of Guadeloupe. In the 16th century, an Indian woman from the village Guadeloupe experienced a miracle. She had been picking flowers, colleting them in her apron, when the miracle occurred. The flowers from the Mexican soil had imprinted upon the apron of the poor Indian woman the face of the Madonna, a Madonna that looks truly Indian, like a daughter of the soil. And from this miracle grew a national legend. The priests understood the value of the legend and had immortalized it in stone. They built a Cathedral of the Madonna of Guadeloupe, and the people had installed the Madonna in the pantheon of their ancient gods.

Galilee and Jerusalem were too far removed from them; they had wanted a Christianity closer to their Cirzalcaty and Vishtilipashtil. And they had found it.

There is a fence around the church. And from this fence, men and women are advancing, on their knees, toward the church altar, holding white, aromatic flowers in their hands, and with Latin prayers on their lips. The same kneeling procession, and the same murmuring of not-understood prayers, have been taking place for 300 years. Mexico is praying to the Madonna for freedom. When, in 1811, the priest Rinaldo raised the flag of revolution, of the battle for Mexican independence, his battle cry had been "Guadeloupe!" And the Madonna helped. Mexico is proceeding, on its knees and in suffering, towards its freedom. Back to its origins, or, maybe, surpassing them and moving further?

The church walls are covered with letters. In one corner hangs a picture of a cot and a message to the Madonna: "I, Zinga, or Maria, have been lying on this cot paralyzed, for a whole year. I beg you, Santisima Madonna, please heal me!" There are many such letters. The last one is dated May 1933. "The letters keep coming," a Mexican standing next to me comments. He has just risen from his knees and is sure that his prayer has been heard, his sin forgiven and that everything will be all right. He is now going to ask a man who is sitting at the gates to write his thank you letter to the Madonna. "He writes so beautifully, the Madonna will enjoy it."

◆   ◆   ◆

We continue across town, on our way to Tashinilk, the "Venice of Mexico." Here once stood a temple to the goddess Satchimilka, the Madonna of ancient Mexico, the goddess of flowers and fruits. There was also once a river here. Long before the arrival of the Spaniards, the Indians had built an island in the river, putting beams into the ground, covering them with intertwined tree branches, topping it all with soil and building houses on top — an island swimming in an artificial lake. It is here that Mexico comes to frolic, or, rather, to search for romance. Entire families come to celebrate festive occasions on large, colorfully decorated boats. Indians in small canoes pass by offering you various Mexican native drinks, cooked food and flowers. Musicians play old romantic Mexican songs.

Reclining on a boat bench, I bask in the mid-afternoon sun, absorbing the sight of the green, shimmering water, the aroma of the flowers and the sound of the sweet, sad, Spanish songs which a blind Indian is singing for me at twenty cents a song. The old, gray-haired Indian who is steering the boat stands with statue-like immobility. He barely lifts a hand as the boat slowly moves over the water, followed on all sides by the sound of Castilian Zimbels playing "*Amore.*"

It reminds me of Venice. Lagoons, palaces and "Death in Venice," Thomas Mann's masterly story of the blending of two images: Venice and death. But the spirit of the lagoons is too beautiful and too sweet, and one is driven to return to reality, be it in the Venice of Italy or in the Venice of Mexico. Thus I am suddenly aroused from my reveries by a familiar, all too familiar sound: "Haksele, haksele, play a cazaksele." I look around and see a boat with a group of young Jewish men and women, and a Litvak is singing the harsh song of their native land. "Oy, oy," sings the man from Lithuania. "Ay, ay," answers the Mexican song from another boat. The "Oy, oy" wins out, plucking me out of my meditations. What does Nietzsche say? One cannot escape the Jews. Not even in Satchinilka.

Mexico's Mother Rachel Laments Her Children's Misfortunes

It is difficult to breathe. Mexico City lies at such a high elevation that the air grows thin, your heart palpitates, and every step is an effort. You want to lie down and relax into a half-slumber. You want to dream about all kind of things, about events of the past, things that have vanished and are hiding somewhere beyond the mountains, the white-capped mountains called Popocatepetl and Iztaccilinatl. Remarkable names, reminding me of the thin geography books of my childhood; names which sound legendary, unreal. Popocatepetl. Iztaccilinatl. These cannot be real names; they must have been made up to torment small children or to stir the imagination of poetic youth. And yet here they are, the two snowy mountains, looking at me so earnestly, so rooted in reality, and yet, somehow, not of this world. These are two giants from a time long past, survivors of a time when the world was…I do not know if it was fresher, bigger, or more fantastic, but, at any rate, it was different. Or, perhaps, this too is fantasy. It may always have been the same. We may always have stared in fear at the top of the mountain, afraid of being swallowed up by the abyss.

I am tired, but I cannot rest, for Mexico City is calling and the enchantment of the old, legend-filled city lures and overcomes my fatigue. I walk along the streets and lanes of the city. It is hot. A recent rain had cleansed the air a bit, and if not for my rapid heartbeat, it would have been an easy walk along the narrow,

450

long, straight lanes of the Palace City. But this time the flowery language is based on reality. This is a city where great determination and an overwhelming romanticism have turned a barbaric dream into reality.

Sitting atop a high mountain, Mexico City, the highest city — or, at least, among the highest cities — in the world, is a representation in iron and stone of the old, proud Castilian motto: "When you want to, you can." A small band of Spanish adventurers, Cortés, Alvares, Benavidez and others, hungry for gold and for power, had made their way into a hard-to-reach land. Braving tropical heat, roaring rivers and dizzyingly high mountains, they came to a strongly organized realm of millions of people, with a well-disciplined army. And in a short time, during the year 1519–1520, they destroyed the Aztec regime, took over the land, tore down their capital city Tenochtitlan, and turned Mexico into a Spanish province.

The puzzling question of how it came to pass that old Mexico let itself so easily be overrun by the Spaniards is still unanswered. The Spaniards themselves found it difficult to account for, and the Indians found it still more difficult. It happened only a few hundred years ago, yet the events remain shrouded in fog. Historians, it is true, tell us that the Aztec regime was about to fall because it was built on loot, force and a segregated caste system. Mexico was not yet a nation, but rather a continent inhabited by twenty-one Indian tribes, or peoples, each with its own language, mores and traditions, forming a variety of societies, all the way from the purely nomadic groups to a firmly organized and structured state. There were Atomis and Torascans, Tchithchinkens and Taltekens, Mayas and Iakis, etc., etc. All preserved legends of wanderings, of being newcomers to a foreign land. They had come from somewhere else, from distant countries without names, from across the ocean, perhaps survivors of the sunken continent of Atlantis. It is said that the Aztec name Aztlan is an allusion to their Atlantis origin. Or perhaps they came from the wide Asian steppes, across the Bering Sea, and are therefore close cousins of the Chinese and other Eastern peoples. Who knows?

Tribe after tribe had come and settled in the valleys amid the mountains of present-day Mexico, until the last tribe, the Aztecs, arrived from the East. Nomads coming from unknown places, they settled on the high plateau of Mexico, there "where the eagle holds the serpent in its claw," there where the palm tree blooms. Here they built their first city, Tenochtitlan, and from there they dispersed, spreading their eagle wings, and becoming the rulers of Mexico. They ruled for 200 years, with a dread lurking in their heart, that new, white men would come from the East, drive them away and take over their land. And the white men from the East did come.

The tribes rebelled against the rule of Montezuma. Five hundred Indians joined the small group of Spaniards. The lion of Castille and Lyon ripped apart the eagle of Mexico and then pursued the millions of Indians, forcing them to serve the Spaniards and their gods.

I am now in the center of Mexico City, on its main plaza, the Palazzo, the seat of the government and of the great Cathedral. And here is also a monument to the last king of the Aztecs, the legendary Montezuma, who was brought down by Cortés. The palace of Montezuma once stood on the same place, as did the main temple of the god Catalcato, the god of fertility. But 400 years ago this had still been an island, a laguna, as was all of Tenochtitlan. Houses nestled on high frames, moored in sand. One used canoes to get from house to house. It was a city built on swampy ground. The Spaniards filled up the canals, dried the land, paved it with stones and built palaces and churches. Those were strongly built Spanish palaces, each one a fortress, the gates displaying the coats of arms of the old Spanish nobility, or of the new *conquistadores*, the conquerors of the land.

I enter the Cathedral. It is very large and empty. The Church is not flourishing in revolutionary Mexico. The Cathedral lacks the gold and diamonds to be found in all of the churches in Spain, and there are only a few valuable pictures and statues. And the style is not altogether a European Catholic one; there seems to be an admixture of another style, of another view of life. One utters prayers to Christ, Jesus of Galilee, but somewhere in the subconscious there is an echo of Cetztalcaso and of Vizlipashtli, ancient Aztec gods. The names have changed, but the essence has remained the same as it was 400 years ago.

In a corner, above the altar, hangs a picture of the Madonna. The people call it the Madonna of Forgiveness, and an interesting legend has grown around it. The story goes that in the 16th century there lived in Mexico a Jew who was so stubbornly devoted to his faith that the Holy Inquisition had to take steps to save his soul form eternal hell fire. He was, naturally, put in the underground dungeon where the Inquisitor held his unfortunate victims. But the Jew was so filled with devotion and pride in his faith that he refused to talk with anyone about his sins. Until one fine day he asked the guard to bring him a brush, some colors and a canvas, and to let him spend his time painting, until his turn came to be burned at the stake. The guard brought him what he asked for, and the Jew began to paint. And there, as if by its own volition, the art of Italy and of the Netherlands, where the Jew formerly lived, had blended to produce a picture of the Madonna, looking as beautiful, mild and sweet as had never been seen in Mexico before.

When the Inquisitor saw the picture he could not tear his eyes from it. He understood that it was a sign from the Madonna, and his heart softened. But the heart of the Jew had also softened; his own work had converted him to Christianity. He was freed, and the picture was named the Madonna of Forgiveness and was hung above the altar in the Cathedral.

It is a naive legend, but one stained with so much blood, Jewish blood. And time has not yet removed the stains.

I continue my walk. Here is the Macubri, the boulevard where Cortés entered Mexico, and here are other streets with old Catholic names, Spanish aristocratic and old Mexican names. Here is the Street of the Mint and the Museum, a small house, a room with a few stones. A giant stone occupies most of the space; this rounded monolithic block is the famous Aztec calendar. It is an artful, very complicated sculpture, with eagles and snakes and human heads with serpents entwined in their hair, surrounding the calendar numbers. The very friendly and highly learned university professor who is accompanying me explains to me the meaning of the figures and the symbols. But I am not listening too attentively. I have no interest in the Aztec calendar; time etched in stone is of less interest to me than the life of the times that produced these symbols.

We walk among the figures, some of which are upright and some of which are lying down, their strange profiles resembling Oriental faces of Assyria and, often, also of ancient Egypt. What was the origin of this mixture of races and of styles? Here is a genuine Chinese figure standing next to an undoubtedly Semitic one. Can it really be true that once, in forgotten times, a tremendous catastrophe had hit the earth and had caused all the peoples to flee and to reassemble and mix in ways which changed the history of mankind? The gaze of the statues goes beyond me, into the distant past, behind the curtain of history, a curtain that, perhaps, will never be lifted.

I step into a room filled with portraits of old Spanish viceroys. Each portrait tells a story of bygone times, romantic stories, naively brutal and barbaric ones. Here is the unfortunate Emperor Maximilian, the blond scion of the House of Hapsburg, who succumbed to the temptation of spending Mexican gold on a luxurious court life and who was shot by revolutionaries. I looked at Maximilian and Carlotta's gilded court chariot and at a few more such historic curiosities, and then I had enough of Mexico's ancient history.

I am back on the street, which is teeming with colorfully attired, barefoot Mexicans and with taverns on every corner. Between the streets Jesus Maria and Jesus Caranza is wedged the Tepito, the thieves market, where all of the knife wielders and pistol shooters ply their trade. Policemen with rifles and watchful detectives are eyeing every person entering the market. Curious and hostile looks follow one. The narrow street is crowded. There are stalls selling the ubiquitous tortillas, enchiladas and all of the delicacies that only the grandchildren of Montezuma can digest. Here and there are watering holes where Mexican natives drink their national drink, a whitish, sweetly distasteful beverage that is said to render one drunk very quickly, whether one drinks a glass or downs a bottle. I cannot imagine anyone doing the latter, but whatever the case, they do get drunk very quickly. Pictures of saints, old almanacs, sandals, shoes, everything can be found in this market. And while a buyer can find many of the things he wants, the police can find even more, if they are willing to look diligently. All of Mexico knows that if anyone is missing anything, it can be found in the Tepito.

Later in the evening I spend hours listening to the Mexican Jewish poet Berliner, telling me about the Tepito, how the least disagreement may result in a stabbing, and how wildly life is being lived there. He had even written a poem about the Tepito. But, truth to tell, the Tepito did not make such a big impression on me. The Galician Bazaar in Kiev, the Moldavanka in Odessa, to say nothing of the Flea Market of Paris, could upstage ten such Tepitos.

The Apaches, of course, did actually come from Mexico, but they had to undergo a lengthy period of absorption into European and French cultural trends in order to become true Parisian Apaches. Thieves had failed to excite interest until the wonderful poems of the 14th century poet-thief François Villon made them a part of national lore.

From the Tepito I come to the long, gray Rosario Street, and to Mexico's oldest church. The Santisima is a fortress-like structure, built for generations to come, for eternity, *Aeternia aeternitatis*, as the Church says. But "eternity" has lasted only for a couple of centuries, for just a moment, because Mexico cannot tolerate alien imposition and swallows it up. The Santisima is sinking deeper and deeper into the ground; soon nothing will remain of it except its spire and its name. The swamps of Tenochtitlan are absorbing the pride of old Castille. The eagle is prevailing over the lion, and this is the remarkable fate of Mexico. No culture endures there for long, not even the modern one. What is being built today will also not last.

Here is the new magnificent National Theater, or, as it is called, The Palace of Fine Arts. Porfirio Diaz, Mexico's last, long-ruling tyrant, laid its groundwork. Diaz was toppled, revolution followed, then civil war. Mexico is restructured now, but the theater is still not quite completed. It is a grandiose building, with white marble on the outside, and red and green marble inside. But it is too ornamental and too small to accommodate contemporary Mexico's theatergoers. It was built for Mexico's elite, which, in Diaz's time comprised merely a few hundred people. Now masses of people are seeking admittance, and there is no room for them. But even this, Mexico's newest palace, is beginning to sink. It is said to be due to faulty architecture and insufficient planning. Possibly, but no plan is good enough if one builds on eroding soil.

I have walked all day, and my heart is palpitating more strongly. I rest for a while at the American cafe where you meet at night "all of Mexico," i.e. tourists and the country's intellectuals. It is a remarkable place, called Casa de Azulejos, the house of mosaic tiles. In the room where I am sitting, sipping my coffee, Europe had, for the first time, made contact with the East. The first Japanese envoys had come to Mexico 200 years ago, and the Viceroy had received them here. Spain then had the opportunity to open the gates to Japan. But Spain was capable only of conquest by the sword and colonization; it had never mastered the art of flexible diplomacy, of gradually pursued negotiations. The Spaniard was too much of a *caballero*, too stiff in the observance of Spanish ceremonials, too little a man of the world.

The following anecdote about the stiff knightliness of old Castille is said to have taken place some 300 years ago. Two young *caballeros,* driving their chariots, accompanied by their splendidly attired servants, arrived at the intersection of Avenue Madera and a narrow lane, next to the cafe where I am now sitting. Chariots faced chariots, with no room to pass to the right or to the left. That meant that one of them had to back out, but which one? One Don cites his ten noble names and insists that his aristocratic heritage is of an older vintage, while the other one replies that in his veins flow the blood of 13th century nobility. And thus they argued for three days and three nights, without either one making a move. Finally the Viceroy himself had to intervene, sending soldiers to separate the stubborn Dons, who otherwise would still be here today, priding themselves on the wilted glories of a long gone past.

Having rested, I take a cab to visit my museum professor who lives in the new, Havana-style, suburb called Hippodrome. Around eleven PM we walk in the moonlight to my hotel. Palms are glowing in silvery light, cypresses are swaying and a cool breeze comes from the mountains. The professor and I talk about distant things, about Heidelberg, philosophy, Europe, and, for a while, I forget that I am in Mexico. Suddenly there comes from somewhere a plaintive cry, almost like a sob. "What is that?" I ask. The Professor smiles: "Probably a cat or, perhaps, a mountain lion, who knows? But had I wanted to tell the story that old women tell to frighten small children into obedience, I would have said that this is *llorona*, the Lamenter. You know there is such a legend in Mexico. Every night a woman in a white robe and a white veil covering her face descends from the mountains. This is Mexico's Mother, the goddess Sivatl. She wanders along the streets of Mexico City and laments: 'How long will the misfortunes of my children last? Woe to my people that has been destroyed!' until she comes to the Plaza Mayor, where there had once been a lake surrounded by reeds which vanished into the mist. Thus she has mourned since Cortés brought down the ruler of the Aztecs. Up to this day, when a lament is heard at night, old Mexican women cross themselves and whisper: '*La llorona.*'"

"A Mother Rachel motif?" I ask. "You know, there is a remarkable similarity between the fate of the Mexican and the Jewish peoples." It is well known that when two young men get together they end up talking about women. But when two middle-aged doctors of philosophy converse for too long, they end up talking about Jews. This, however, is a topic for another time. I am too tired for it right now....

In the Streets of the Virtues:
About the New Jewish Community of Cuba

Havana's new neighborhoods, with their wide avenues and well-kept, ornamental buildings, aim at a literary and political ambience — at least to judge by its streets, named after poets and politicians. But old Havana, with its long, narrow streets, and its severe, faded houses accompanied by balconies, is "virtuous." All the streets have uplifting names. One street is called *Vertud* (virtue), a second *Merced* (mercy), a third *Perseverencia* (perseverance), with all seven virtues duly represented. It is a wonder that the seven sins are missing. But the residents of Havana explain that it is precisely on the streets named after the loftiest virtues that the most frolicsome of sins make their abode. They peacefully co-exist as neighbors, the virtues and the sins, and no one sees it as a contradiction. Havana naively symbolizes an attitude that other communities cover up, namely that things are better this way, lest the virtues become too overbearing. And it is amid these narrow streets that a remarkable event is taking place, a new scene in the drama of Jewish history.

There once was a large, blossoming Jewish community in Spain. Jews carried themselves with pride. They had famous names, a great culture; they were the elite of the Jewish people. But then there came a storm that eradicated them,

457

leaving not the smallest trace of the existence of the Spanish-Jewish tree. The Spanish exiles however, though persecuted and expelled, did not want to, or were unable to, forget. They carried the Spanish language and the traditions of old Castille with them to the farthest corners of the earth. Spain itself, however, remained anathema; there would be no going back. When, in later years, Spanish Jews living in the Balkans, or Portuguese Jews living in Holland, were approached by emissaries from the Spanish government with offers to return, these Sephardim turned them down. The Sephardim remember and do not forgive.

But in a roundabout way, across the wide ocean, Jews have found themselves unintentionally becoming participants in Spanish culture. And this holds true not only for the old, the exiles, for whom Judeo-Spanish, or Ladino, is still the mother tongue, but also for the recently arrived Jews from Russia and Poland who never dreamed that they would have any connection with the language and culture of Itzhak Abravanel and Uriel Acosta, with the language spoken by Torquemada. And yet...and still....

In Argentina, in Peru, in Chile, in all of Spanish-speaking American and in Portuguese-speaking Brazil a new Jewish life is being brought into being. The Jewish Colonization Association embarked on this task 40 years ago, and the work is still proceeding. The appeal of those sunny, hot countries has acquired an elemental force, and Jews are daily leaving their cold, damp houses in Poland to make their way toward the equator, toward the tropics, going to Venezuela, Ecuador, Columbia, Uruguay, and especially to Argentina and Brazil. Wherever you find groups of Jews, you find Jewish newspapers sprouting out of the tropical soil; the process of acculturation is beginning. In Argentina this process is well underway, in Brazil it has already begun, and it has even reached Cuba, that small, hot, distant island. Whoever heard of it or thought about it in the shtetls of Poland and Lithuania? But necessity is a good teacher, teaching us everything from baking bagels to geography. Jews have suddenly become aware that somewhere in the wide world there is an island where Jews are unknown, an island only six hours away from America, yes America, the golden country. How does one get there?

Jews are sitting waiting for American visas. When they get tired of waiting, however, they settle for Cuban visas. They have to sit and wait there too, but at least it is closer. They wait a year; they wait two. In the beginning relatives in America send a few dollars. But after a while hopes for a visa start to fade, and relatives in America become impatient: How long will this money drain last? And the "temporary" immigrant who had thought of Cuba as merely a waiting room, and a very hot one at that, begins to understand that he has to do something, to settle somewhere, to make a place for himself. Thus, the hotels on the Avenues Acosta and Merced, in the old Havana quarter, are transformed into apartments, and the erstwhile guests become residents. The immigrant accustoms himself to the thought, he begins to like the tropical climate, and he starts to feel at home. He looks around him, and it seems to him that he is surrounded by Jews — all of the natives talk with their hands, everyone exhibits the "Jewish" temperament, and everyone looks like a Jew. Thus, the Jews do not stand out here. Thus, unlike in Europe or in America, the Jew here is free from the burden of carrying the mark of an outsider on his forehead. No one in the streets notices that he is a stranger — until he starts talking. And even then the naive Cubans assume that he speaks German. And they have great respect for Germans.

Thus the Jew soon begins to feel at home on the Acosta, the old street that carries such a famous, tragic Jewish name. The street is named in honor of a Cuban poet, and, according to his poems, he must truly be one of the Acostas, from one of the old Spanish or Portuguese Marrano families. You can find Marranos everywhere, only they themselves do not even know it. I met a lady in Havana, a lawyer by the name of Cardozo. "Where does your name come from?" I asked her.

"We come from an old Italian family," she answers.

"Italian? You are mistaken; you come from Jews." And I tell her the story of the old, great Spanish-Jewish Cardozo family.

The Cuban lawyer with the coal-black eyes responds enthusiastically: "I am of Jewish origin! How lovely, how romantic! I have aristocratic blood in my veins!"

Around the Avenues Acosta and Vertud a new Jewish world is forming, a young world. You see many young people, mostly under 30, and few are bearded. A young community, young in years and young in experience. Six or seven years ago it was the home of a handful of Jews. Today, it is estimated that about eight to ten thousand Polish and Sephardic Jews now live here. The Sephardim, whom the Polish Jews call Turks, have acclimated quickly, since they speak the language of the land, albeit in its old, slightly archaic form. Thus, instead of the Spanish *mucho*, the Sephardim say *muntcho* — but there are so many Spanish dialects in Cuba that one more or less makes little difference. They feel at home, and they are the majority.

Yet they are not the ones to set the tone. The leadership role has been assumed by the new arrivals, the *arrivistes*: Polish and Lithuanian Jews, who had started out for New York but remained in Havana. They even managed to create their own Spanish-Yiddish jargon. It is remarkable what a knack Jews have to mess up a language. Can one think of an easier Spanish word than *bueno* ("good") or *puedo* ("I can")? But the Jew must blunder and change it, thus *bueno* becomes, in Jewish parlance, *boino*, and *puedo* becomes *poide*, and *Cuba* becomes *Cube*. And this, I am told, also happens in Argentina, where a Jew is recognized by his *boino*. One soon will do so in Cuba as well, but one will recognize him not only by his *boino*, but also by the bundle he carries around.

There they are, in growing numbers, on the streets of Havana, driving wagons from village to village, peddling. Almost everyone is a peddler or, a step higher, a small merchant. One day I came across two Jewish peddlers on the street. They offered me their wares, shoelaces, knives, glass beads: "Buy, señor, buy!" There were two of them, quite burned by the sun. I was terribly hot myself, and I could hardly fathom how people walked the street peddling. I started talking with the peddlers. One was a simple Polish Jew, who had become accustomed to peddling, and was content, as long as he could make a profit.

The second peddler, a young man around 28, started talking to me. He did not look at me as a stranger, and began pouring his heart out to me. He struck me as highly intelligent. Having lived for twelve years in Leipzig, he was well-versed in German literature and was also *au courant* in modern psychology. He had come to Cuba in the hopes of going on to America, and here he was, living on the Acosta and peddling his wares. "And what will be the outcome?" he asked about his predicament. "God only knows."

I put his question of "What will be the outcome?" to two Jewish communal workers at the Jewish Center, which is the social club of the young community. "One must not allow the new Jewish community to grow like a tropical forest. Jews here must not become a people of peddlers," I pleaded. "What then shall they do?" the director of the Center asked me. He told me that the Cuban government, which up till now had been very sympathetic to Jewish immigrants, has begun to change its attitude. It, too, does not want thousands of new peddlers. They had thought, at first, that Jews would bring in fresh initiative, new work and industries into the country. But as they now say about the Jews in Cuba, "they merely sell potatoes and grow scissors...."

The country is too small for so many peddlers. It has enough scissors and knives already. Cuba needs work and new energy, and the Jews have disappointed them. "But what are the Jewish communal leaders in Europe and in America doing?" I ask the head of the Cuban Immigration Bureau. "Why are they not thinking about this problem? Cuba is, as it were, the key to the new and great Latin American world, to the new center of Jewish emigration. Why are they not preparing for it? I wish you would start putting pressure on the leadership in New York and in Paris." But I know, already, that this will be to no avail. As the old saying goes, "It is given us only to want and to desire. To do — this is not our lot."

There is a new, manifold life bubbling and sizzling here. The Jewish Center is a beehive of activity: A Yiddish theater puts on plays, children are taught Yiddish, Spanish and Hebrew, and Jews receive counseling of all kinds. On the Casa Jesus y Maria two rabbis are arguing with the butcher. "I am simply ashamed to write home," one of the rabbis tells me. "To be a rabbi on the street of Jesus and Maria! But what can I do?" On a street named Inquisador, Polish and Sephardi Jews come together in the Zionist Center, where Zionists hold meeting in Spanish and in Yiddish, and where each speech must be translated, because one part of the membership does not understand the other. Young poets are wandering on the streets of Havana, dreaming of Jewish literature on Cuban soil, or in Detroit, should that come to pass.

And everything is so new and fresh, truly as if emerging out of Genesis. For the first time we can witness a Jewish community in the process of coming into being…among the "old virtues." And this, in itself, may have made their trip to Cuba worthwhile, turning it into a manifestation of the ability Jews have of reconstructing Jewish life.

Cuban Miniatures

I
Milagra and Imaculata

It is 4 o'clock in the afternoon. The heat has already abated a bit, a breeze is coming from the ocean, and it is pleasant to walk along the streets of Havana, streets named after saints and all the virtues. And on the street actually named *Virtudad* there reaches me from every "virtuous" house a quietly whispered: "Psst, psst, señor, mister," and burning mulatto eyes wink at me from behind the half-opened shutters. The street is so narrow that my elbows almost touch the houses on both sides of the street, houses from which temptresses behind the shutters cast out their lures.

People are passing by, young and old, women and children, and no one pays any attention. But having still not managed to outlive the bashful self-consciousness of my early youth, I feel that everyone is laughing at me, and I can feel my face turning red.

I walk uphill to the Avenida de la Republica, toward the university. Here, too, are the half-closed shutters, but no one calls out to me. This is the abode of Havana's poverty, of its tropical indolence, of a way of life that is so alien to us northerners, that is such an unintelligible, oppressive, disquieting puzzle.

It is almost evening, and the shutters are slowly opening up. Here and there you see women — black, brown and white, old and young — a world of women. Where are the Cuban men? What are they doing? Where are they spending the hot days and warm evenings? They are not working. One very rarely sees a man at work in Havana. Are they in bars? In cafes? Who knows? I look at the faces, and I feel that I ought not to, for they immediately recognize me as a stranger. "Your skin is still too white," the taxi driver who drove me around Havana explained. I know I am viewed as a "Yankee," and Yankees are not very popular in the lower class quarters of Havana. And, actually, there is nothing much to see here. It may be just a matter of taste, but I have found nothing here to gladden my eye and arrest my attention. Yet here I come to a doorstep where two women are sitting — and all my roaming along these streets has become worthwhile. At first I hear only twittering noises, like the piping of two birds: "Juanito, my child, my boy," and Juanito, a big, blond boy of about sixteen, who is leaning against the door of the house, shrugs his shoulders and says: "All right, aunt Milagra, all right aunt Imaculata." And the small voices keep on piping.

I turn around, take a look and see a remarkable sight: Two small, thin, almost doll-like women, with small gray heads and deeply lined, parchment faces, are sitting attired in the crinoline and lace of times gone by. Two small, gray, bird-like creatures, whose combined age must add up to 180 years. I cannot tear myself away from this sight, but the old women have noticed me, and, bashfully lowering their heads, they rise — one body with four legs — and enter the house, closing the door behind them. Only Juanito remains outside, shaking his head in wonderment at the sudden end of the sing-song.

"Hey, Juanito," I call out to him. "Do you want to earn a *media?*"

Juanito's eyes light up. It must be a rare event for him to have such a treasure rain down upon him. "Si, señor, and what shall I do for it?"

"Nothing, my son," I say in the Cuban manner, pretending that I am a resident. But Juanito is not fooled.

"Yes, mister," he answers, and I am found out.

"Listen, Juanito, I am selling lottery tickets, and I would like to sell a couple of tickets to the señoritas who were sitting here; just tell me who they are."

Juanito starts laughing. "You want to sell them lottery tickets? All right, I will ask them." And, opening the door, he calls out: "Tia Milagra, Tia Imaculata, there is a Frenchman here who wants to see you." The old women are frightened and begin to consult agitatedly with each other. Juanito, in the meanwhile, tells me that the Señoras Suares are twin sisters, maiden ladies, about a hundred years old. One is called Milagra, meaning miracle, and the other Imaculata, as in the immaculate conception. No, they are not his aunts; he is an orphan, and they have taken him into their home. Milagra and Imaculata have finally reached a decision, and we are invited in, Juanito leading the way.

Entering the room I am immersed in the atmosphere of the Spanish past. The walls are covered with pictures of saints and portraits of generals in Spanish uniforms. The old women are trembling like leaves in the wind, and they twitter: "What do you want, señor Frenchman?" And I come up with a tale out of the thousand and one nights about a lottery being held somewhere. There is nothing I want, only to know whether and when they would like to buy a ticket. I get a bit mixed up, but they do not notice it. To the contrary, the more egregious my lies, the more they believe me, and we soon are sitting around the table, sipping black Cuban coffee and talking. "Oh yes, in former times…alas…once.…" Milagra's shrill voice fills the room while Imaculata nods her head.

"Once" means when Cuba was still part of Spain, when there still was a viceroy, and uniforms. "Remember, Imaculata, Captain Figaro el Montelabo, remember his black mustache and golden epaulettes?" And behind the half-closed shutters in a small house on the Avenida de la Republica unrolls the magic carpet of a time gone by, a time when Milagra and Imaculata had been young and when Cuba had been a province of Spain. A forgotten, dust-covered world revived for a short time had brought a sparkle to the tear-dimmed eyes of the old sisters.

"Alas, my Spain is gone," sighs Milagra, and her sister sighs too. An old Velasquez picture had come to life for a brief moment.

"Well, what do you have to say Juanito?" I ask the young blond Cuban as I leave. And the 16-year-old — perhaps he is even younger? — answers with utter simplicity: "Mister Frenchman, if you give me two more *medeiras* I will show you houses where Frenchwomen live who, upon my word, are a lot younger than the aunts Suares." I lightly kick him in the ankle and walk on.

II
In the Capitol

About a week has passed since I was granted a blue ticket, a special permission to enter the capitol to attend a session of Congress. This is my third visit to Havana in the course of eight years. Each time I have tried to attend a session of Congress, in order to witness Cuban's democracy in action, and have, so far, been unsuccessful. This holds true not only for Cuba but also for other Latin American countries that I have visited. In Mexico and in Guatemala my question "When can I attend a session of Parliament?" was met with a "Not now, the Parliament is not in session; the Government has dismissed it." "Dismissed by edict or by force of arms?" And the usual answer was a shrug of the shoulders and a smile, as if to say: Why do you ask such a silly question? Is anything in our Latin American republic done without soldiers and bayonets?

My first trip to Cuba took place during the regime of the dictator Machado, when the capitol had just been completed. It is a magnificent edifice, one of the most beautiful in all of the Americas. But what purpose did it serve? Who needed it? Machado and his cronies, of course, were said to have made a profit of about $20 million. It required profound cynicism to disregard contemptuously the elementary human rights guaranteed by the constitution while erecting a splendid palace to house the parliament — the symbol of freedom and democracy.

On my second trip, a few years later, Machado had just been toppled, and Carlos M. Céspedes had assumed the presidency. "Can one now attend a session of Congress?" I asked, and the answer was the usual: "This is still a dictatorship; one must get along without a parliament for a while longer." Oh well, I could wait.

And this time, after all the revolutions, calm and order prevails, and my patience is rewarded. The Parliament's chief press representative is very amiable, beaming with happiness. He has, undoubtedly, waited for a long time for such an event. "Si, señor, tomorrow, at the first session." This is the first session following the removal of the constitutionally elected president, Miguel Mariano Gomez, and his replacement with Federico Laredo Bru. Everyone knows, of course, that Gomez had been president in name only and that Bru, in his turn, lacked all presidential power. It is common knowledge that the presidency and the constitution are mere stage settings and that the real power is wielded backstage by the dictator and the country's actual ruler, Colonel Fulgencio Batista, the head of the army. But it is also known that the erstwhile wig-maker, and current dictator, Colonel Batista, is himself merely a puppet in the hands of the real string-puller, the American envoy. Not Washington, not Cordel Hull, not even President Roosevelt is the determining force — the fate of Cuba lies in the hands of the American ambassador.

In the meantime, however, there is still a constitution, on paper, and a building for the use of parliament, so the comedy must be properly enacted. One does act, but one takes one's time. I wait a whole week for the "tomorrow" promised me by the affable press chief. Every day the deputies assemble in the capitol, and every day they are told that there would be no session, at which point they crowd into committee rooms and conduct their business behind closed doors, being in no hurry to make their deliberations public. And they are right, for such a parliament, without a quorum and without a constitution, is merely a political carnival, and not a joyful one.

I keep on waiting. Finally the deputies assemble, and a majority comes together to enact the will of the dictator. There are long, passionate speeches by liberals and brief, sharp, self-assured answers by conservatives, or maybe the other way around. Who in Cuba can listen to a speech and be sure who is speaking and why? The result is that the former liberals or moderate conservatives, led by Dr. Marcus Sperling, lose their leadership position in the parliament, something they have certainly deserved. Cuban liberals and conservatives are no politicians; they mostly were, and still are today, simply followers and partisans of certain herd-leaders, whether they call themselves Machado, Céspedes, Miguel Mariano Gomez, or the self-proclaimed "true revolutionary," Dr. Ramon Grau San Martin, a former professor of philosophy, former president of Cuba, and currently an exile in Miami. They all are part of the same dough, a Cuban dough — without yeast, just water, air and flour from America.

There was a time when Spanish or Italian rhetoric made a great impression on me. Now it leaves me cold. All the sonorous phrases, the dance-like gyrations, the hand clapping and the dramatics of Dr. Marcus Sperling, or of his opponent Dr. B. Acosta, have failed to impress me, or, I think, anyone else in the room. One knows that it is a shadow play, the shadow of the constitution doing combat with the shadow of dictatorship, a mere shadow struggle projected onto the screen; so what difference does it make who emerges victorious? Mr. Caperi, the American ambassador, is the one who determines the outcome of the real play going on backstage.

As we leave the "historic" session, I say quietly to a Cuban colleague, "You know, my friend, Machado was really the smartest of them all. He did build a palace for the parliament, but he didn't allow it to become a parliament."

"Shush, don't talk like that!" my Cuban friend says as he looks around cautiously. "Walls have ears and so do stones. And, besides, what did our teacher, the 'apostle' Martin say about Cuba? 'Our wine is sour, but it is our own.'"

"Are you sure that this is your wine?" But my friend pretends not to hear. In the cafe opposite El Capitola a band of young mulatto women was playing black jazz, and my Cuban colleague drowns his political cares in the intoxicating jazz. And this may be the right thing to do.

III
Chico and the Goat

In Cuba you have to bargain with the cab driver. Since the car has all the usual equipment, including a meter, you would think it would be the simplest thing in the world just to get into the car and let the meter count the miles as they come along. But this is not the Cuban way, either because Cubans are not too good at reading numbers, or because this procedure does not suit the Cuban temperament. Therefore, before getting into the car you have to settle the amount of the fare. Yet a Cuban does not haggle, he does not demand an outlandish fare, nor is he out to skin you. One can easily come to terms with him; ten cents more or less do not greatly affect him. "How much will a couple of hours' drive around Havana come to?" I ask one of the drivers of the cars lined up alongside the Parque Central, in the center of the city. The driver looks at me, rubs his nose and names a sum which to me, I can see, is astronomical, but which is, in truth, very modest. As a matter of form, and in order not to lower his self-esteem, I make a counteroffer less ten cents.

The short, dark-skinned, thin driver immediately agrees, and his smiling eyes attest that he is satisfied. I also am satisfied, and we start out. Only it appears that the satisfaction does not extend to the car, a respectable, rather aged, small Ford, the likes of which we do not see in the U.S. anymore. The car moans and groans, and the wheels barely move.

"Señor Americano," the driver says as he turns to me, "You must excuse me, but you see, the car needs a drink."

"Well, let it have it."

"Yes, but…." and he turns up his empty hands. I take the hint and give him an "extra." I am already familiar with the way Cuban drivers operate. They never have enough gasoline, and when they buy some they do not get a gallon but a ladle, a small glass full, like a dose of medicine. And small wonder, since gasoline in Cuba costs three times as much as in the U.S. This is what being a colony means: one has to give everything, but one gets nothing in return.

After the car gets its drink we proceed.

"What is your name?" I ask.

"My name? Oh, it is a long one, my name is Alexandro Damaso Juan Nepemoseno Torquemodo. Torquemodo is my family name, the first four names I was given in church, but I am called Chico; it is easier this way." And he turns his thin, dark face towards me and laughs.

"And how old are you, Chico?"

"Who can tell, Señor? The years are like waves, they come and they go, and who can count them? I only know that I can remember when Spain was still here, and I was then already among the fighters for independence, for freedom for our Cubita, our little Cuba."

"Oh, Chico, then you must be already rather advanced in years." A quick calculation tells me that he must be around 58 or 60 years old.

As we drive along the streets of Havana, Chico tells me that he has three children, two boys and a girl. The oldest boy, Paco, is ill and spends his days warming himself in the sun. His second son works as a tourist guide, leading visitors to all of the fun places of Havana, and the girl works in a cigar factory. She already has a *novio*, a fiancé, and the wedding will be soon. I do not ask about his wife; one does not pose such a question to a Cuban, since you most likely will be asked, in turn, "Which one?" and get a recital of names.

"Where are we going, Señor?" my driver suddenly remembers to ask. In the U.S. this is the first, matter-of-course question the driver asks. In Cuba the destination, the direction, plays a minor role. One goes wherever the road leads; what difference does it make? I, myself, do not know just where to go, so I say, "Go straight ahead, this is a beautiful road. Who built it?"

"This is the road built by General Machado." It is a smooth, American style asphalt road, leading between green fields and idyllic small villages.

"Oh, Machado. Well, then let's go to the town that he has built." And off we go, slowly, since his old Ford is not aiming to achieve any speed record, but, then, I am not in a hurry either.

We arrive at a planned city, built in style and with a purpose. There is a linen mill, a leather factory, and a few other plants — new, clean, technologically up-to-date. Around the plants are offices, housing for employees, a school, a church, and in the center of the city, a park with all of the amenities, including a waterfall. But all of this is vacant, abandoned; it is like a miniature Pompeii, a city struck down by sudden death. The only thing that is still in use is a cinema where, three times a week, movies are shown to the people living in the surrounding villages. And even then one feels traces of Pompeian destruction. The marquee once bore the name of General Machado's mother, and this, too, has been torn down, leaving only traces of the once proud, golden letters.

Chico tells me that "the general" built all this, but when he was thrown out of Havana, the entire city was destroyed, the factories were closed, the trees in the park were uprooted, and the benches beneath them chopped up. "It is fortunate that they did not tear up this road he laid out."

"Was the general really that bad?" I ask Chico.

He looks around; the air is clear, not a person in sight for miles, and he starts talking.

"See, Señor, this is how it has been all of my life, since I can remember, one revolution after another. My father was a Spaniard, my mother a mulatto. They called my father Pancho, Pancho the coachman, and he used to scold me for running to join the revolutionary army, of joining Marti and Mateo: 'Why are you doing this, Chico, what do you have against the Spaniards? Truly they are better than our Creoles. Don't you know that the Yankees have planned this in order to take over our Cuba? What do we need freedom for? We have the sun, black beans, and, on some days, a cupful of rice — what more do we need? Think about it, Chico, someday you will regret it.' This was some thirty years ago, Señor, and I still don't understand what is going on in Cuba. One president comes, another goes; there is shooting in the streets, and young people are arrested and put into prisons — for the sake of what? I don't understand, do you understand it? They say that Machado was a bad general. I really don't know why. He laid roads, built factories and houses. Did he put money into his own pockets? Of course, what else? But he gained something, and we gained something. So he was driven out, his name was erased.

"And now?" I ask.

"Oh, señor, don't loosen my tongue. Not only walls have ears, but even trees can betray you, you know." And Chico bends towards me, with his garlic and cheap tobacco breath hitting me in the face. "You know, since the Greek has become such an important person, things have become nearly unbearable." "The Greek" is the name bestowed by the populace on the erstwhile wig-maker Fulgencio Batista. "Everywhere there are soldiers, and more and more restrictions and discipline are being imposed. What for? Who is asking him? What is it that the wig-maker wants?"

Chico was so busy talking that he did not notice that we had entered a village. Two soldiers, or gendarmes, give us a keen look. They surely do not mean anything by it, but Chico grows pale with fright and firmly closes his lips. At this moment he is suddenly hailed: "*Bueno*, Chico!" Chico turns around, and a smile spreads over his face. "*Bueno*, Paco!" The car stops. We get out, and an idyllic reunion takes place in the middle of the road. Paco, an old mulatto, leads us to his family waiting across the way. There is a woman, two pretty girls, and a boy who is sitting in a wagon with a load of bananas and all kinds of tropical vegetables and fruits. The wagon is pulled by a goat.

Chico and his friend embrace and embark on a long conversation about family, relatives and friends. I, too, am included in the reunion, especially after I invite everyone into a tavern and treat some with wine, some with *mantecata*, and others with ice cream. "A good American," Paco remarks to his friend Chico, and the goat utters "Meh...meh" in agreement.

"Now this is living," Chico says dreamily as we set out to return to Havana. "This is happiness — a wagon, a hut in the field, beneath the blue skies, and a goat, right, Señor?" But in the meantime we have arrived in Havana.

"Hey, Chico, be careful!" The idyll of the goat had gotten Chico so caught up that he almost hit an American tour bus.

"Oh, these Americans," sighs Chico, adding some colorful Cuban expressions. "What do they want from us?" And, really, what do they want from Chico?

IV
The Emperor's Grandson

"*Permettez monsieur!*" Since for two weeks I have heard only Spanish and had to discipline my tongue to a correct use of a foreign language, the sudden sound of a familiar language has a liberating effect. I do not know why it is that of all the languages in the world, French is the one I feel closest to, even though it is also a foreign language, one I had to learn. It may be because of the French books in my father's house — Voltaire, Diderot and, of course, the thick tome of Maxim de Cassan's descriptions and photogravures of Paris. Or it may be due to the fact that the Mediterranean cadences strike Jewish ears as such familiar sounds that the French language has always evoked in me a kind of "remembrance."

"*Permettez-moi*," says the lady at the dinner table in the hotel where I am staying, in a suburb of Havana. The hotel is built like a monastery, between clusters of flowers, surrounded by trees, in a cemetery-like quiet. The lady knows that I am a foreigner and assumed that I may be "pretty close" to being a Frenchman. I did not look to her like an American, and the fact that I was a Jew did not even occur to her. I was glad to drop the burden of speaking Spanish for a while. Actually, all she had wanted was for me to pass the salt, but, salt or sugar, it served as an introduction.

We begin to talk and to get acquainted. The French-speaking lady came from Belgium, and fate transplanted her to Havana, where she has lived for several years already, waiting...waiting for a miracle. She tells me her name, and I am astounded.

"Is it possible? Or is this a fictitious name?" I ask.

The lady shakes her head: "No my name is not fictitious, it is real. You are not mistaken, my name is one of the oldest names in Europe, that is, not my, but my husband's name. You see, we come from an old Venetian family. There were Doges and Papists among them, and a great-great-great grandfather was the Emperor of Rome who issued all the laws governing the Western world." The family wandered about from Rome to Byzantium, from Venice to Spain, until it landed in Cuba, becoming a part of its highest aristocracy. One of them served as a senior diplomat in Brussels, where they were introduced, and where they got married. But her happiness turned out to be Cuban-style: closed shutters, jealousy, a harem-like life. Until the ancient blood reached a point of degeneration and her husband was stricken with insanity. The ancient tree had grown tired, and the great-great-great-grandson of the Emperor of Rome was languishing in an insane asylum. And she, the Belgian, was sitting in Havana, waiting, waiting for liberation.

We talk, we leaf through the latest books of French writers: Gide, Malraux, Catholic communists — she knows it all, she is a European, through and through.

"Madame, perhaps you would like to come to a movie with me? Marlene Dietrich is playing in 'The Garden of Eden.'"

"I would like to, but I am afraid."

"Afraid of what?"

"Of Cuba. You have no idea of the medieval atmosphere that prevails here." But I persuade her, and we go. The next day, as we meet at breakfast, she tells me: "Unfortunately, Monsieur, I was right. I have had three telephone calls already this morning. And you saw the black carriage and the lady in black lace, this was my sister-in-law — a part of the imperial family. You must understand, someone saw us last night, and the tight-knit world of the Havana aristocracy has gone into action."

"Do they enact a reverse French Revolution? Are we in the year 1937 or 1789?"

"You are laughing, Monsieur. You have never sought to be the Emperor's grandson in Havana." And the aristocratic prisoner withdrew to her room to read revolutionary literature.

V

The Drumsticks of the Nianigas

"Ta-ta-tak-ta-ta." Try to take two smooth, rounded, polished pieces of wood, and clap one against the other in a rhythmic beat, and you will be holding two sticks made to beat a drum. The drum is missing, and your thoughts must supply it; it is purely an imaginary drum. But all over Cuba, from morning till late at night, these drumsticks are clapping. No matter where you may be, in a restaurant, in a cafe, on the seashore, everywhere is heard the unavoidable beat of the drumsticks. And the size of the orchestra does not matter. Whether it is an entire jazz band, with drums, trumpets, even a saxophone, or just a lone mulatto or negro playing the fiddle or the flute, the accompanying drumsticks are ever-present, the *obligato* to every performance.

On the wharf, next to the tavern where one drinks beer or Coca-Cola, two black men are improvising. They are on the alert, and the moment a car stops, or someone enters the tavern, they approach him, smiling broadly. One of them is a "poet," which means that he makes up songs for any occasion you might want, and will sing for ten minutes or half the night. His companion, meanwhile, is clapping the drumsticks, which he holds in the shape of a cross, before the upper one descends on the lower one and he starts beating out the rhythm. I listen. The lyrics are limping along, and the singsong, as monotonous as the African steppes, is feebly accompanying the words, but the drumsticks go on inexorably...tak-tak-ta-ta-ta-tak.

I beckon to the improvisers to come closer, and their tired muse seems to be glad of a moment's respite.

"Where do these drumsticks come from, and what kind of rhythm is this?" I ask. But the players merely smile and do not answer.

Then the drumstick player says, "This is how we played it when there were still nianigas."

But the singer, who seems to be older and wiser, steps on his toes and hisses, "Be quiet, you...." This is followed by an avalanche of choice Cuban name-calling. The drumstick player bites his lips and walks away.

"Who are these nianigas?" I ask the singer, flitting a coin before his eyes.

"Eh, señor, who knows what that fool is talking about. You must understand that we Cubans do not believe in such things anymore." I can see the poor mulatto is squirming to be off, and I let him go. I would, surely, not learn anything more from him.

My Cuban friends have, of course, never heard of this. They are, after all, still "green," strangers who had come to this land only a few years ago, and are not interested in anthropological questions. But among my acquaintances there is a resident who is knowledgeable about Cuba, though he acknowledges that he still does not know the whole story.

Years ago entire tribes were brought from Africa, in chains, to work in the sugar and tobacco fields. Having been slaves in their homeland, they soon came to feel at home in Cuba. The sun shone here the same as in Africa, the skies were as blue, there were palms, dense forests, and there were the same myths. Their Spanish bosses were also superstitious, believing in magic, ghosts and demons. And the Africans brought to Cuba their entire religious baggage. On the surface they are Christians, Catholics, but on the inside they still worship the pagan gods Ecue, Tchanga, Imaia — the trinity of African theology.

Spirits appear from the skies, the woods, the sea, spirits which pursue men at night, to be held in check by the tam-tam of the drums, by the clapping of the drumsticks, while dancing attracts them. This African religion has maintained itself under the cover of the church altars, the two drumsticks forming a cross as it was before the two sticks of the cross had been nailed together. In the daytime they profess Catholicism, but at night the greater power belongs to the nianigas, to the sorcerers in the negro quarters, in the *campos* of the Sugar factories, and in the almost exclusively negro province Oriente. There, in the depth of the night, the nianigas practice in the woods and fields their ancient, wild African rituals. "Tam-tam" goes the drum, and "tak-tak" go the overpowering drumsticks; black feet follow the rhythm while black bodies writhe in ecstasy.

"I cannot show you genuine negro nianigas," my Cuban friend says. "The police prosecute them, but I will show you an imitation which is almost the real thing." And late at night we go somewhere far out of the city, to a so-called "Afro-Cuban cabaret." Of course, this is only a cabaret set up to make money off tourists, off Americans who get drunk and sing "Sweet Adeline," but Africa is not to be suppressed, not even by America.

The musicians play what has been announced as a rumba, but this rumba differs from any dancehall rumba, and I hardly recognize the melody. Two negroes are dancing. The male is dressed in a white lace robe, artfully fashioned to resemble ostrich feathers, while the female wears a white dress and a veil. He dances towards her, comes close, then pushes her away. She approaches him, raising her hands in slavish supplication. He turns away from her and proudly dances around her, and she falls to the ground, at his feet. He stands still for a moment, then raises her up and they both begin to spin around in a wild dance.

The "African waltz" comes to an end, the night is far advanced, and the heat is suffocating. Lovers are whispering beneath the trees, and even the inebriated Americans are falling under the spell of the place. Suddenly there is heard the tam-tam of the drums and the tak-tak of the sticks, and the moon emerges, enveloping everything in silvery magic. From somewhere comes the sound of steps, but I do not see anyone as I look around me. Suddenly a procession emerges from one of the gardens. First come some negro men carrying lanterns, their faces painted as masks of idols. They are followed by about 30 women, four to five in a row, a seemingly endless multitude, and, finally, men with banners, and with sticks in their upraised hands. The melody is wild, and I seem to distinguish the words: where there is a flame, there is the magic spirit. The voice of the singer is shrill, the drums are beating, the sticks are clapping, and the dancers are twirling in a dance, one stepping to the right, one to the left, and with a twist of the body rejoining the circle. Soon everybody is dancing, and I begin to feel my own limbs responding, and that, any minute now, I may join in.

Having materialized from somewhere out of the night, the group is, just as mysteriously, absorbed by the night. "This is called the Conga dance," my guide explains. "And this is just a civilized version, fit for a cabaret. You can imagine how this would be danced in an open field, by and for negroes. To tell the truth, nianiga is the only power ruling the Cuban negroes."

"And the negroes are in the majority, aren't they?"

"Sure, and this is, really, Cuba's gravest problem, one that is ignored because it has been forgotten. But it does exist. The revolution under President Grau San Martin was actually a rebellion of the blacks, mainly of the mulattos. They were beaten back, but for how long? Sooner or later Cuba is going to become a Spanish Africa. Nianiga is awaiting its hour. And you still wonder why it is so difficult to understand Cuba!"

I had wanted to tell my Cuban friend that this was not just a Cuban problem, that nianiga, the magic culture, has revolutionized the entire world, and that we are going to pay a price for it. But the hour was late, and I was too tired for a discussion. The drumsticks made me sleepy — the sticks that form a cross before they begin their beat.

VI
The Penitent of Mosara

My Jewish friends give me no peace. They want answers to problems. I plead with them: "My friends, look, the stars are so golden in the tropical sky, the air is soft, and I am so tired of thinking. Let's just go for a ride and sing the song we once sang, remember?" But my friends demand their pound of flesh. And they have a point, as they are isolated in Cuba, leading an impoverished, humdrum life, and they are eager for a bit of intellectual stimulation. They are young, relatively speaking. The entire Cuban Jewish community is still relatively young, mere 30 or 40 years old. But a 40-year-old is old here. And in the tropics young blood sizzles and demands the absolute — absolute justice, absolute faithfulness.

The five people in the car with me, sitting almost in each other's laps, are urging me: Tell us, explain it to us, we cannot tolerate such uncertainties.

I give in. "What is it that is bothering you so much, my friends? Let us worry about it together."

And they start talking, all at the same time. "The process, Radek, Piatikov, Raskolnikov, Trotsky, the Seventeen…" A deeply felt sigh escapes me. This is just the topic I do not want to talk or even to think about. I had read in the Cuban paper a brief account of the events and had put it out of my mind — it is too difficult, too burdensome to deal with.

But my friends insist. To them it is a problem of an absolute value judgment. "How can we go on, how can we keep the faith when such things can happen, when such great people can confess to such horrible crimes?" asks one of the passengers, on the verge of shedding tears. I do not want to enter into any discussion, especially since I may not know much more about it than they do. I, too, am far removed from it all, and, in addition, I do not in the least share their respect for these "great people," nor for many others on the other side of the barricades. But…

"You know, my friends, I want to tell you a short story which has some connection to your country. Yesterday I went with an acquaintance to one of Cuba's most interesting places, a place that you, undoubtedly, know about. It is called Mosara, and it is an institution for the insane. There is one pavilion for the moderately disturbed and another one for the seriously ill. There are small cottages for the quiet and harmless patients, and ones ringed by stone walls for the violent ones. Wherever you go you see insane people in their blue robes.

"You see, having studied psychiatry in my youth, I have always been tremendously interested in this subject, and so I visit insane asylums wherever I travel. It was, therefore, natural to use the opportunity of being in Havana to visit the famous Mosara. A young, nicely dressed doctor showed me around, describing various cases, of half-idiots, of mutes who refuse to speak, and, in contrast, those who cannot stop their parrot-like talking. 'There are many interesting, tropical variations of insanity,' he said, 'but I will not afflict you with details. I want to tell you only of one patient who, I am sure, will interest you. We call him the Penitent of Mosara.'

"And my guide leads me to a pavilion. There, amid, dull, apathetic patients, a man is sitting on his cot, his head lowered, his hands locked in chains. 'We had no intention of handcuffing him, but he implored us to do it,' explained the doctor. We approach him, and he turns away. The doctor puts his hand on his shoulders: 'Hey, Juan Pedro, don't be so rude, here is a guest from America who wants to see you.' Juan Pedro lifts his pale, sharply etched Spanish face and stretches out his manacled hands. 'Good, I confess, I am guilty. I have killed him!' 'Who did you kill?' 'Who? Lindbergh's baby, President McKinley. I am guilty, so shoot me. I beg you.'

"'This is the strangest psychiatric abnormality I have ever seen,' says the doctor as we walk out. 'We call him the Penitent of Mosara, or sometimes we call him Dostoevsky. He has a mania of self-incrimination, of piling on himself all kind of false accusations, of assuming responsibility for everything and, therefore, everyone's guilt.'

'What is the origin of this illness? What is the patient's background?' I ask the doctor. And he tells me that this man had once been a politician with a great imagination and even greater ambitions. He had wanted to take on so much, that in the end, he collapsed, and this is where he is now…"

My listeners understand the parable, but it does not satisfy them: How can one compare Russia with Mosara, world figures with political maniacs? They are about to engage in a lively dispute when suddenly one of them notices that a car is following us, shining its lights upon us. "Ssh," one whispers into my ear, "a secret police car is following us, we better stop talking." And, for the first time in my life, I came to appreciate the arrival of the secret police to stop questions that no one can answer…at least for the time being.

A Detour to Egypt

The Dying Sphinx

Egypt, the ancient land of wonders and of mystery, produces a new enigma, but only a few, a very few, hear — and even they do no understand it, do not know how to approach it. The Sphinx is dying. The ancient Sphinx, with the body of an animal and the head of a human, is not merely a thousand years old, as Napoleon told his soldiers when they reached Egypt, but four, six, who knows how many thousand years old. The Sphinx, who had become an enigma and a question mark for thinking humans, is dying. The granite statue, half-covered by thousand-year-old waves of sand, has cracked, and some fine morning it will break apart. Thus will the oldest witness of universal history tumble into the abyss of time.

What wonderful stories could the Sphinx of Giza have told us, had he been able to speak? Tales of Egypt when the world was still young, of Asia when it was at its mightiest. He had seen the Asian herdsmen who occupied Egypt for several hundred years. He had seen the ancient Hebrews, that remarkable tribe that, on their way from somewhere, had beaten all those that stood in their way, as they were heading from the desert, through the desert, to the desert. The caravans of Hiram, the king of Tyre, Alexander the Great and his soldiers, Cambyses the Persian, Caesar the Roman, the Turks, the Arabs, Napoleon — they all passed before his eyes. They all came to view him and, stilled by his dead, stony gaze, searched for an answer to the ancient, eternal riddle: Whence do we come, and where are we going? What is the meaning, and what is the purpose of life? They had questioned and were left unanswered. And so they departed in despair, yet hopeful. They despaired because life vouchsafes no answers; they remained hopeful because life is eternal. The very existence of the stone Sphinx was a guarantee of stability and perpetuity.

We do not know what the Egyptians were thinking when they created the Sphinx. Perhaps they had not given it much thought. It is possible that the Egyptians artists merely wanted to embody the force and the greatness of two natural elements, the body of an animal and the mind of man. What the Egyptians did not make explicit was spun out by others. The Greeks took on the Sphinx and elevated it to a symbol. Coming down the mountain path leading to the city of Thebes, the traveler was stopped at the city gate by a Sphinx, a lion with the head of a woman, asking for the answer to the riddle: "What crawls on all fours in the morning, walks on two legs at noon, and on three legs in the evening?" The traveler, unable to solve the riddle, was dispatched by one shove of the mighty lion's paw into the abyss. Until Oedipus came to solve the riddle, and the Sphinx, deeply humiliated, hurled itself into the chasm. The answer was: man in his infancy, as an adult, and in old age, leaning on his cane.

A primitive, childish riddle, but this very fact makes it, such a profoundly searching one. It is the first time that man had asked himself: What is man? An animal at the outset, with animal instincts and animal cravings, yet not an animal, something more than an animal. When does the animal become human? As long as the riddle remains unsolved, man remains helpless, the animal flattens him and sends him into the abyss. Man frees himself only when he comes to understand himself, and then it is the animal that disappears.

Out of the old, Greek-Oriental riddle, whose origin is lost in the chasm of time, sprouted forth human culture. And no matter how straight or crookedly the mind proceeds, it always returns to the same, eternal core, the Sphinx riddle: What is man?

One cannot, however, always ask the same question. One does not want to be like the man in Heine's poem who, sitting on a rock on the shore of the roaring gray ocean, asks: "Whence and whereto?" He asks and "is still awaiting an answer." Human thought has developed. Having grown tired of peering through telescopes and microscopes into his own depth, man reversed course and began to explore the world around him. Heaven and earth, oceans and mountains, the nature of objects and the laws of nature. Man stepped out of the narrow mountain pass of Thebes and entered the broad, free-ranging planes. It is an easier journey. It is easier to explore the nature of crystals than the nature of man. It may, perhaps, be possible to discover the basic elements of atoms, but it is impossible to find the key to oneself, to that living "I" that is the mystery of all mysteries, the beginning of all beginnings, the core of creativity and its sole aim.

It has been more than sixty years since sand began to cover up the Sphinx — literally and metaphorically. The world has dismissed all searching, all philosophic quests as fruitless, ineffectual, as being mere words, castles in the sand. What is needed, it was said, are facts, data and concrete, solid matter. Anything that cannot be seen, measured or tested in laboratories is scientifically invalid, is considered by science as mere literature. It is true that all of us are, to a certain degree, materialists, and that we adhere, in varying degrees, to the doctrine of the "human machine," which is the final, strongest anti-Sphinx tenet. It acclaims man as a machine, an interplay of atoms and forces, an organization of definable material forces. We cannot, as yet, define it, but only because our instruments are still not precise enough, because we have not yet perfected our research methods. But, sooner or later, we will reach the mysterious core, and we will know man — as a machine. Yet even at this point, the Sphinx raises its voice again: You say man is a machine? Well, do we really know the secret of its composition? We can observe, we can, to a certain degree, understand how it works, but is this truly comprehension? And when we talk about electricity, power, energy, do we really know what it is we are talking about? Are these not also mere words we are saying? Do these words not conceal rather than reveal the secret meaning of the world? And when we say "development," do we know what this means? Development from what starting point, toward what goal, for what purpose?

We have, however, grown tired of the eternal questing and probing in the dark. And rather than going on searching without ever finding an answer, we stop searching. Somewhere in the quiet, hidden recesses of our mind, or, as it is more commonly referred to, our heart, the struggle between the animal and the human elements lives on. Each one must fight out this struggle within oneself. Each one must answer the Sphinx-question for oneself. Man must either prevail over the animal or lose out to it. When the struggle becomes too exhausting, then one seeks to compromise and tells oneself: So what if I am an animal? What is our human claim to greatness? Why must we stifle and suppress our deepest, most natural, flesh-and-blood instincts? To what extent is that small light burning somewhere within us more valuable than the bright light our body emits, a light we can see and a warmth we can touch? And there arises the teaching of the "blond beast."

Friedrich Nietzsche, the greatest Oedipus of our time, the only one who has tragically submitted to the piercing, fatal gaze of the Sphinx, could find no other answer, no other way out, than to roar back at the Sphinx: Do not threaten me, do not question me. I am not afraid of you. You ask: What is man? And I say to you: Man is nothing, man must first come into being. And from Mount Sils-Maria came the ringing, pathetic, despairing word: superman. Man must die; the superman must be born. And the Sphinx asked, once again: What is the super-man? Nietzsche had no answer, and the Sphinx consumed him.

Silence has fallen. We have grown weary, and so has the Sphinx. It is futile to keep on asking because there is no answer. And the Sphinx is longing for the end. The eternal witness does not want to be a witness anymore. Built by human hands, it wants to be like everything else made by man, a thing, and each thing has a beginning and an end. But what does not have a beginning? And when the Sphinx splinters, when the sand covers the questing eye, will the questioning voice within us also fall silent?

Life goes its own way. More deserts, more sand, solitude and time…and out of time emerge two stony eyes which ask: What is man? And thus it will be till the end of time, till the sands run out.

The Relics of Egypt

We are reaching port in Egypt. We see flat, sandy shores, with tall, bare palms, topped by leafy crowns mirrored in a narrow ribbon of water. After days spent on blue water and under clear skies, after passing by stony, gray islands, ocean rocks, witnesses of stormy, fiery happenings, of earth revolutions which tore continents apart and filled the divide with blue water — we come across the white-yellow plane of Egypt. Egypt greets you from afar. Egypt, the relic of the world.

The first person I encounter in Alexandria, even before the ship casts anchor, is also a relic. Pharaoh himself is coming toward me; Pharaoh as he is pictured on the obelisks, on the ancient Egyptian wall paintings. A bit of ancient Egypt is suddenly before me, as if arising from the sea: a copper-brown apparition with a narrow, slightly pointed head, a thin face, smooth and shiny, with high cheekbones and full lips. The head rests on broad shoulders, the figure narrowing down from the chest. The attire is also of remarkable, Asian-Oriental width: colorful black, apron-like trousers held up by a broad orange belt, a green jacket with narrow lavender sleeves, and the whole orgy of colors topped by a red fez with a black tassel. The ears are adorned with silver earrings, and one can just feel that the nose is yearning for a ring as well. But Egypt, the African Egypt, stops short of that. This is, after all, not barbaric Africa; we are in Egypt.

"Who is this Potiphar?" I ask a fellow passenger, a Romanian-Egyptian merchant who was born in Egypt and speaks only French, albeit with the idiosyncratic accent of a true child of the French city street.

483

"This is not Potiphar," the merchant replies with a serious mien (obviously immune to my "wit"), "this is the oldest of the haven porters."

"Is he also an Arab?"

"No, he is a Copt." Which means that I am not mistaken. It is, really, the Biblical Potiphar, or perhaps even Pharaoh, just in a different garb. Because the Copt, the Christian Egyptian, is a direct descendent of ancient Egypt. The Copts escaped the Arabic flood that had overrun Egypt. They did, it is true, lose their language, as they also speak Arabic — who in Egypt does not speak Arabic? — but their religion saved them from a complete integration into the Egyptian surroundings. And, from time to time, they hear in their churches the language of the Pharaohs, of the Hartumis, and of the hieroglyphics. This is not at all surprising since Christianity is, in the final analysis, a grandchild, or an *ur*-grandchild, of the most idiosyncratic Egyptian religion, the religion of Mother Isis, Father Ammon and, yes, the Son Osiris.

I make my way without incident through the noisy, colorful, barefoot, grimy multitude of Arab-Egyptian porters, cigarette venders and lottery sellers and seek refuge in the quiet of an Egyptian hotel. After a rest and some refreshment, I venture out again into the hot Egyptian sun and set out toward the old city of Alexandria. My mind is filled with awe-inspired visions of Alexandria and Egypt. How many names, how many events do these words evoke! Asia, Africa and Europe form here a trinity of universal culture. Egypt had not been a barren field to be cultivated, but, rather, a barn where the ripe grain was stored, a trough where the dough of all the cultures was kneaded.

I walk, following street after street, boulevard after boulevard, searching for traces of the past. And I find none. Arabic, French, Greek, Hebrew, Italian, all the Mediterranean languages assault my ears. But I see only stores and cafes, grubby shopkeepers, unsightly Arab women with green-painted faces, but nowhere is there even a sign of the wondrous Alexandria of Egypt.

This is a surprise and a puzzle for all travelers. What happened to ancient Alexandria? You come to Rome and the entire history of the city unrolls itself before your eyes. You see a small bridge here, a column there, and then a temple (or its remnants), yet they still exist, and ancient Rome lives on in its gravestones. One layer of culture joined with another, co-existing, and wherever you look, you see living history. But Alexandria and all of Egypt have undergone the miracle of Korah: the earth opened up and engulfed all of it, buried it beneath the sand, as if it had never existed, leaving no mementos.

A traveler visiting Alexandria 150 years ago would have been able to see not only the new city but also the stones and relics of old Alexandria. One hundred and fifty years after his trip, even the last remnants of the past have vanished. An ancient lighthouse, the column of Pompeii, and one or two other columns are all that is left of Alexandria, the metropolis of the ancient world. And reading what Greek and Roman writers tell us about Alexandria, about its great temples and beautiful palaces, built by the Ptolemaic dynasty, about the wonderful library with its 700,000 books, the mausoleum where the body of Alexander the Great lay in a gold coffin placed inside a crystal one, about the bourse and the gigantic stores where merchandise from all over the world was stored, reading all this, one understands the words of the old Roman writer Aurelius Tacitus: "My eyes were overwhelmed."

One understands and one feels, once again, that all this greatness and beauty have vanished without a trace. The library of the Roman Emperor, philosopher and book lover Marcus Aurelius was burned by Greek monks and, once again, by Mohammedan generals. The temples were raised to the ground; the entire ancient Greek, Hellenic culture vanished, as if claimed by the ocean. And who knows, perhaps it needed to disappear. It was a late fruit of a tree that had already stopped blooming, that was dying while still young and full of sap. The beauty of Greece, its intelligence, its philosophy could not take root in the sandy shores of the Nile; there was too much sun, too much heat; the desert was too near. The desert wind had come upon Greek thought, set it aflame and scorched it. Because culture is measure and order, but Egypt is measureless, like the desert. Therefore Plato, transplanted to Egypt, led to Plotinus, who gave rise to Philo and then Iamblichus — all of them mystical, enigmatic, too poetical and lacking in cadence.

I am walking through the old city. Where once a Greek-Alexandrian temple had stood next to a mosque, I see a barefoot, ragged Arab or, perhaps, an Egyptian (it is difficult to distinguish them in the glaring sunshine). He lies there, lost in thought, in dreams, in complete surrender to the light of the sun. The sight of this Arab brings to my mind a personage of olden times, the most remarkable thinker that the Alexandrian culture produced, Ammonios Sakas, the Socrates of the Hellenic period. He, too, was a peripatetic teacher. He, too, put nothing in writing yet founded a school. Socrates had led to Plato; Sakas, the taciturn, barefoot, half-naked Egyptian porter, had led to the Neo-Platonic school, to mysticism and ecstasy. And between the two, between Greece and Egypt, stood Philo, the Alexandrian Jew, who had wanted to merge Greek-Egyptian mysticism with Jewish acuity of reason, who had wanted to bring together the spirit of the Egyptian desert with the living pulse of mountainous Judea. But he had been no match for the force of the desert sand, and his ideas remained rootless and sapless, producing no fruit.

"They are on the same side, the Jews, the Egyptians and the Greeks, on the side of the seraphim," the Roman Emperor Arvandus had once written from Alexandria to his general Servenious. Seraphim — this is rather symbolic of the incomprehensibility, age, taciturnity and mysteriousness of Egypt. A seraph had buried himself in the sand and had become a relic.

Having lost all hope of finding some of Alexandria's ancient beauty, which has survived only in a few old books and literary memoirs, I return to the new city, to the French-Greek-Arab bazaar and the unintelligible African-Mediterranean Egyptian life. The tall houses are barring the view of the desert and the palm trees, but I did see them, behind me, as they stand and wait. They await their hour, the time when they will swallow up new Alexandria, adding a new relic to the old one. This is the fate of Egypt.

From Moses to Moses

Perhaps it really did happen this way. Why should we accord greater credibility to the German historian Edward Maier, who is sitting in a Berlin library, casuistically interpreting reams of books, than we accord the old anonymous historian who has told so artistically and so grippingly the wondrous story of Moses and the epic of Egypt? Egyptian literature, it is true, contains no testimony; no memories are etched into stone or put down on parchment in colorful hieroglyphics. But has everything that has ever happened been recorded? And what do we know about Egypt? Out of a ten-thousand-year-long history there remain a small number of monuments, a few written pages which European scholars have only half understood but have gone on to transform into quasi-history.

Furthermore, not everything that has been written down is true, and it is, often, just the untold and the forgotten events that have truly occurred. We Jews are especially inclined to forget many things that happen to us; we have always understood the advantage of blending in.

When you are in Egypt, it is very easy to imagine that the remarkable story the Bible tells us happened just as it is written. A tribe from Asia wandered through the desert, traversed the mountains of Canaan, and descended into the valley of the Nile. They gained power, lost it, became enslaved, and were forced to carry heavy stones to build the pyramids. I can see them, so life-like, just as if it were happening today. Breaking up stones beneath the burning sun, they pass them along a long line of brown human bodies, bent down to the earth by the weight

of the slab. Around their heads they wear a string recalling a superhuman prophecy. And I can see the dark, bronzed Egyptian waving his whip over their heads.
But then there arrives from the city of Memphis a tall, proud son of the desert,
clad in a dark robe, on his head a scarf tied with two black strings. He
approaches, looks on and cannot bear to see the shame of his brethren. He kills
the Egyptian and buries him in the sand. I can see them leaving: camels, sheep
and cows followed by the human wanderers, making their way through the hot
desert. It all seems so natural, so simple; it fits so well into the Egyptian landscape, and it establishes a new, closer link to the Bible.

I recalled these ancient events — or legends — when the Arab guide leading
our troupe of American tourists pointed out the place where Pharaoh's daughter
supposedly found Moses in the bushes at the shore of the Nile. Everyone
laughed, even the American lady who had been gazing, enraptured, at the black-
eyed Ali, in his blue robe and white turban, ready to believe everything he told us.
Even she shook her head and murmured, "Oh well, that is too much." It may
well be that she was not quite clear about who Pharaoh was, or the identity of the
Moses — or Musa — as Ali was calling him. But she had understood that, no
matter the exact details, Ali had overstepped the bound of credibility.

We continued on to the Sahara desert, to the ruins of the old imperial city of
Memphis, swaying from side to side atop camels in this dirty, living ship of the
desert. It seemed interminably long until we reached the pyramids. It was the first
pyramid I saw, and I was disappointed. This is always the problem with world-
famous places; out of all that we have read and heard about them, we tend to
construct a vision which reality cannot match. It may have been due to the heat,
the Arabs or the tourists, but the pyramids of the Sahara did not impress me — I
saw only big, gray, pointed gravestones, nothing more.

I came a second time, the night lit by the moon, alone except for an Arab
guide to whom I had offered a double *baksheesh* if he would refrain from all tour
talk. And this time, when I approached the pyramids of Giza from another direction and saw the great pyramids next to the sphinx…I will not, I cannot, describe
the impact. Silence enveloped me — the silence of the night, of the pyramids, of
the desert, smiling so softly beneath the moonlight and the silence of the terrifying sphinx. Terrifying. In the daytime it is merely a curiosity, a pedestal upon
which a stone-hewn animal rests, an animal with a human face. Its nose is missing, the eyes are dead, and the work is carelessly executed. I could not summon
up any feeling of ecstasy, and I knew that even what I thought I was feeling was
merely a literary response.

But at night, in moonlight, all alone, eye to eye with the desert, the pyramids and the sphinx! "At night all streams are talking." And from the nearby Nile to the stream of my own thoughts and feelings could be heard a murmur and a soft song. Why do they say that the sphinx does not sing at sunset? Is he not singing now — at a time that only I can hear it, I and the silvery sky above me? He sings of all times, of eternities, of what could have occurred, and of what almost did happen. He sings about the sand that covers all things, and the desert that swallows all. Eyeless, he yet looks at me. He? She? I do not know. But it was not a riddle for me, or a legend; it was the experience of myself and the desert, the moon and pharaoh, and everything, old and new.

When I finally tore myself away from the sphinx and turned around, I saw an enchanting sight. On the steps of the Great Pyramid, the Cheops Pyramid, stood a white-robed figure. It was only the Arab "pyramid sheikh" waiting for a *baksheesh*. But for a moment it seemed to me that this was a high priest of Ra-Amon, of Isis and Osiris, an old Egyptian *Hartun*, one of those who advised the biblical Pharaoh. Everything seemed possible at that moment. And why not? Had the desert, the white desert, not seen everything and swallowed everything? I began to understand why Egypt has always been the classic land of magic, mystery and mysticism, and I began to feel Egypt's intoxicating effect taking hold of me.

My Arab guide had been awaiting me impatiently and was happy when he finally got the chance to talk on our way back to town. And how he talked! In all languages he spouted all the lies and foolish tales that only an Egyptian can concoct, and I did not stop him. It is sweet to listen to nonsense when one returns from the bare, stern desert of the Sphinx.

Now I am again where Moses lived, not Moses ben Amram, but Moses ben Maimon, the Rambam. I am in the business district of Cairo, noisy with the clang of streetcars and automobiles rushing past the donkeys, camels and man-drawn wagons. Arab women are carrying baskets on their heads; men are selling water. Arab shopkeepers are standing at the doors of their shops. (Arabs? or are these, perhaps, Jews?) It is hot, dusty and what a smell! A tobacco smell from the nargilas, coffee, onion, garlic, body odor, the stench of graves, and who knows what else. And then there is the dirt — a truly Egyptian one, seemingly left over from the time of the Ten Plagues. Amidst this labyrinth of streets there is a small, dirty lane, the Zorb al-Muhammad. "This is it," points out the old respectable Sephardic merchant who accompanies me on my Jewish sights of Cairo. "This" meant the synagogue of Rabbi Moses, the synagogue the Rambam built, and where his coffin is.

We walk into a crowd of barefoot, dirty Jewish men, women and children, and we are immediately besieged by dozens of outstretched hands, begging to be filled with Egyptian piasters. The Rambam's synagogue is built in an idiosyncratic, ancient Oriental style, not in an Arabic or any other style I know of. Perhaps it is an ancient Jewish one? The Jews of Egypt had then not as yet relinquished the memories of their past.

In a room behind the sanctuary stands a kind of podium, and next to it hangs the picture of the Rambam. It is a very different picture from the ones we are accustomed to. There is no white beard and no turban. We see a thin face with a spare beard. The garments are Eastern-Spanish, not Egyptian-Arabic. And it portrays a more serious, finer, nobler demeanor than the more familiar likenesses. Beneath the portrait is an inscription, telling in a pure, fulsome Hebrew the life of Moses ben Maimon, from his birth in Córdoba till his death in Cairo. Behind the picture, separated by a curtain, is another small room. My Sephardic guide carefully washes his hands, kisses the wall and bows himself into the room. He is almost kneeling as he prays quietly, his lips barely moving, but the trembling of his shoulders and the movement of his whole body testify that the prayer comes from the very depth of his heart — an ecstatic prayer. And he was praying at the grave of the greatest rationalist that Judaism has brought forth, of our clearest thinker, the Rambam!

My guide, however, as do all of the Jewish men and women in Egypt, was praying not at the grave of Maimonides, who was the author of the *Guide for the Perplexed*, the Aristotelian, the scholar, the interpreter; he was praying at the grave of Rav Moshe, the saintly doctor who cured most serious illnesses and who has the power to cure even after his death.

What an ironic twist of fate: the Rambam serving as a source of superstition! But do not great personalities have the ability to open various ways of the world to us? Did the first Moses not lead us on the way to the Sinai, the way to Golgotha, the way to Mecca? Everything flows from him, even the events that have turned against him. "From Moses to Moses there was no one like Moses...." The road followed by the second Moses, the one who was not born in Egypt but who lived and died there, not far from Goshen, a brief distance from Memphis, was a shorter, narrower one, remaining within the Jewish domain. But not all of the roads have yet been traveled, and the Rambam blazed some paths that are still open to pursuit. From Moses to Moses — the cycle of Egypt has been completed.

Chronology of Essays

The essays in *Across the Great Divide* are culled from two Yiddish compilations of Abraham Coralnik's work — one from Warsaw, published in1928, and another from New York, published in 1938. The 1938 anthology includes fairly exact dates for an essay's appearance in the Yiddish newspaper *Der Tog*, while the 1928 one indicates only the decade during which an essay first appeared.

A Budapest Dreyfusiade (*1920's*)
A Bundle of Keys (*1926*)
A Legend Destroyed (*1926*)
A Time for Soul Searching (*July, 1933*)
A Treasury of Allusions (*January, 1930*)
About a World that is No More (*1920's*)
About the Jewish Spirit (*November, 1936*)
About the Pillar of Gezer (*1927*)
About the Wide and the Narrow Road (*October 23, 1933*)
Achad Ha'am: The Thinker (*1927*)
Amid the Fog (*1929*)
Among Old Friends (*1926*)
Among Old Houses (*1927*)
And Nathan Talks On (*July 27, 1935*)
Anski: Russia's Negotiator (*1922*)
Around the Center (*1920's*)
Around the Sinai (*February 10, 1935*)
At the Foot of the Old Mountain (*1930's*)
Between Heaven and Water (*June 5, 1926*)
Chaim Weizman (*1922*)
Civilization and "Kugelization"(*1920's*)
Cuban Miniatures (*February, 1937*)
David Lubin (*1920's*)
Desert (*October, 1924*)
E Finita La Commedia? (*1934*)
From Moses to Moses (*1920's*)

In a Small Room (*1933*)
In Jerusalem: Among Gray Stones and Eternities (*October 5, 1933*)
In the Streets of the Virtues: About the New Jewish Community of Cuba (*December, 1929*)
In Whose Name? (*1920's*)
In Wondrous Bimini: Impressions of Florida (*December, 1929*)
Israel: Old and New (*October, 1926*)
Josephus and Simeon (*1923*)
Just to Stay Alive? (*1920's*)
Kohelet (*October 30, 1931*)
Lacking Pepper (*December, 1931*)
Leafing Through Graetz (*October, 1931*)
Legendary Prague (*1923*)
Mexico's Mother Rachel Laments Her Children's Misfortunes (*1934*)
Mitzpah (*October 5,1924*)
Moses (*1926*)
Mountains, Cities, and Men (*October 16, 1927*)
Nachman Syrkin: 1868–1924 (*1924*)
New Heavens and Old Clothes (*1920's*)
Oedipus is Still Seeking (*April, 1931*)
Old Nooks (*1924*)
On the Island of Love: A Lead from Cyprus (*November, 1933*)
On the Road (*1925*)
Our Golden Legend (*October 27, 1935*)
Over the Abyss (*October 30, 1932*)
Paul (*1925*)
Pouring Salt on Open Wounds (*1920's*)
Prescriptions for Judaism (*1920's*)
Reading the Book of Ruth (*June 7, 1930*)
Round and Round the Book of Books (*May 14, 1927*)
Shalom (*September 23, 1926*)
Sights of Paris (*September, 1933*)
Still Older? (*1920's*)
Stromboli (*1926*)
Telling Throughout the Night (*April 5, 1936*)
The Akiba Smile (*August 15,1929*)
The Essayist (*1928*)
The Eternal Sacrifice (*1920's*)

The Damp Cellars of the Inquisition and the Swimming Island of Song (*July, 1934*)
The Dying Sphinx (*1925*)
The Gaon of Neswicz: Shlomo Maimon (*May 19, 1928*)
The Heaven-Goer (*1920's*)
The Hidden Away Ezra (*October, 1936*)
The Iron Maiden (*1927*)
The Jewish Form (*1920's*)
The Jewish Illusion (*1920's*)
The Jewish Intellect (*1920's*)
The Land Phoenix (*1930*)
The Loyal Ones (*October 17, 1927*)
The Middle Way (*February, 1933*)
The New God (*1920's*)
The Paradox of Judaism (*September 22, 1934*)
The Petrified Branch (*October, 1929*)
The Relics of Egypt (*1926*)
The Sage (*1927*)
The Sealed Book (*1920's*)
The Second Nation (*May 1, 1937*)
The Sixth Death of an Illusion (*1935*)
The Spirit of our Time (*1920's*)
The Stone (*1926*)
The Third Pool of Light (*July 4, 1936*)
The Tragedy of Hasidism (*1920's*)
The Transmigration of a Shekel (*1930's*)
The Two Walls (*December 21, 1924*)
The Unknown Sanctuary (*1927*)
The Wider Circle Early (*1920's*)
The Wreath of the Holy Ark (*1920's*)
The "Yesterday Jews" and the "Tomorrow Jews" (*1920's*)
Theodore Herzl (*1925*)
Together (*1931*)
When Abraham was Still Young (*October 4, 1929*)
Without a Melody? (*1928*)
Without a Preface (*November 4, 1927*)

About the Author

Abraham Coralnik, born in the Ukraine in 1883, received both a Yeshiva education and a Ph.D. in philosophy from the University of Vienna. He was an editor of Theodore Herzl's newspaper *Die Welt* (The World), a senior minister in the short-lived first Soviet government, and an essayist for the New York Yiddish daily *Der Tog* (the Day).

978-0-595-34573-1
0-595-34573-5

Printed in the United States
34604LVS00005B/118-132